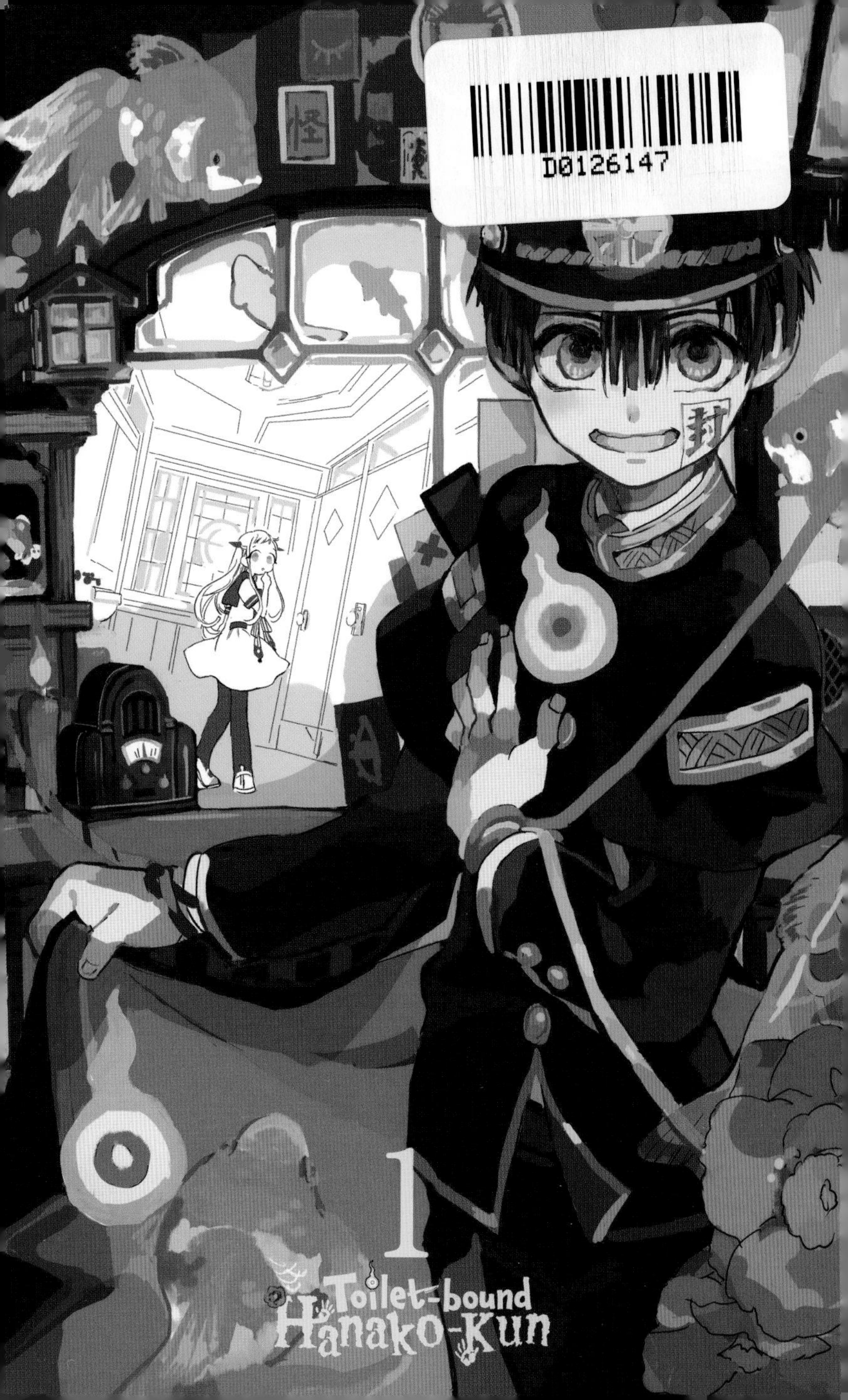

1
Toilet-bound
Hanako-Kun

Contents

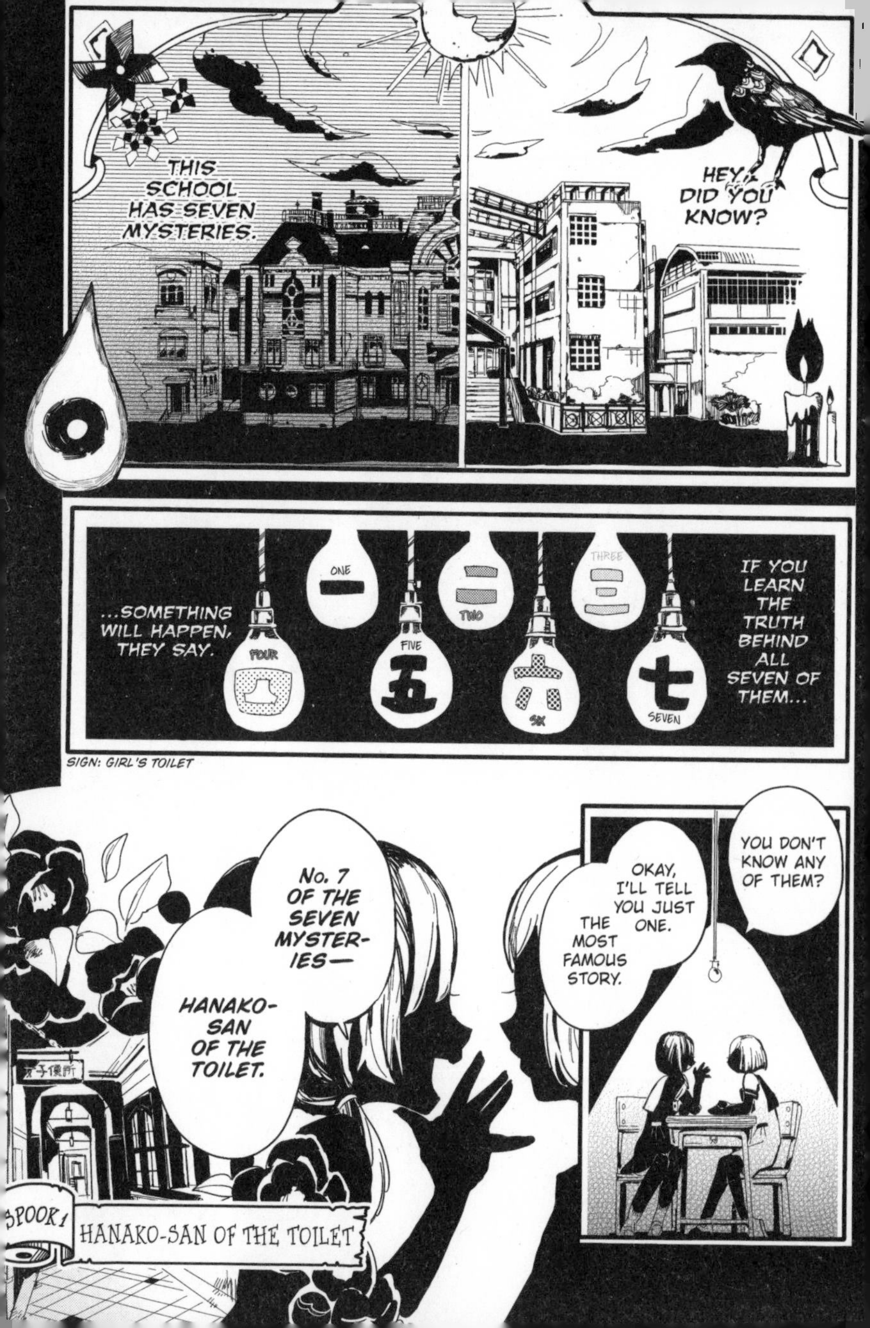
HEY, DID YOU KNOW?
THIS SCHOOL HAS SEVEN MYSTERIES.
IF YOU LEARN THE TRUTH BEHIND ALL SEVEN OF THEM...
ONE
TWO
THREE
FOUR
FIVE
SIX
SEVEN
...SOMETHING WILL HAPPEN, THEY SAY.
SIGN: GIRL'S TOILET
YOU DON'T KNOW ANY OF THEM?
OKAY, I'LL TELL YOU JUST ONE.
THE MOST FAMOUS STORY.
No. 7 OF THE SEVEN MYSTERIES—
HANAKO-SAN OF THE TOILET.
SPOOK 1
HANAKO-SAN OF THE TOILET

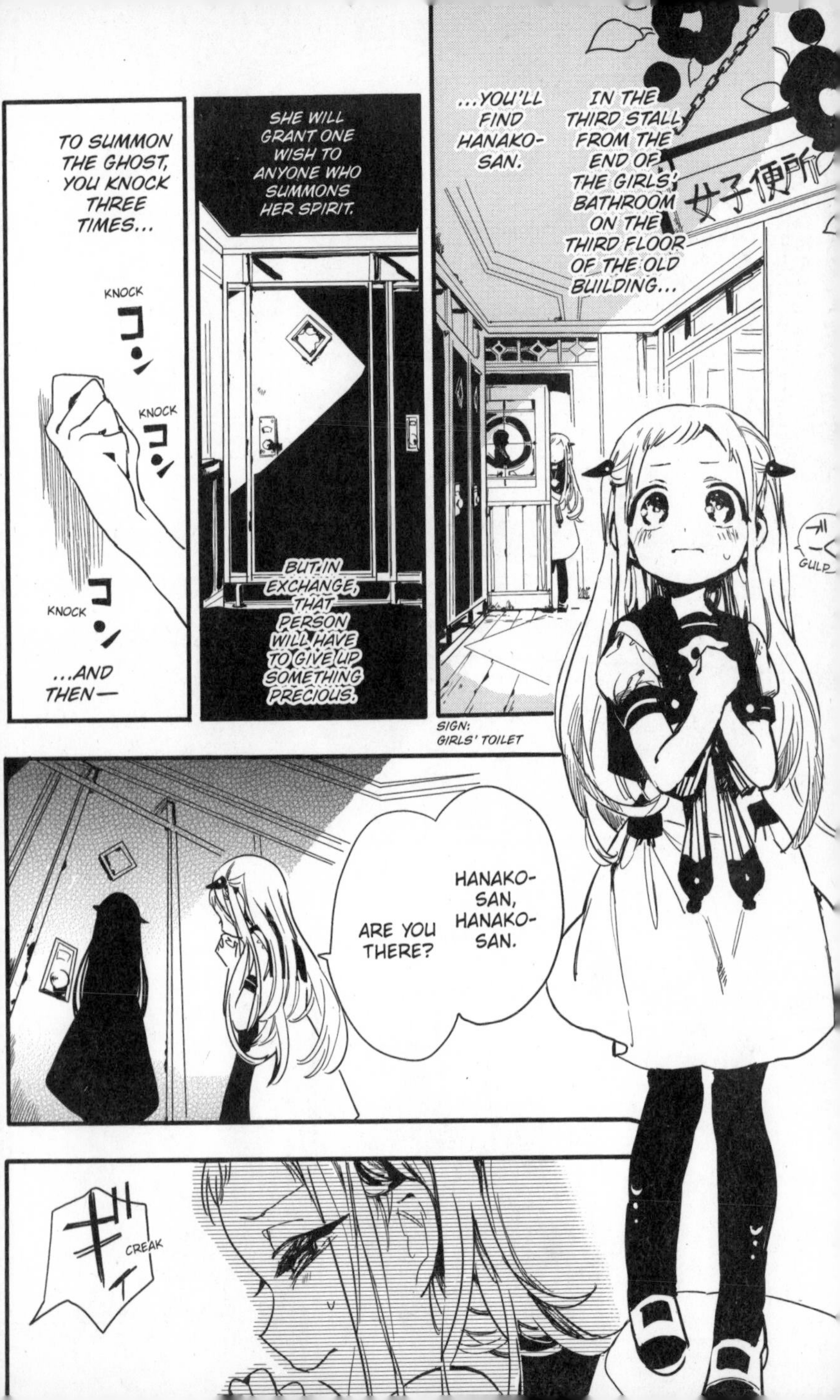

IN THE THIRD STALL FROM THE END OF THE GIRLS' BATHROOM ON THE THIRD FLOOR OF THE OLD BUILDING...
...YOU'LL FIND HANAKO-SAN.
女子便所
SIGN: GIRLS' TOILET
GULP
SHE WILL GRANT ONE WISH TO ANYONE WHO SUMMONS HER SPIRIT.
BUT IN EXCHANGE, THAT PERSON WILL HAVE TO GIVE UP SOMETHING PRECIOUS.
TO SUMMON THE GHOST, YOU KNOCK THREE TIMES...
コン
KNOCK
コン
KNOCK
コン
KNOCK
...AND THEN—
HANAKO-SAN, HANAKO-SAN.
ARE YOU THERE?
ギィ
CREAK

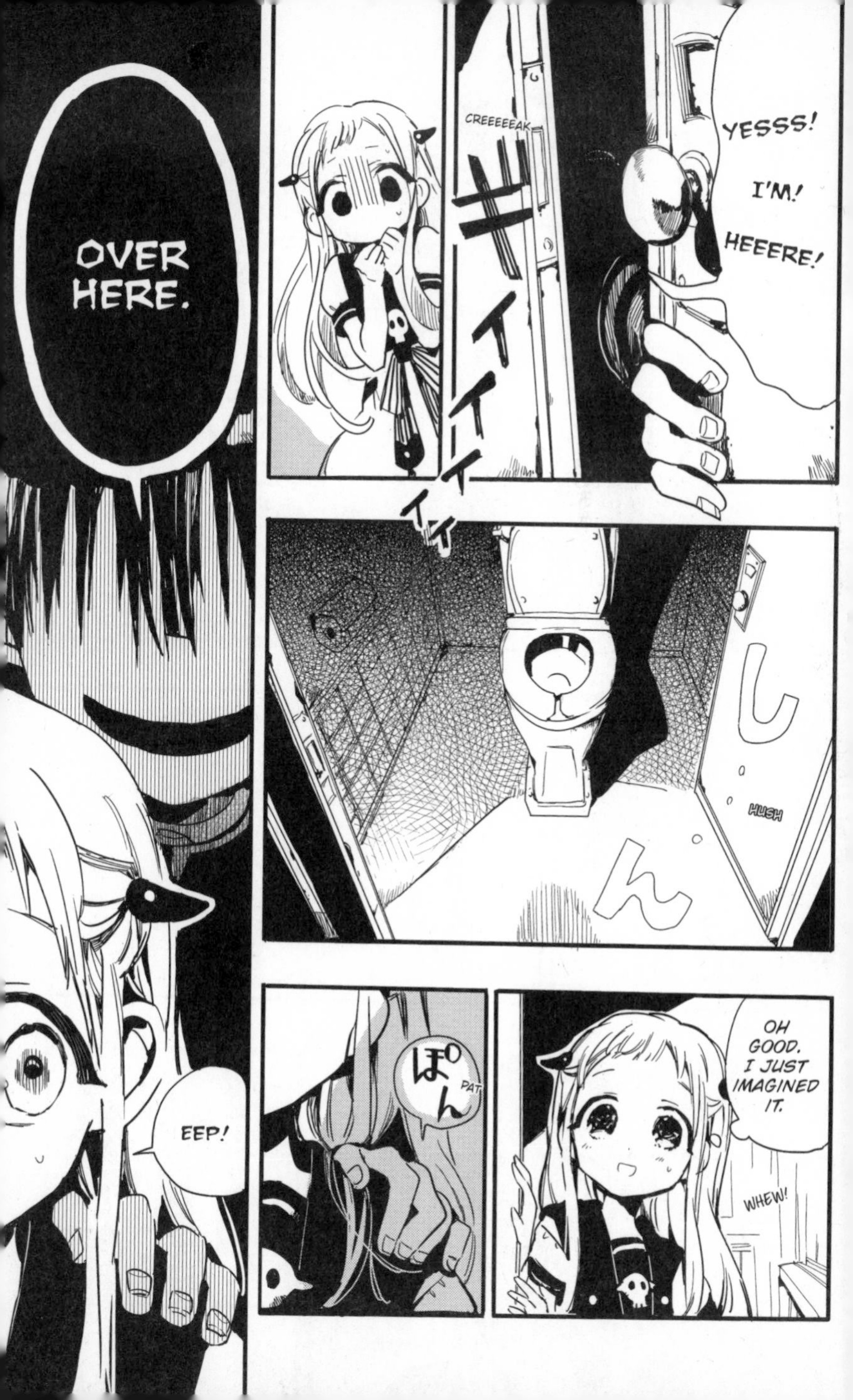
YESSS!
I'M!
HEEERE!
CREEEEEAK
ギイイイイイ
しん
HUSH
OH GOOD. I JUST IMAGINED IT.
WHEW!
ぽん
PAT
OVER HERE.
EEP!

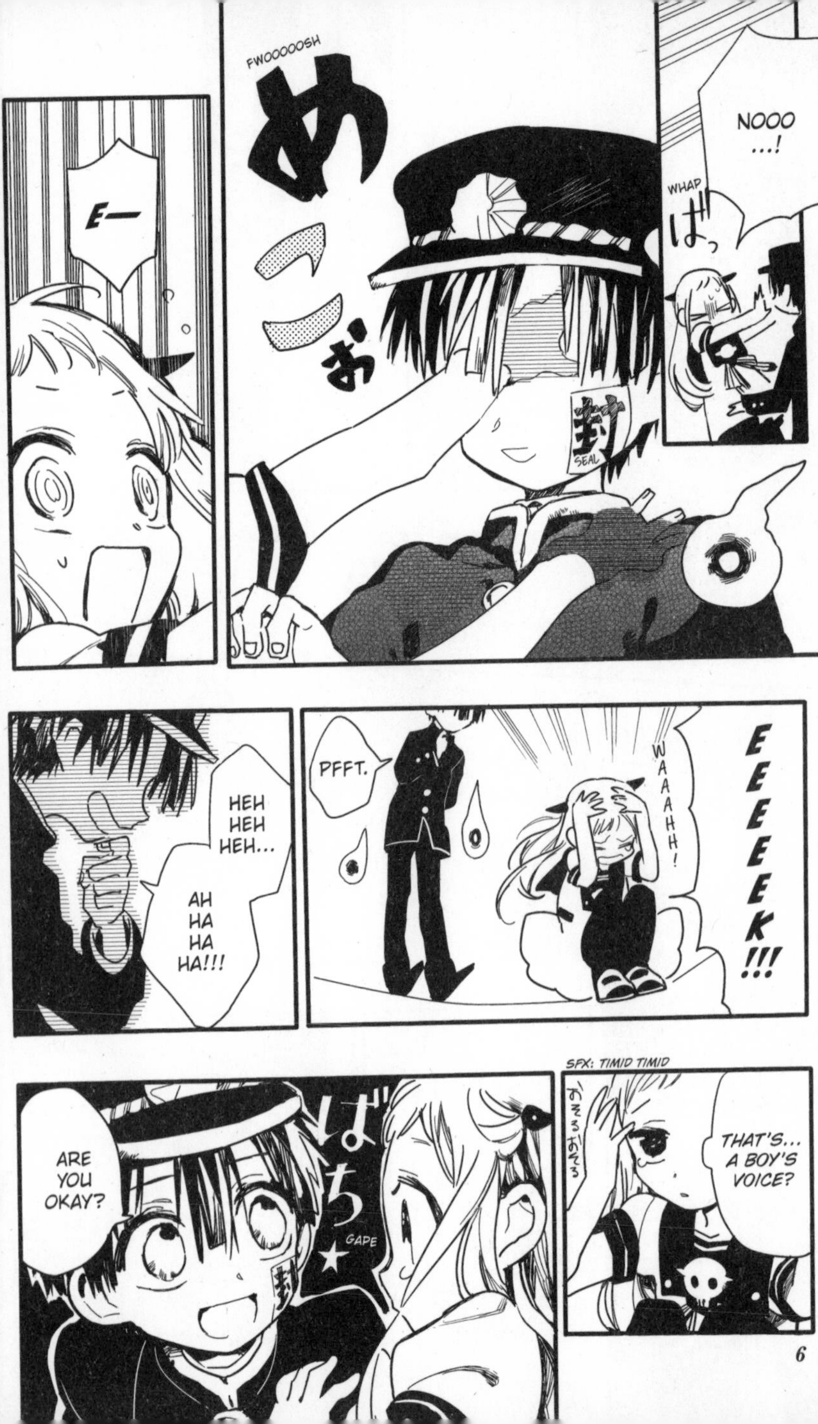
NOOO ...!
WHAP
ばっ
FWOOOOOSH
SEAL
E—
EEEEEEK!!!
WAAAAHH!
PFFT.
HEH HEH HEH...
AH HA HA HA!!!
SFX: TIMID TIMID
THAT'S... A BOY'S VOICE?
GAPE
ARE YOU OKAY?

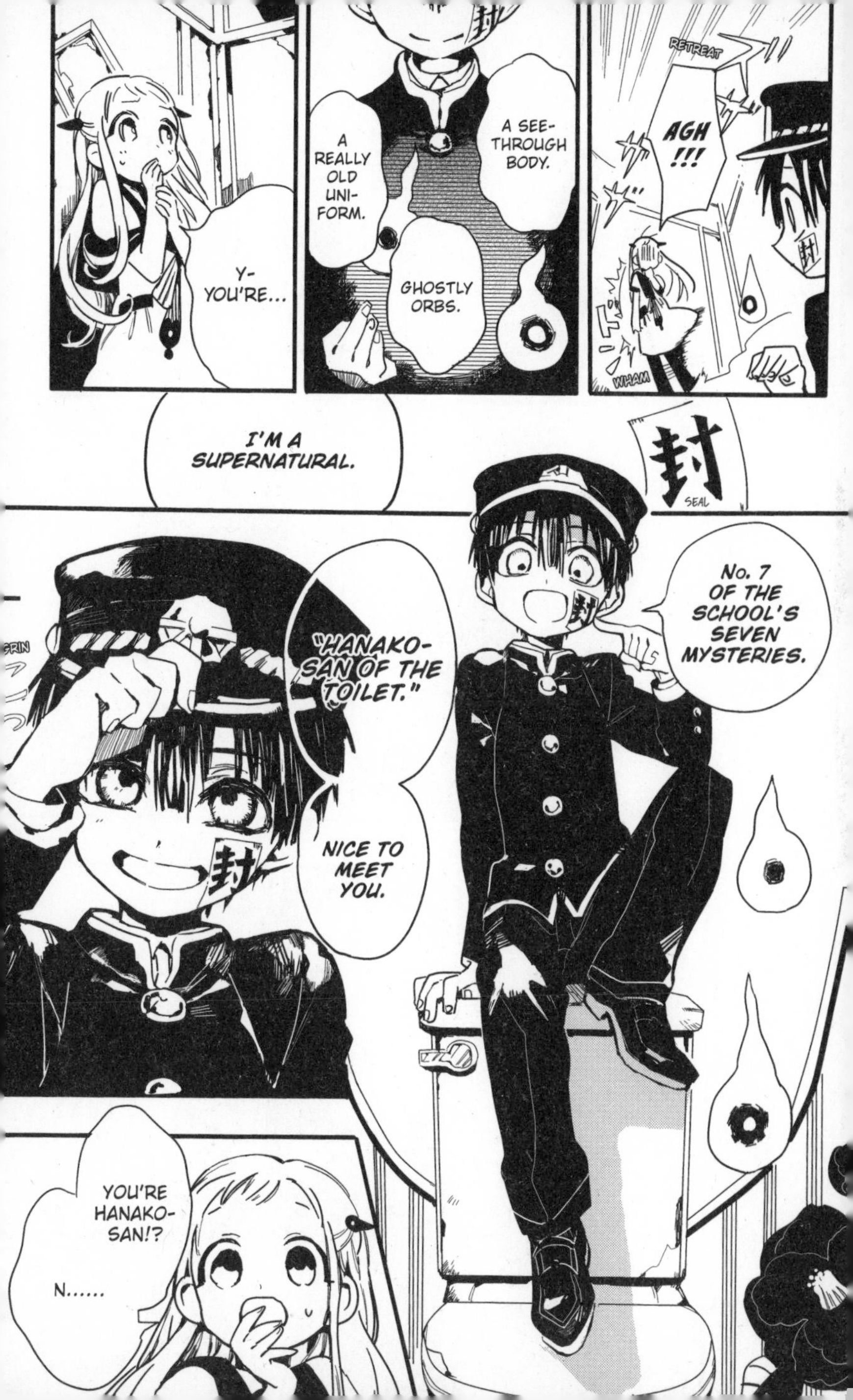
RETREAT
AGH!!!
WHAM
A SEE-THROUGH BODY.
A REALLY OLD UNIFORM.
GHOSTLY ORBS.
Y-YOU'RE...
I'M A SUPERNATURAL.
SEAL
No. 7 OF THE SCHOOL'S SEVEN MYSTERIES.
"HANAKO-SAN OF THE TOILET."
NICE TO MEET YOU.
GRIN
YOU'RE HANAKO-SAN!?
N......

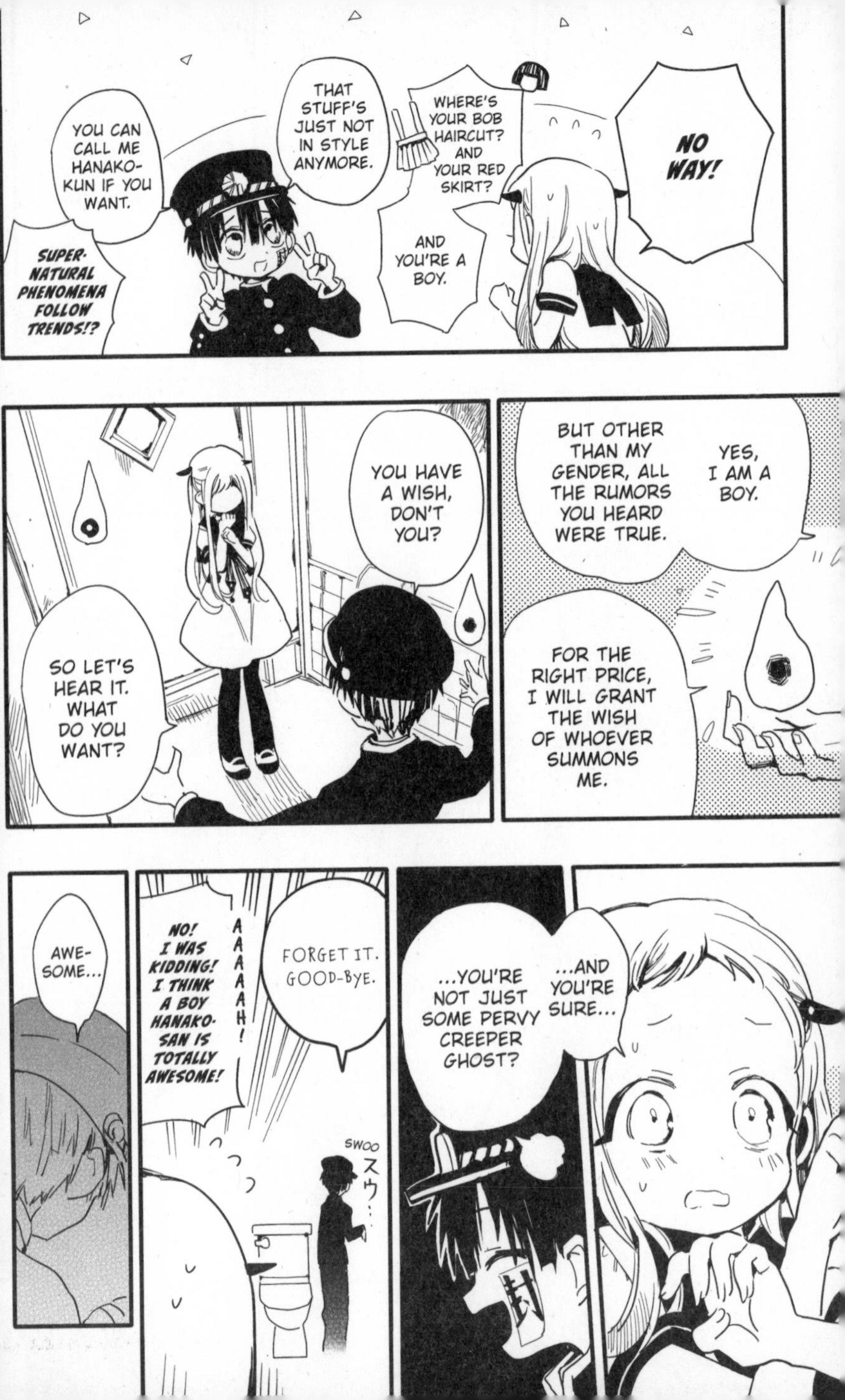
NO WAY!
WHERE'S YOUR BOB HAIRCUT? AND YOUR RED SKIRT?
AND YOU'RE A BOY.
THAT STUFF'S JUST NOT IN STYLE ANYMORE.
YOU CAN CALL ME HANAKO-KUN IF YOU WANT.
SUPER-NATURAL PHENOMENA FOLLOW TRENDS!?
YES, I AM A BOY.
BUT OTHER THAN MY GENDER, ALL THE RUMORS YOU HEARD WERE TRUE.
FOR THE RIGHT PRICE, I WILL GRANT THE WISH OF WHOEVER SUMMONS ME.
YOU HAVE A WISH, DON'T YOU?
SO LET'S HEAR IT. WHAT DO YOU WANT?
...AND YOU'RE SURE...
...YOU'RE NOT JUST SOME PERVY CREEPER GHOST?
FORGET IT. GOOD-BYE.
AAAAAAH!
NO! I WAS KIDDING! I THINK A BOY HANAKO-SAN IS TOTALLY AWESOME!
SWOO
スウ…
AWE-SOME...

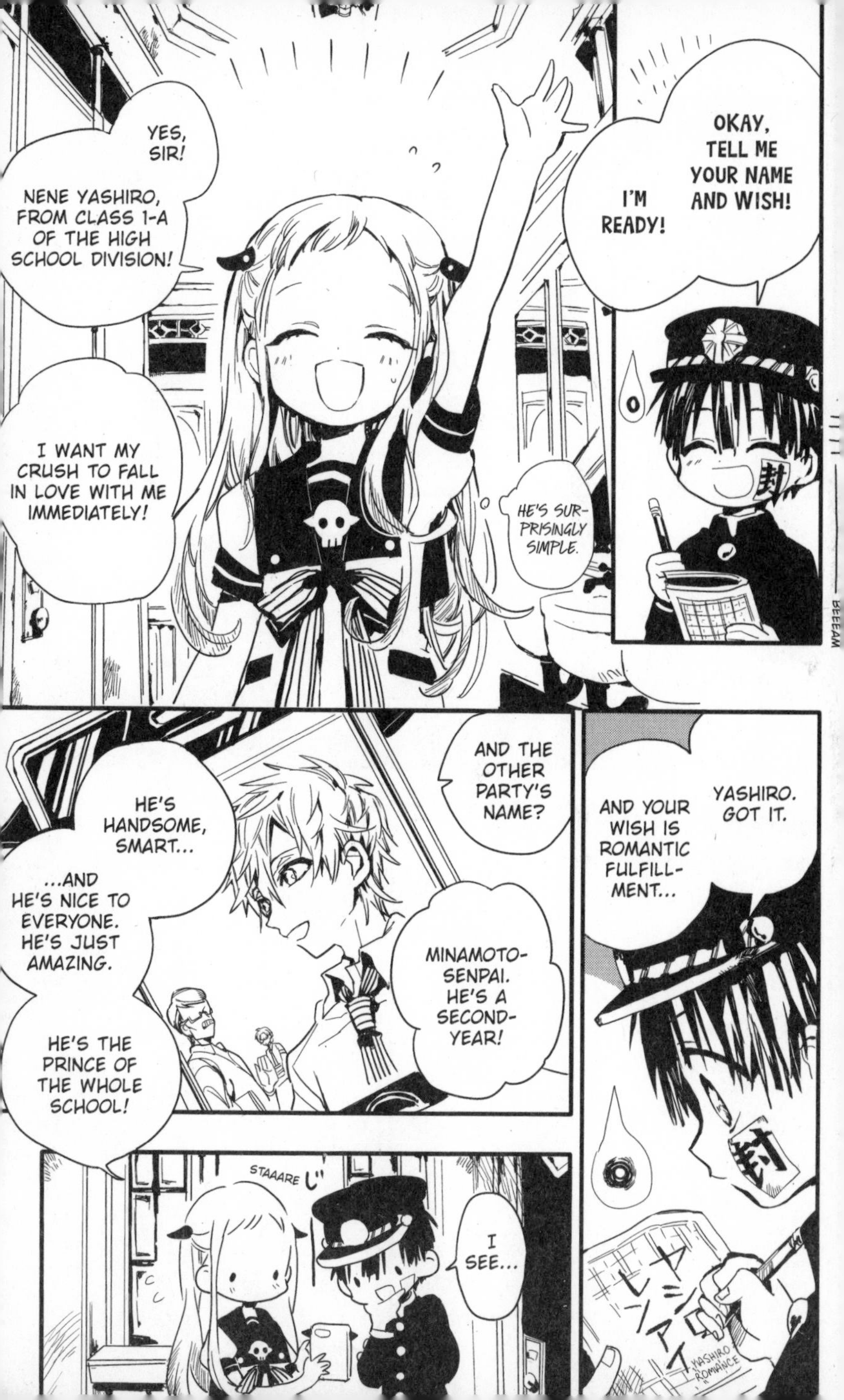
OKAY, TELL ME YOUR NAME AND WISH!
I'M READY!
BEEEAM
YES, SIR!
NENE YASHIRO, FROM CLASS 1-A OF THE HIGH SCHOOL DIVISION!
I WANT MY CRUSH TO FALL IN LOVE WITH ME IMMEDIATELY!
HE'S SURPRISINGLY SIMPLE.
YASHIRO. GOT IT.
AND YOUR WISH IS ROMANTIC FULFILL-MENT...
YASHIRO ROMANCE
AND THE OTHER PARTY'S NAME?
MINAMOTO-SENPAI. HE'S A SECOND-YEAR!
HE'S HANDSOME, SMART...
...AND HE'S NICE TO EVERYONE. HE'S JUST AMAZING.
HE'S THE PRINCE OF THE WHOLE SCHOOL!
STAAARE
I SEE...

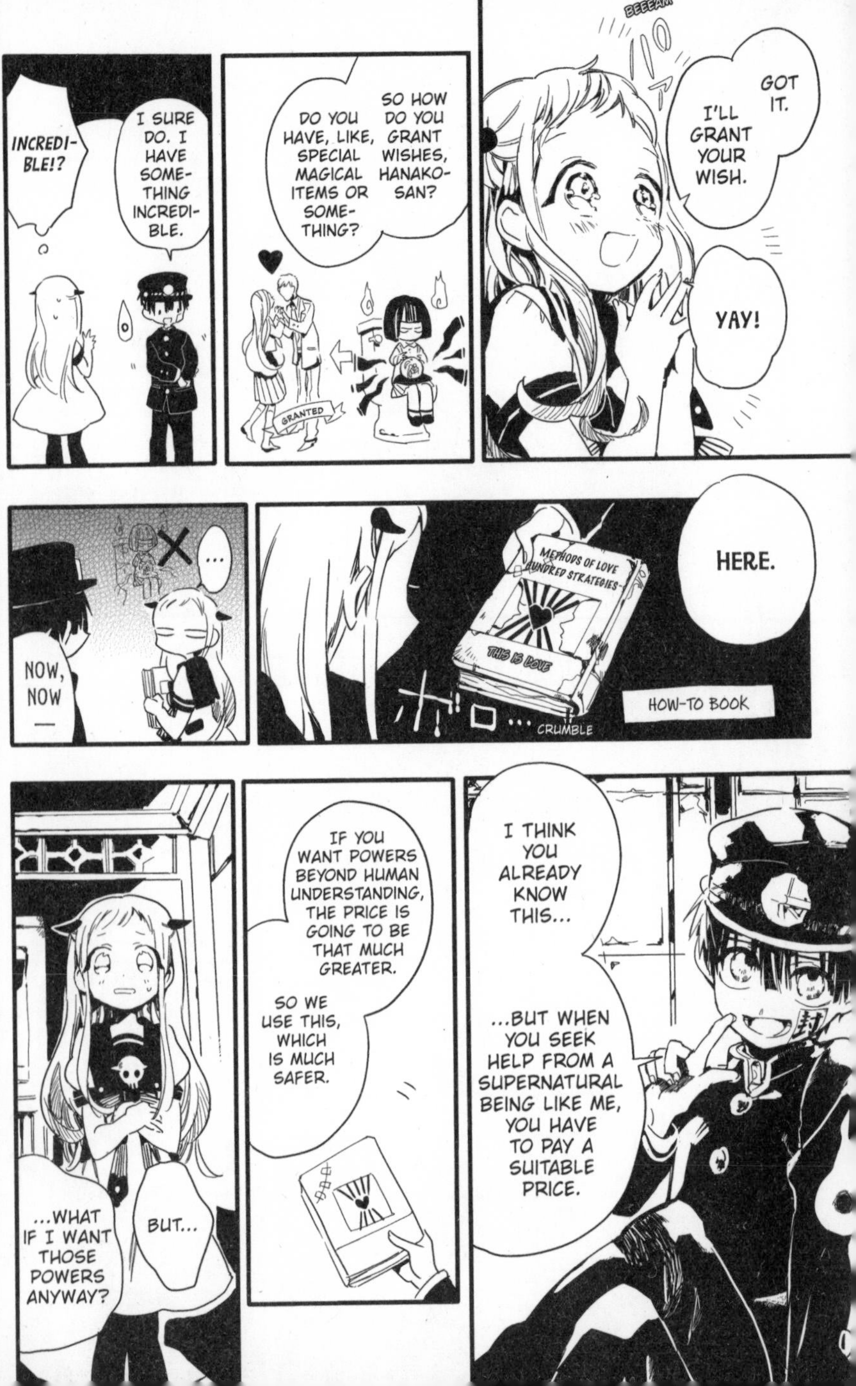
BEEEAM
GOT IT.
I'LL GRANT YOUR WISH.
YAY!
SO HOW DO YOU GRANT WISHES, HANAKO-SAN?
DO YOU HAVE, LIKE, SPECIAL MAGICAL ITEMS OR SOMETHING?
GRANTED
I SURE DO. I HAVE SOMETHING INCREDIBLE.
INCREDIBLE!?
HERE.
METHODS OF LOVE —HUNDRED STRATEGIES—
THIS IS LOVE
HOW-TO BOOK
CRUMBLE
...
NOW, NOW —
I THINK YOU ALREADY KNOW THIS...
...BUT WHEN YOU SEEK HELP FROM A SUPERNATURAL BEING LIKE ME, YOU HAVE TO PAY A SUITABLE PRICE.
IF YOU WANT POWERS BEYOND HUMAN UNDERSTANDING, THE PRICE IS GOING TO BE THAT MUCH GREATER.
SO WE USE THIS, WHICH IS MUCH SAFER.
BUT...
...WHAT IF I WANT THOSE POWERS ANYWAY?

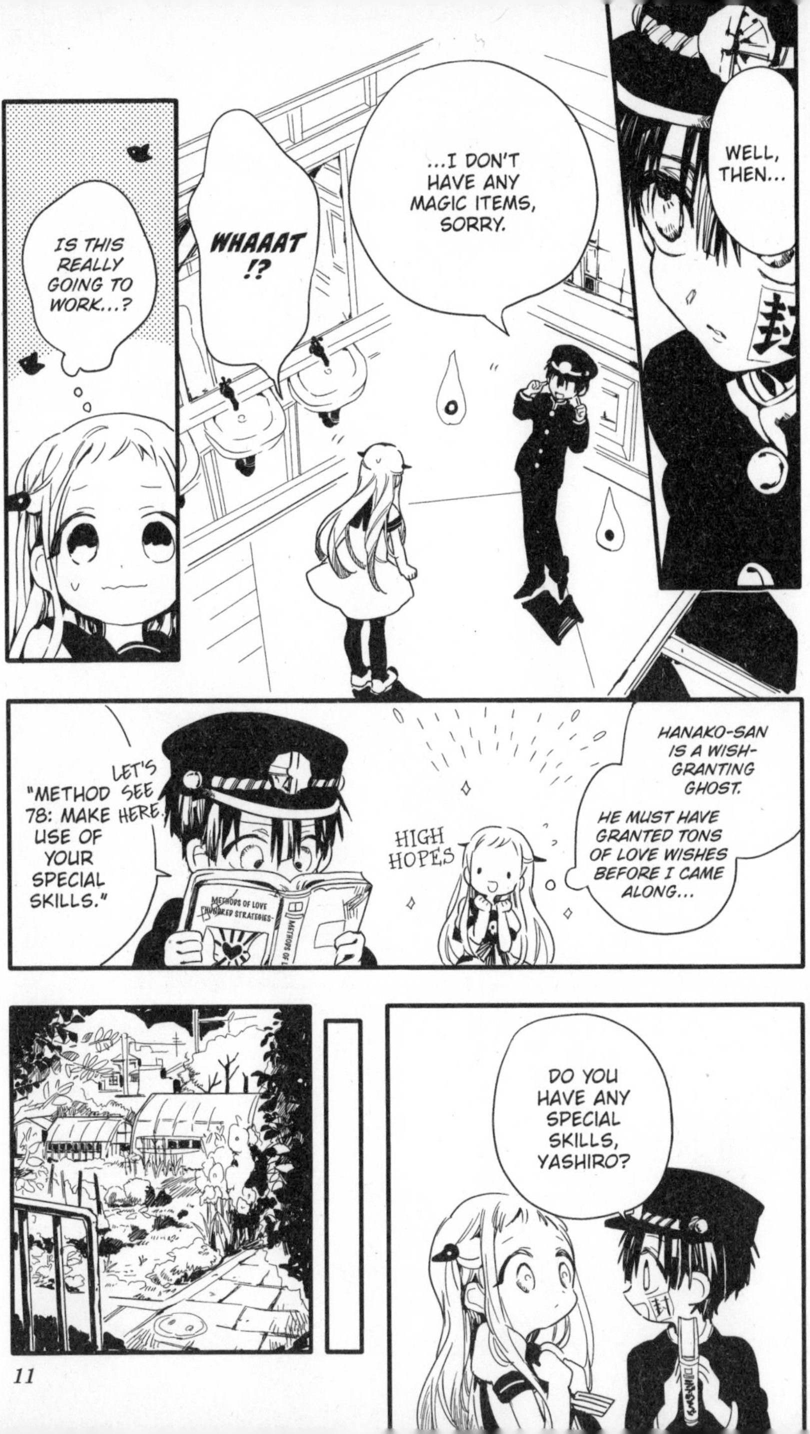
WELL, THEN...
...I DON'T HAVE ANY MAGIC ITEMS, SORRY.
WHAAAT!?
IS THIS REALLY GOING TO WORK...?
HANAKO-SAN IS A WISH-GRANTING GHOST.
HE MUST HAVE GRANTED TONS OF LOVE WISHES BEFORE I CAME ALONG...
HIGH HOPES
LET'S SEE HERE.
"METHOD 78: MAKE USE OF YOUR SPECIAL SKILLS."
METHODS OF LOVE
HUNDRED STRATEGIES
DO YOU HAVE ANY SPECIAL SKILLS, YASHIRO?

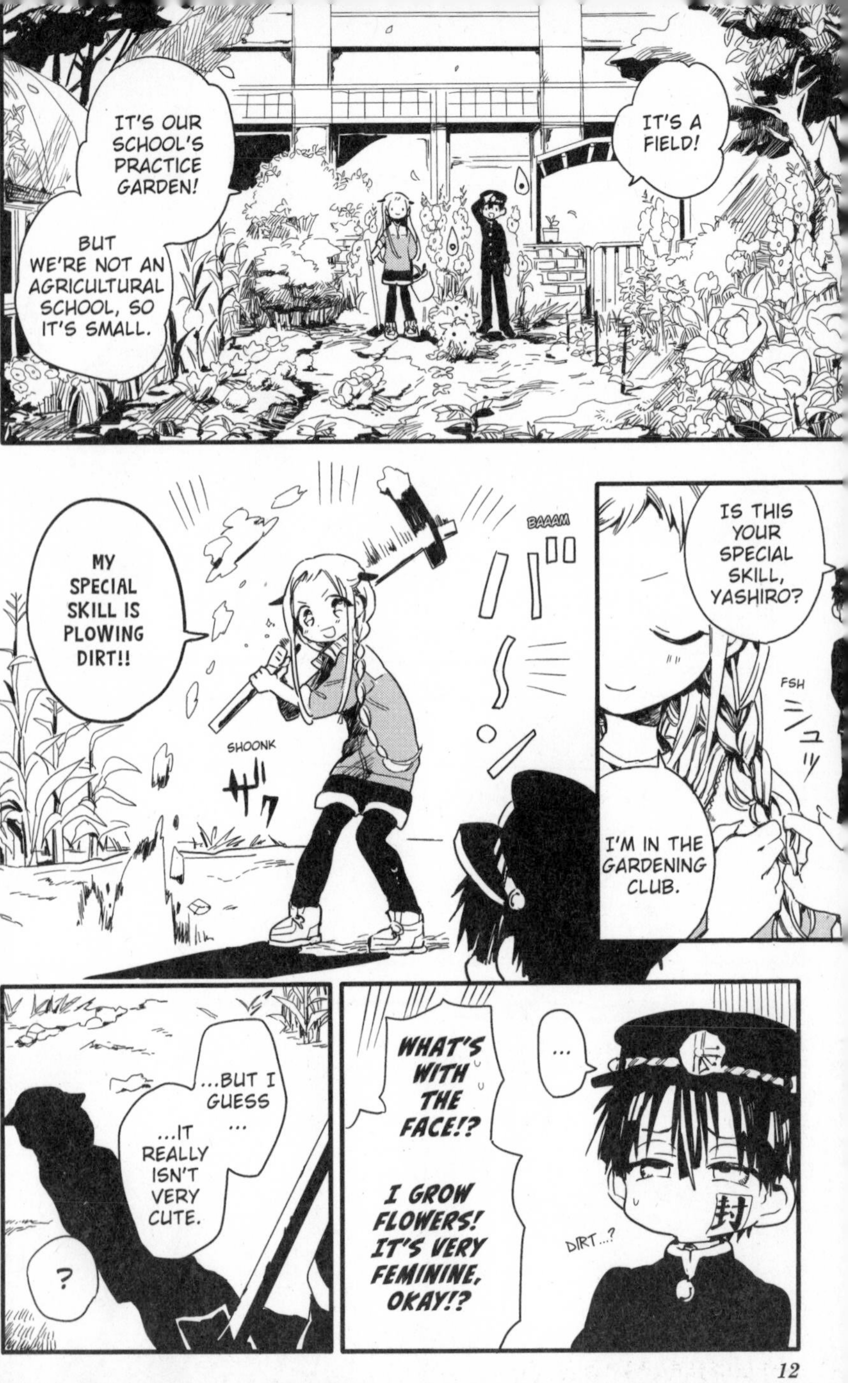
IT'S A FIELD!
IT'S OUR SCHOOL'S PRACTICE GARDEN!
BUT WE'RE NOT AN AGRICULTURAL SCHOOL, SO IT'S SMALL.
IS THIS YOUR SPECIAL SKILL, YASHIRO?
FSH
I'M IN THE GARDENING CLUB.
BAAAM
MY SPECIAL SKILL IS PLOWING DIRT!!
SHOONK
...
DIRT...?
WHAT'S WITH THE FACE!?
I GROW FLOWERS! IT'S VERY FEMININE, OKAY!?
...BUT I GUESS...
...IT REALLY ISN'T VERY CUTE.
?

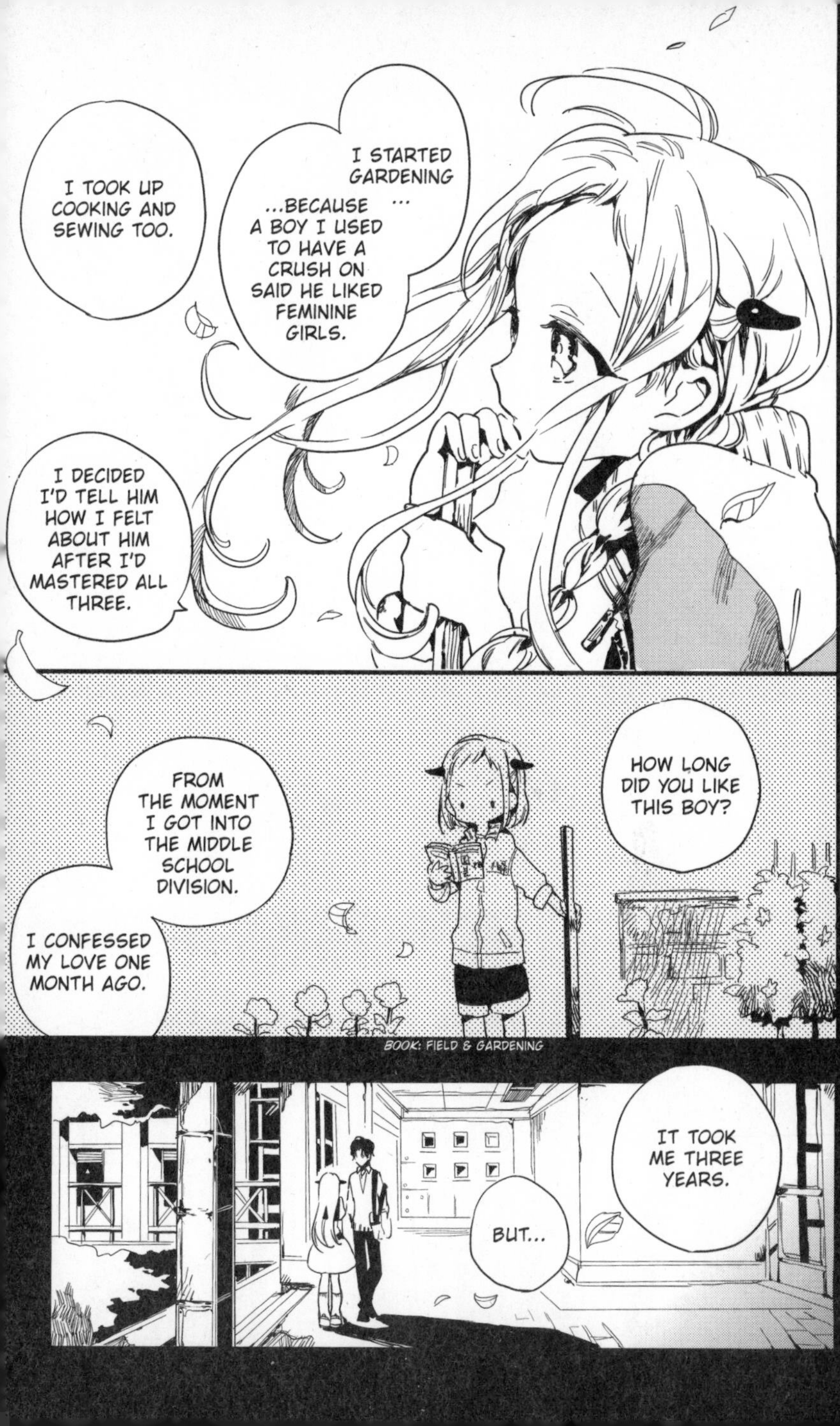
I STARTED GARDENING ... ...BECAUSE A BOY I USED TO HAVE A CRUSH ON SAID HE LIKED FEMININE GIRLS.
I TOOK UP COOKING AND SEWING TOO.
I DECIDED I'D TELL HIM HOW I FELT ABOUT HIM AFTER I'D MASTERED ALL THREE.
HOW LONG DID YOU LIKE THIS BOY?
FROM THE MOMENT I GOT INTO THE MIDDLE SCHOOL DIVISION.
I CONFESSED MY LOVE ONE MONTH AGO.
BOOK: FIELD & GARDENING
IT TOOK ME THREE YEARS.
BUT...

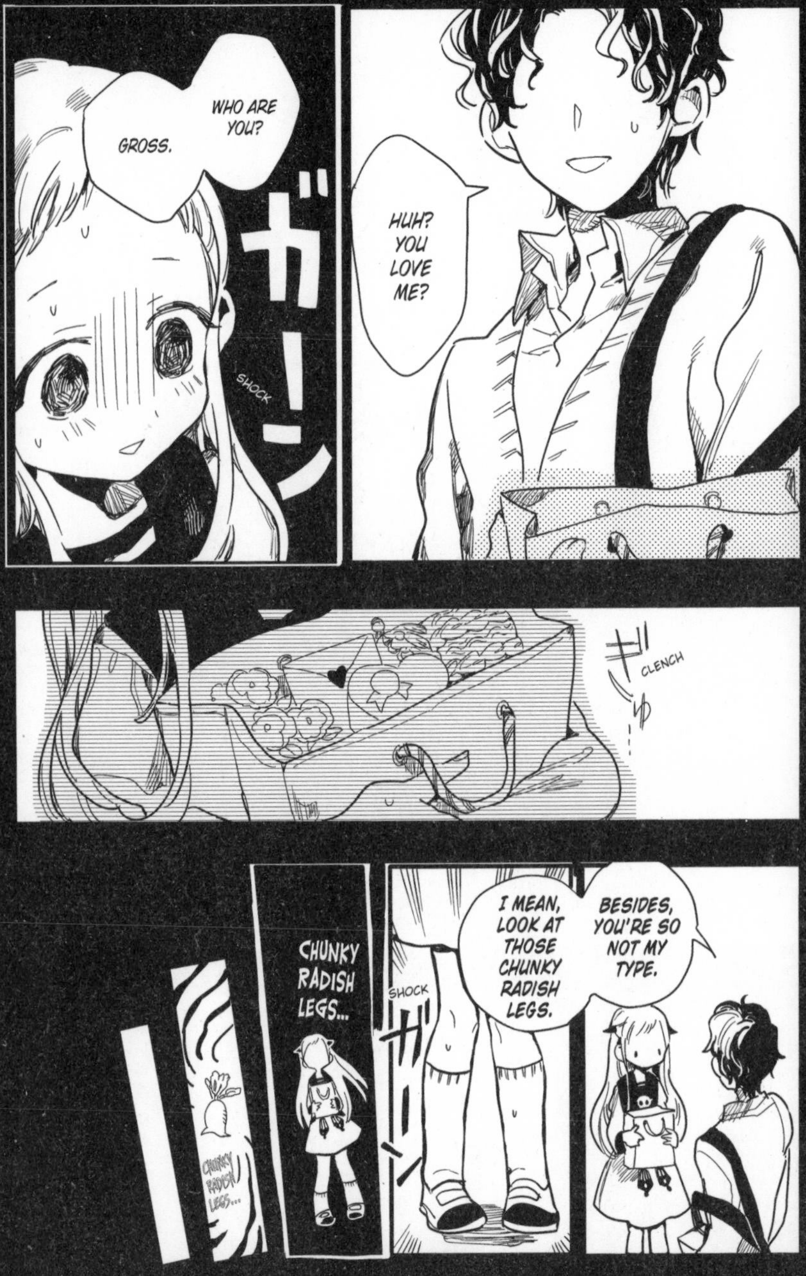
HUH? YOU LOVE ME?
WHO ARE YOU?
GROSS.
ガーン
SHOCK
CLENCH
BESIDES, YOU'RE SO NOT MY TYPE.
I MEAN, LOOK AT THOSE CHUNKY RADISH LEGS.
SHOCK
CHUNKY RADISH LEGS...
CHUNKY RADISH LEGS...

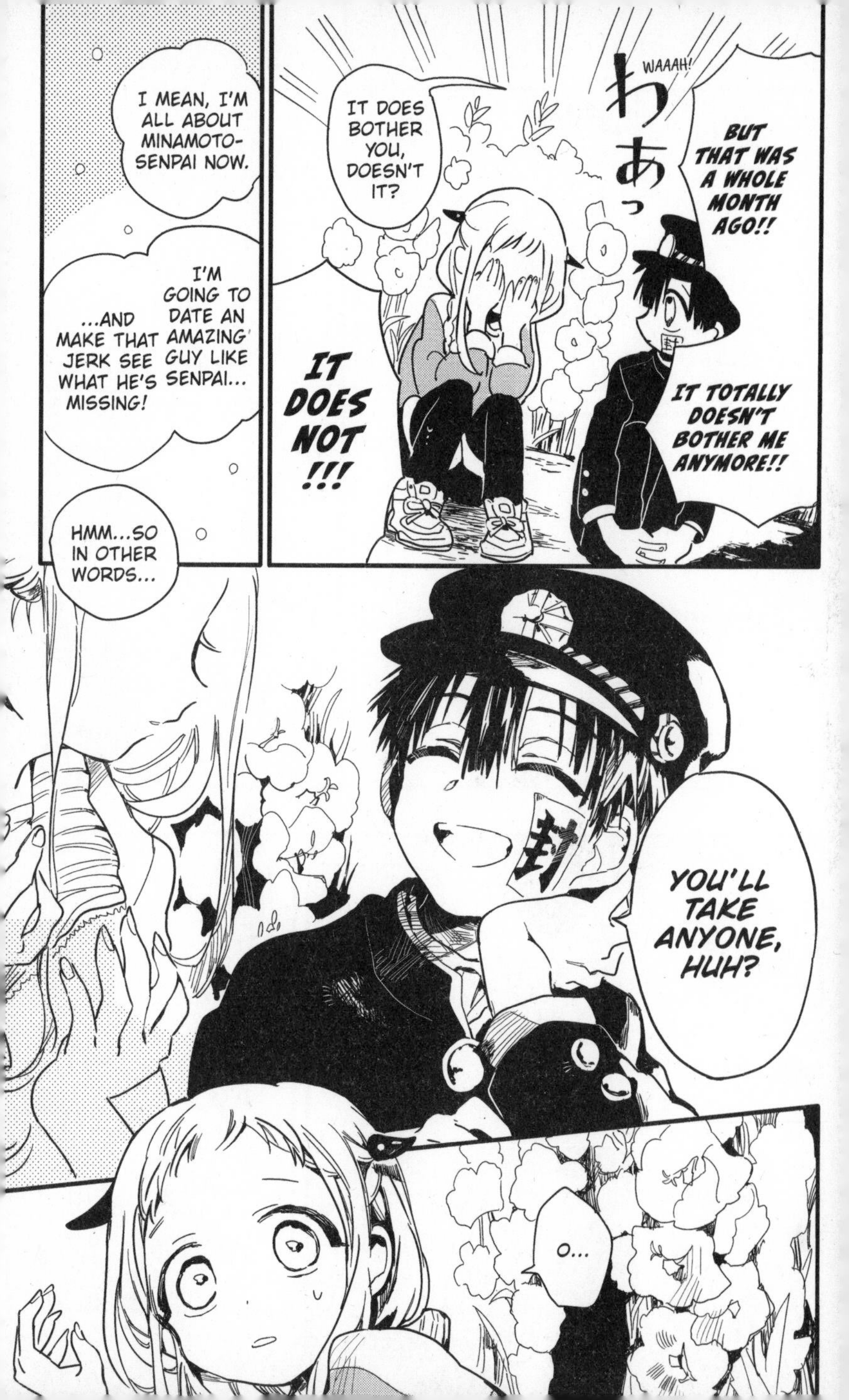
IT DOES BOTHER YOU, DOESN'T IT?
わぁっ
WAAAH!
BUT THAT WAS A WHOLE MONTH AGO!!
IT TOTALLY DOESN'T BOTHER ME ANYMORE!!
IT DOES NOT!!!
I MEAN, I'M ALL ABOUT MINAMOTO-SENPAI NOW.
I'M GOING TO DATE AN AMAZING GUY LIKE SENPAI...
...AND MAKE THAT JERK SEE WHAT HE'S MISSING!
HMM...SO IN OTHER WORDS...
YOU'LL TAKE ANYONE, HUH?
O...

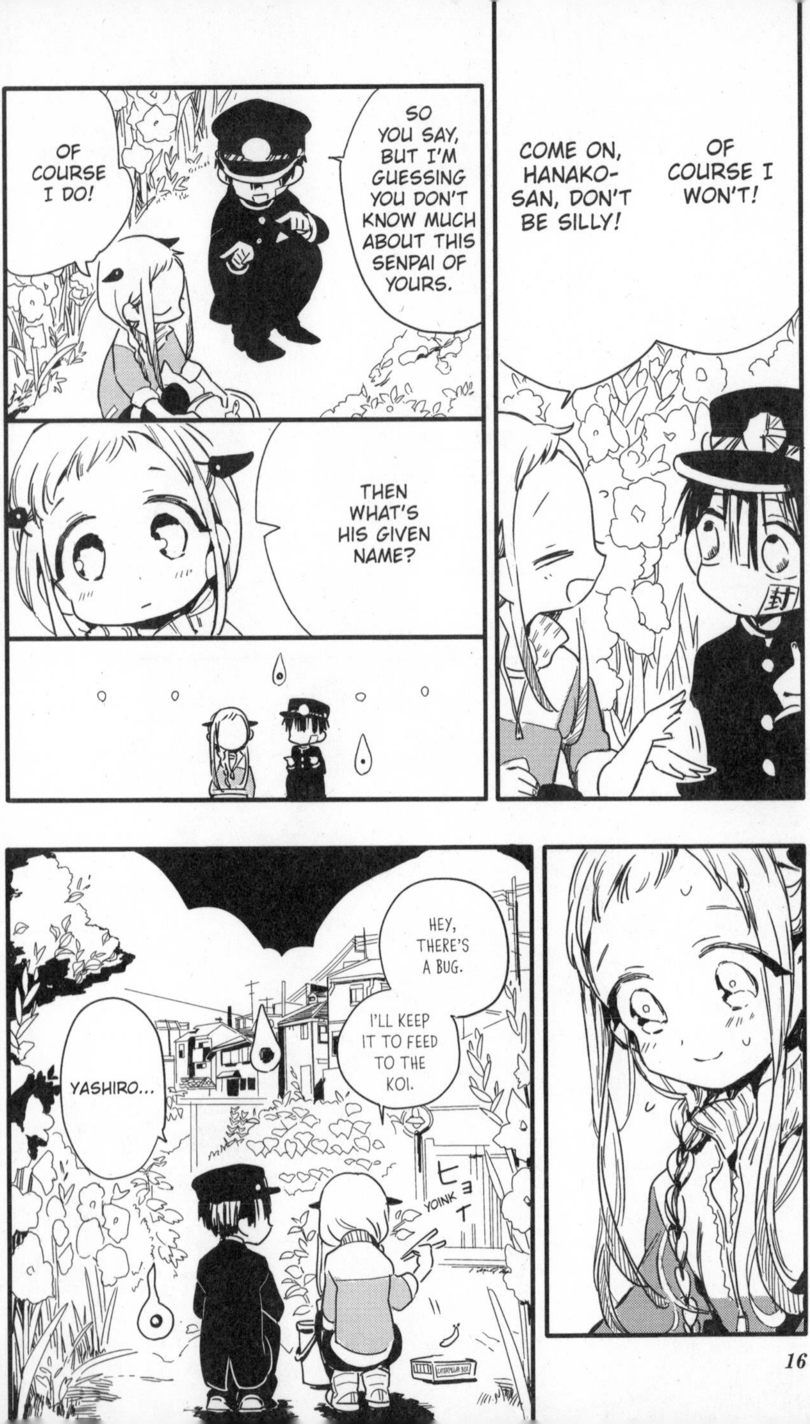
OF COURSE I WON'T!
COME ON, HANAKO-SAN, DON'T BE SILLY!
SO YOU SAY, BUT I'M GUESSING YOU DON'T KNOW MUCH ABOUT THIS SENPAI OF YOURS.
OF COURSE I DO!
THEN WHAT'S HIS GIVEN NAME?
HEY, THERE'S A BUG.
I'LL KEEP IT TO FEED TO THE KOI.
YASHIRO...
ヒョイ
YOINK
CATERPILLAR BOX

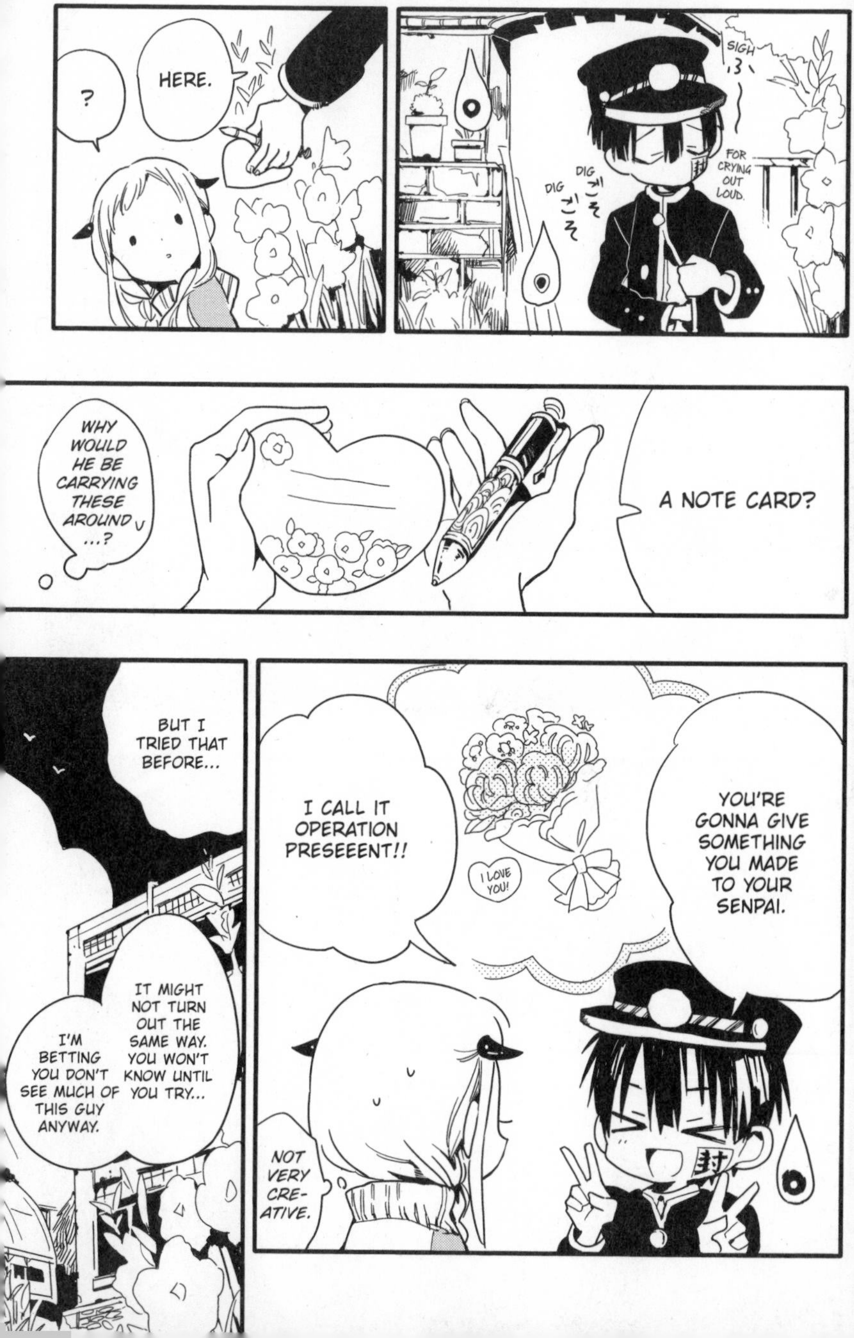
SIGH
FOR CRYING OUT LOUD.
DIG
DIG
HERE.
?
A NOTE CARD?
WHY WOULD HE BE CARRYING THESE AROUND...?
YOU'RE GONNA GIVE SOMETHING YOU MADE TO YOUR SENPAI.
I LOVE YOU!
I CALL IT OPERATION PRESEEENT!!
NOT VERY CRE-ATIVE.
BUT I TRIED THAT BEFORE...
IT MIGHT NOT TURN OUT THE SAME WAY. YOU WON'T KNOW UNTIL YOU TRY...
I'M BETTING YOU DON'T SEE MUCH OF THIS GUY ANYWAY.

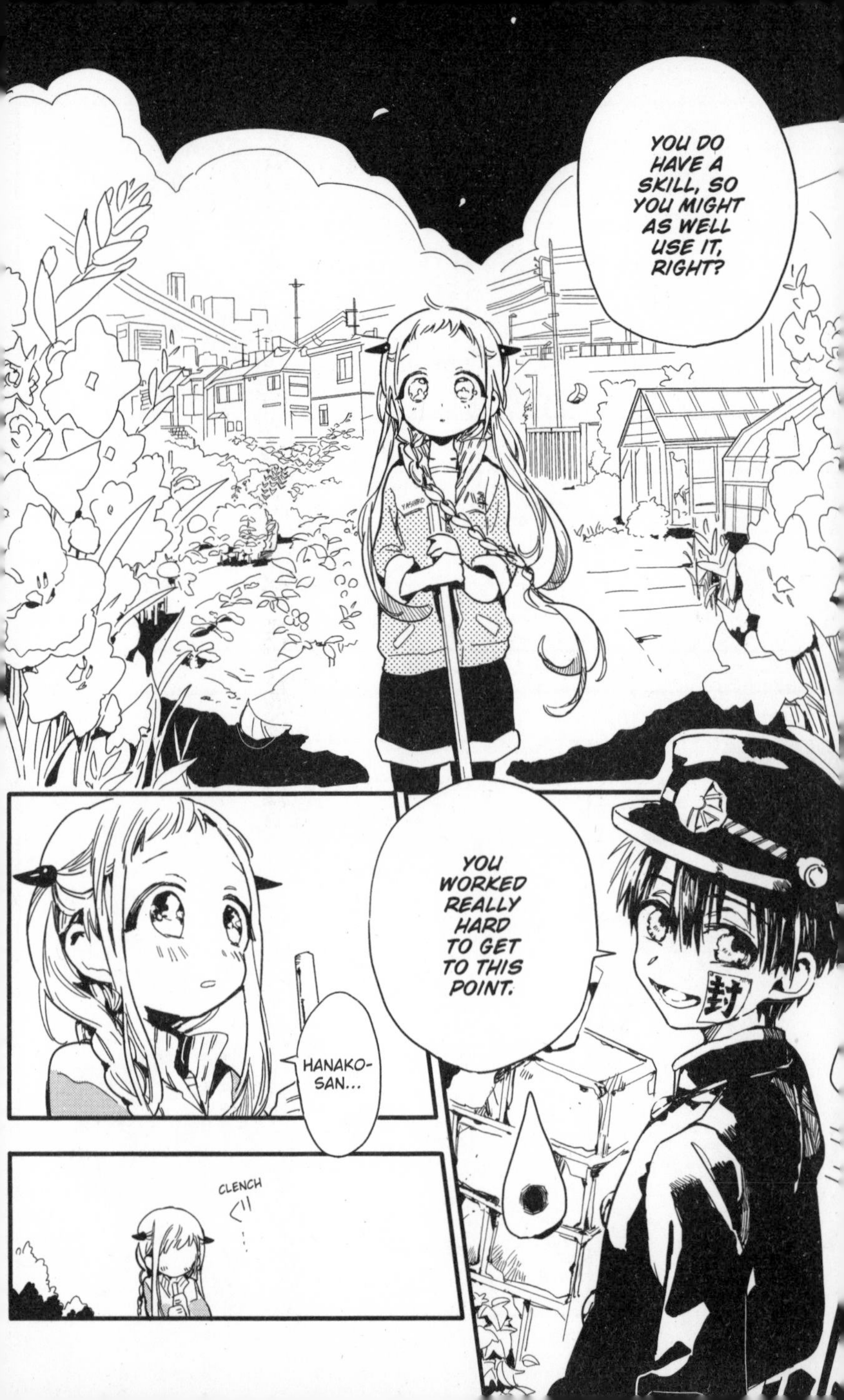
YOU DO HAVE A SKILL, SO YOU MIGHT AS WELL USE IT, RIGHT?
YASHIRO
YOU WORKED REALLY HARD TO GET TO THIS POINT.
HANAKO-SAN...
CLENCH

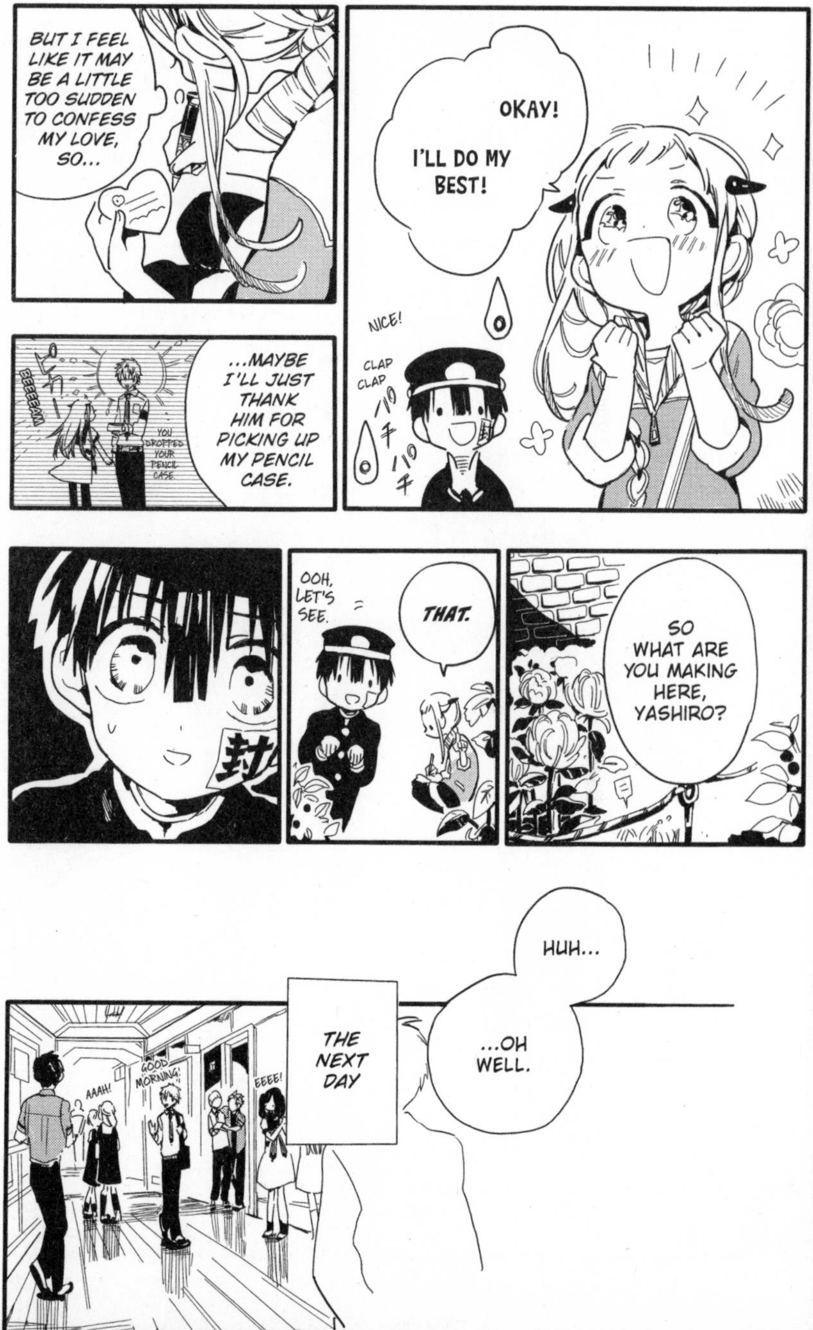
OKAY!
I'LL DO MY BEST!
NICE!
CLAP CLAP
BUT I FEEL LIKE IT MAY BE A LITTLE TOO SUDDEN TO CONFESS MY LOVE, SO...
...MAYBE I'LL JUST THANK HIM FOR PICKING UP MY PENCIL CASE.
BEEEEAM
YOU DROPPED YOUR PENCIL CASE.
SO WHAT ARE YOU MAKING HERE, YASHIRO?
THAT.
OOH, LET'S SEE.
HUH...
...OH WELL.
THE NEXT DAY
EEEE!
GOOD MORNING!
AAAH!

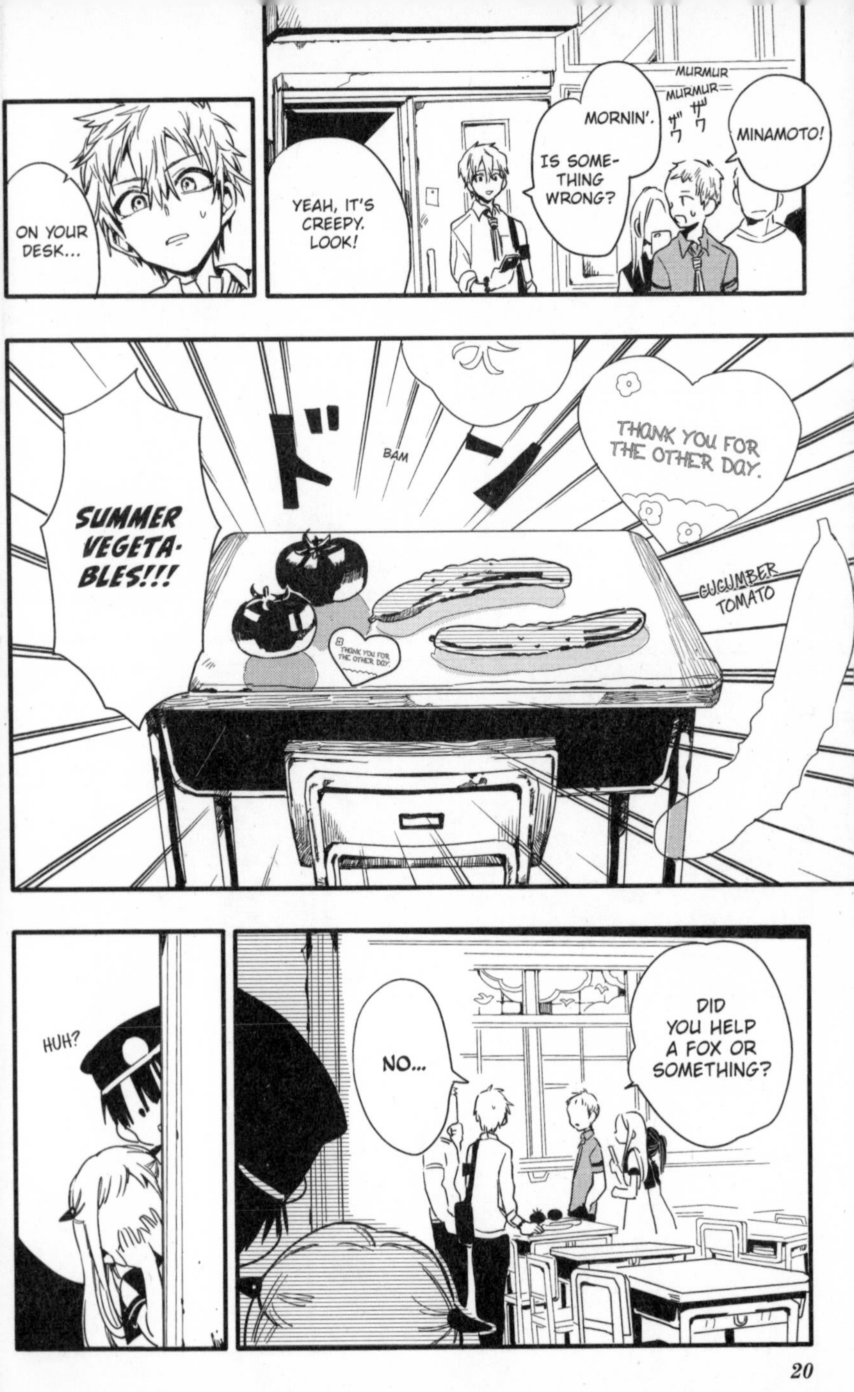
MINAMOTO!
MURMUR MURMUR
ザワ ザワ
MORNIN'.
IS SOMETHING WRONG?
YEAH, IT'S CREEPY. LOOK!
ON YOUR DESK...
THANK YOU FOR THE OTHER DAY.
CUCUMBER TOMATO
ド
BAM
SUMMER VEGETABLES!!!
THANK YOU FOR THE OTHER DAY.
DID YOU HELP A FOX OR SOMETHING?
NO...
HUH?

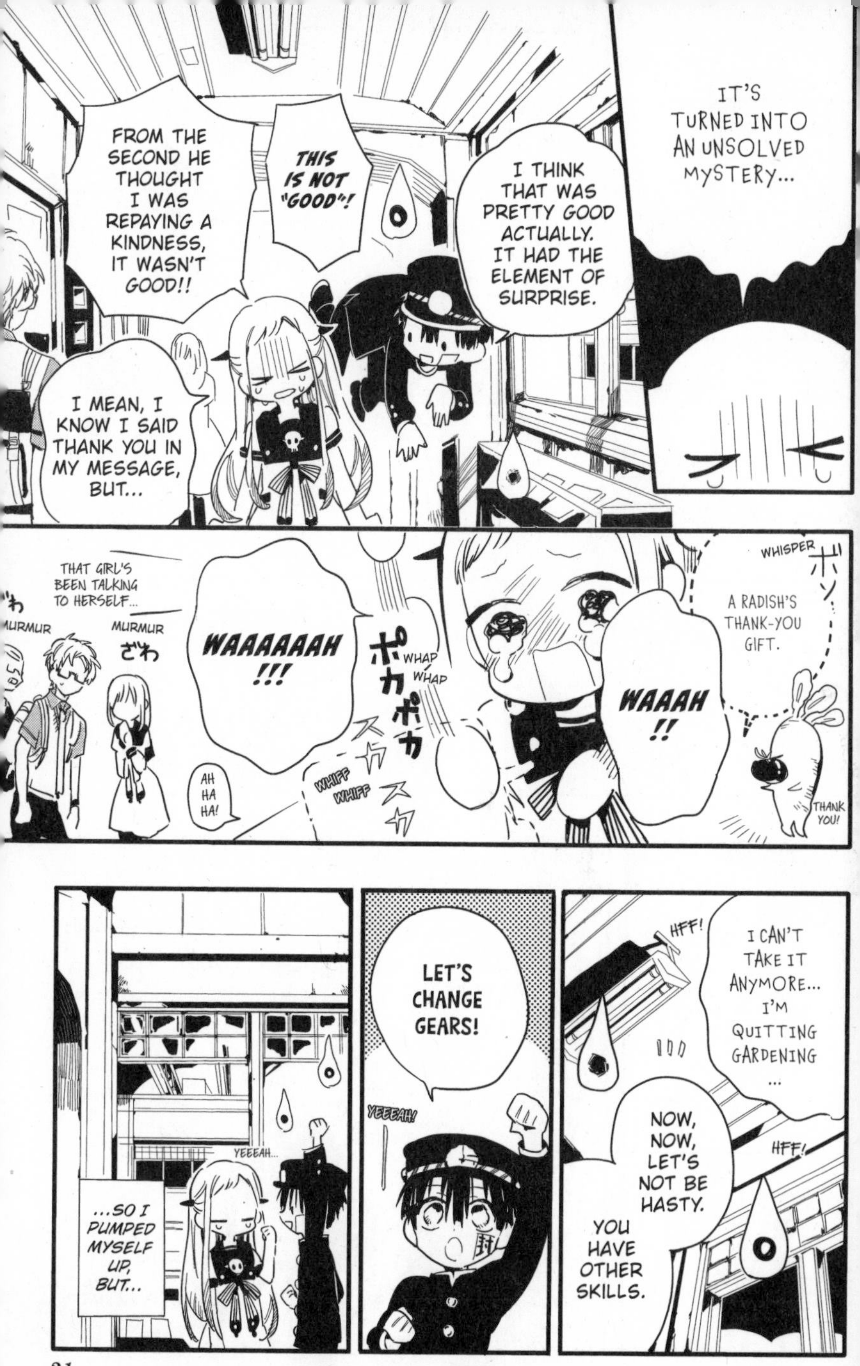
IT'S TURNED INTO AN UNSOLVED MYSTERY...
I THINK THAT WAS PRETTY GOOD ACTUALLY. IT HAD THE ELEMENT OF SURPRISE.
THIS IS NOT "GOOD"!
FROM THE SECOND HE THOUGHT I WAS REPAYING A KINDNESS, IT WASN'T GOOD!!
I MEAN, I KNOW I SAID THANK YOU IN MY MESSAGE, BUT...
WHISPER ボソ
A RADISH'S THANK-YOU GIFT.
THANK YOU!
WAAAH!!
ポカポカ WHAP WHAP
スカスカ WHIFF WHIFF
WAAAAAAH!!!
AH HA HA!
THAT GIRL'S BEEN TALKING TO HERSELF...
MURMUR ざわ
MURMUR ざわ
HFF!
I CAN'T TAKE IT ANYMORE... I'M QUITTING GARDENING...
NOW, NOW, LET'S NOT BE HASTY. YOU HAVE OTHER SKILLS.
HFF!
LET'S CHANGE GEARS!
YEEEAH!
YEEEAH...
...SO I PUMPED MYSELF UP, BUT...

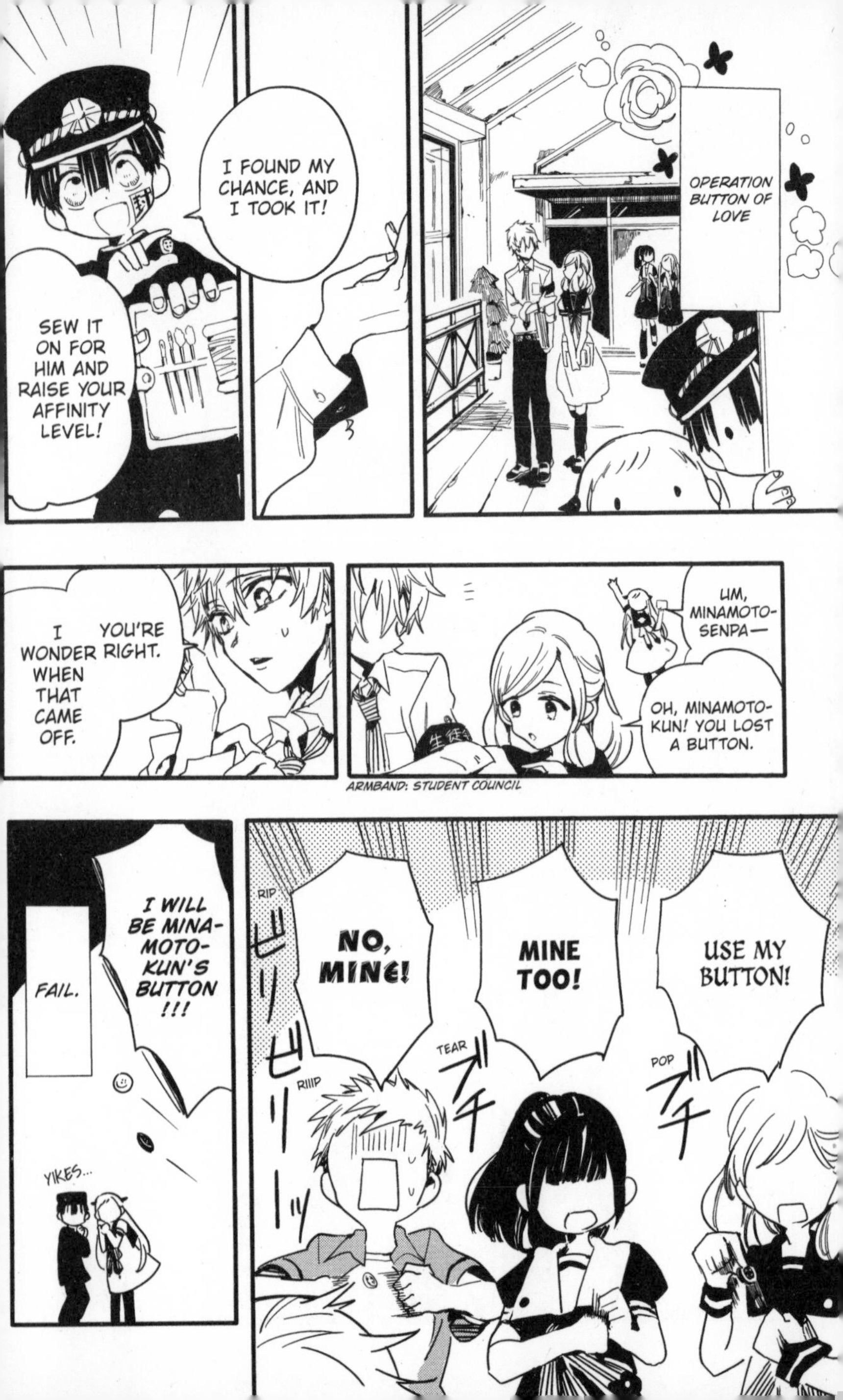
OPERATION BUTTON OF LOVE
I FOUND MY CHANCE, AND I TOOK IT!
SEW IT ON FOR HIM AND RAISE YOUR AFFINITY LEVEL!
UM, MINAMOTO-SENPA—
OH, MINAMOTO-KUN! YOU LOST A BUTTON.
ARMBAND: STUDENT COUNCIL
YOU'RE RIGHT.
I WONDER WHEN THAT CAME OFF.
USE MY BUTTON!
POP
MINE TOO!
TEAR
NO, MINE!
RIP
RIIIP
I WILL BE MINA-MOTO-KUN'S BUTTON!!!
FAIL.
YIKES...

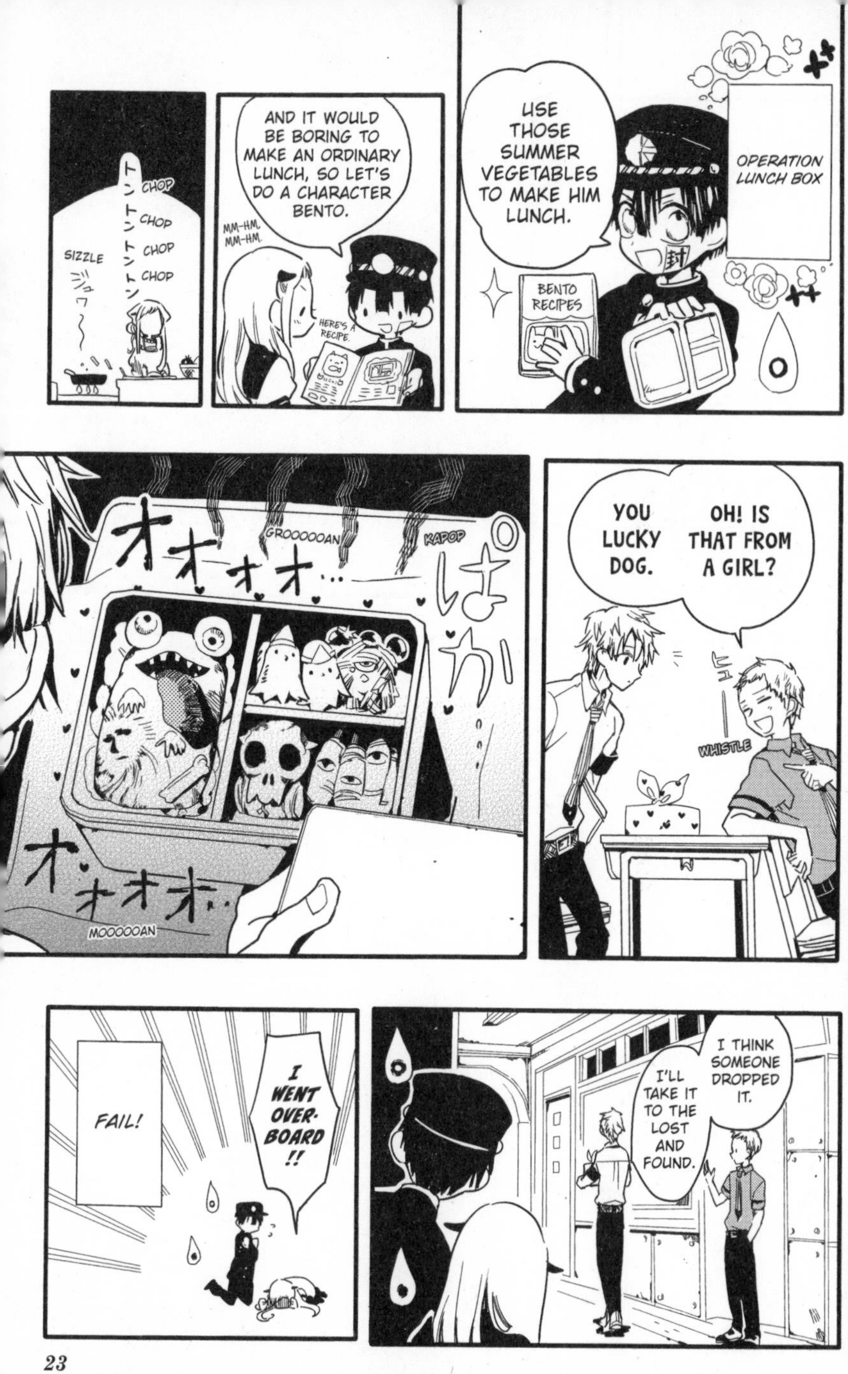
OPERATION LUNCH BOX
USE THOSE SUMMER VEGETABLES TO MAKE HIM LUNCH.
BENTO RECIPES
AND IT WOULD BE BORING TO MAKE AN ORDINARY LUNCH, SO LET'S DO A CHARACTER BENTO.
MM-HM, MM-HM.
HERE'S A RECIPE.
トントントントン
CHOP
CHOP
CHOP
CHOP
ジュワ〜
SIZZLE
OH! IS THAT FROM A GIRL?
YOU LUCKY DOG.
ヒュ
WHISTLE
ぱか
KAPOP
オオオオ…
GROOOOOAN
オオオオ…
MOOOOOAN
I THINK SOMEONE DROPPED IT.
I'LL TAKE IT TO THE LOST AND FOUND.
I WENT OVER-BOARD!!
FAIL!

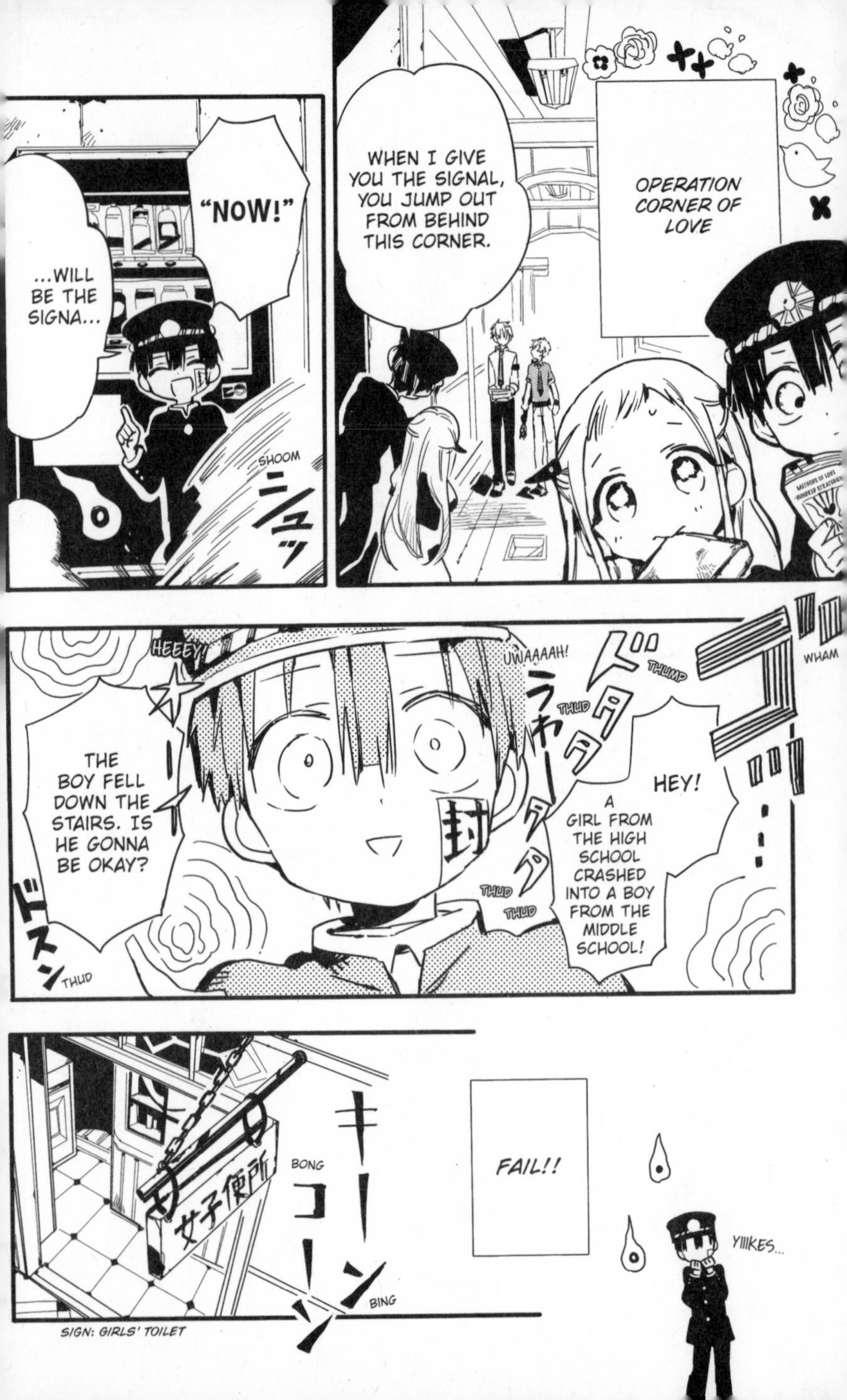
OPERATION CORNER OF LOVE
WHEN I GIVE YOU THE SIGNAL, YOU JUMP OUT FROM BEHIND THIS CORNER.
"NOW!"
...WILL BE THE SIGNA...
SHOOM
シュッ
WHAM
ゴッ
THUMP
ドッ
UWAAAAH!
うわーっ
THUD
タタタ
HEY! A GIRL FROM THE HIGH SCHOOL CRASHED INTO A BOY FROM THE MIDDLE SCHOOL!
THUD
THUD
HEEEY!
THE BOY FELL DOWN THE STAIRS. IS HE GONNA BE OKAY?
ドスン
THUD
FAIL!!
YIIIKES...
BONG
キーンコーン
BING
女子便所
SIGN: GIRLS' TOILET

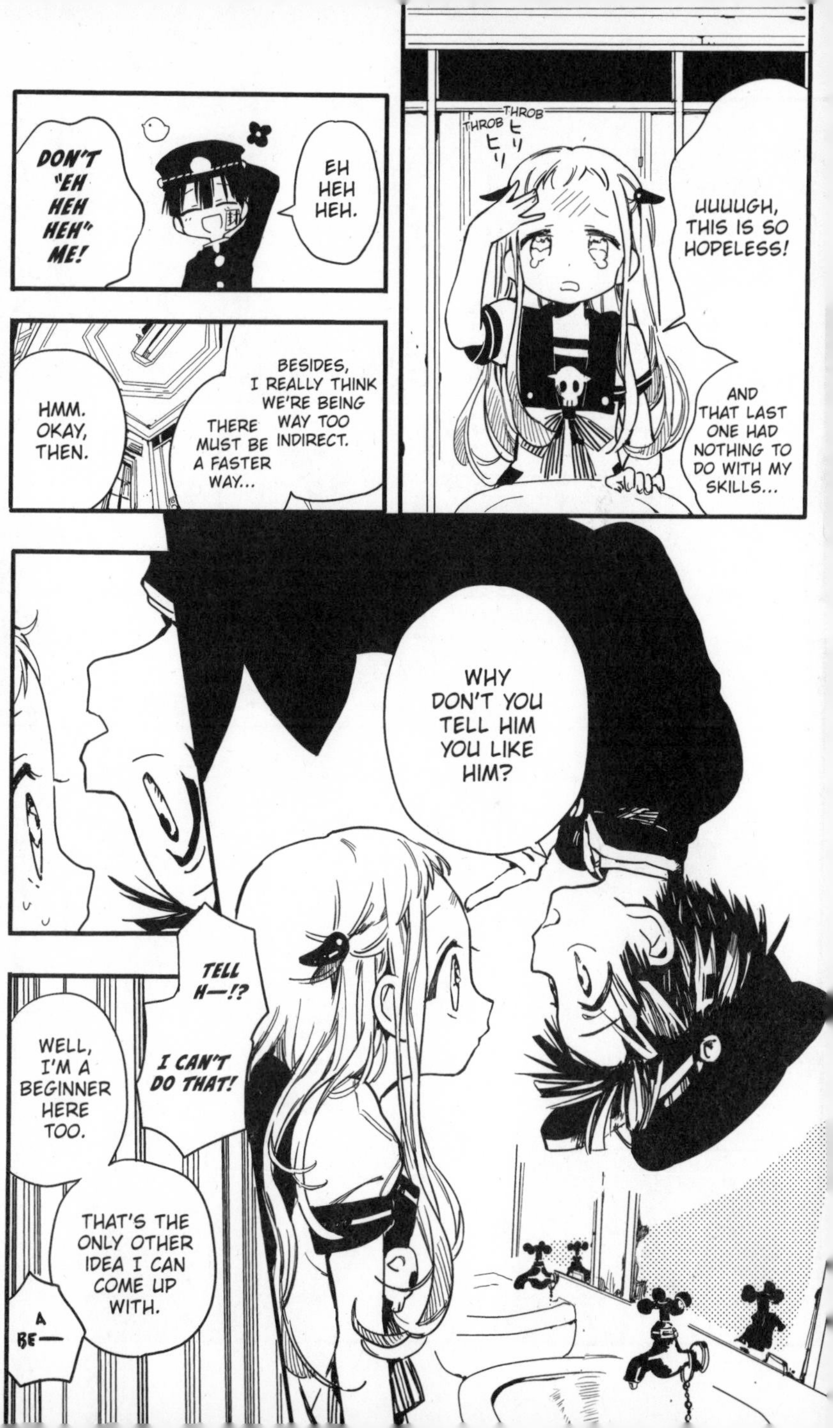
THROB ヒリ
THROB ヒリ
UUUUGH, THIS IS SO HOPELESS!
AND THAT LAST ONE HAD NOTHING TO DO WITH MY SKILLS...
EH HEH HEH.
DON'T "EH HEH HEH" ME!
BESIDES, I REALLY THINK WE'RE BEING WAY TOO INDIRECT.
THERE MUST BE A FASTER WAY...
HMM. OKAY, THEN.
WHY DON'T YOU TELL HIM YOU LIKE HIM?
TELL H—!?
I CAN'T DO THAT!
WELL, I'M A BEGINNER HERE TOO.
THAT'S THE ONLY OTHER IDEA I CAN COME UP WITH.
A BE—

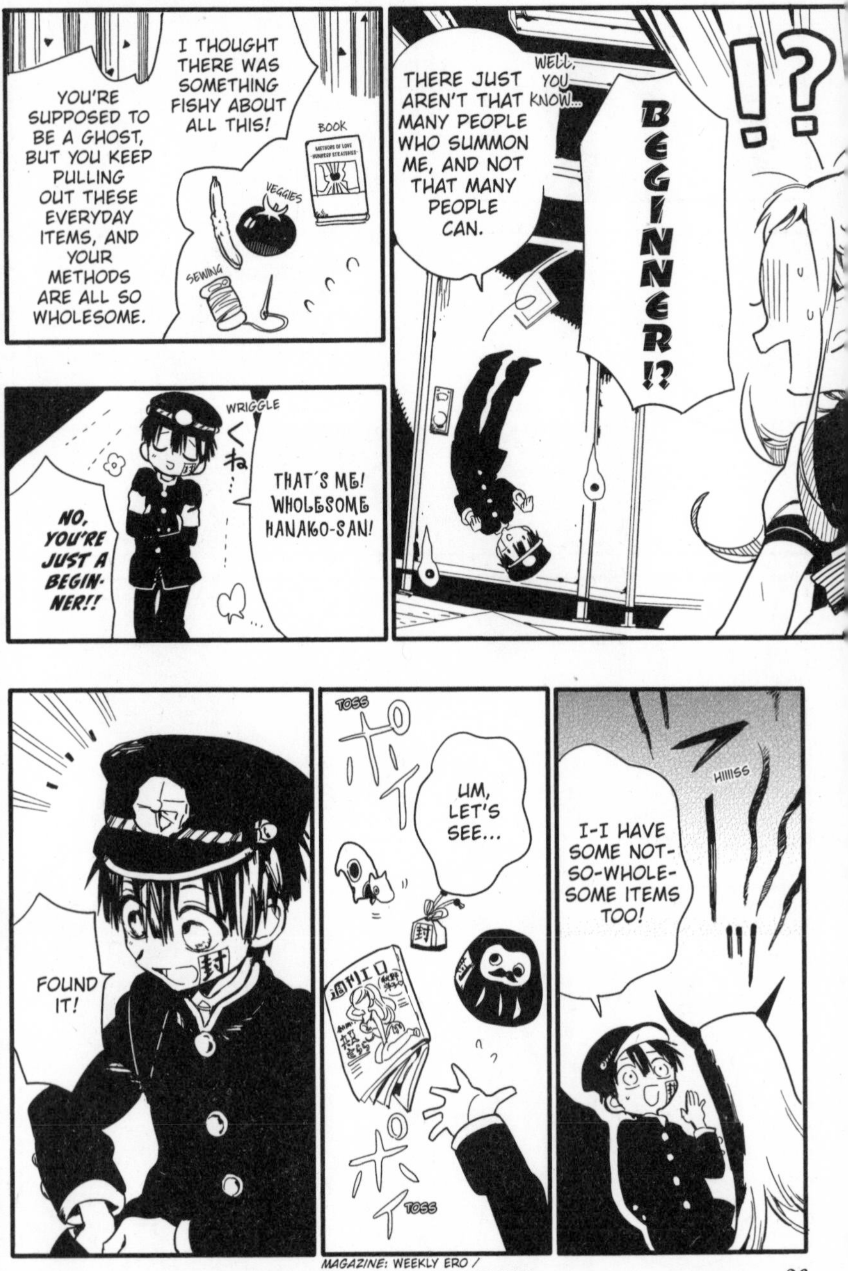
!?
WELL, YOU KNOW...
THERE JUST AREN'T THAT MANY PEOPLE WHO SUMMON ME, AND NOT THAT MANY PEOPLE CAN.
BEGINNER!?
I THOUGHT THERE WAS SOMETHING FISHY ABOUT ALL THIS!
YOU'RE SUPPOSED TO BE A GHOST, BUT YOU KEEP PULLING OUT THESE EVERYDAY ITEMS, AND YOUR METHODS ARE ALL SO WHOLESOME.
BOOK
VEGGIES
SEWING
WRIGGLE
THAT'S ME! WHOLESOME HANAKO-SAN!
NO, YOU'RE JUST A BEGINNER!!
HIIIISS
I-I HAVE SOME NOT-SO-WHOLESOME ITEMS TOO!
TOSS
UM, LET'S SEE...
TOSS
FOUND IT!

MAGAZINE: WEEKLY ERO / YOUKO AKINO / SARARA MANATSU

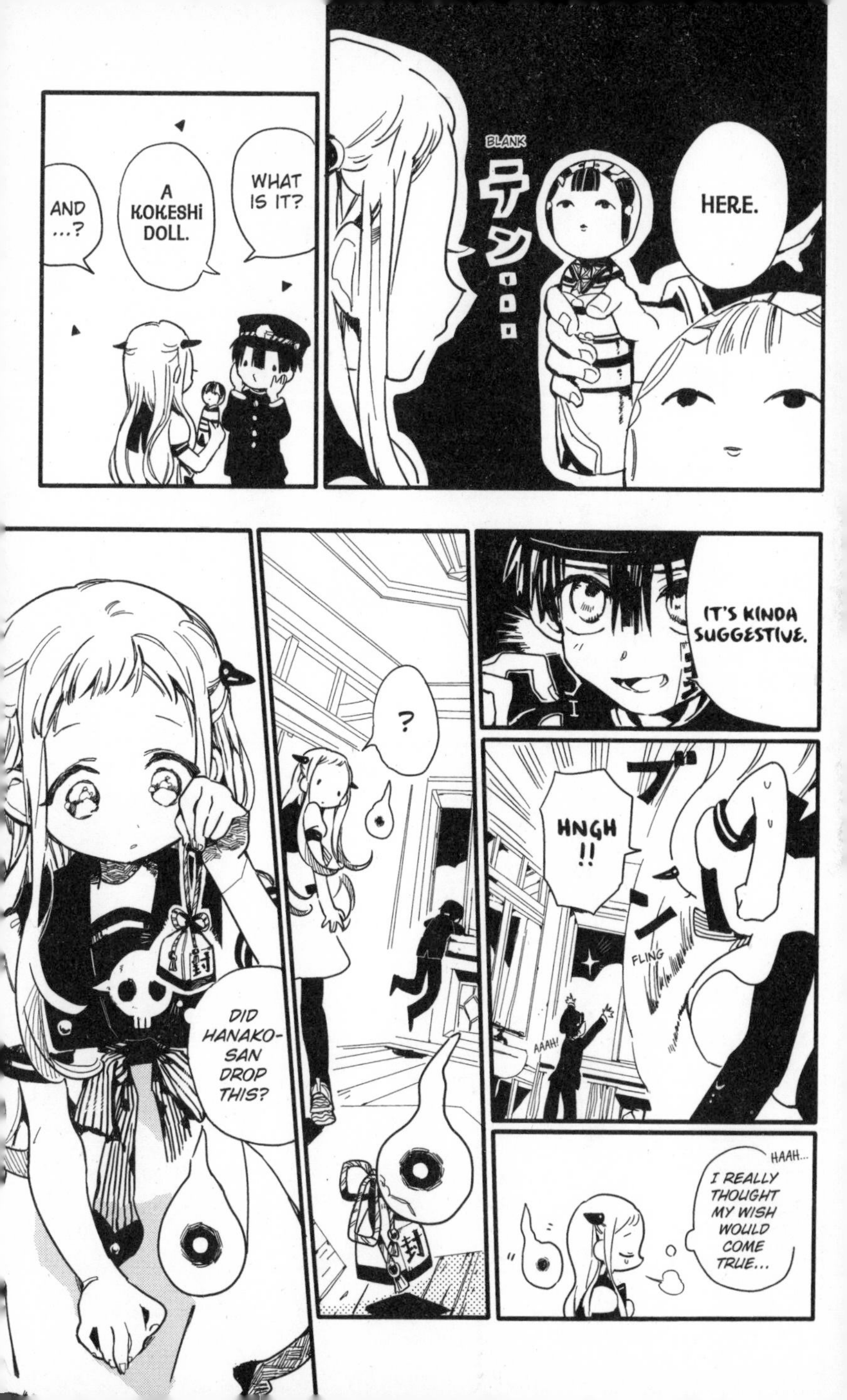
HERE.
BLANK
テン
WHAT IS IT?
A KOKESHI DOLL.
AND ...?
IT'S KINDA SUGGESTIVE.
HNGH !!
ブン
FLING
AAAH!
HAAH...
I REALLY THOUGHT MY WISH WOULD COME TRUE...
?
DID HANAKO-SAN DROP THIS?

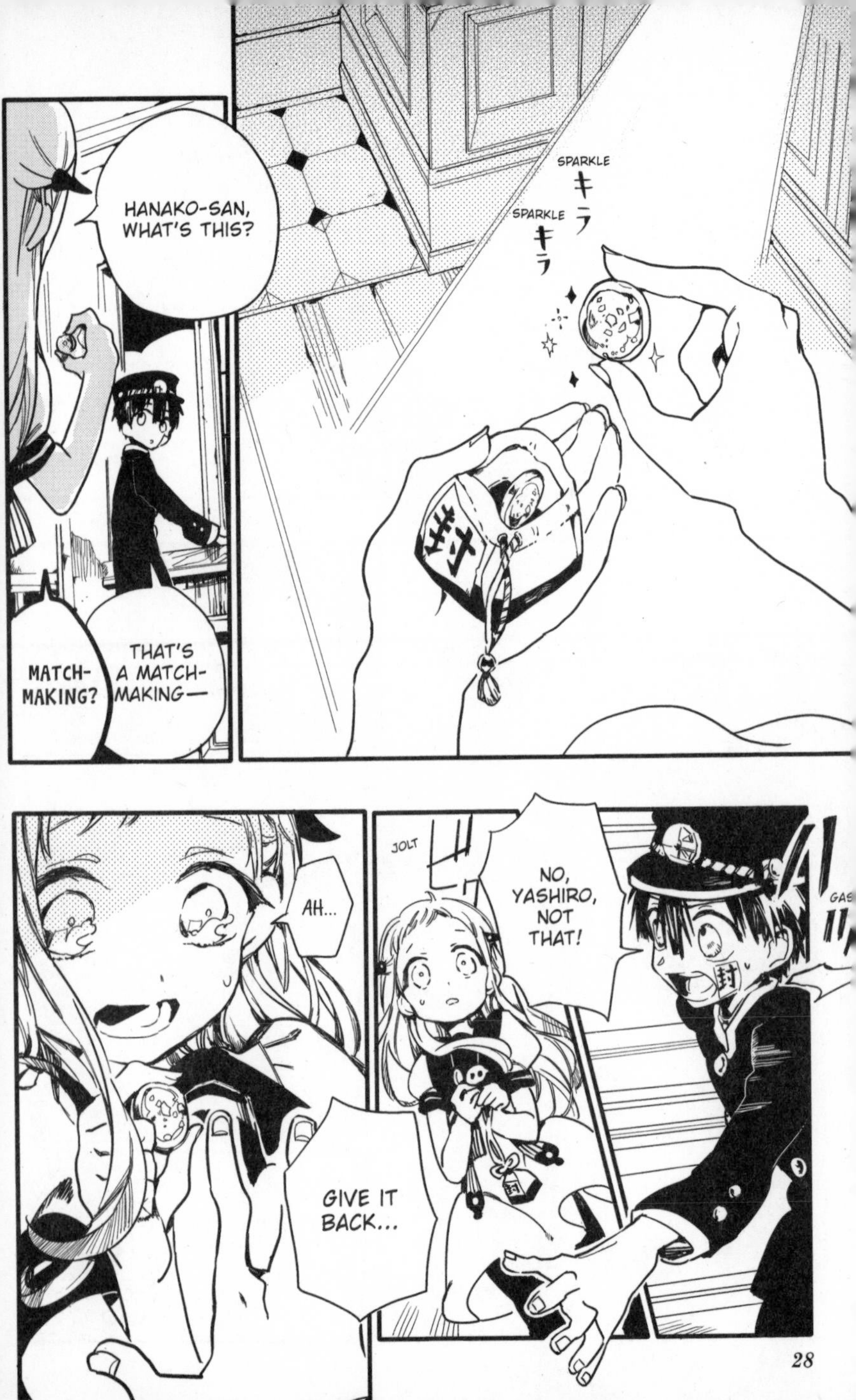
SPARKLE キラ
SPARKLE キラ
HANAKO-SAN, WHAT'S THIS?
THAT'S A MATCH-MAKING—
MATCH-MAKING?
JOLT
NO, YASHIRO, NOT THAT!
GIVE IT BACK...
AH...

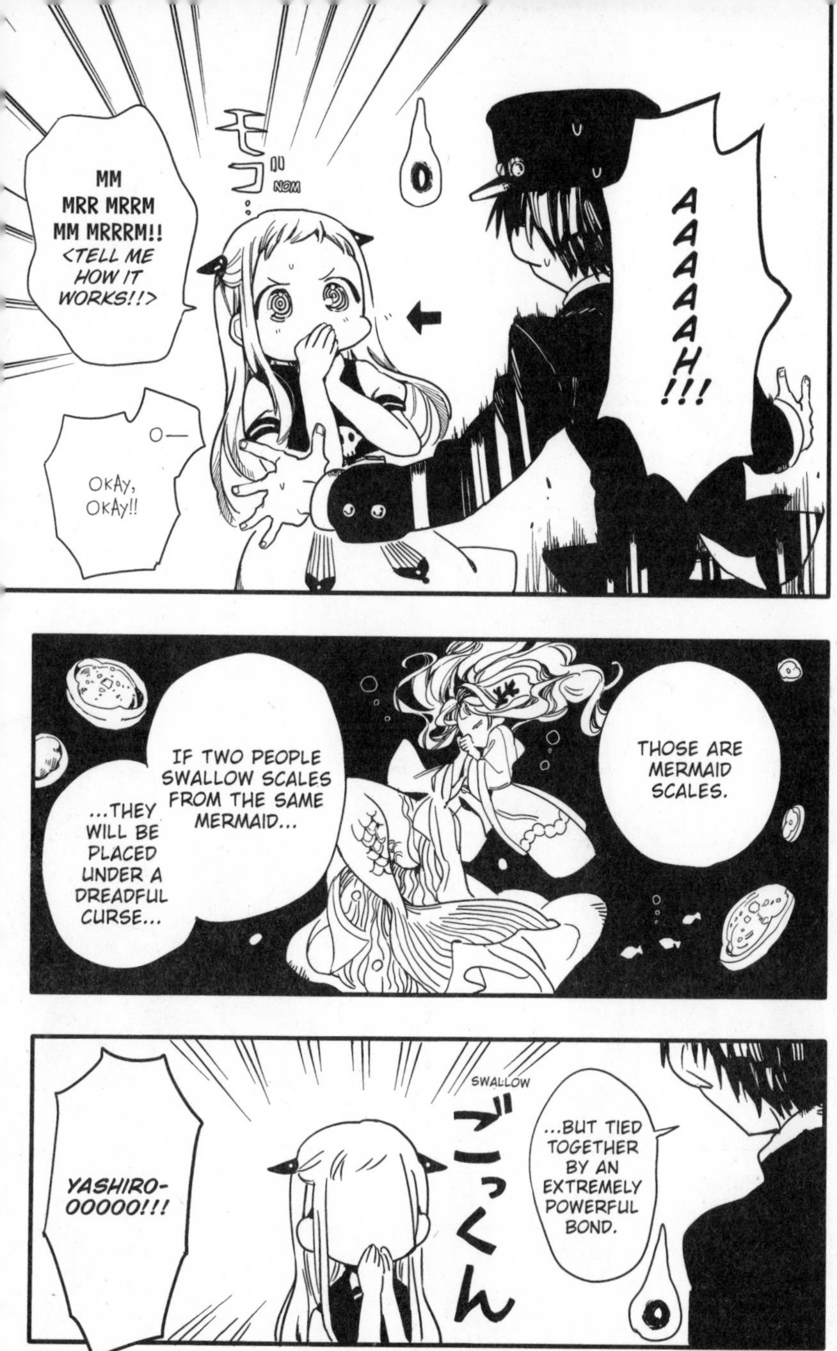
AAAAAAH!!!
モゴ NOM
MM MRR MRRM MM MRRRM!! <TELL ME HOW IT WORKS!!>
O—
OKAY, OKAY!!
THOSE ARE MERMAID SCALES.
IF TWO PEOPLE SWALLOW SCALES FROM THE SAME MERMAID...
...THEY WILL BE PLACED UNDER A DREADFUL CURSE...
...BUT TIED TOGETHER BY AN EXTREMELY POWERFUL BOND.
ごっくん SWALLOW
YASHIRO-OOOOO!!!

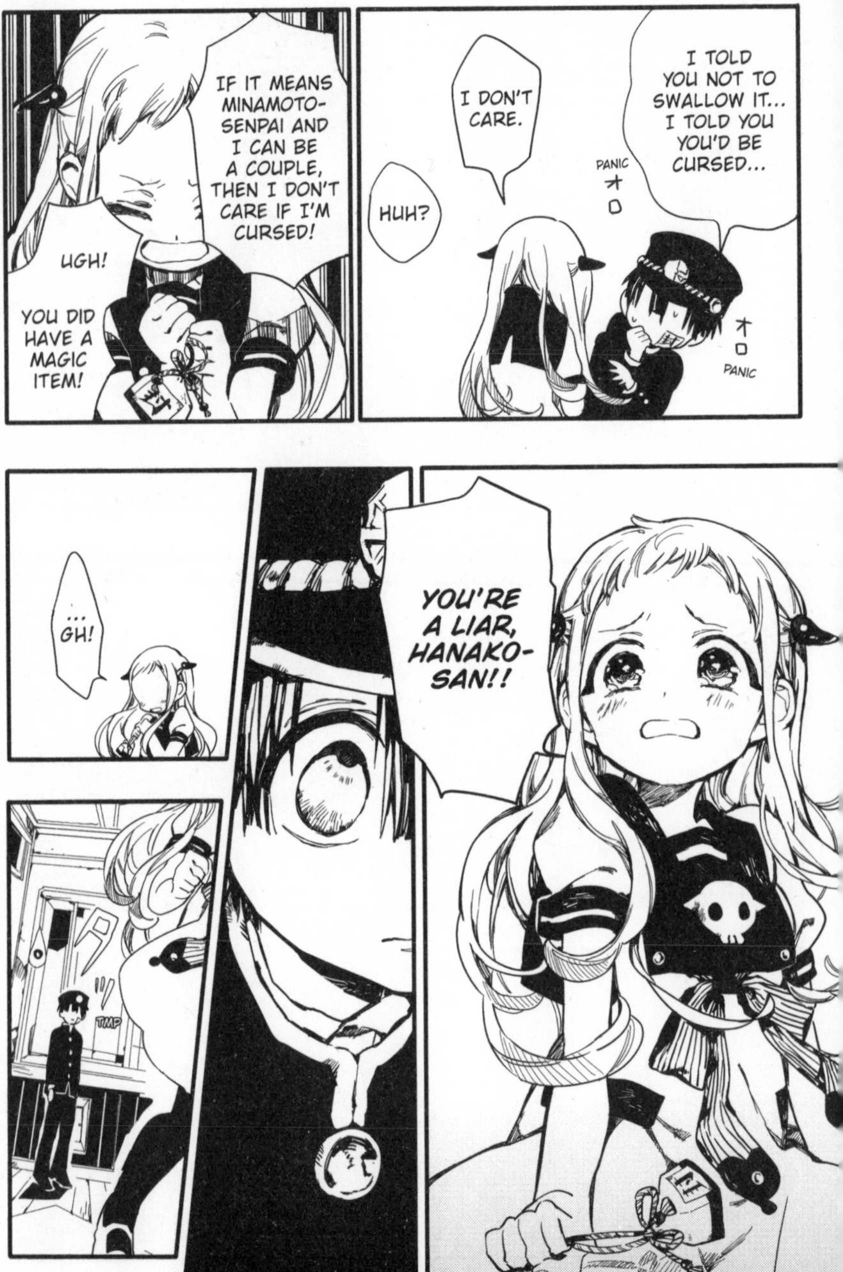
I TOLD YOU NOT TO SWALLOW IT... I TOLD YOU YOU'D BE CURSED...
PANIC
PANIC
I DON'T CARE.
HUH?
IF IT MEANS MINAMOTO-SENPAI AND I CAN BE A COUPLE, THEN I DON'T CARE IF I'M CURSED!
UGH!
YOU DID HAVE A MAGIC ITEM!
YOU'RE A LIAR, HANAKO-SAN!!
...GH!
TMP

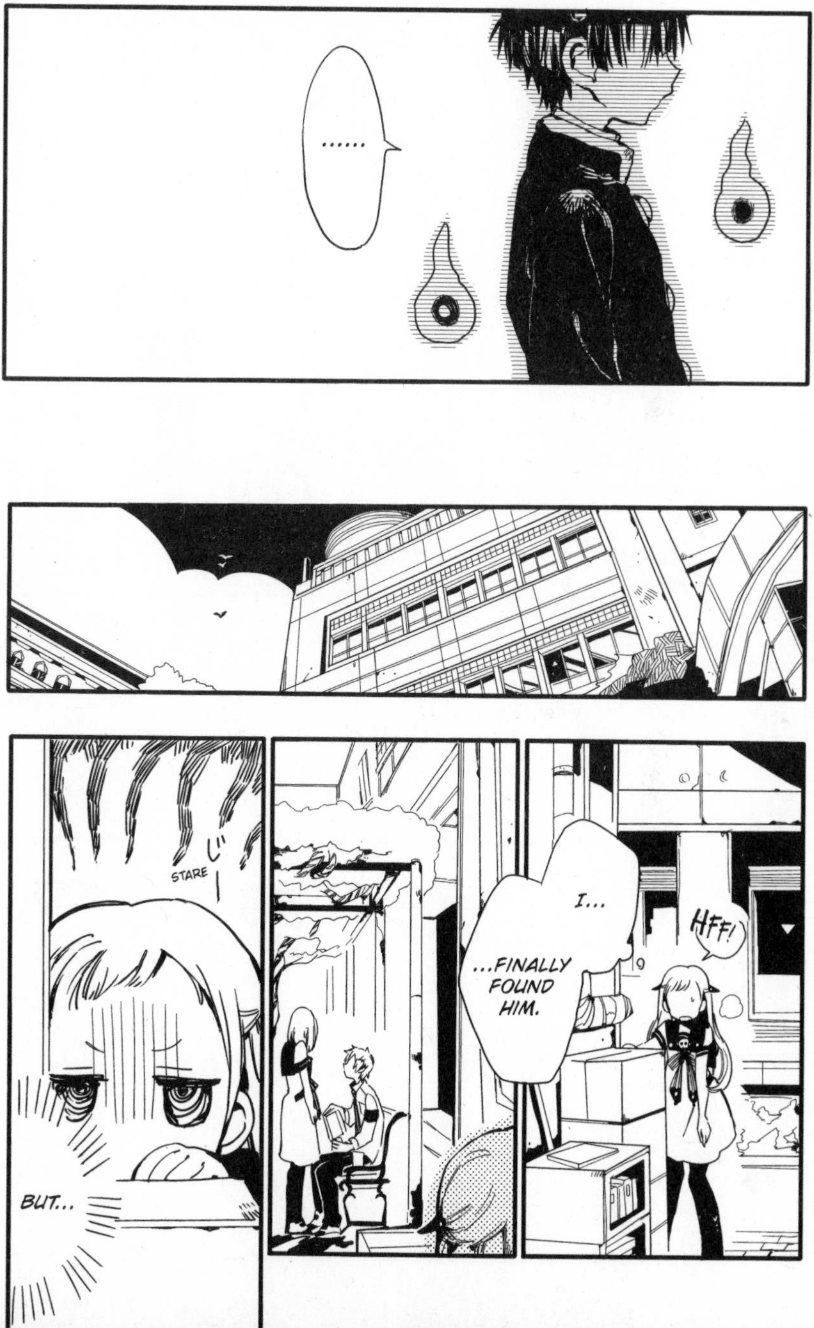
......
HFF!
I...
...FINALLY FOUND HIM.
STARE
BUT...

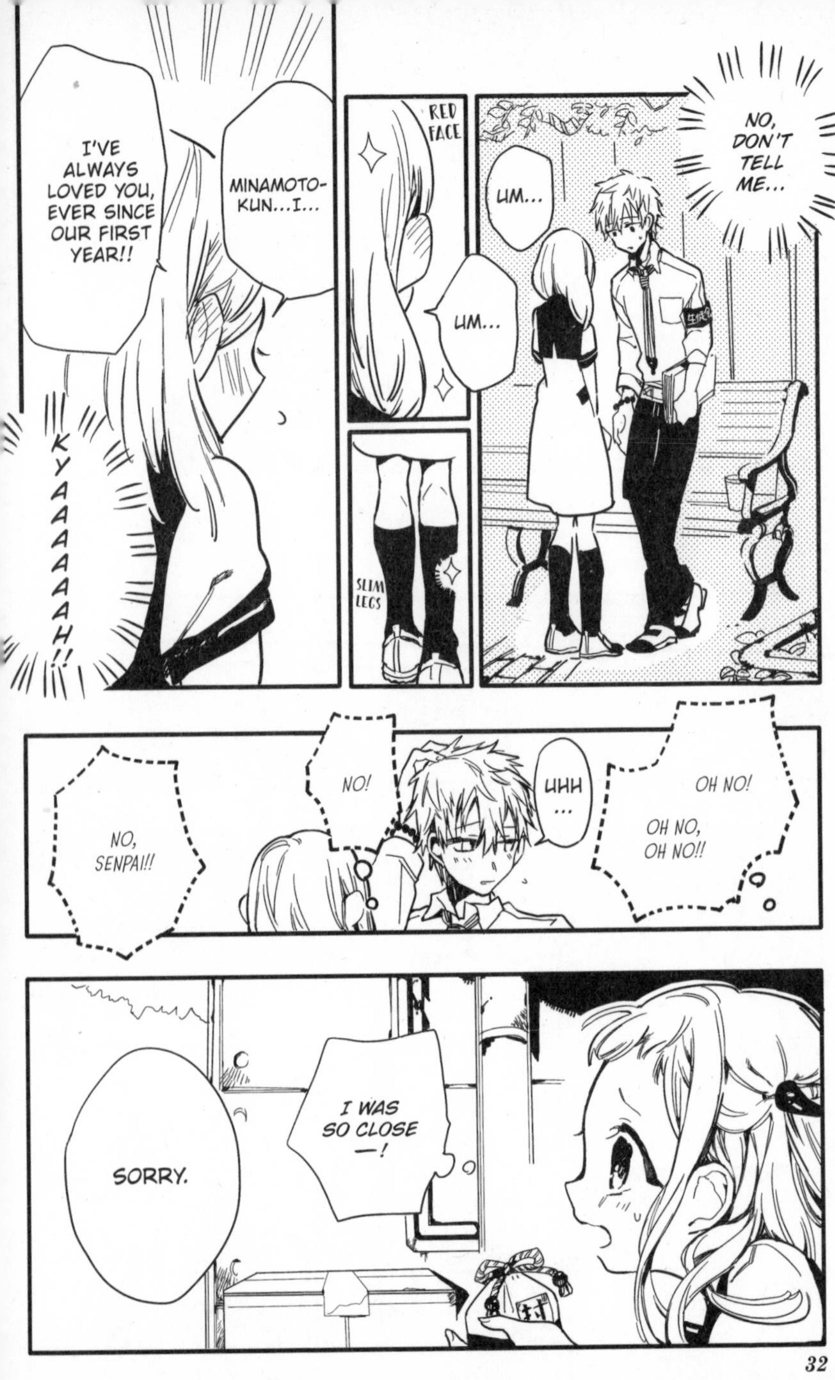
NO, DON'T TELL ME...
UM...
RED FACE
UM...
SLIM LEGS
MINAMOTO-KUN...I...
I'VE ALWAYS LOVED YOU, EVER SINCE OUR FIRST YEAR!!
KYAAAAAAH!!
OH NO! OH NO, OH NO!!
UHH ...
NO!
NO, SENPAI!!
I WAS SO CLOSE—!
SORRY.

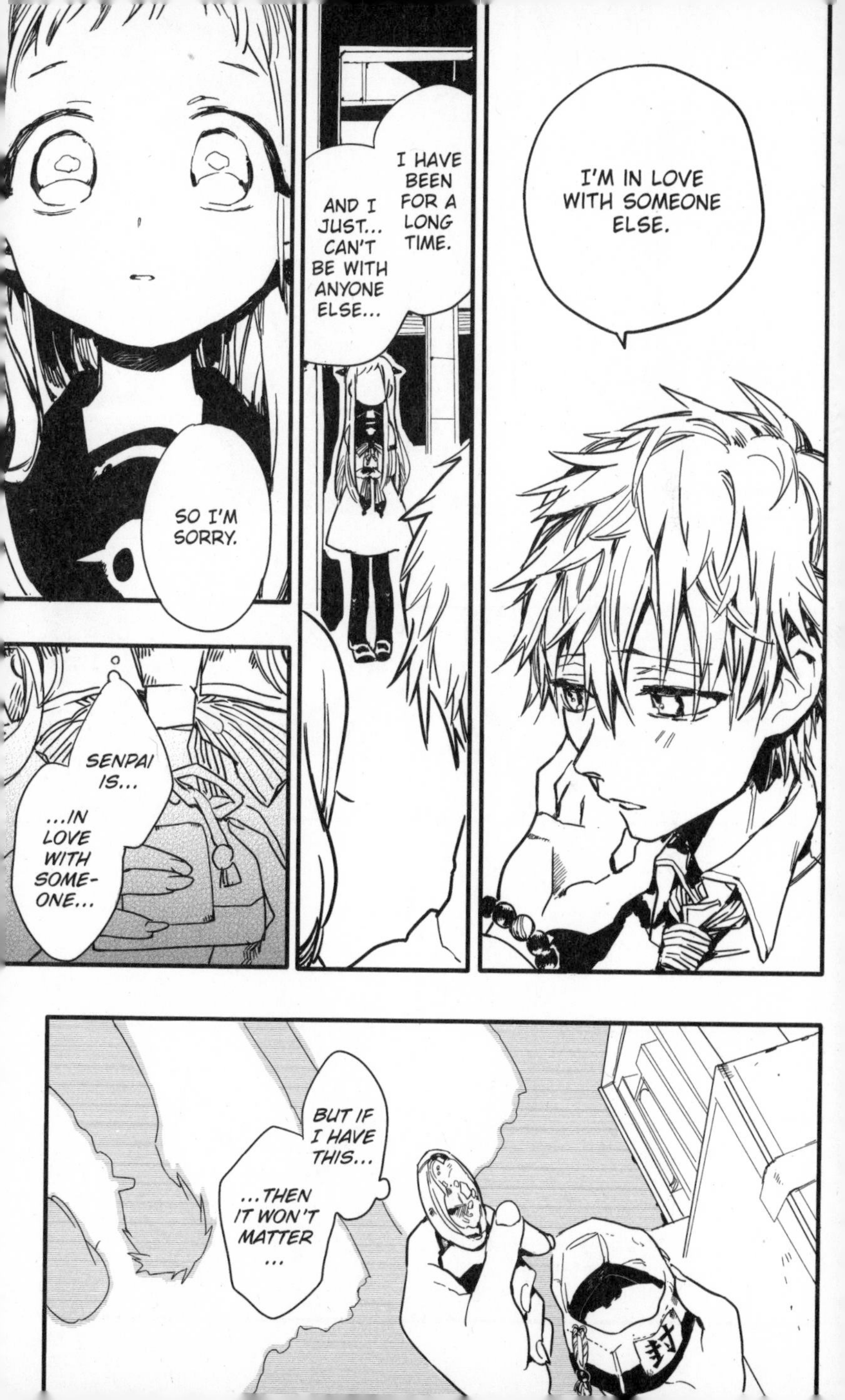

I'M IN LOVE WITH SOMEONE ELSE.
I HAVE BEEN FOR A LONG TIME.
AND I JUST... CAN'T BE WITH ANYONE ELSE...
SO I'M SORRY.
SENPAI IS...
...IN LOVE WITH SOME-ONE...
BUT IF I HAVE THIS...
...THEN IT WON'T MATTER ...

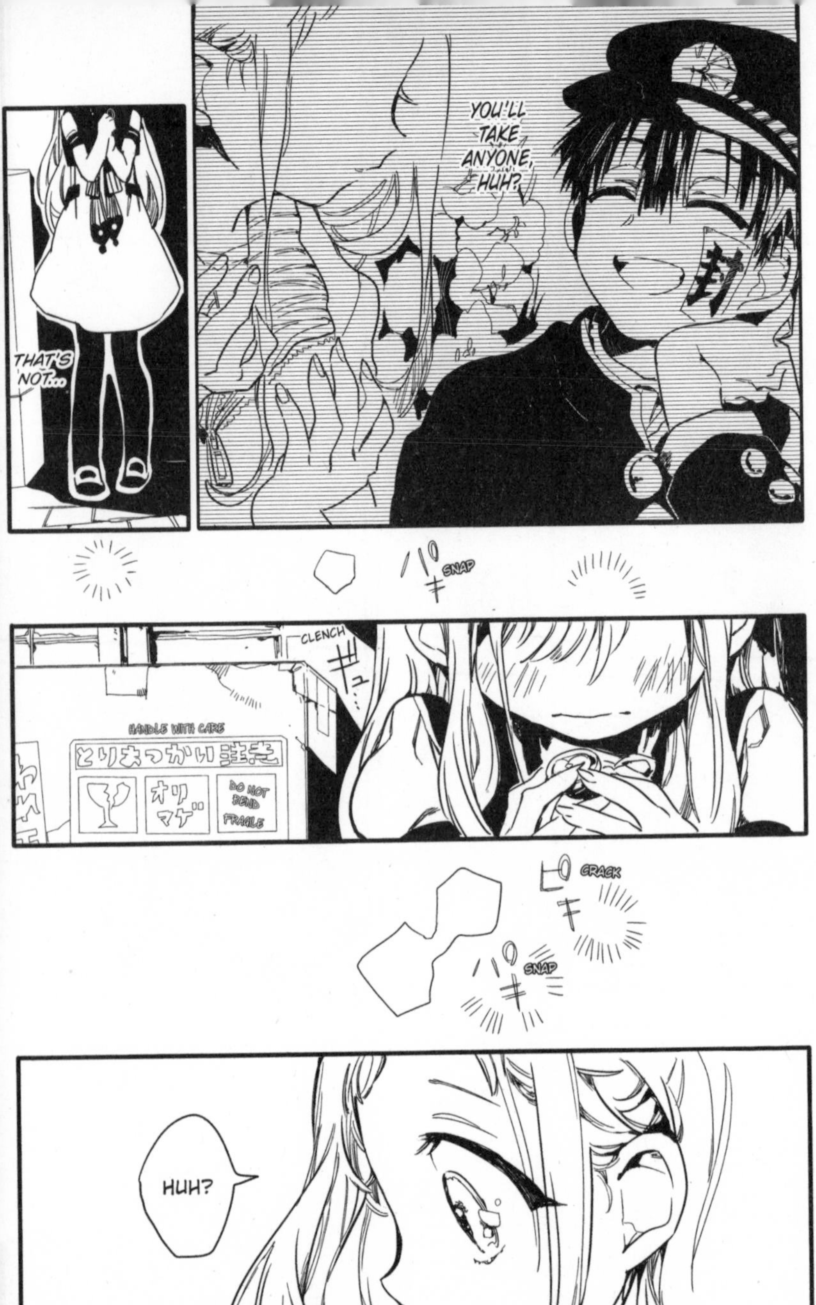
YOU'LL TAKE ANYONE, HUH?
THAT'S NOT...
SNAP
CLENCH
HANDLE WITH CARE
とりあつかい注意
オリマゲ
DO NOT BEND
FRAGILE
CRACK
SNAP
HUH?

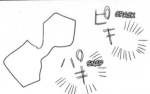

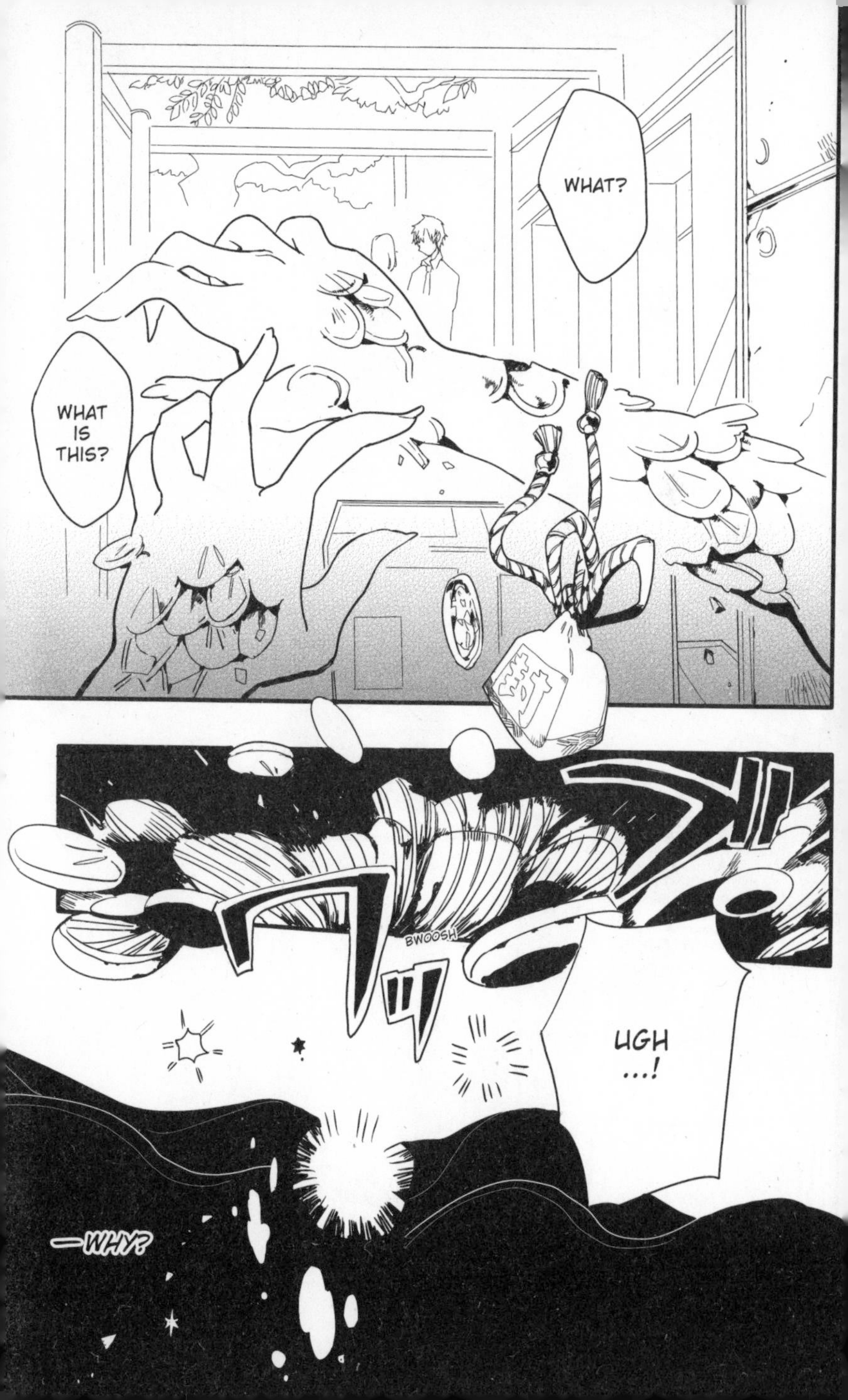
WHAT?
WHAT IS THIS?
BWOOSH
UGH ...!
—WHY?

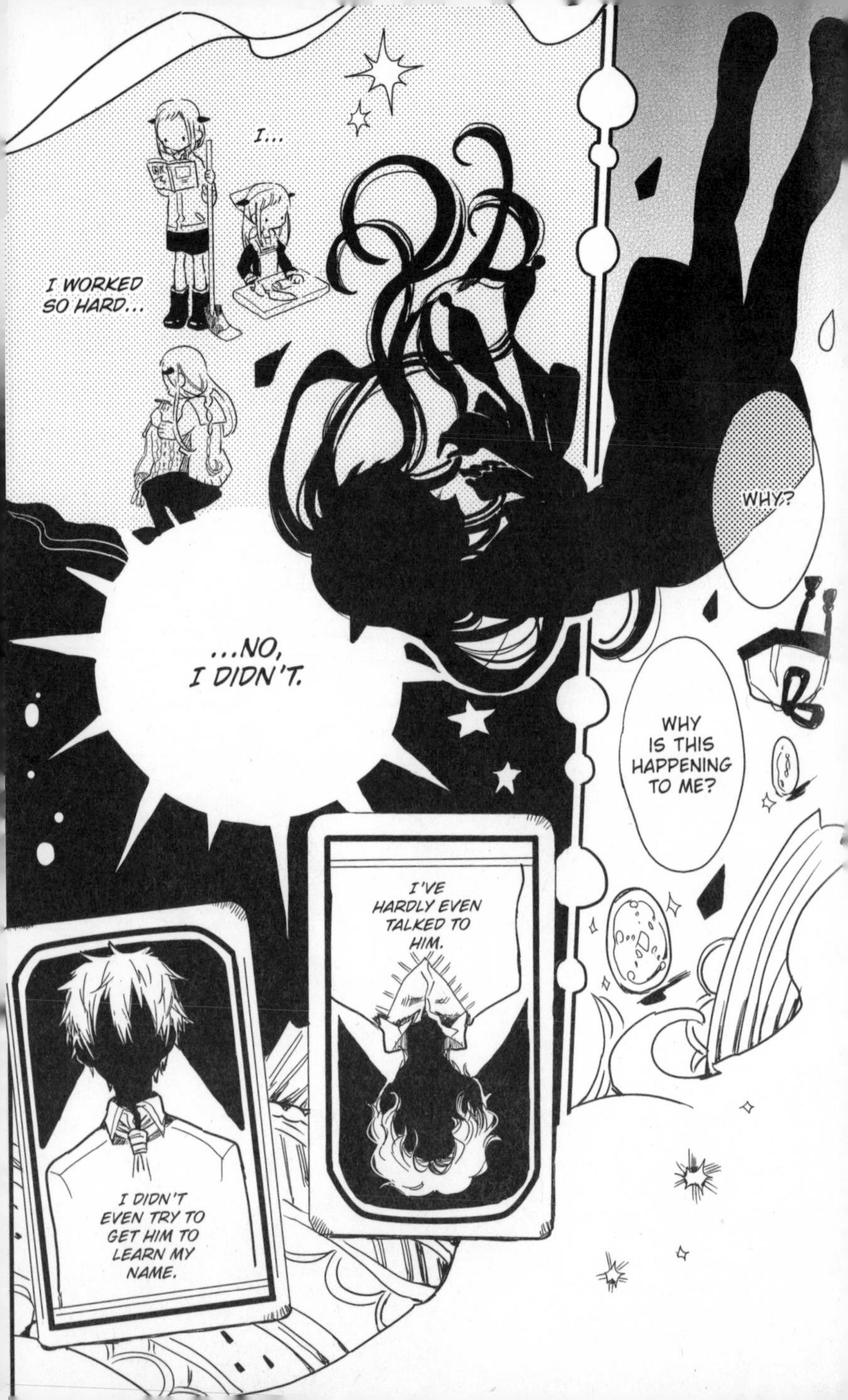
WHY?
WHY IS THIS HAPPENING TO ME?
I...
I WORKED SO HARD...
...NO, I DIDN'T.
I'VE HARDLY EVEN TALKED TO HIM.
I DIDN'T EVEN TRY TO GET HIM TO LEARN MY NAME.

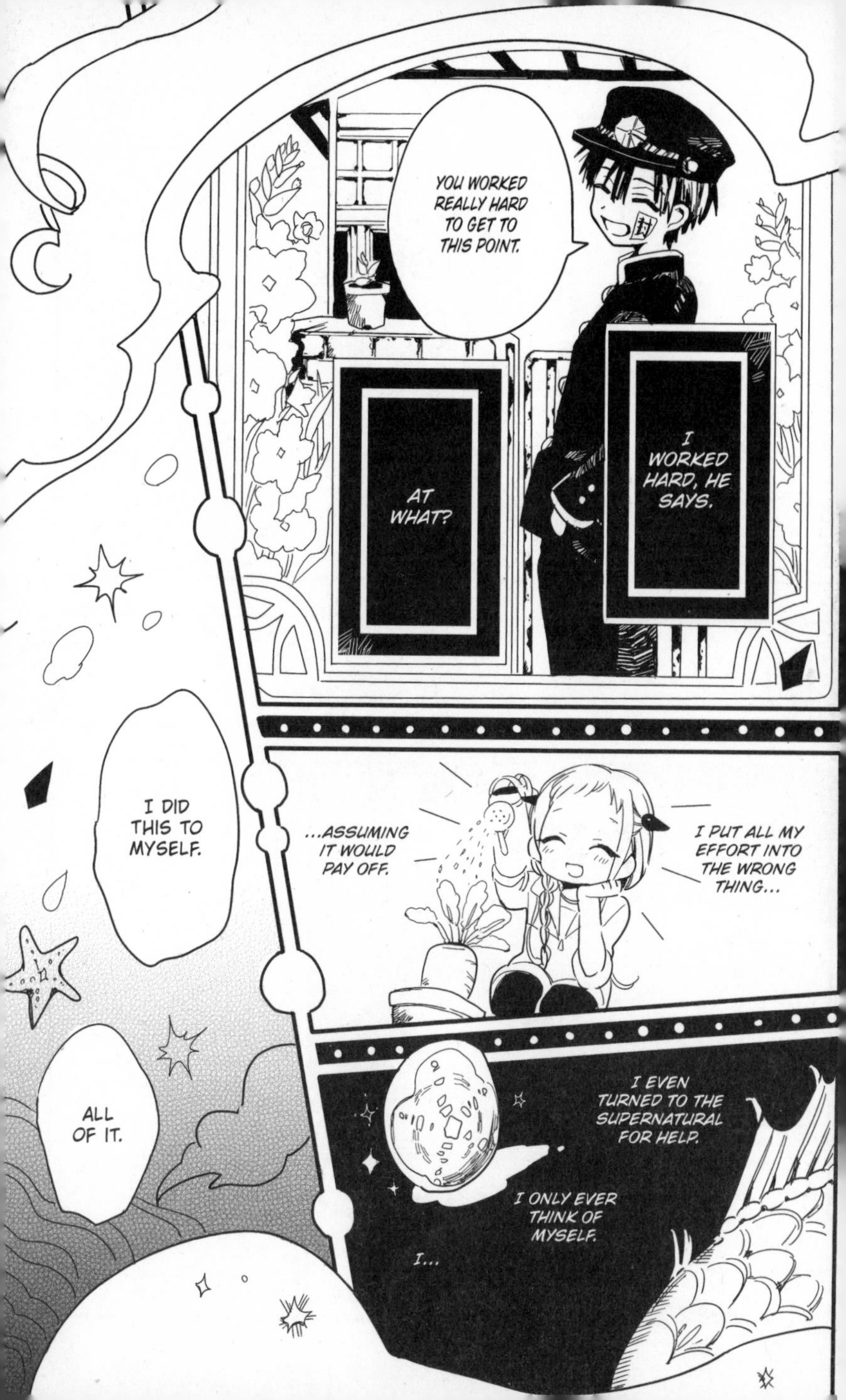
YOU WORKED REALLY HARD TO GET TO THIS POINT.
I WORKED HARD, HE SAYS.
AT WHAT?
I PUT ALL MY EFFORT INTO THE WRONG THING...
...ASSUMING IT WOULD PAY OFF.
I EVEN TURNED TO THE SUPERNATURAL FOR HELP.
I ONLY EVER THINK OF MYSELF.
I...
I DID THIS TO MYSELF.
ALL OF IT.

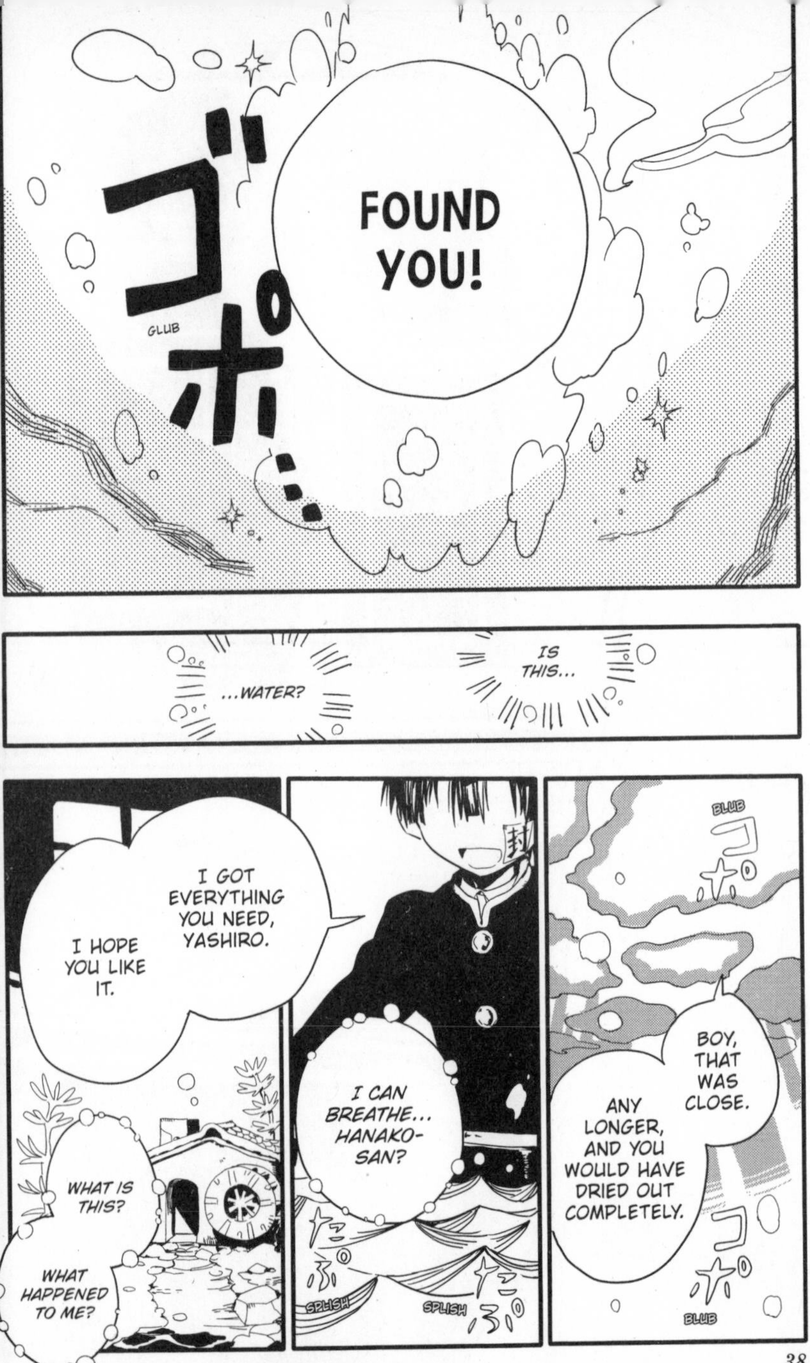
FOUND YOU!
GLUB
IS THIS...
...WATER?
BLUB
BOY, THAT WAS CLOSE.
ANY LONGER, AND YOU WOULD HAVE DRIED OUT COMPLETELY.
BLUB
I CAN BREATHE... HANAKO-SAN?
SPLISH
SPLISH
I GOT EVERYTHING YOU NEED, YASHIRO.
I HOPE YOU LIKE IT.
WHAT IS THIS?
WHAT HAPPENED TO ME?

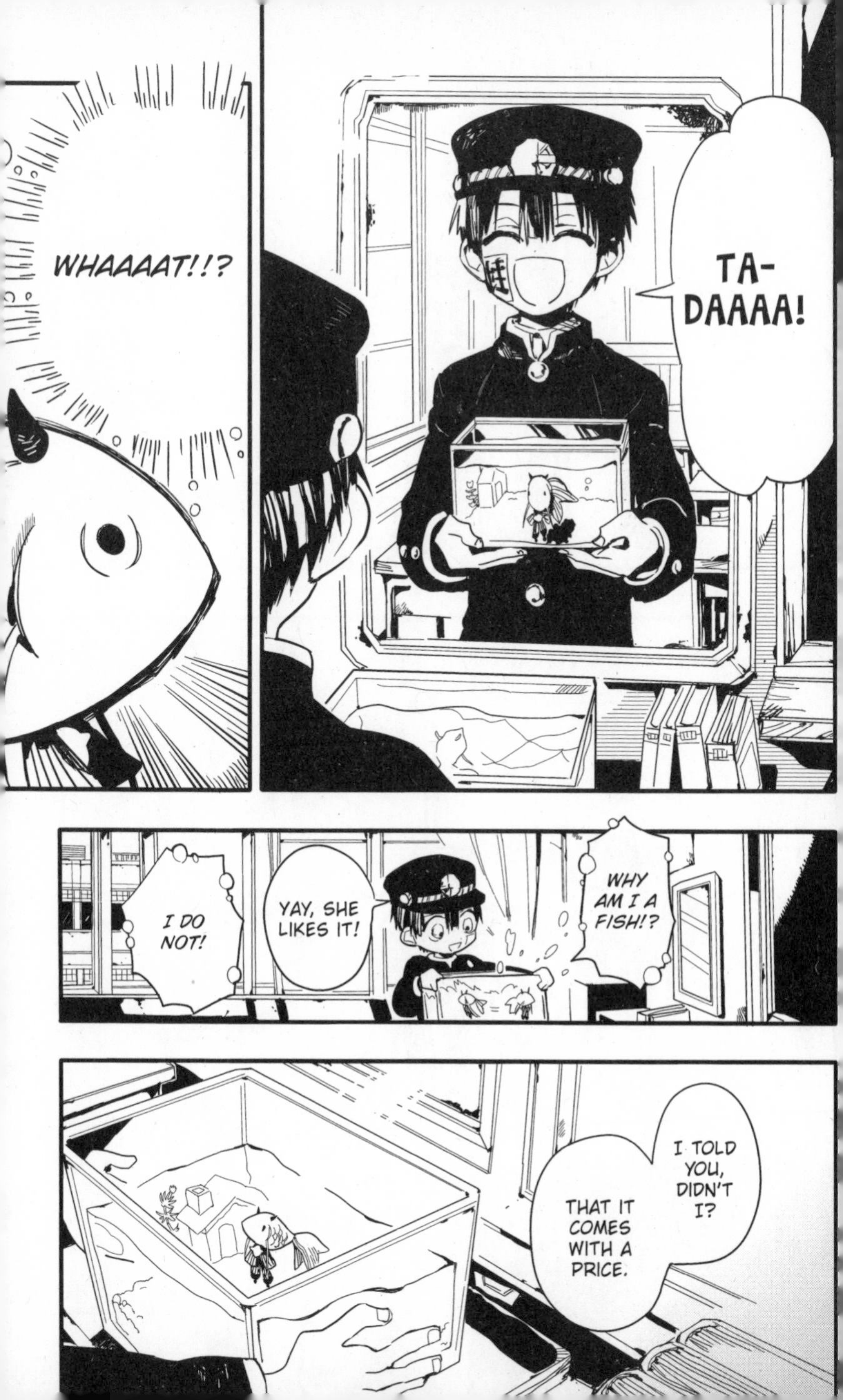
TA-DAAAA!
WHAAAAT!!?
WHY AM I A FISH!?
YAY, SHE LIKES IT!
I DO NOT!
I TOLD YOU, DIDN'T I?
THAT IT COMES WITH A PRICE.

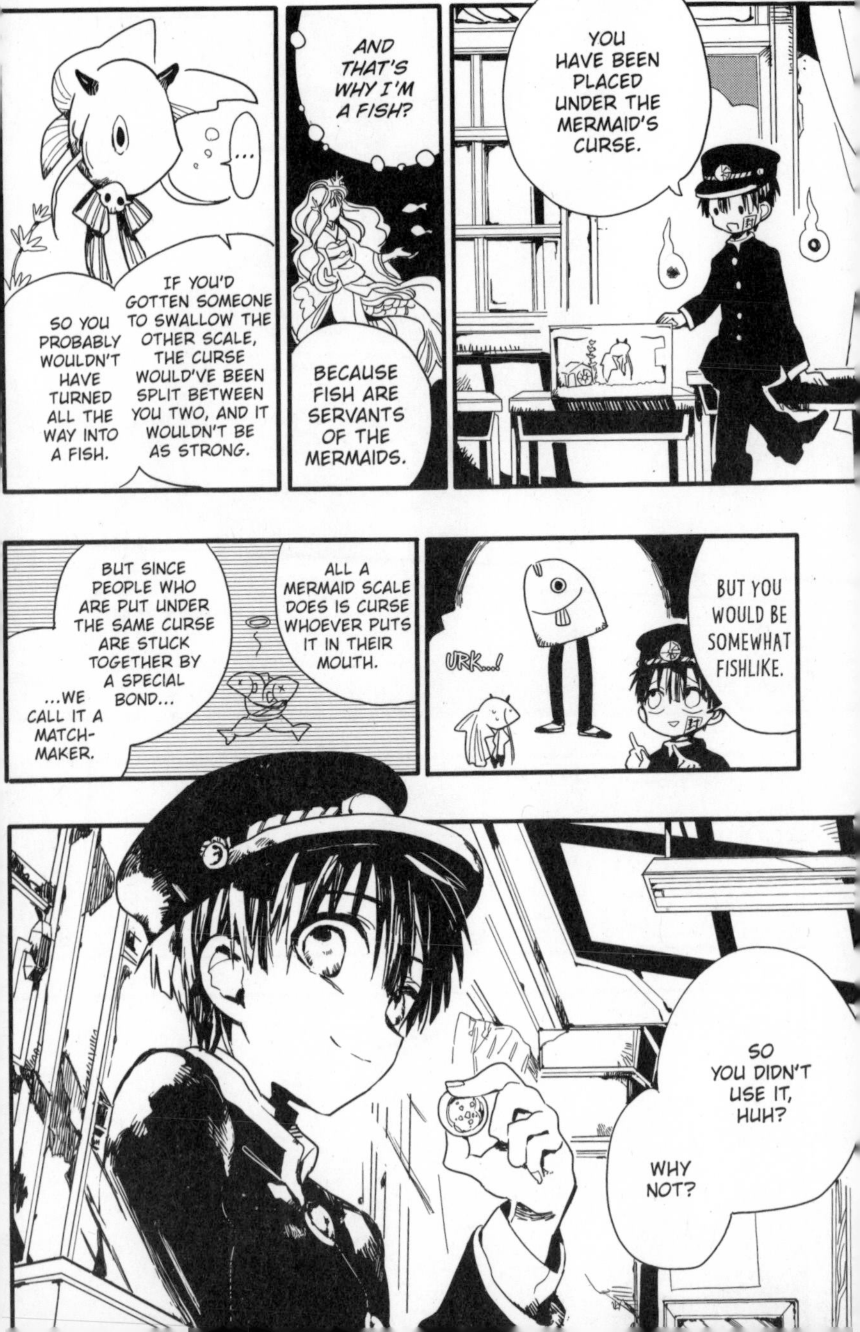
YOU HAVE BEEN PLACED UNDER THE MERMAID'S CURSE.
AND THAT'S WHY I'M A FISH?
BECAUSE FISH ARE SERVANTS OF THE MERMAIDS.
...
IF YOU'D GOTTEN SOMEONE TO SWALLOW THE OTHER SCALE, THE CURSE WOULD'VE BEEN SPLIT BETWEEN YOU TWO, AND IT WOULDN'T BE AS STRONG.
SO YOU PROBABLY WOULDN'T HAVE TURNED ALL THE WAY INTO A FISH.
BUT YOU WOULD BE SOMEWHAT FISHLIKE.
URK...!
ALL A MERMAID SCALE DOES IS CURSE WHOEVER PUTS IT IN THEIR MOUTH.
BUT SINCE PEOPLE WHO ARE PUT UNDER THE SAME CURSE ARE STUCK TOGETHER BY A SPECIAL BOND...
...WE CALL IT A MATCH-MAKER.
SO YOU DIDN'T USE IT, HUH?
WHY NOT?

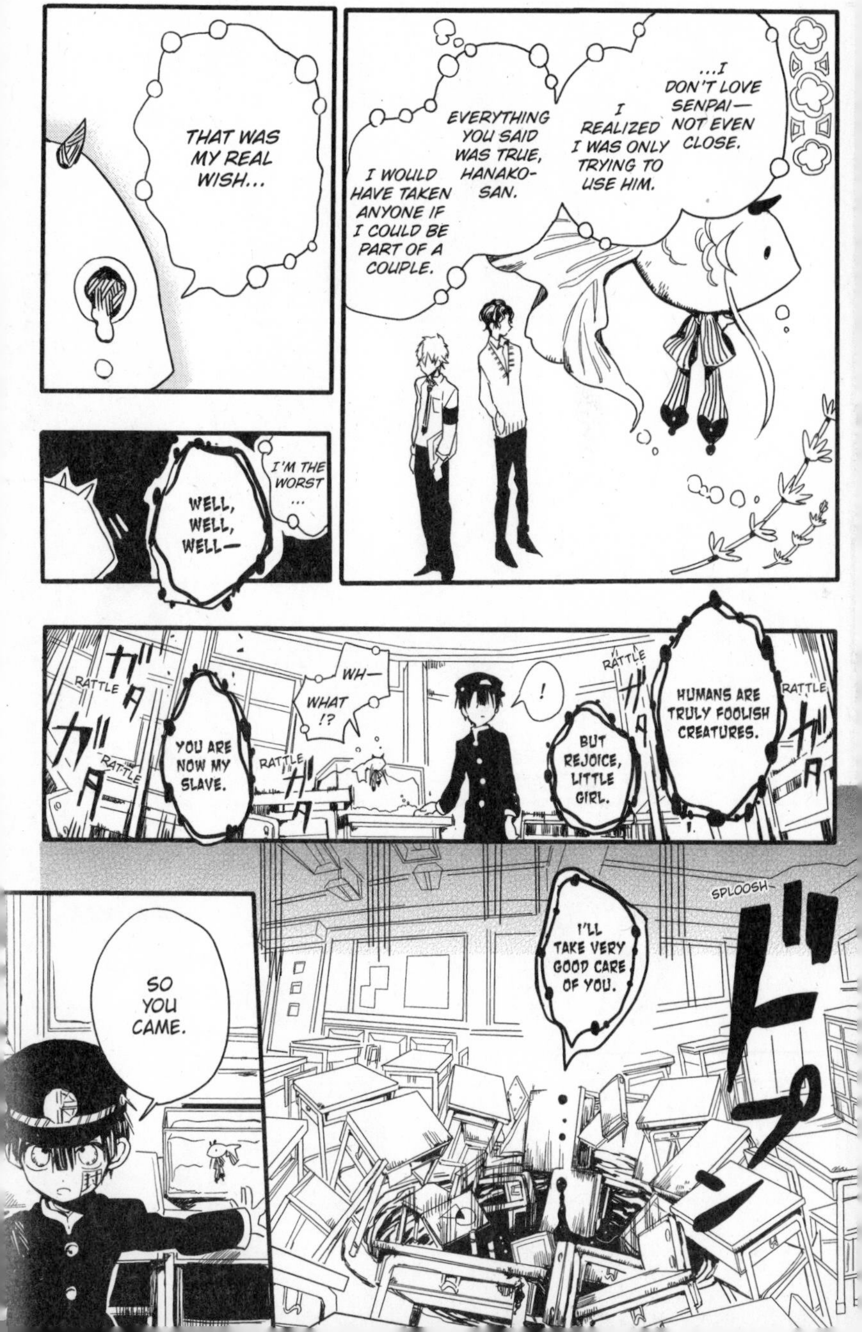
...I DON'T LOVE SENPAI—NOT EVEN CLOSE.
I REALIZED I WAS ONLY TRYING TO USE HIM.
EVERYTHING YOU SAID WAS TRUE, HANAKO-SAN.
I WOULD HAVE TAKEN ANYONE IF I COULD BE PART OF A COUPLE.
THAT WAS MY REAL WISH...
I'M THE WORST...
WELL, WELL, WELL—
RATTLE
RATTLE
HUMANS ARE TRULY FOOLISH CREATURES.
BUT REJOICE, LITTLE GIRL.
!
WH— WHAT!?
RATTLE
YOU ARE NOW MY SLAVE.
RATTLE
RATTLE
SPLOOSH
I'LL TAKE VERY GOOD CARE OF YOU.
SO YOU CAME.

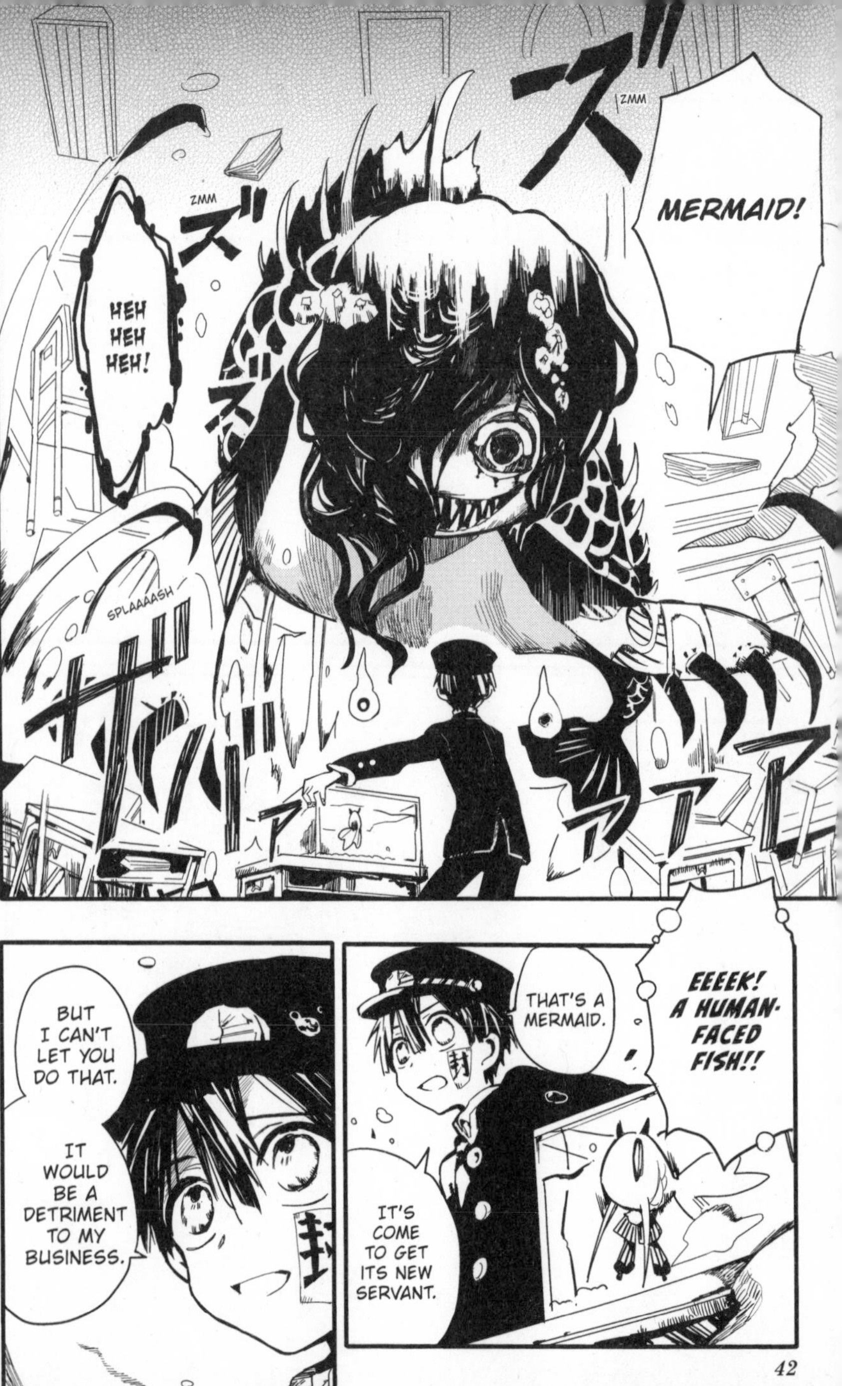
ZMM
MERMAID!
ZMM
HEH HEH HEH!
SPLAAAASH
EEEEK! A HUMAN-FACED FISH!!
THAT'S A MERMAID.
IT'S COME TO GET ITS NEW SERVANT.
BUT I CAN'T LET YOU DO THAT.
IT WOULD BE A DETRIMENT TO MY BUSINESS.

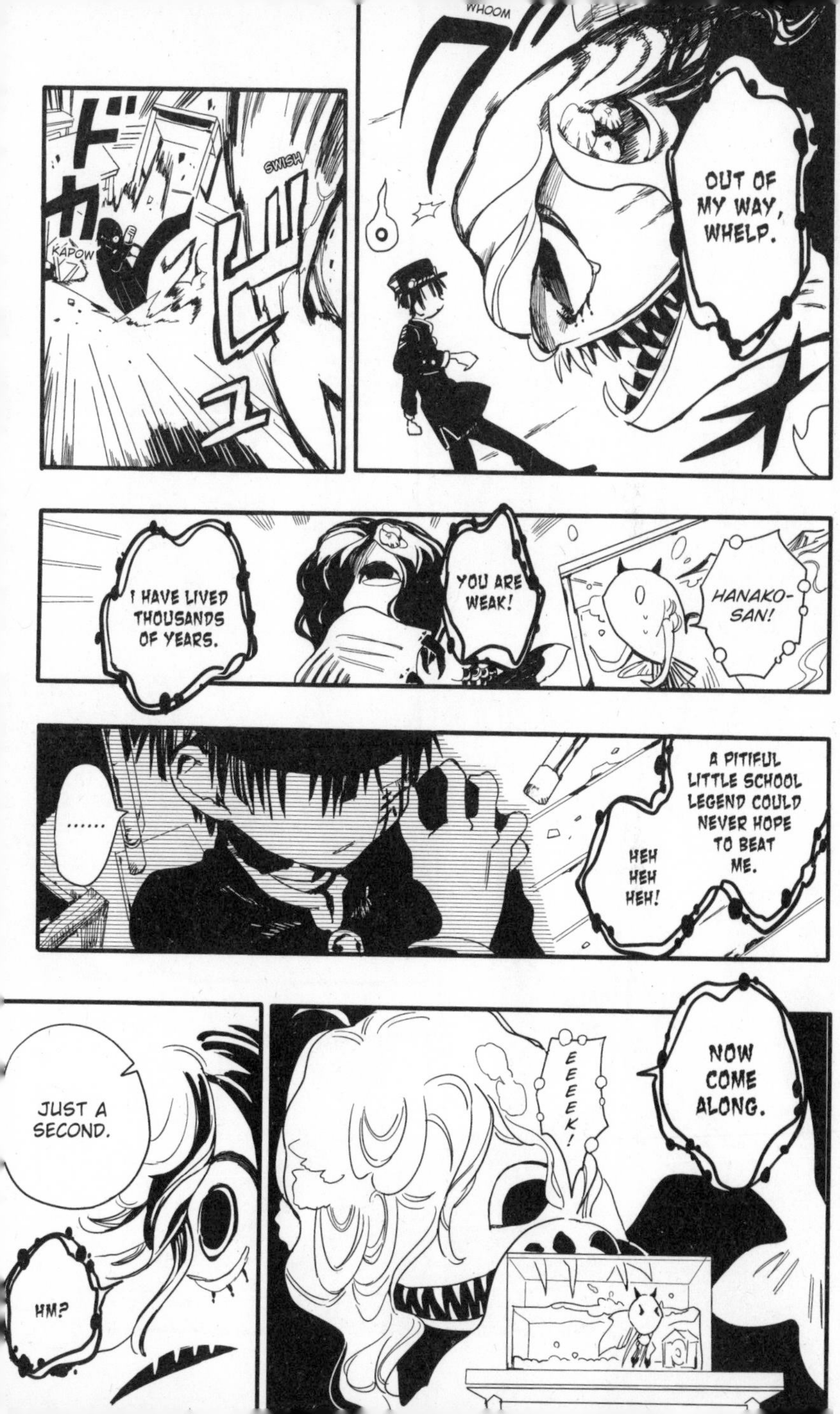
WHOOM
OUT OF MY WAY, WHELP.
SWISH
ビュ
ドカ
KAPOW
HANAKO-SAN!
YOU ARE WEAK!
I HAVE LIVED THOUSANDS OF YEARS.
A PITIFUL LITTLE SCHOOL LEGEND COULD NEVER HOPE TO BEAT ME.
HEH HEH HEH!
......
NOW COME ALONG.
EEEEK!
JUST A SECOND.
HM?

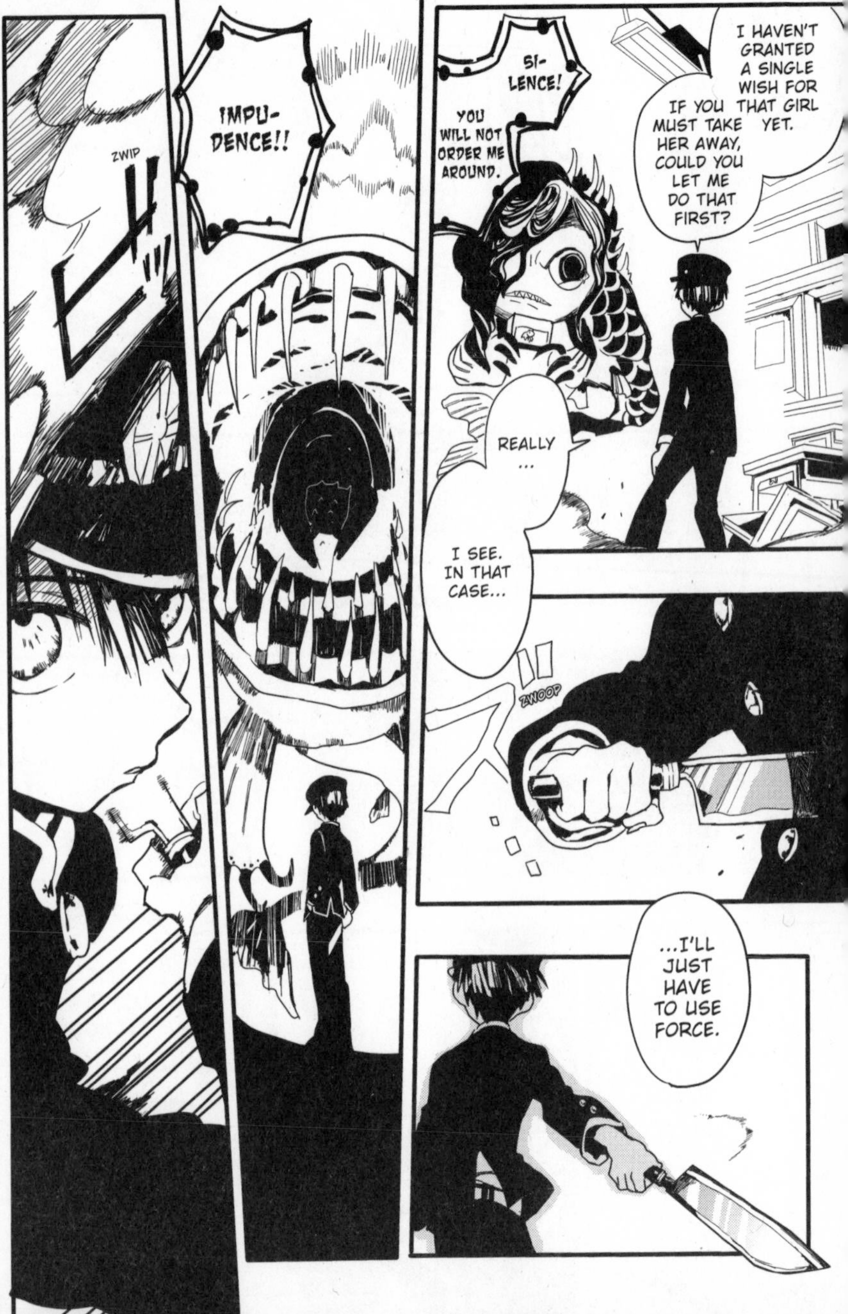
I HAVEN'T GRANTED A SINGLE WISH FOR THAT GIRL YET.
IF YOU MUST TAKE HER AWAY, COULD YOU LET ME DO THAT FIRST?
SI-LENCE!
YOU WILL NOT ORDER ME AROUND.
IMPU-DENCE!!
ZWIP
REALLY...
I SEE. IN THAT CASE...
ZWOOP
...I'LL JUST HAVE TO USE FORCE.

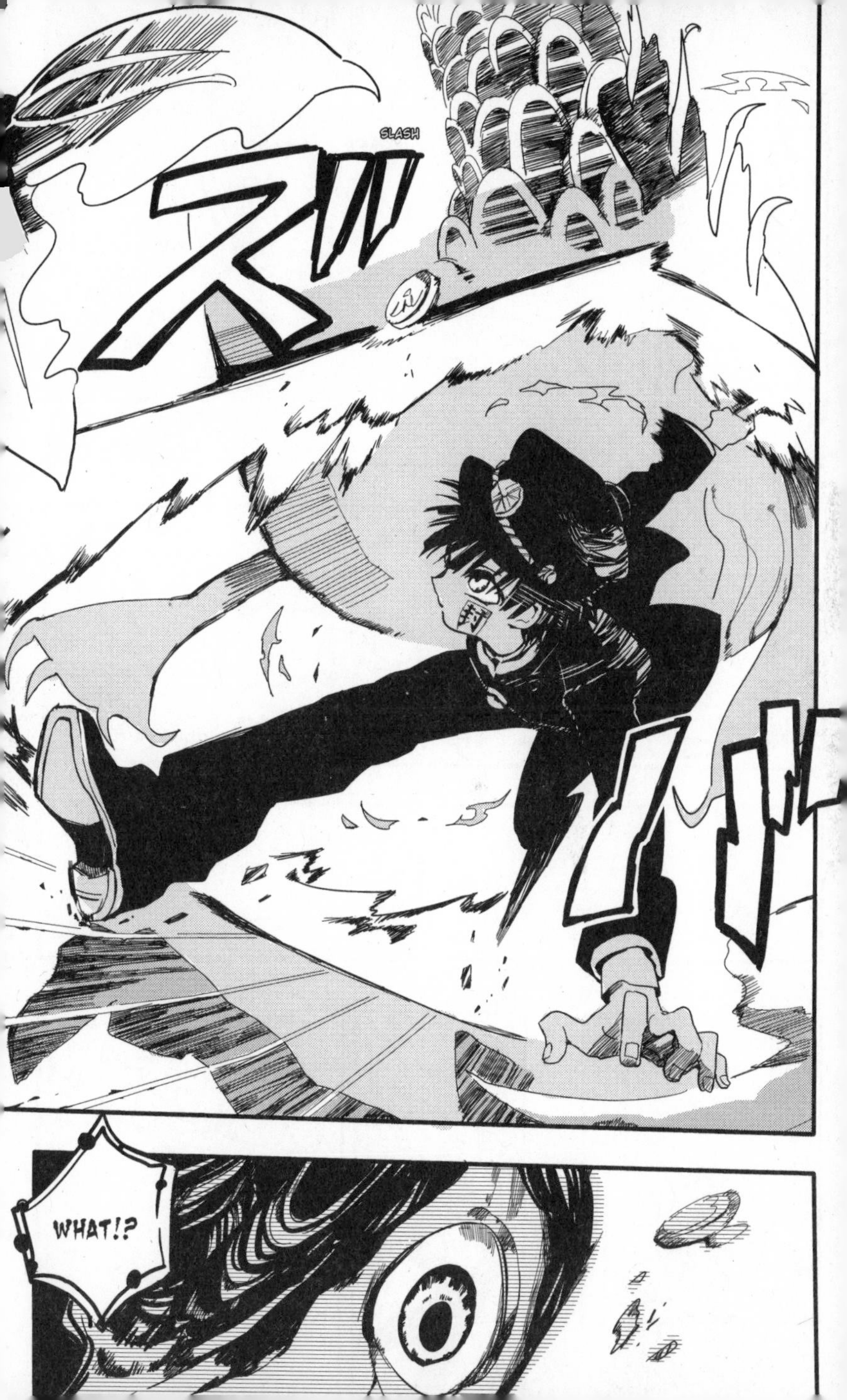
SLASH
WHAT!?

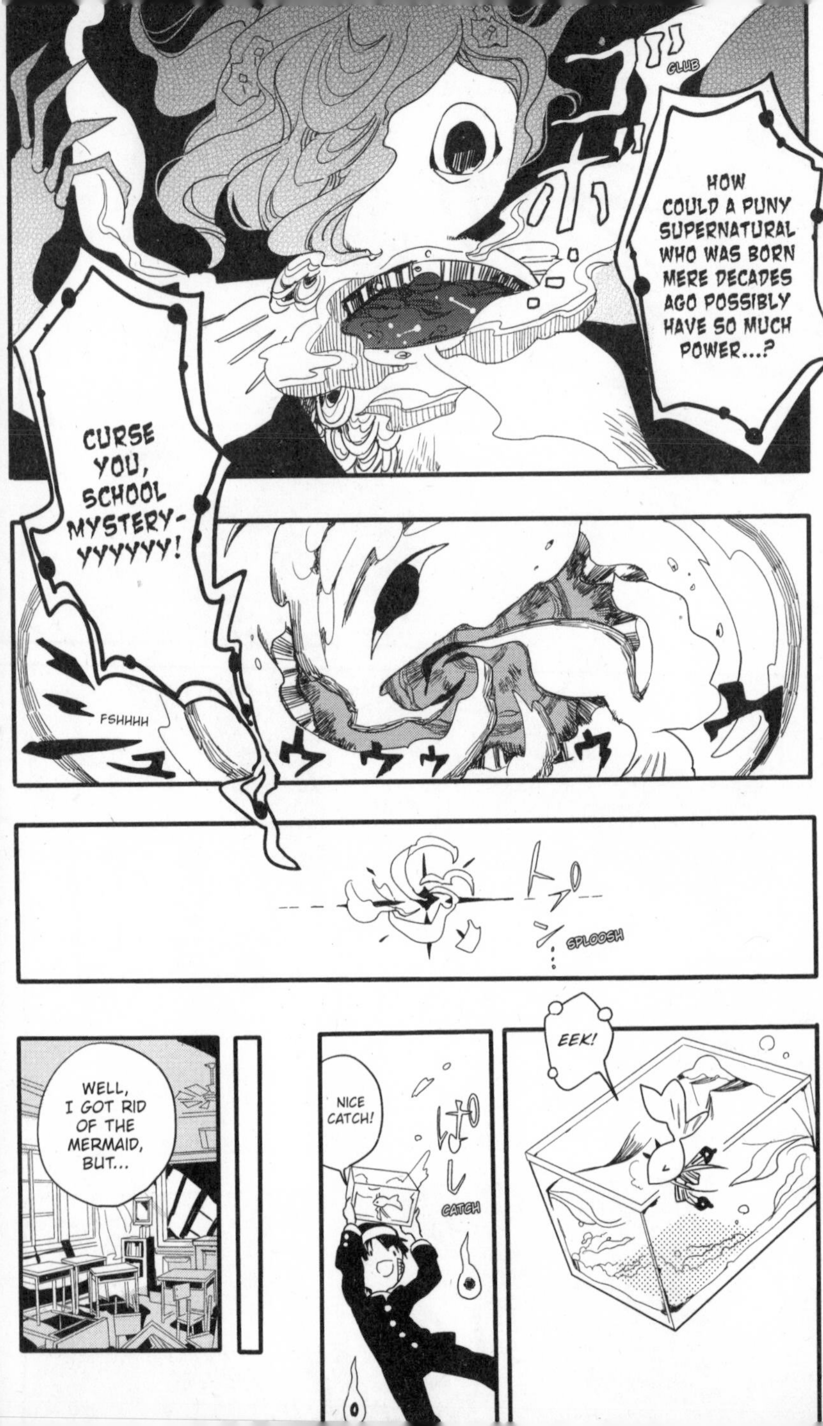
GLUB
HOW COULD A PUNY SUPERNATURAL WHO WAS BORN MERE DECADES AGO POSSIBLY HAVE SO MUCH POWER...?
CURSE YOU, SCHOOL MYSTERY-YYYYYY!
FSHHHH
SPLOOSH
EEK!
NICE CATCH!
CATCH
WELL, I GOT RID OF THE MERMAID, BUT...

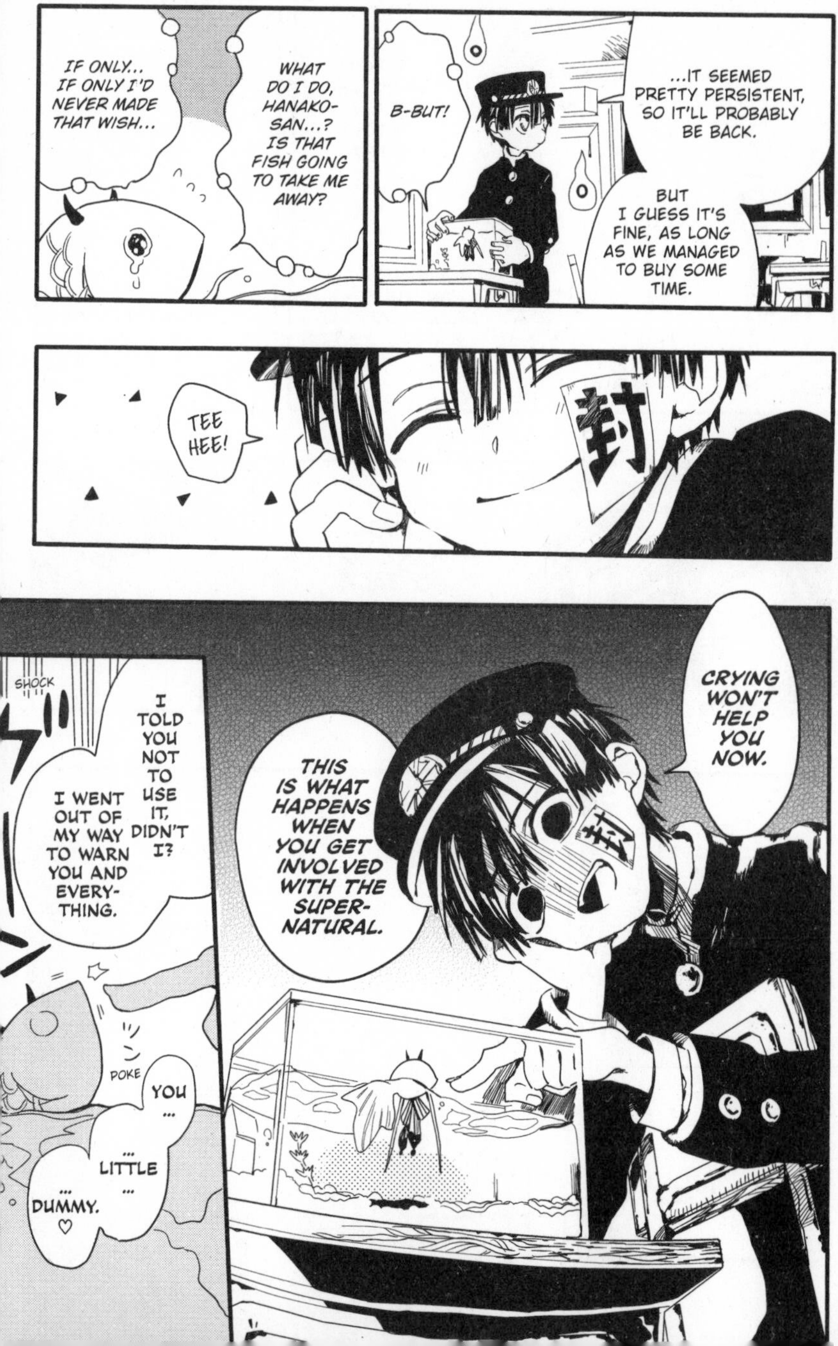
...IT SEEMED PRETTY PERSISTENT, SO IT'LL PROBABLY BE BACK.
BUT I GUESS IT'S FINE, AS LONG AS WE MANAGED TO BUY SOME TIME.
B-BUT!
WHAT DO I DO, HANAKO-SAN...? IS THAT FISH GOING TO TAKE ME AWAY?
IF ONLY... IF ONLY I'D NEVER MADE THAT WISH...
TEE HEE!
CRYING WON'T HELP YOU NOW.
THIS IS WHAT HAPPENS WHEN YOU GET INVOLVED WITH THE SUPER-NATURAL.
I TOLD YOU NOT TO USE IT, DIDN'T I?
I WENT OUT OF MY WAY TO WARN YOU AND EVERYTHING.
SHOCK
POKE
YOU...
...LITTLE...
...DUMMY. ♡

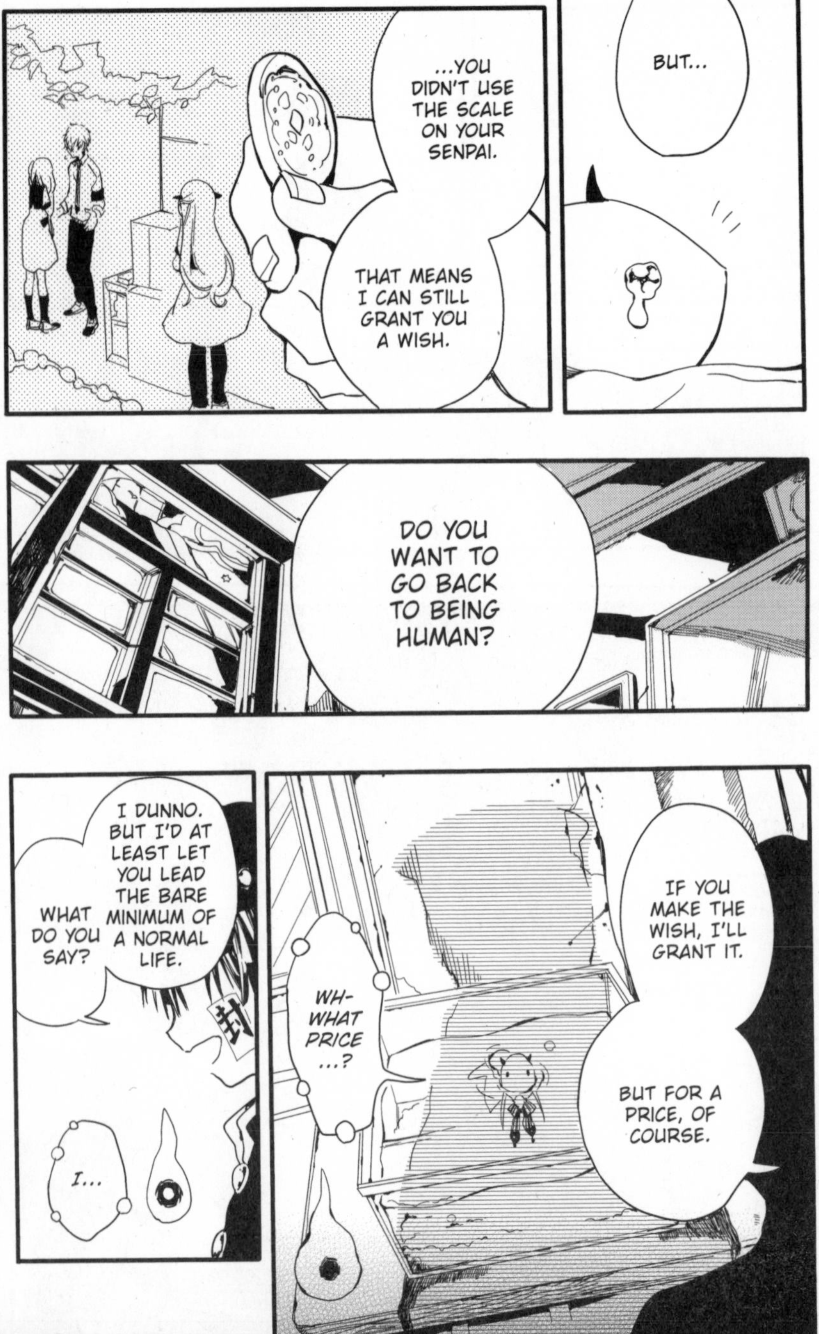
BUT...
...YOU DIDN'T USE THE SCALE ON YOUR SENPAI.
THAT MEANS I CAN STILL GRANT YOU A WISH.
DO YOU WANT TO GO BACK TO BEING HUMAN?
IF YOU MAKE THE WISH, I'LL GRANT IT.
BUT FOR A PRICE, OF COURSE.
WH-WHAT PRICE...?
I DUNNO. BUT I'D AT LEAST LET YOU LEAD THE BARE MINIMUM OF A NORMAL LIFE.
WHAT DO YOU SAY?
I...

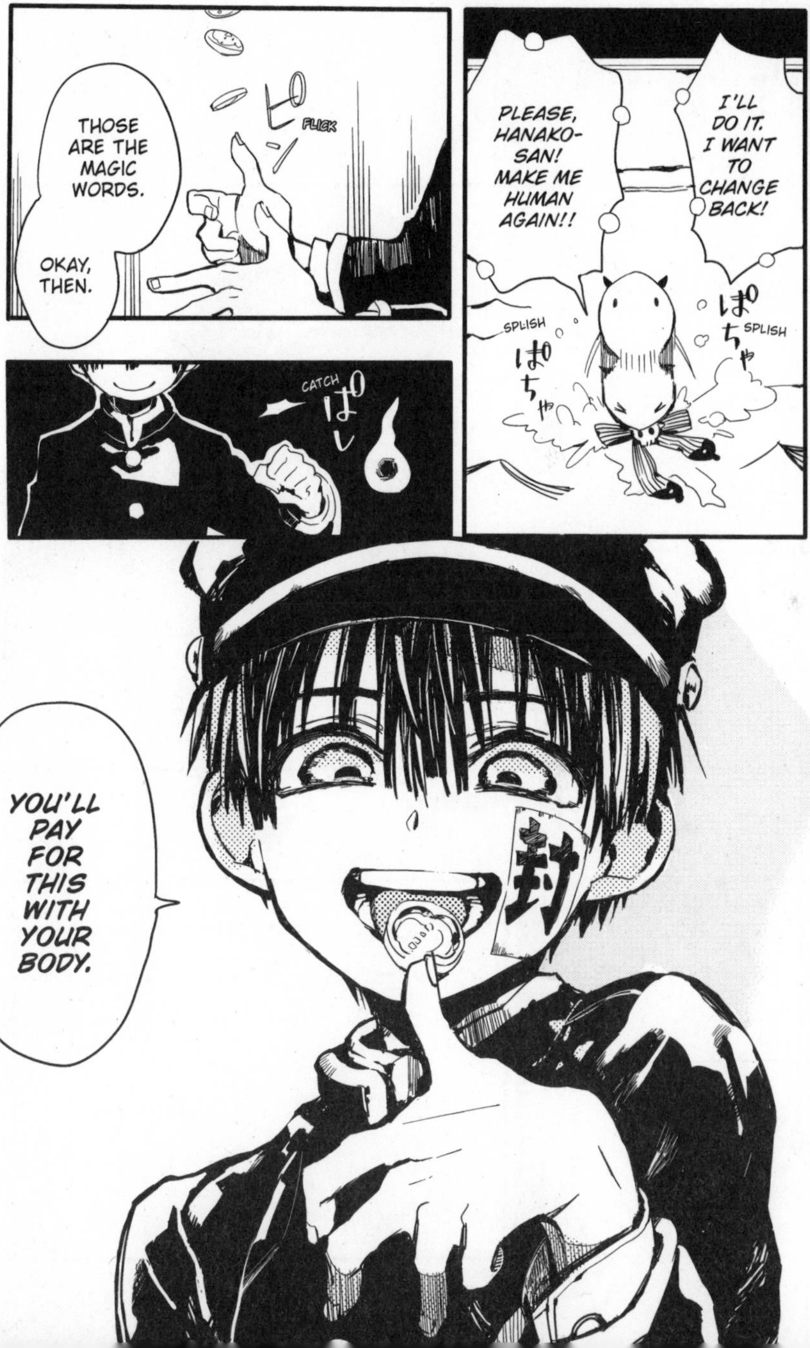

I'LL DO IT. I WANT TO CHANGE BACK!
PLEASE, HANAKO-SAN! MAKE ME HUMAN AGAIN!!
ぱちゃ SPLISH
ぱちゃ SPLISH
THOSE ARE THE MAGIC WORDS.
OKAY, THEN.
ピッ FLICK
ぱし CATCH
YOU'LL PAY FOR THIS WITH YOUR BODY.

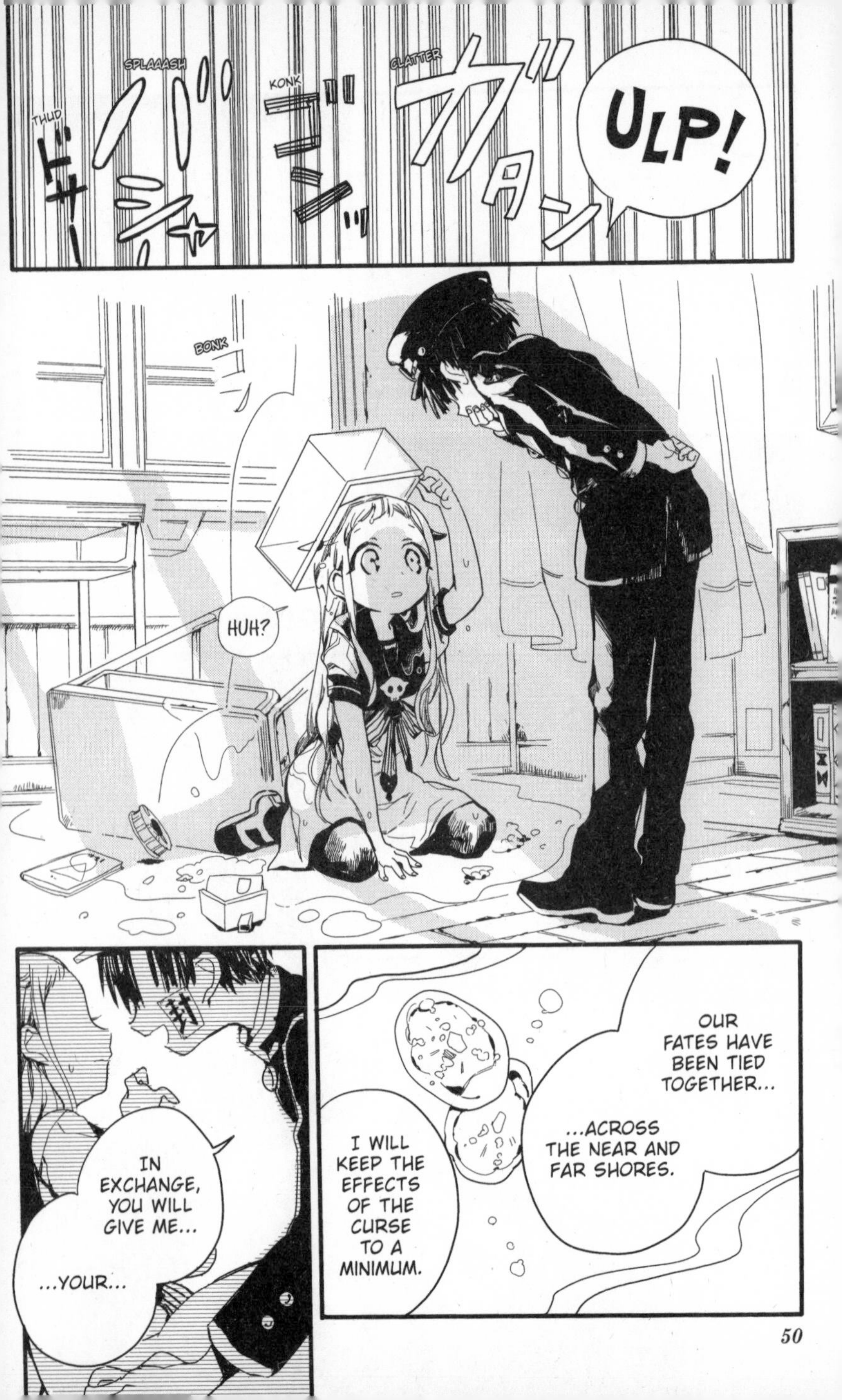

ULP!
CLATTER
KONK
SPLAAASH
THUD
BONK
HUH?
OUR FATES HAVE BEEN TIED TOGETHER...
...ACROSS THE NEAR AND FAR SHORES.
I WILL KEEP THE EFFECTS OF THE CURSE TO A MINIMUM.
封
IN EXCHANGE, YOU WILL GIVE ME...
...YOUR...

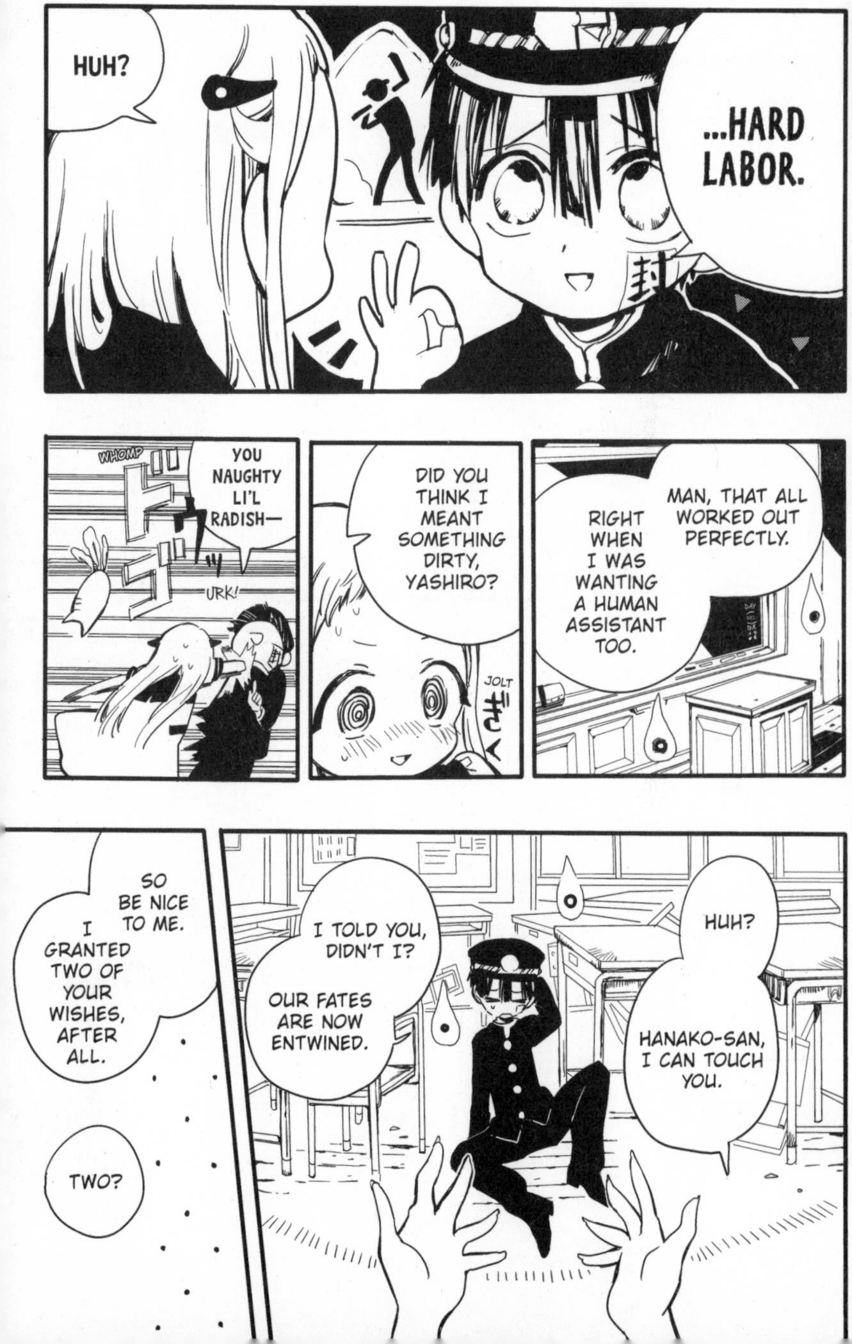

...HARD LABOR.
HUH?
MAN, THAT ALL WORKED OUT PERFECTLY.
RIGHT WHEN I WAS WANTING A HUMAN ASSISTANT TOO.
DID YOU THINK I MEANT SOMETHING DIRTY, YASHIRO?
JOLT
YOU NAUGHTY LI'L RADISH—
WHOMP
URK!
HUH?
HANAKO-SAN, I CAN TOUCH YOU.
I TOLD YOU, DIDN'T I?
OUR FATES ARE NOW ENTWINED.
SO BE NICE TO ME.
I GRANTED TWO OF YOUR WISHES, AFTER ALL.
TWO?

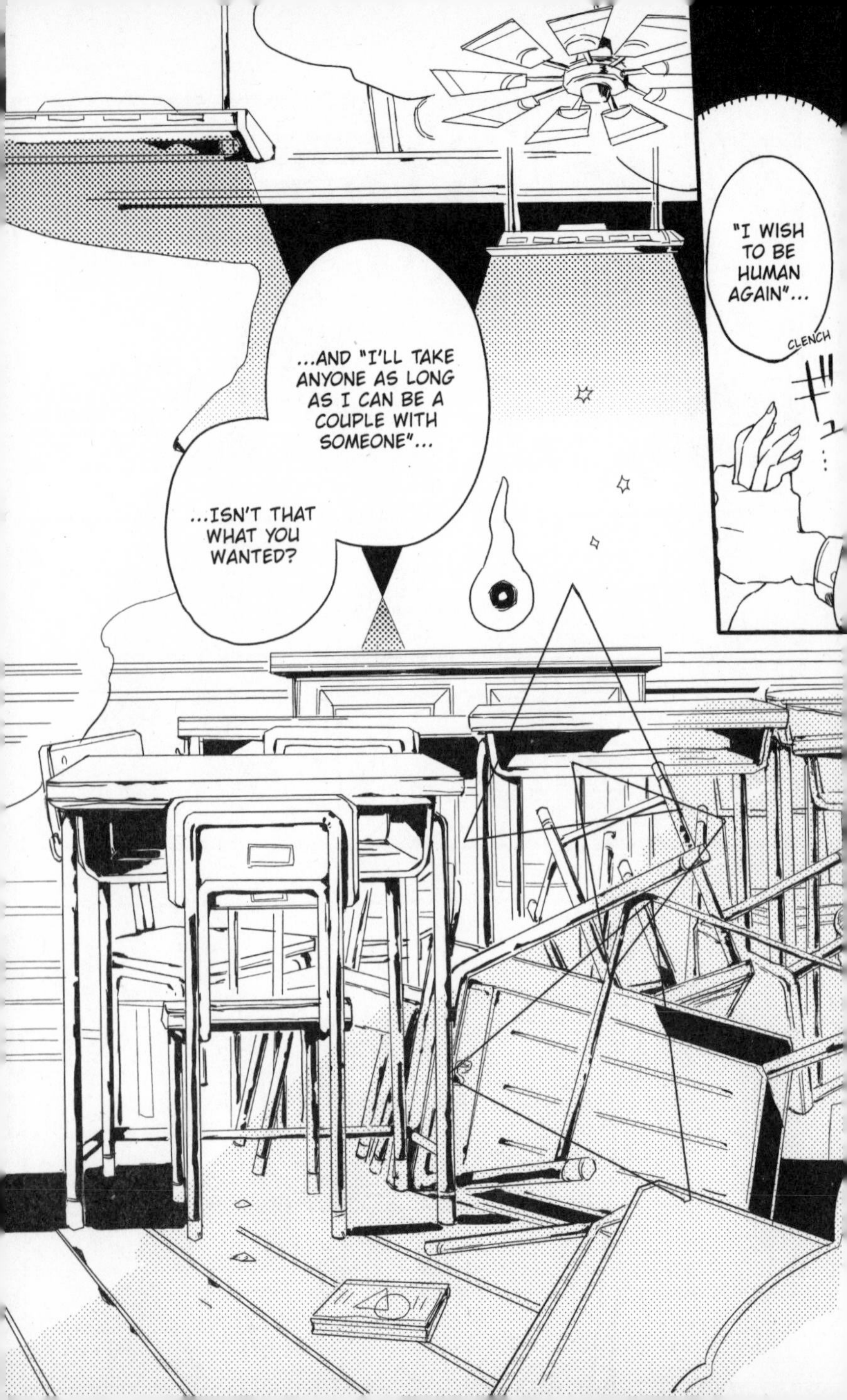
"I WISH TO BE HUMAN AGAIN"...
CLENCH
...AND "I'LL TAKE ANYONE AS LONG AS I CAN BE A COUPLE WITH SOMEONE"...
...ISN'T THAT WHAT YOU WANTED?

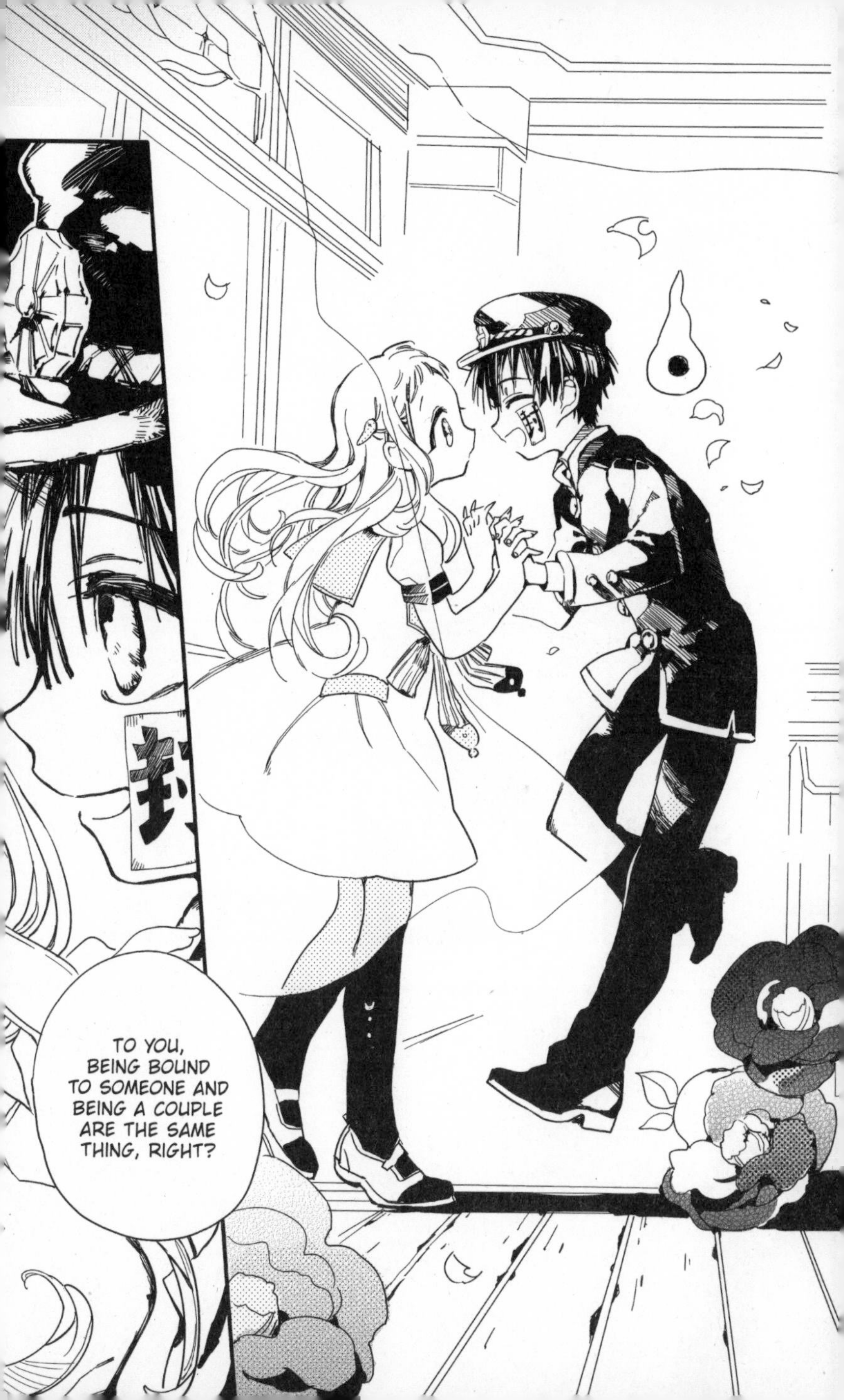
TO YOU, BEING BOUND TO SOMEONE AND BEING A COUPLE ARE THE SAME THING, RIGHT?

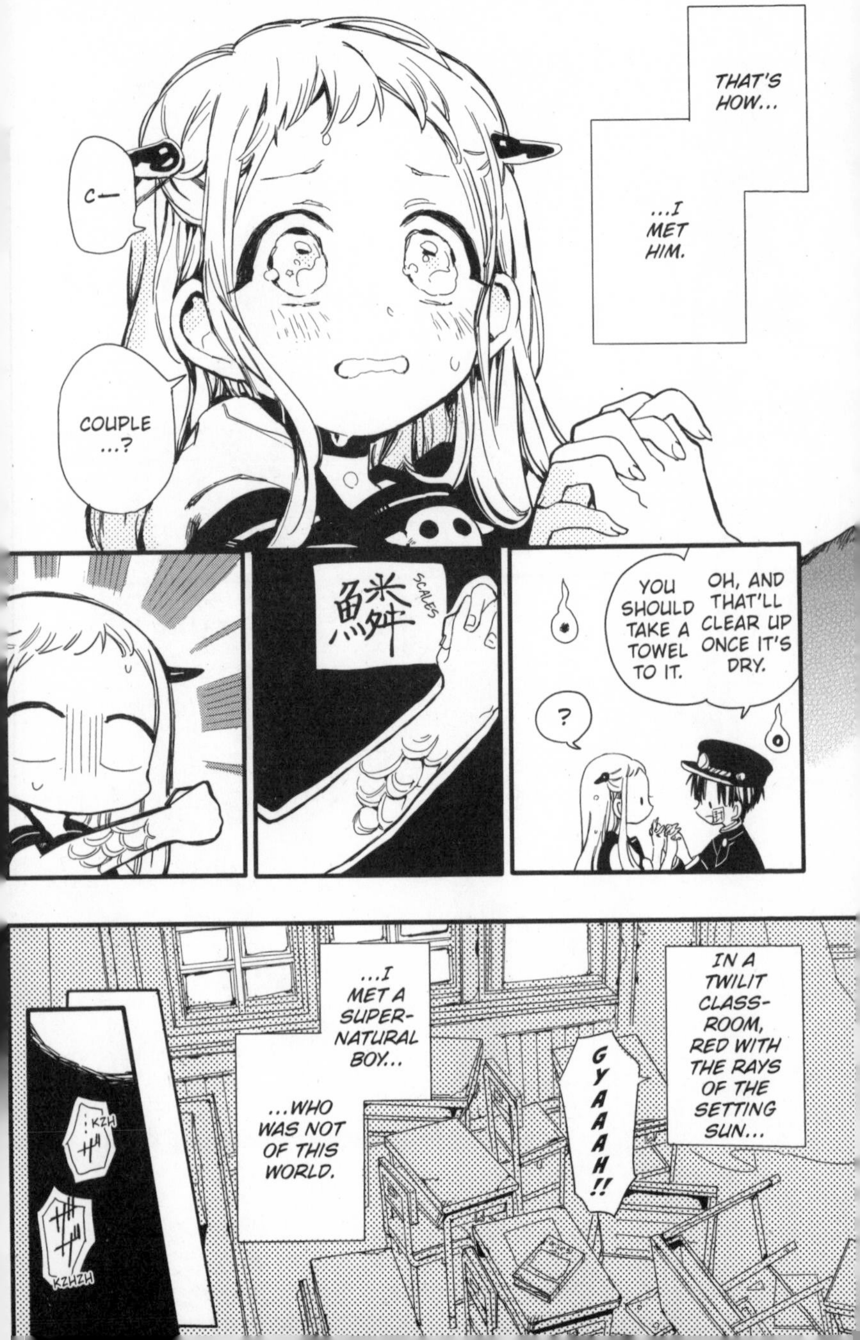
THAT'S HOW...
...I MET HIM.
C—
COUPLE ...?
OH, AND THAT'LL CLEAR UP ONCE IT'S DRY.
YOU SHOULD TAKE A TOWEL TO IT.
?
鱗 SCALES
IN A TWILIT CLASS-ROOM, RED WITH THE RAYS OF THE SETTING SUN...
GYAAAAH!!
...I MET A SUPER-NATURAL BOY...
...WHO WAS NOT OF THIS WORLD.
KZH
KZHZH

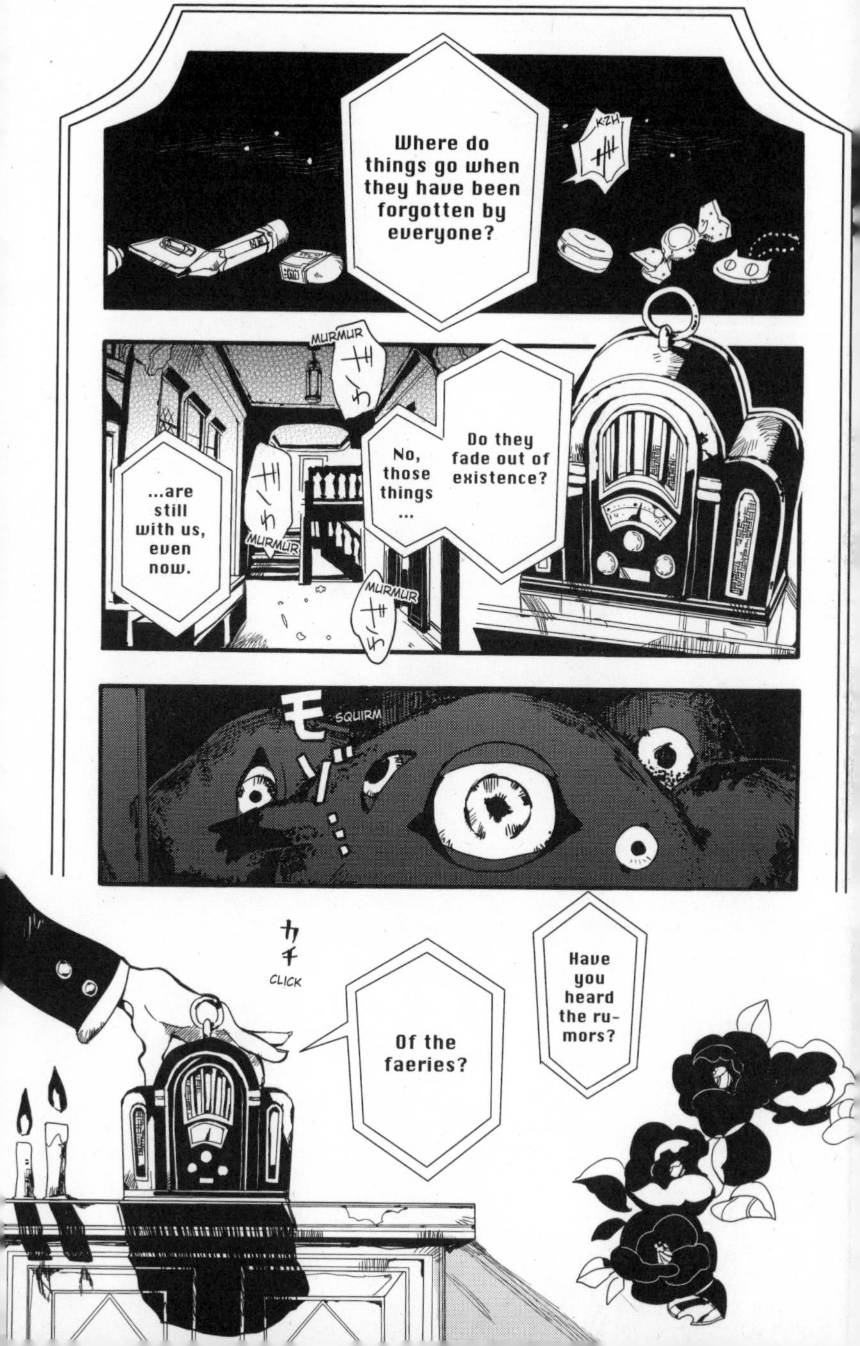
KZH
Where do things go when they have been forgotten by everyone?
MURMUR
Do they fade out of existence?
No, those things ...
...are still with us, even now.
MURMUR
MURMUR
SQUIRM
Have you heard the rumors?
Of the faeries?
CLICK

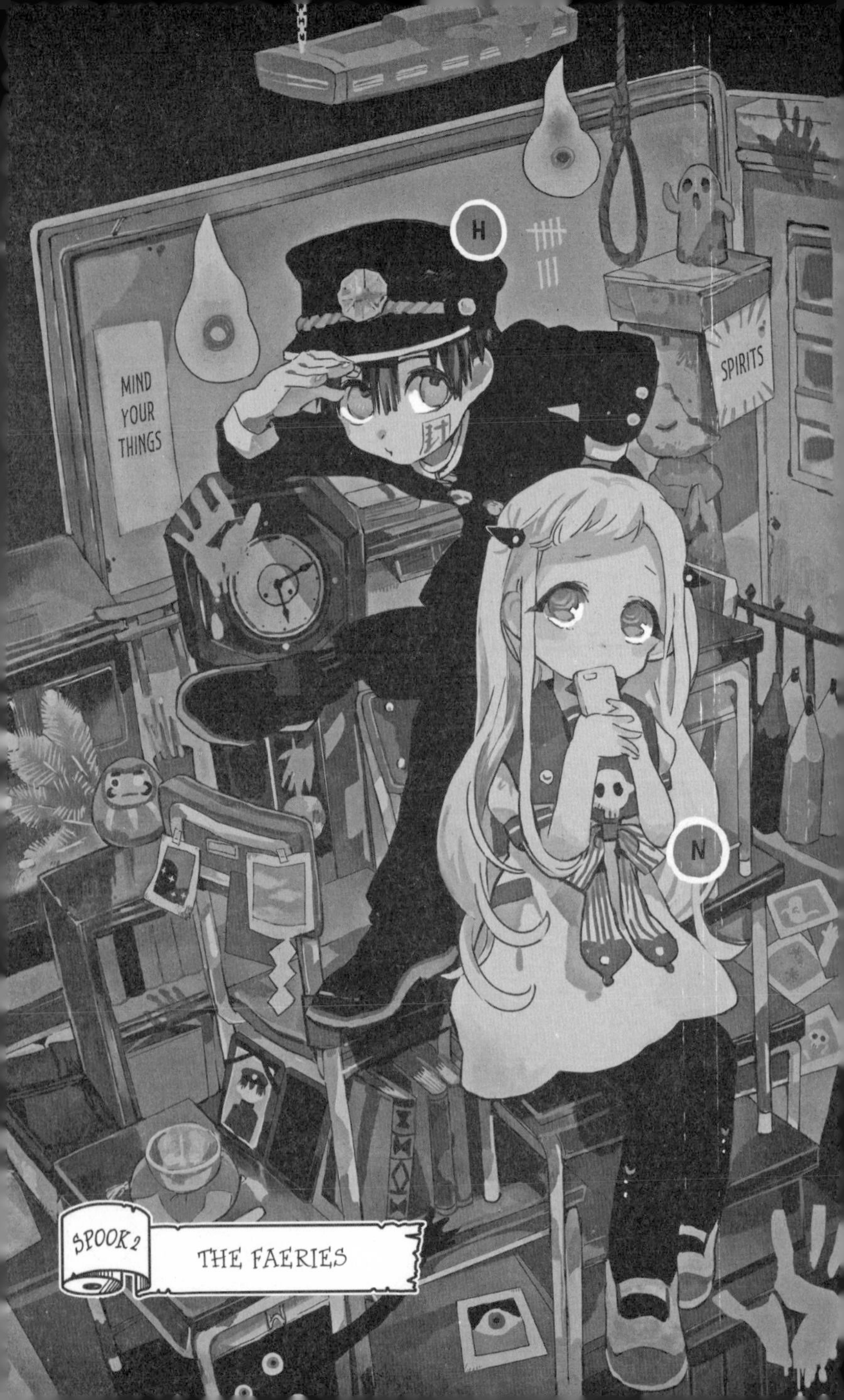
H
MIND YOUR THINGS
SPIRITS
N
SPOOK 2
THE FAERIES

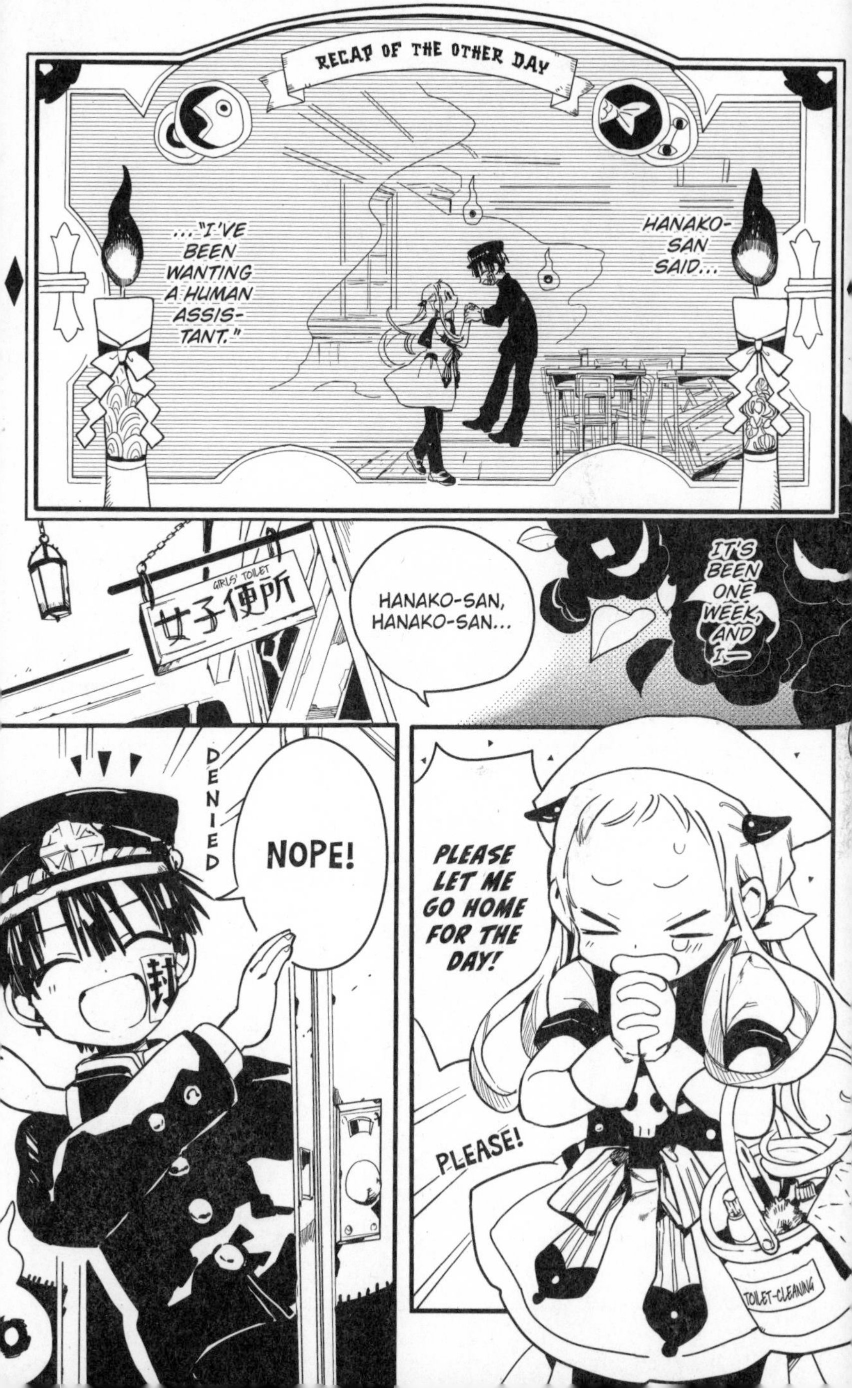
RECAP OF THE OTHER DAY
HANAKO-SAN SAID...
..."I'VE BEEN WANTING A HUMAN ASSISTANT."
IT'S BEEN ONE WEEK, AND I—
HANAKO-SAN, HANAKO-SAN...
GIRLS' TOILET
女子便所
PLEASE LET ME GO HOME FOR THE DAY!
PLEASE!
TOILET-CLEANING
DENIED
NOPE!
封

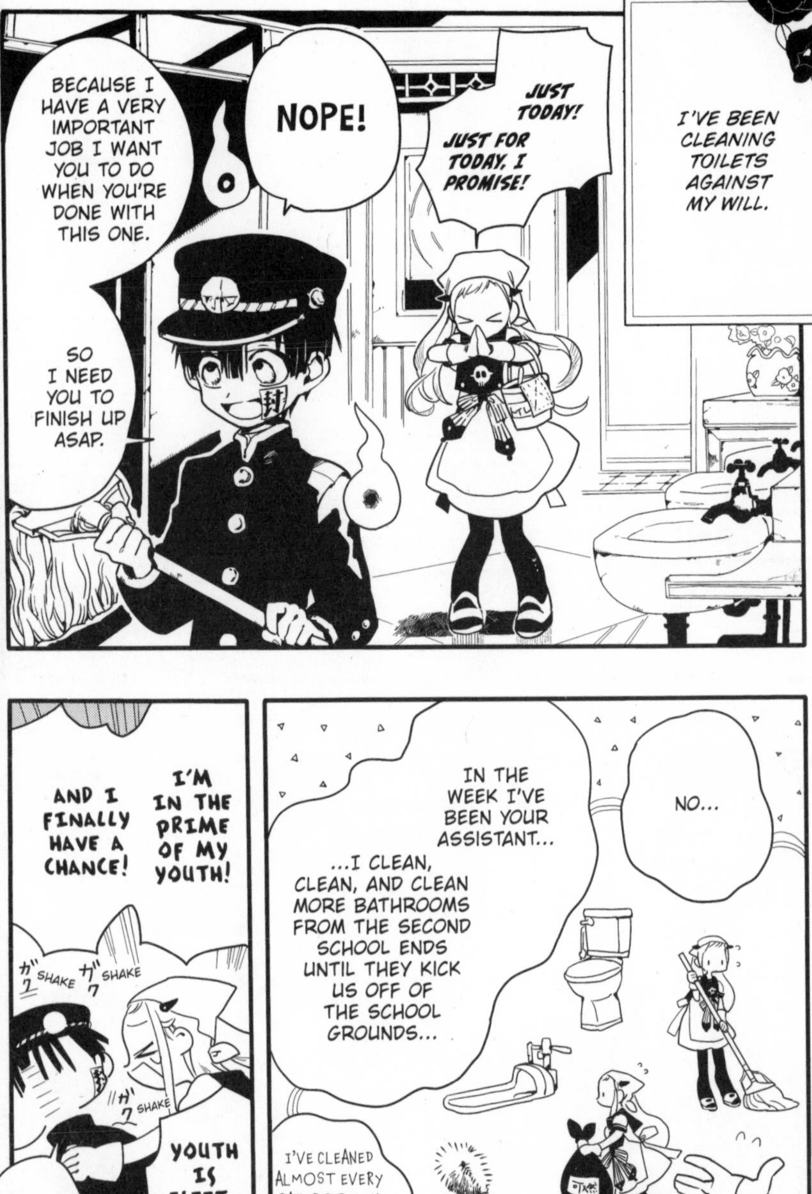
I'VE BEEN CLEANING TOILETS AGAINST MY WILL.
JUST TODAY!
JUST FOR TODAY, I PROMISE!
NOPE!
BECAUSE I HAVE A VERY IMPORTANT JOB I WANT YOU TO DO WHEN YOU'RE DONE WITH THIS ONE.
SO I NEED YOU TO FINISH UP ASAP.
NO...
IN THE WEEK I'VE BEEN YOUR ASSISTANT...
...I CLEAN, CLEAN, AND CLEAN MORE BATHROOMS FROM THE SECOND SCHOOL ENDS UNTIL THEY KICK US OFF OF THE SCHOOL GROUNDS...
I'VE CLEANED ALMOST EVERY BATHROOM IN THE ENTIRE SCHOOL.
I'M IN THE PRIME OF MY YOUTH!
AND I FINALLY HAVE A CHANCE!
ガク SHAKE ガク SHAKE
ガク SHAKE
YOUTH IS FLEET-ING!
CHANCE?

BAG: COMBUSTIBLE

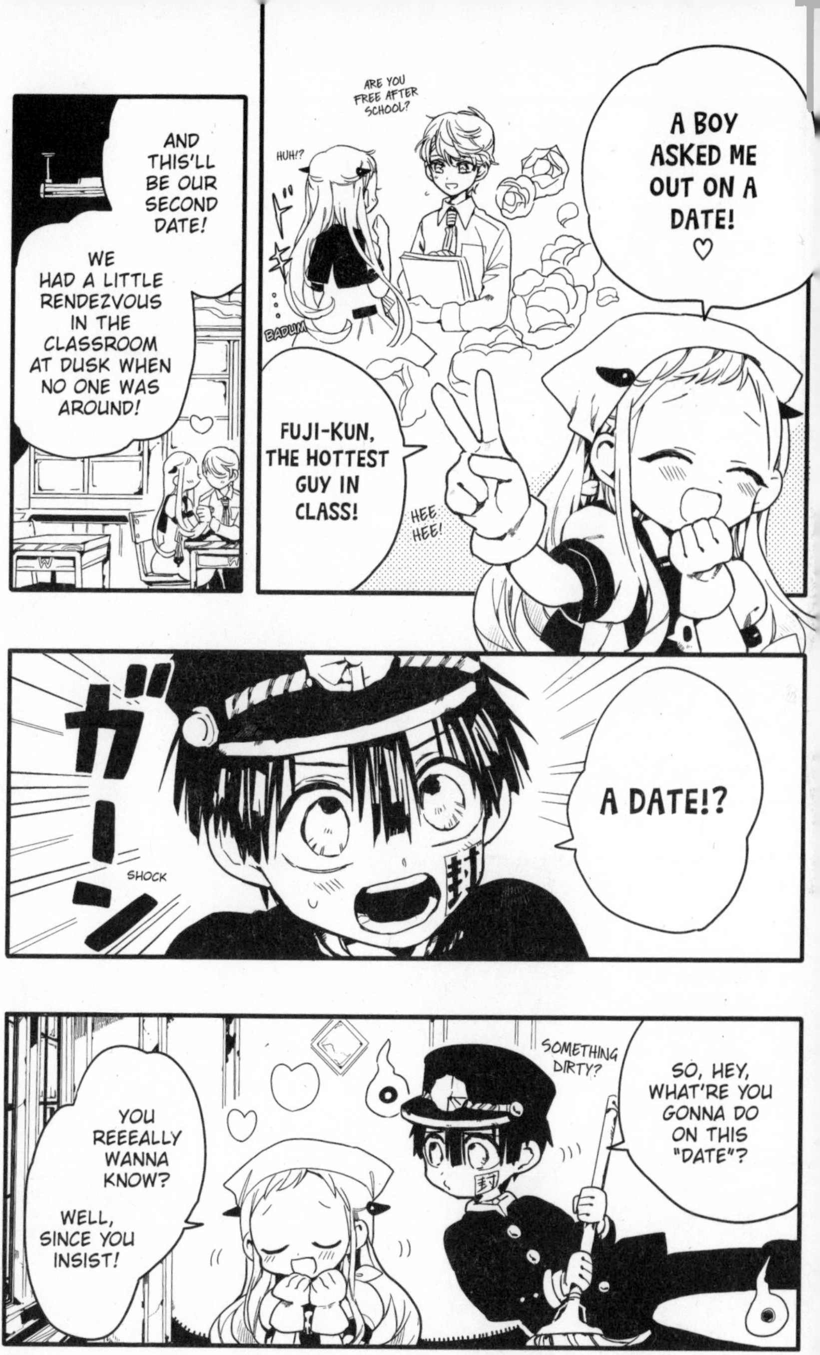
A BOY ASKED ME OUT ON A DATE! ♡
ARE YOU FREE AFTER SCHOOL?
HUH!?
BADUM
FUJI-KUN, THE HOTTEST GUY IN CLASS!
HEE HEE!
AND THIS'LL BE OUR SECOND DATE!
WE HAD A LITTLE RENDEZVOUS IN THE CLASSROOM AT DUSK WHEN NO ONE WAS AROUND!
A DATE!?
SHOCK
SO, HEY, WHAT'RE YOU GONNA DO ON THIS "DATE"?
SOMETHING DIRTY?
YOU REEEALLY WANNA KNOW?
WELL, SINCE YOU INSIST!

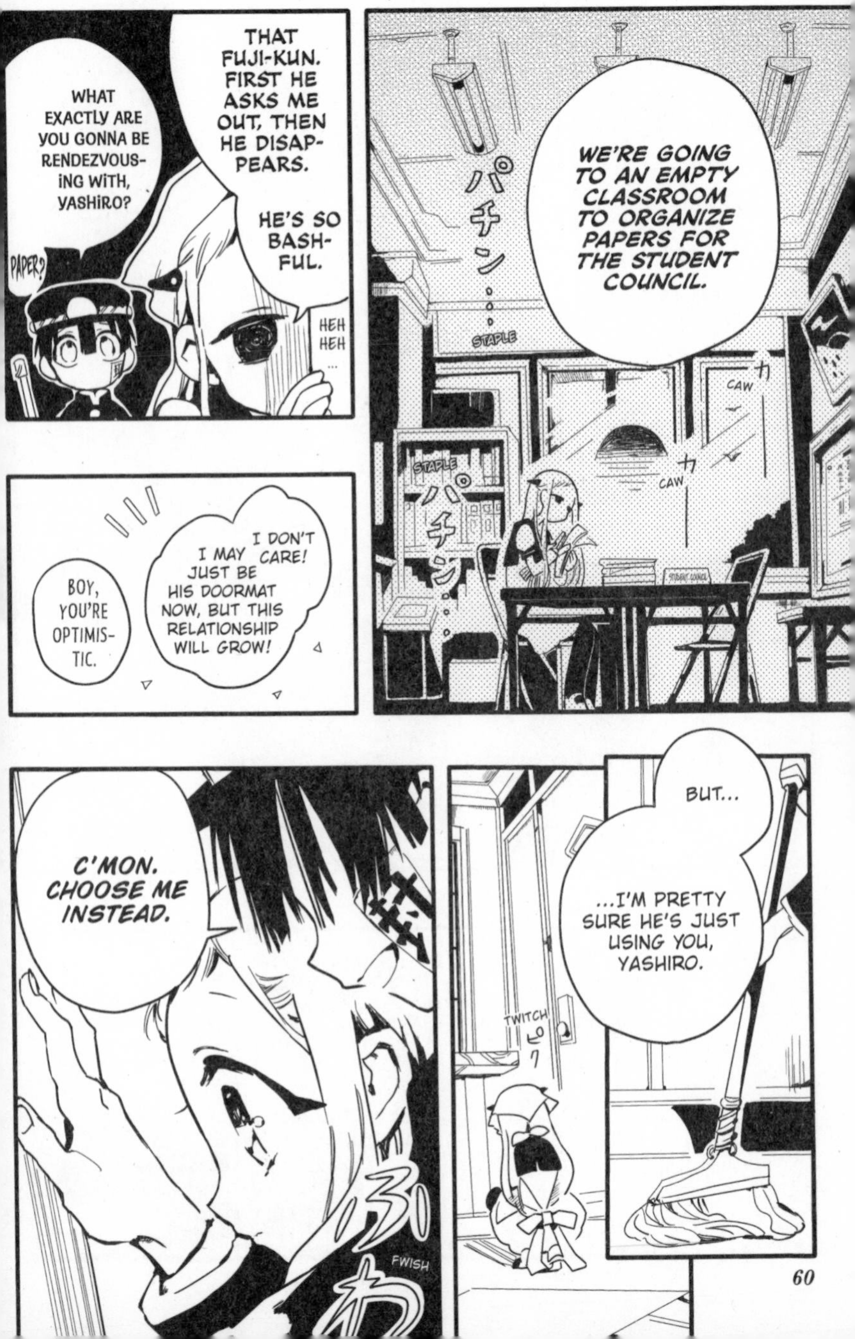

WE'RE GOING TO AN EMPTY CLASSROOM TO ORGANIZE PAPERS FOR THE STUDENT COUNCIL.
パチン…
STAPLE
パチン…
STAPLE
カ
CAW
カ
CAW
STUDENT COUNCIL
THAT FUJI-KUN. FIRST HE ASKS ME OUT, THEN HE DISAPPEARS.
HE'S SO BASHFUL.
HEH HEH ...
WHAT EXACTLY ARE YOU GONNA BE RENDEZVOUSING WITH, YASHIRO?
PAPER?
I DON'T CARE!
I MAY JUST BE HIS DOORMAT NOW, BUT THIS RELATIONSHIP WILL GROW!
BOY, YOU'RE OPTIMISTIC.
BUT...
...I'M PRETTY SURE HE'S JUST USING YOU, YASHIRO.
TWITCH
ピク
C'MON. CHOOSE ME INSTEAD.
ふわ
FWISH

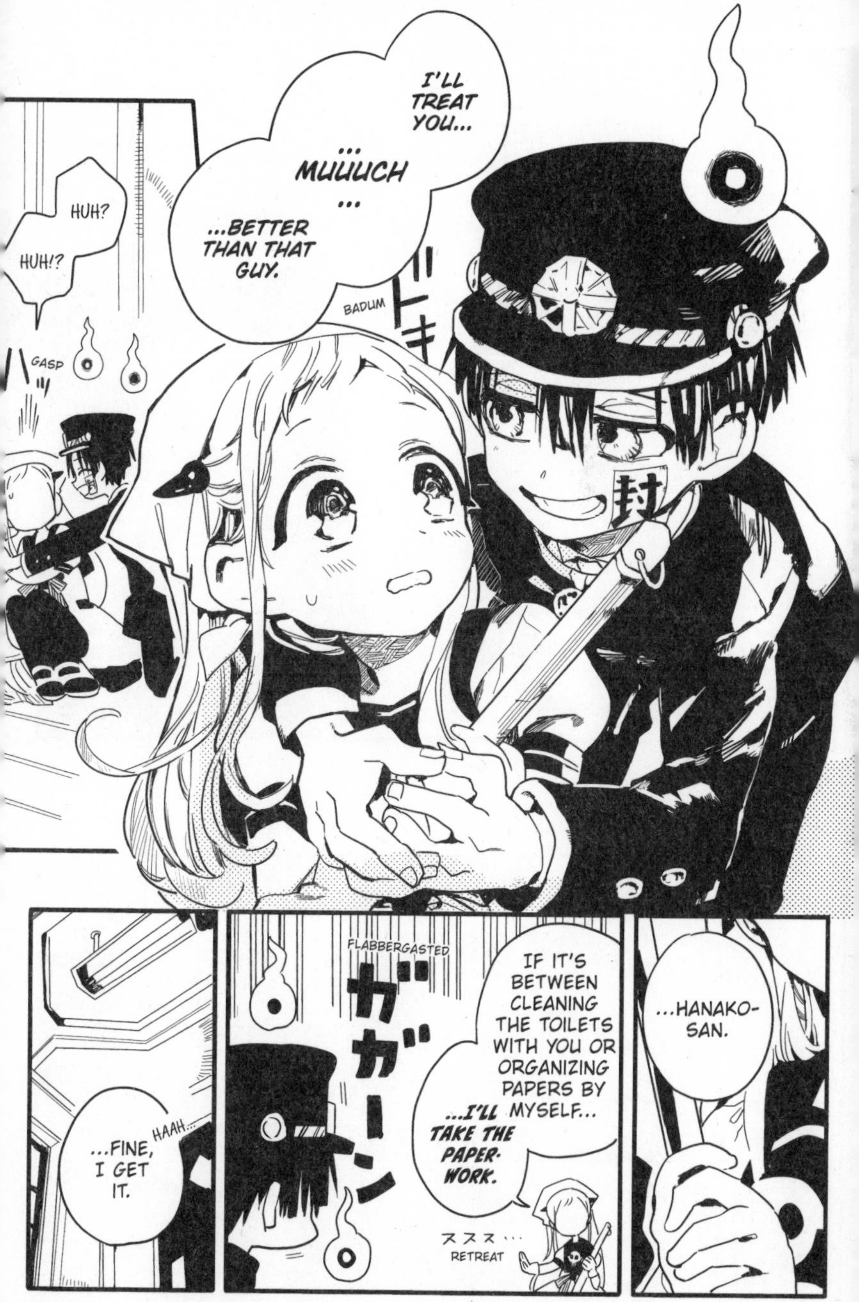
I'LL TREAT YOU...
... MUUUCH ...
...BETTER THAN THAT GUY.
ドキ
BADUM
HUH?
HUH!?
GASP
...HANAKO-SAN.
IF IT'S BETWEEN CLEANING THE TOILETS WITH YOU OR ORGANIZING PAPERS BY MYSELF... ...I'LL TAKE THE PAPER-WORK.
ガガーン
FLABBERGASTED
ススス...
RETREAT
...FINE, I GET IT.
HAAH...

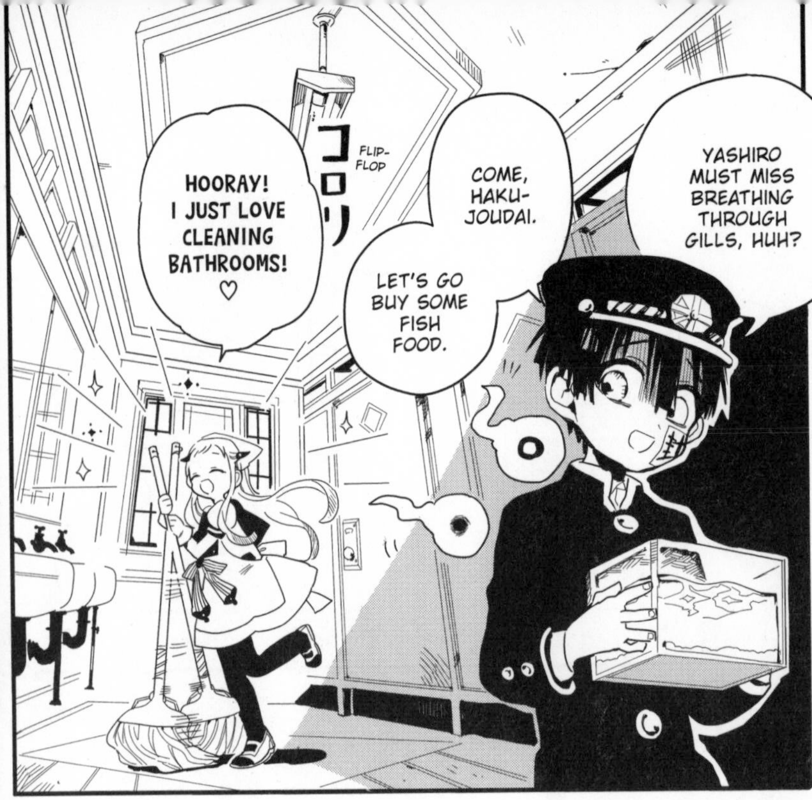
YASHIRO MUST MISS BREATHING THROUGH GILLS, HUH?
COME, HAKU-JOUDAI.
LET'S GO BUY SOME FISH FOOD.
コロリ
FLIP-FLOP
HOORAY! I JUST LOVE CLEANING BATHROOMS! ♡

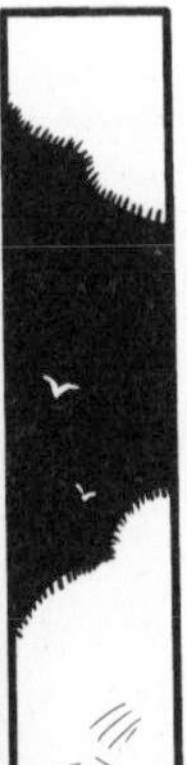

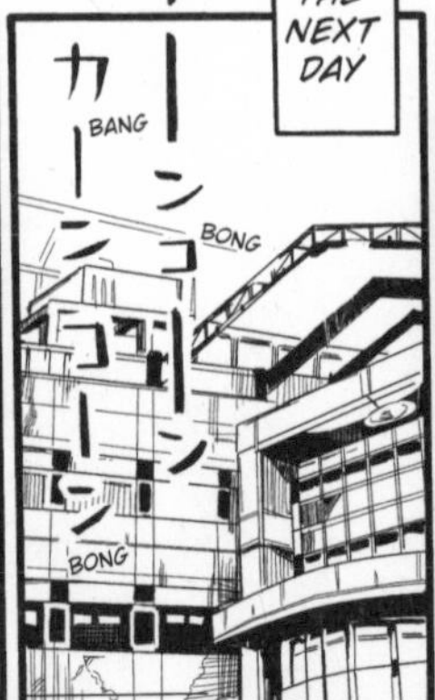
THE NEXT DAY
キーンコーン
BING
BONG
カーンコーン
BANG
BONG

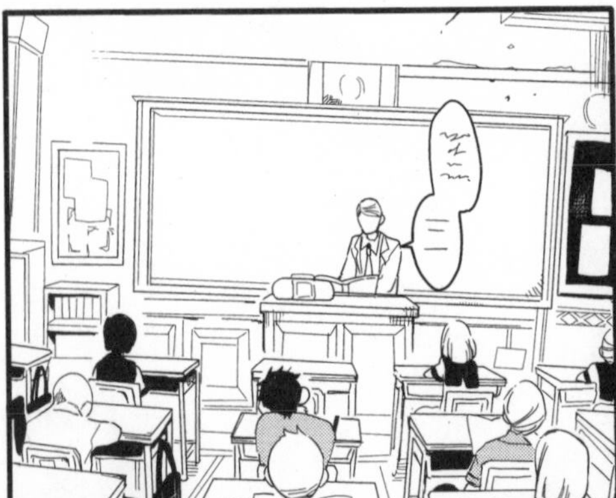

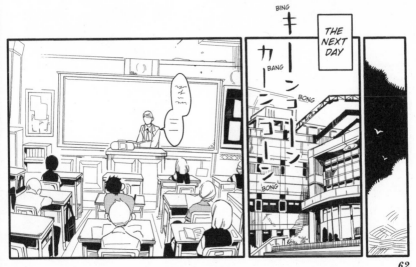

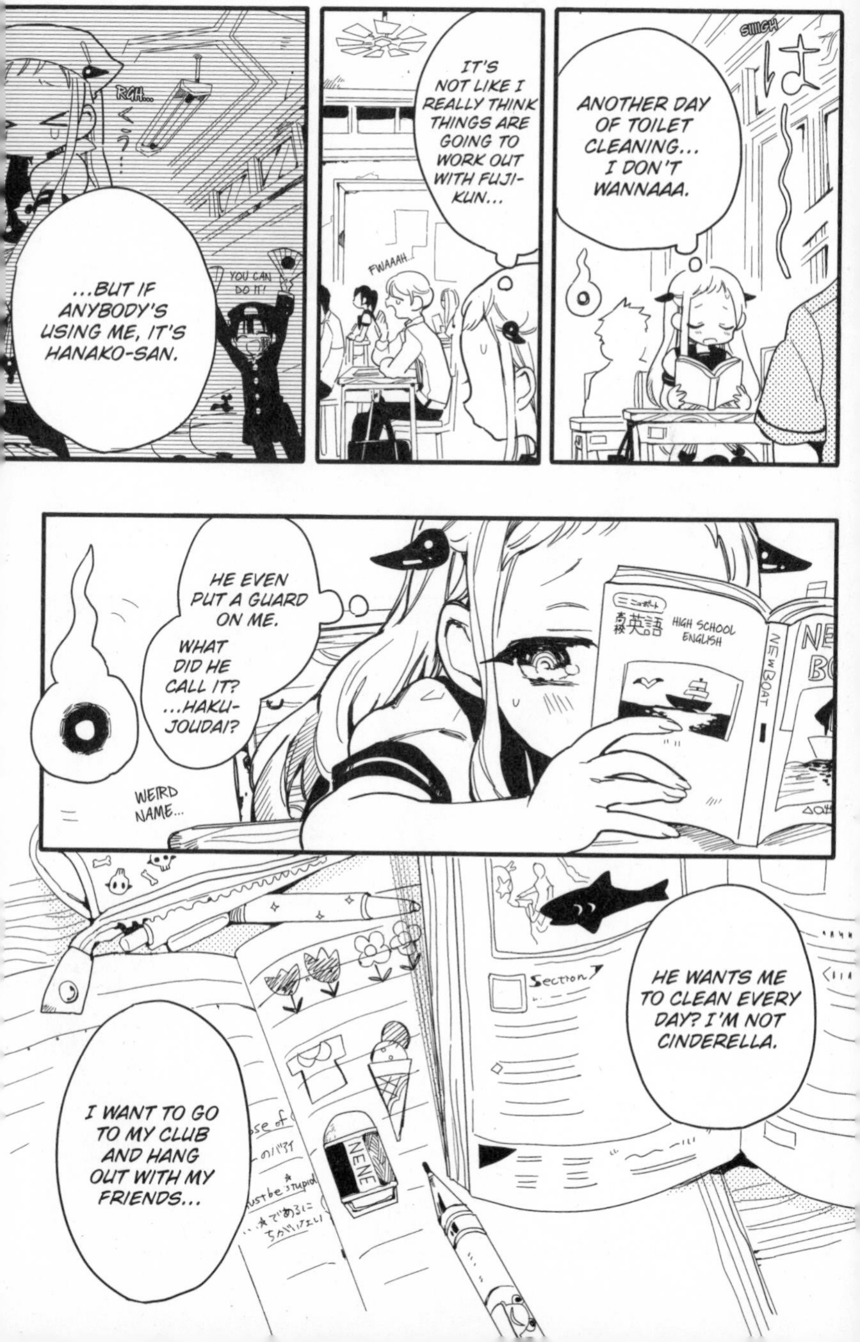
SIIIIGH
ANOTHER DAY OF TOILET CLEANING... I DON'T WANNAAA.
IT'S NOT LIKE I REALLY THINK THINGS ARE GOING TO WORK OUT WITH FUJI-KUN...
FWAAAH...
RGH...
YOU CAN DO IT!
...BUT IF ANYBODY'S USING ME, IT'S HANAKO-SAN.
HIGH SCHOOL ENGLISH
NEW BOAT
HE EVEN PUT A GUARD ON ME.
WHAT DID HE CALL IT? ...HAKU-JOUDAI?
WEIRD NAME...
HE WANTS ME TO CLEAN EVERY DAY? I'M NOT CINDERELLA.
Section 7
I WANT TO GO TO MY CLUB AND HANG OUT WITH MY FRIENDS...
NENE

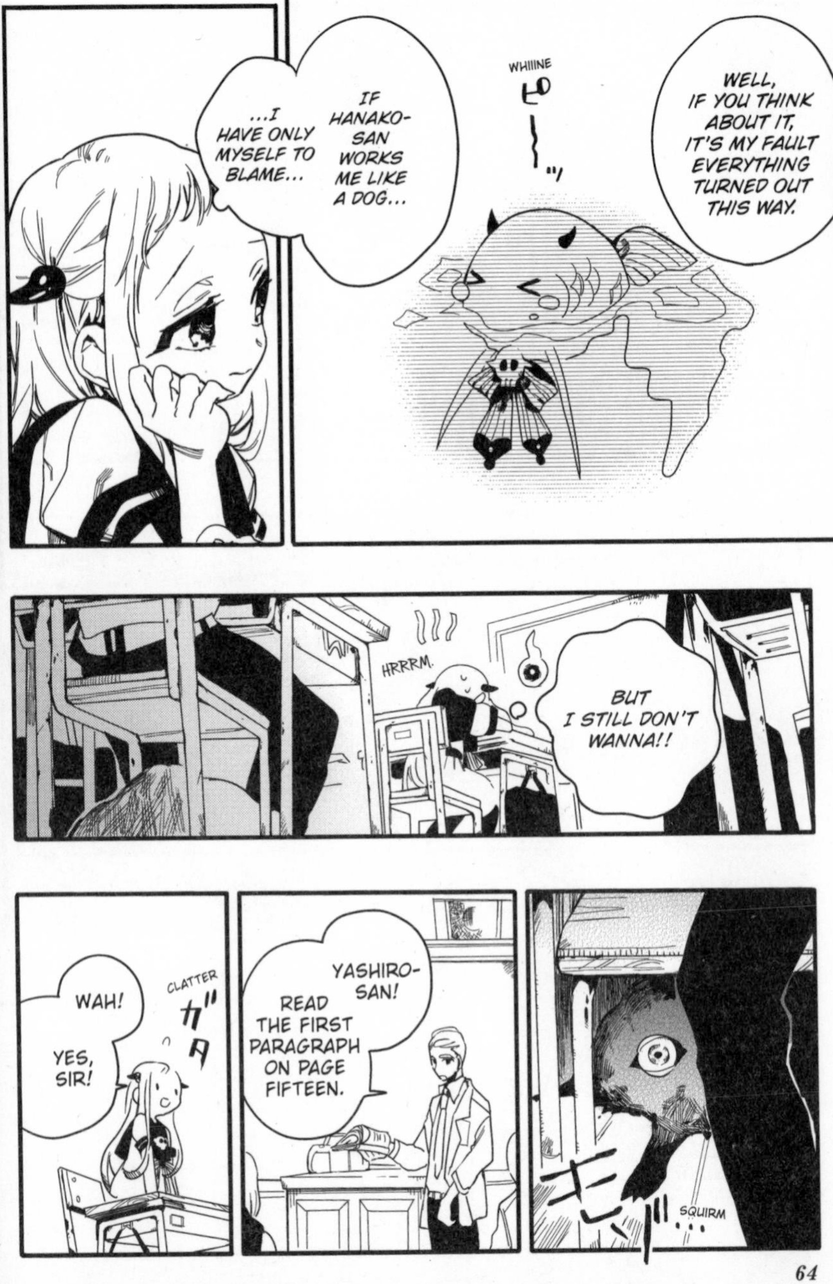
WELL, IF YOU THINK ABOUT IT, IT'S MY FAULT EVERYTHING TURNED OUT THIS WAY.
WHIIINE
IF HANAKO-SAN WORKS ME LIKE A DOG...
...I HAVE ONLY MYSELF TO BLAME...
BUT I STILL DON'T WANNA!!
HRRRM.
SQUIRM
YASHIRO-SAN!
READ THE FIRST PARAGRAPH ON PAGE FIFTEEN.
CLATTER
WAH!
YES, SIR!

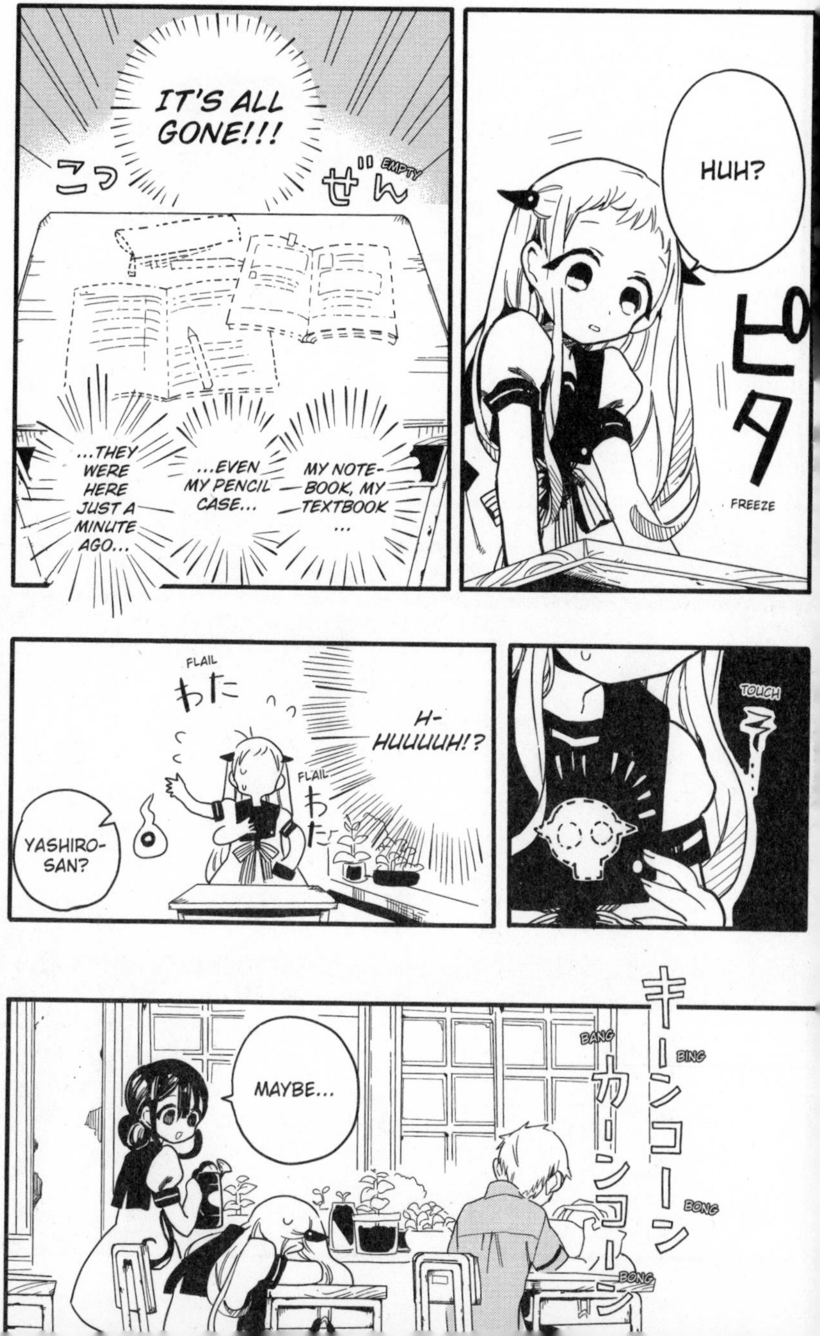
HUH?
ピタ
FREEZE
IT'S ALL GONE!!!
こつ
ぜん
EMPTY
MY NOTE-BOOK, MY TEXTBOOK ...
...EVEN MY PENCIL CASE...
...THEY WERE HERE JUST A MINUTE AGO...
TOUCH
H-HUUUUUH!?
わた
FLAIL
わた
FLAIL
YASHIRO-SAN?
キーンコーン
BANG
BING
カーンコーン
BONG
BONG
MAYBE...

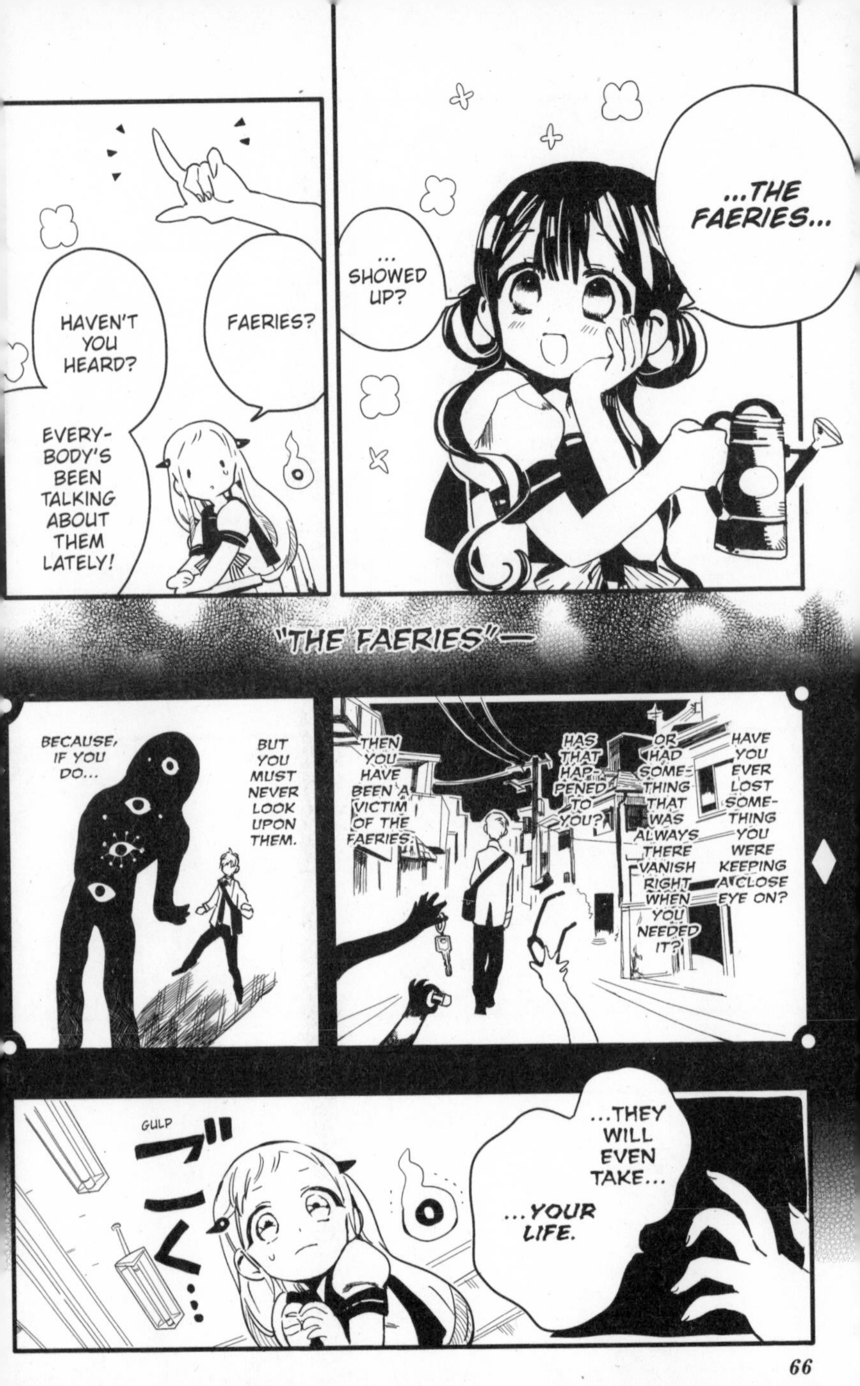
...THE FAERIES...
...SHOWED UP?
FAERIES?
HAVEN'T YOU HEARD?
EVERY-BODY'S BEEN TALKING ABOUT THEM LATELY!
"THE FAERIES"—
HAVE YOU EVER LOST SOME-THING YOU WERE KEEPING A CLOSE EYE ON?
OR HAD SOME-THING THAT WAS ALWAYS THERE VANISH RIGHT WHEN YOU NEEDED IT?
HAS THAT HAP-PENED TO YOU?
THEN YOU HAVE BEEN A VICTIM OF THE FAERIES.
BUT YOU MUST NEVER LOOK UPON THEM.
BECAUSE, IF YOU DO...
...THEY WILL EVEN TAKE...
...YOUR LIFE.
GULP
ゴく...

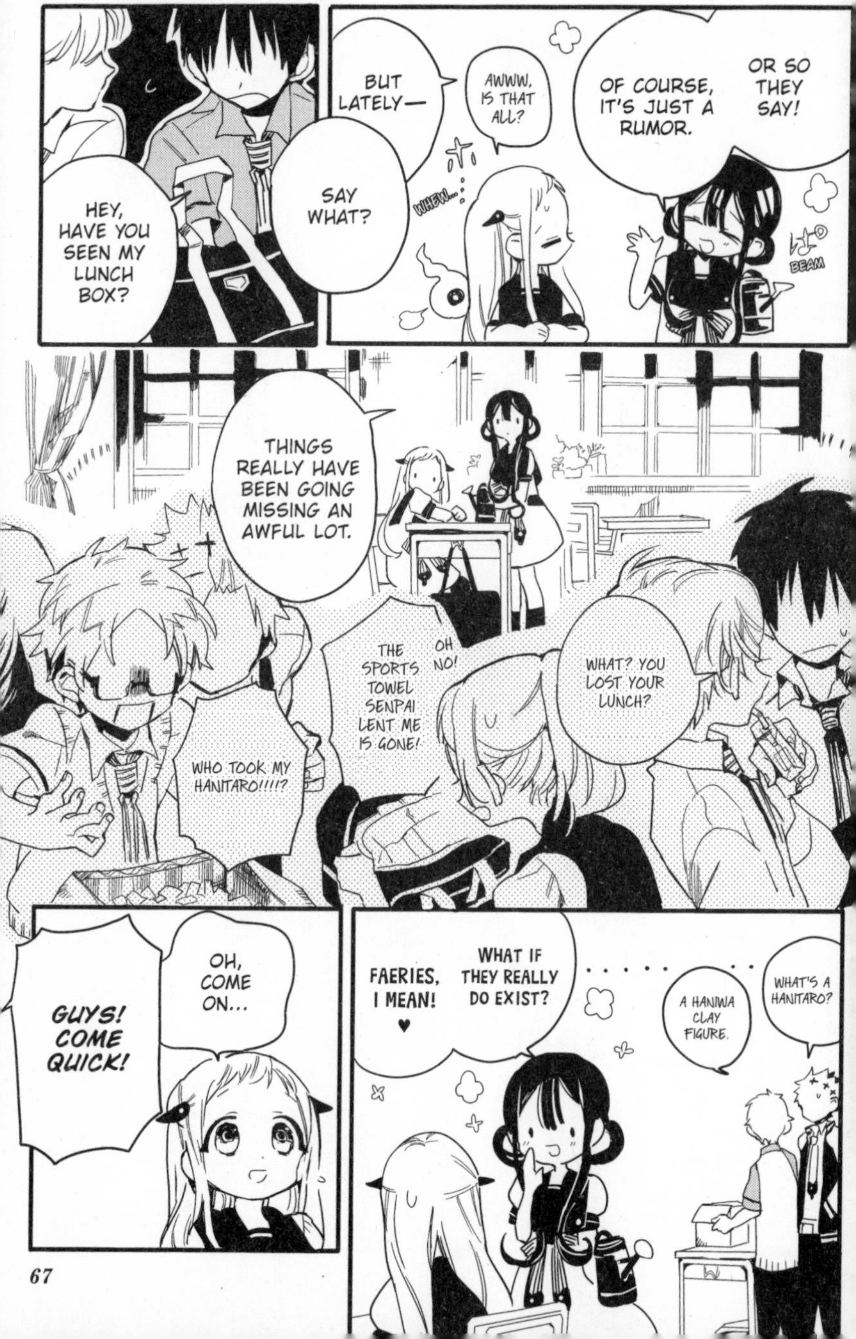
OF COURSE, IT'S JUST A RUMOR. OR SO THEY SAY!
BEAM
AWWW, IS THAT ALL?
WHEW...
BUT LATELY—
SAY WHAT?
HEY, HAVE YOU SEEN MY LUNCH BOX?
THINGS REALLY HAVE BEEN GOING MISSING AN AWFUL LOT.
WHAT? YOU LOST YOUR LUNCH?
OH NO!
THE SPORTS TOWEL SENPAI LENT ME IS GONE!
WHO TOOK MY HANITARO!!!!?
WHAT'S A HANITARO?
A HANIWA CLAY FIGURE.
. . . .
WHAT IF THEY REALLY DO EXIST? FAERIES, I MEAN! ♥
OH, COME ON...
GUYS! COME QUICK!

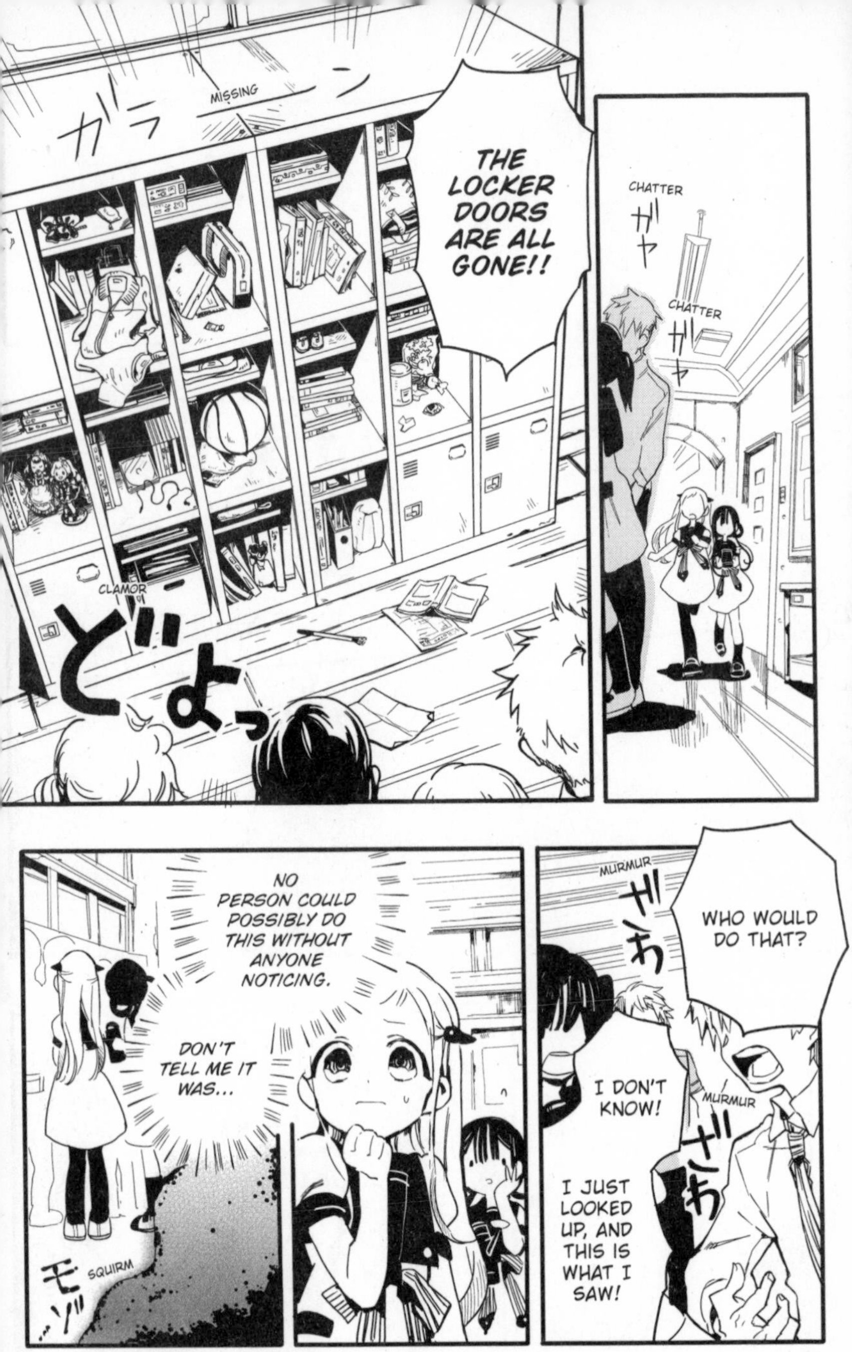
CHATTER
ガヤ
CHATTER
ガヤ
THE LOCKER DOORS ARE ALL GONE!!
MISSING
ガラーン
CLAMOR
どよっ
WHO WOULD DO THAT?
MURMUR
ざわ
I DON'T KNOW!
MURMUR
ざわ
I JUST LOOKED UP, AND THIS IS WHAT I SAW!
NO PERSON COULD POSSIBLY DO THIS WITHOUT ANYONE NOTICING.
DON'T TELL ME IT WAS...
SQUIRM
モゾ

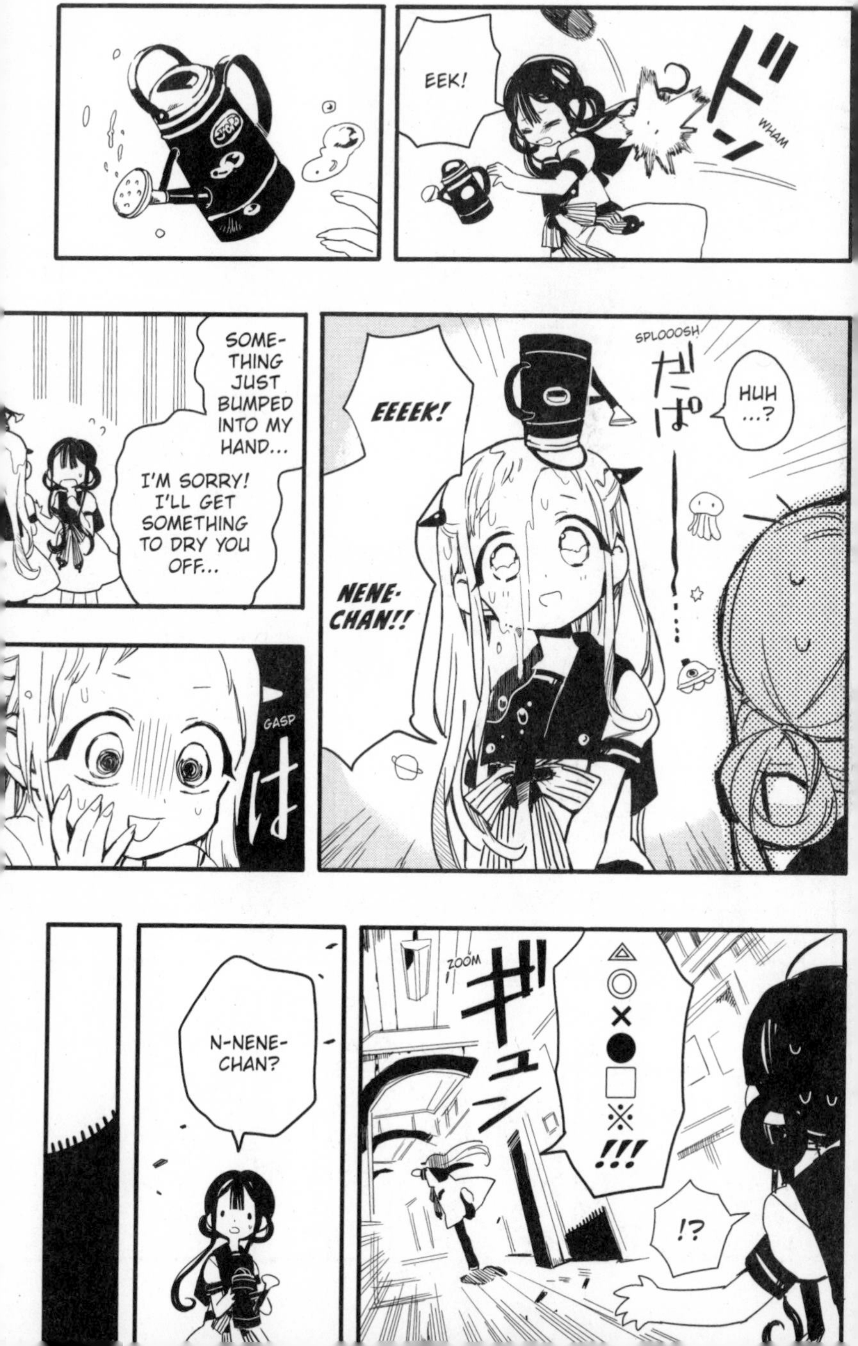
EEK!
ドン
WHAM
SPLOOOSH
だぱ
HUH ...?
EEEEK!
NENE-CHAN!!
SOME-THING JUST BUMPED INTO MY HAND...
I'M SORRY! I'LL GET SOMETHING TO DRY YOU OFF...
GASP
は
ZOOM
ギュン
△○×●□※!!!
!?
N-NENE-CHAN?

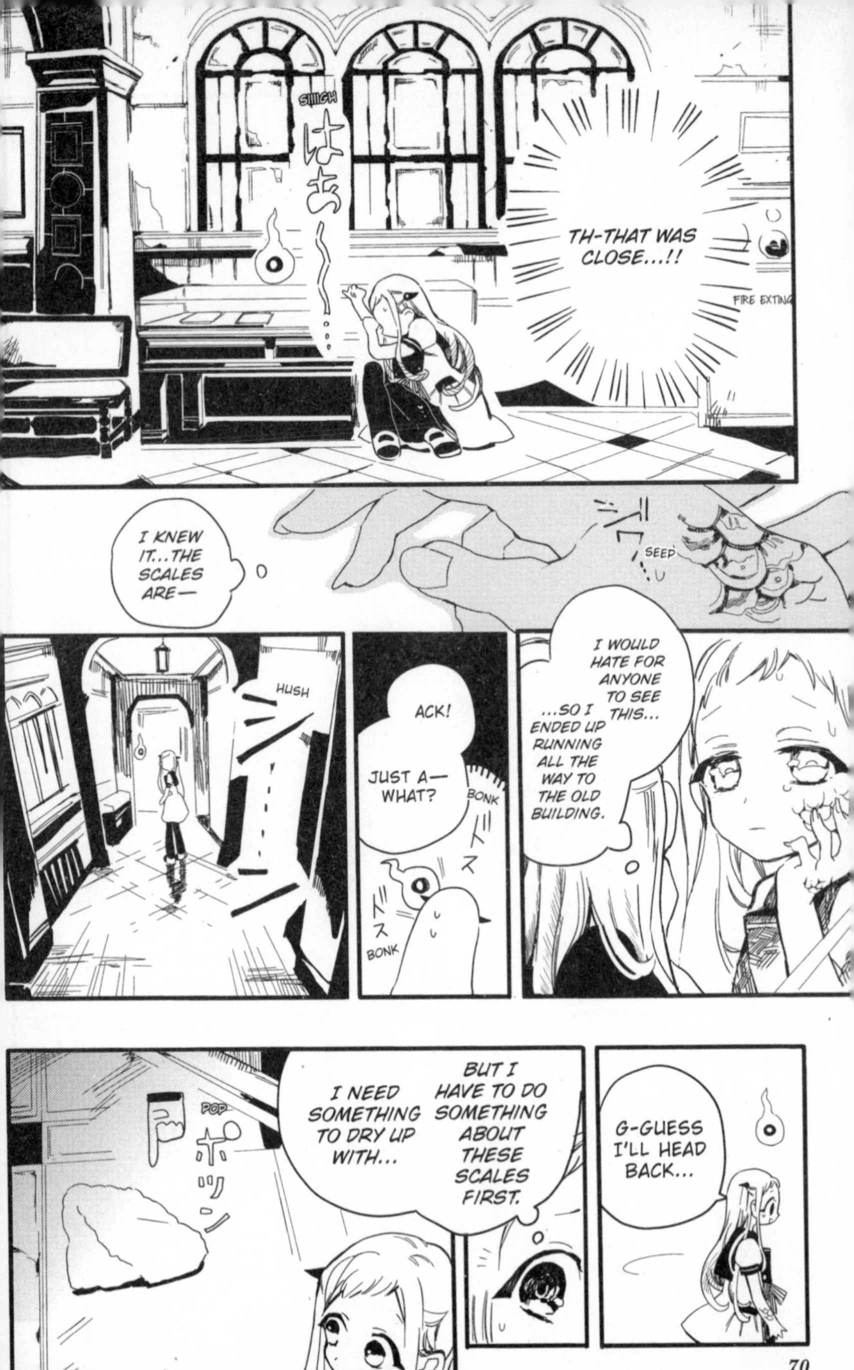
SIIIGH
はぁ~
TH-THAT WAS CLOSE...!!
FIRE EXTING
SEEP
I KNEW IT...THE SCALES ARE—
I WOULD HATE FOR ANYONE TO SEE THIS...
...SO I ENDED UP RUNNING ALL THE WAY TO THE OLD BUILDING.
ACK!
JUST A— WHAT?
BONK
BONK
HUSH
G-GUESS I'LL HEAD BACK...
BUT I HAVE TO DO SOMETHING ABOUT THESE SCALES FIRST.
I NEED SOMETHING TO DRY UP WITH...
POP

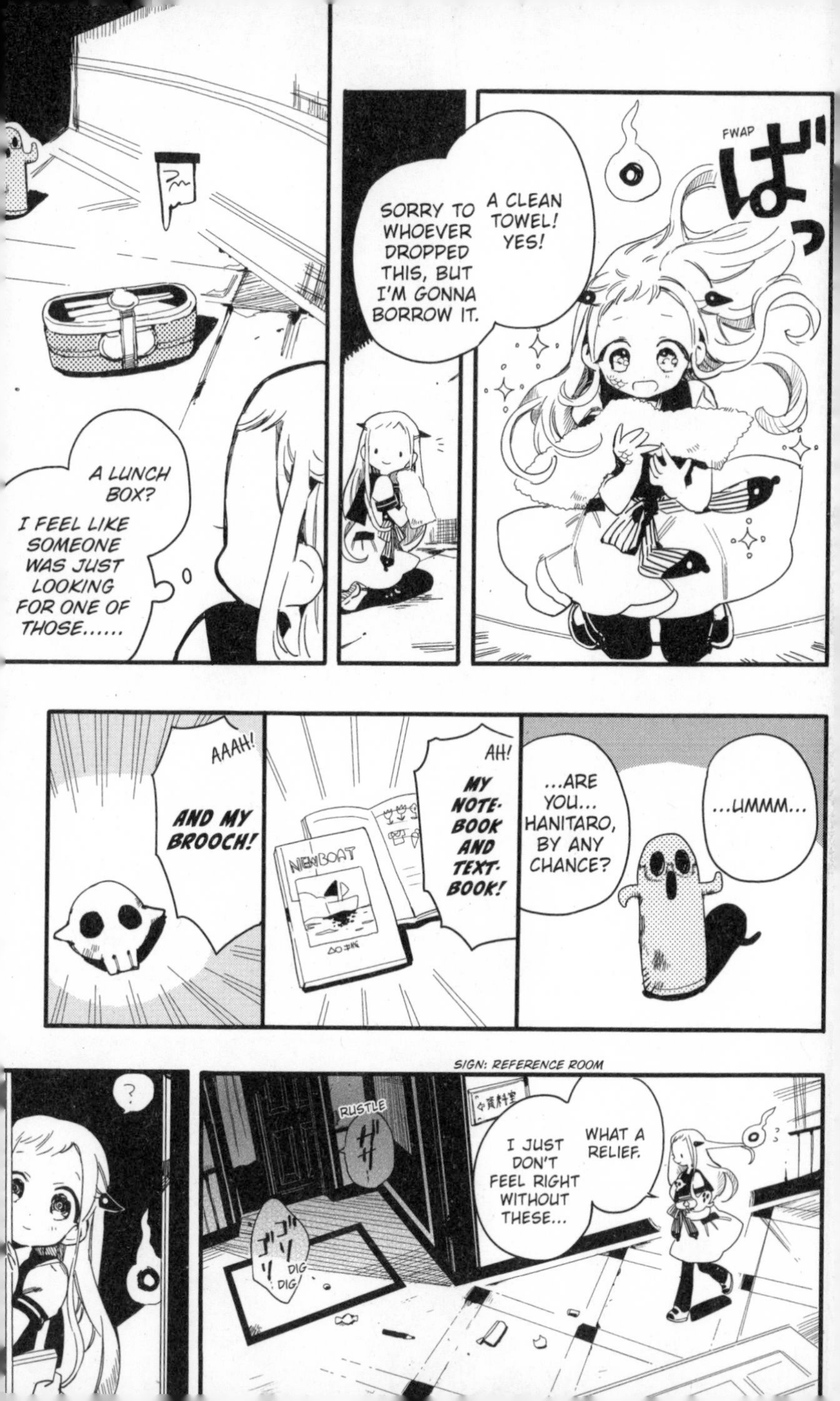
FWAP
ぱっ
A CLEAN TOWEL! YES!
SORRY TO WHOEVER DROPPED THIS, BUT I'M GONNA BORROW IT.
A LUNCH BOX?
I FEEL LIKE SOMEONE WAS JUST LOOKING FOR ONE OF THOSE......
...UMMM...
...ARE YOU... HANITARO, BY ANY CHANCE?
AH!
MY NOTEBOOK AND TEXTBOOK!
NEWBOAT
AAAH!
AND MY BROOCH!
SIGN: REFERENCE ROOM
資料室
WHAT A RELIEF.
I JUST DON'T FEEL RIGHT WITHOUT THESE...
RUSTLE
DIG DIG
?

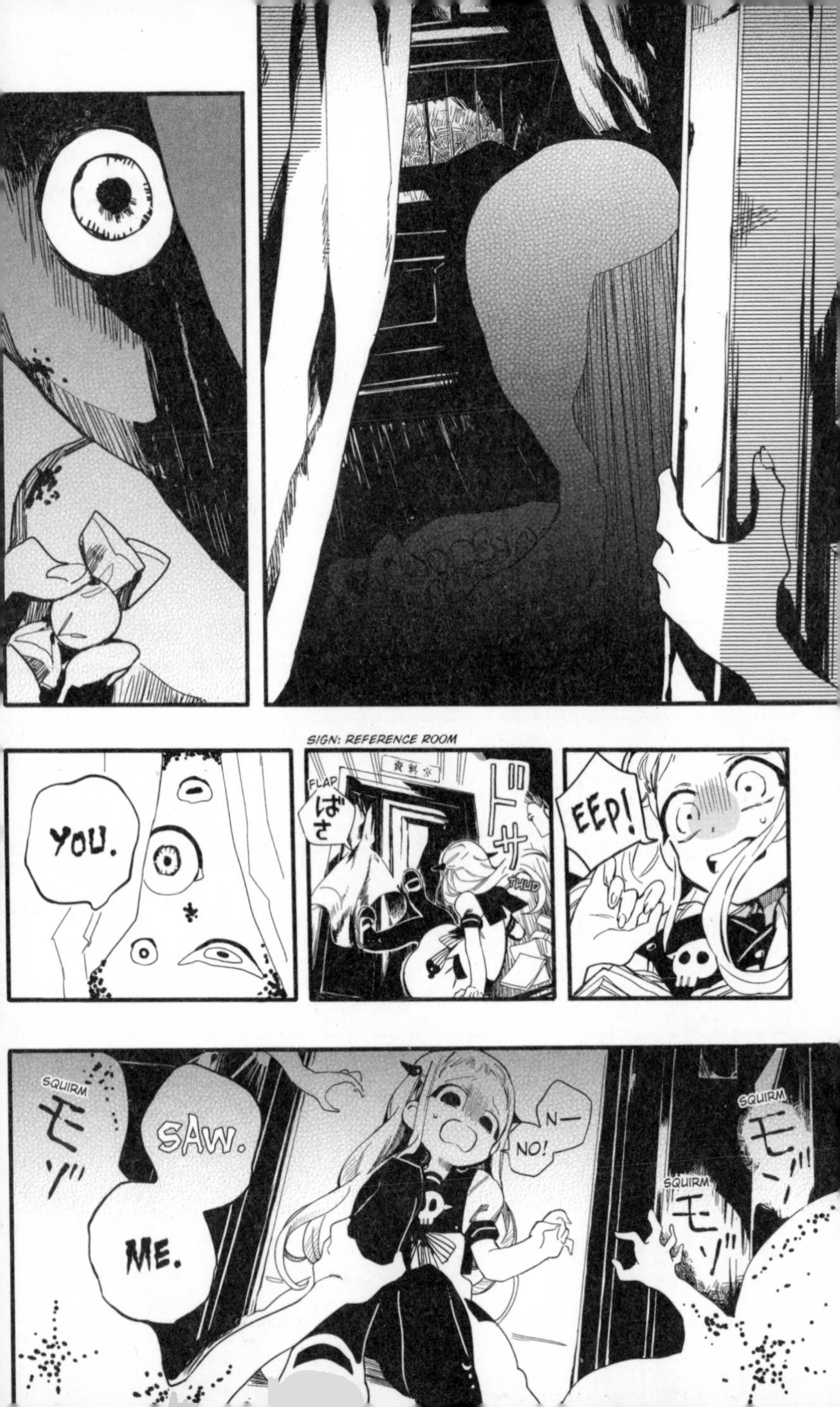
EEP!
SIGN: REFERENCE ROOM
FLAP
ばさ
ドサ
THUD
YOU.
SQUIRM
モゾ!!
SQUIRM
モゾ
N—
NO!
SAW.
ME.
SQUIRM
モゾ

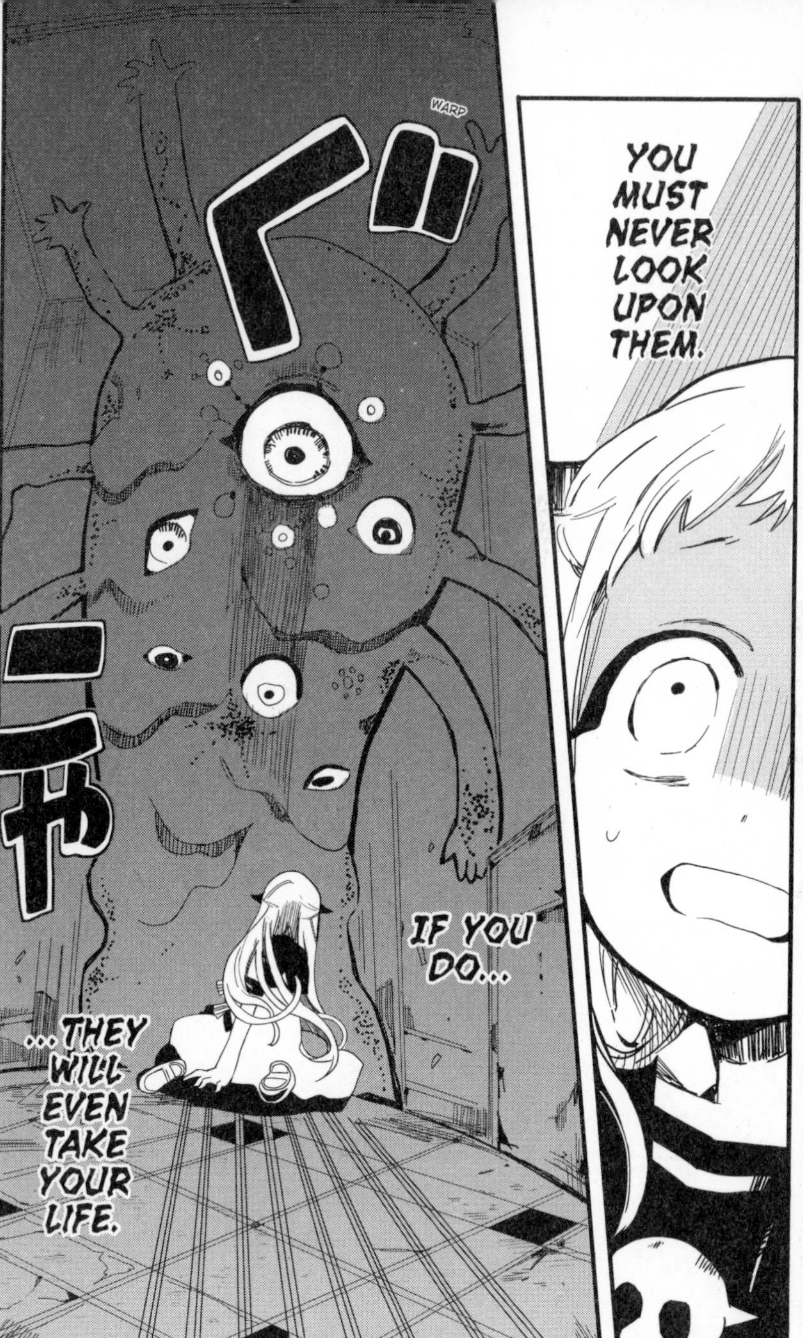
YOU MUST NEVER LOOK UPON THEM.
WARP
IF YOU DO...
...THEY WILL EVEN TAKE YOUR LIFE.

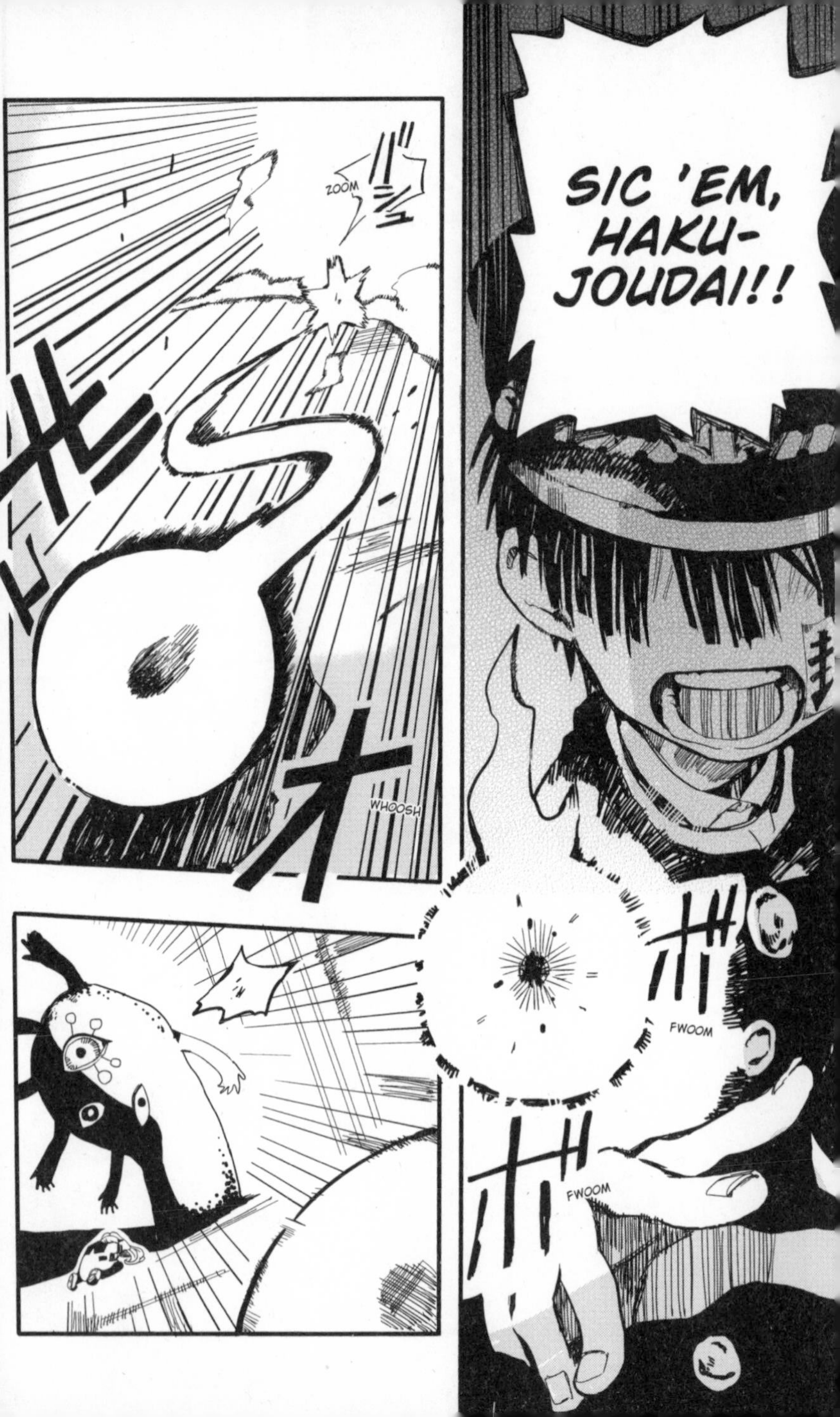
SIC 'EM, HAKU-JOUDAI!!
FWOOM
FWOOM
ZOOM
WHOOSH

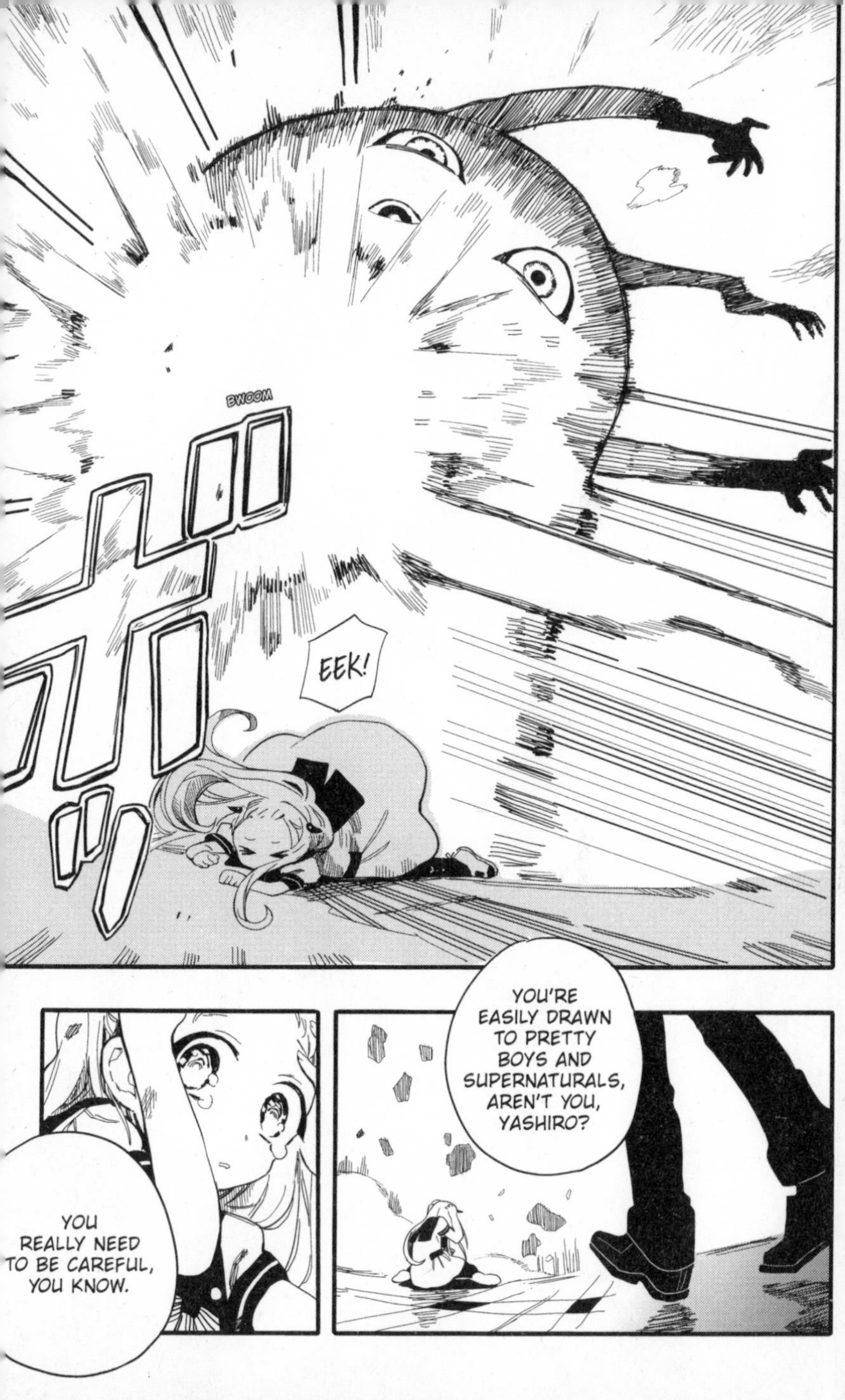
BWOOM
EEK!
YOU'RE EASILY DRAWN TO PRETTY BOYS AND SUPERNATURALS, AREN'T YOU, YASHIRO?
YOU REALLY NEED TO BE CAREFUL, YOU KNOW.

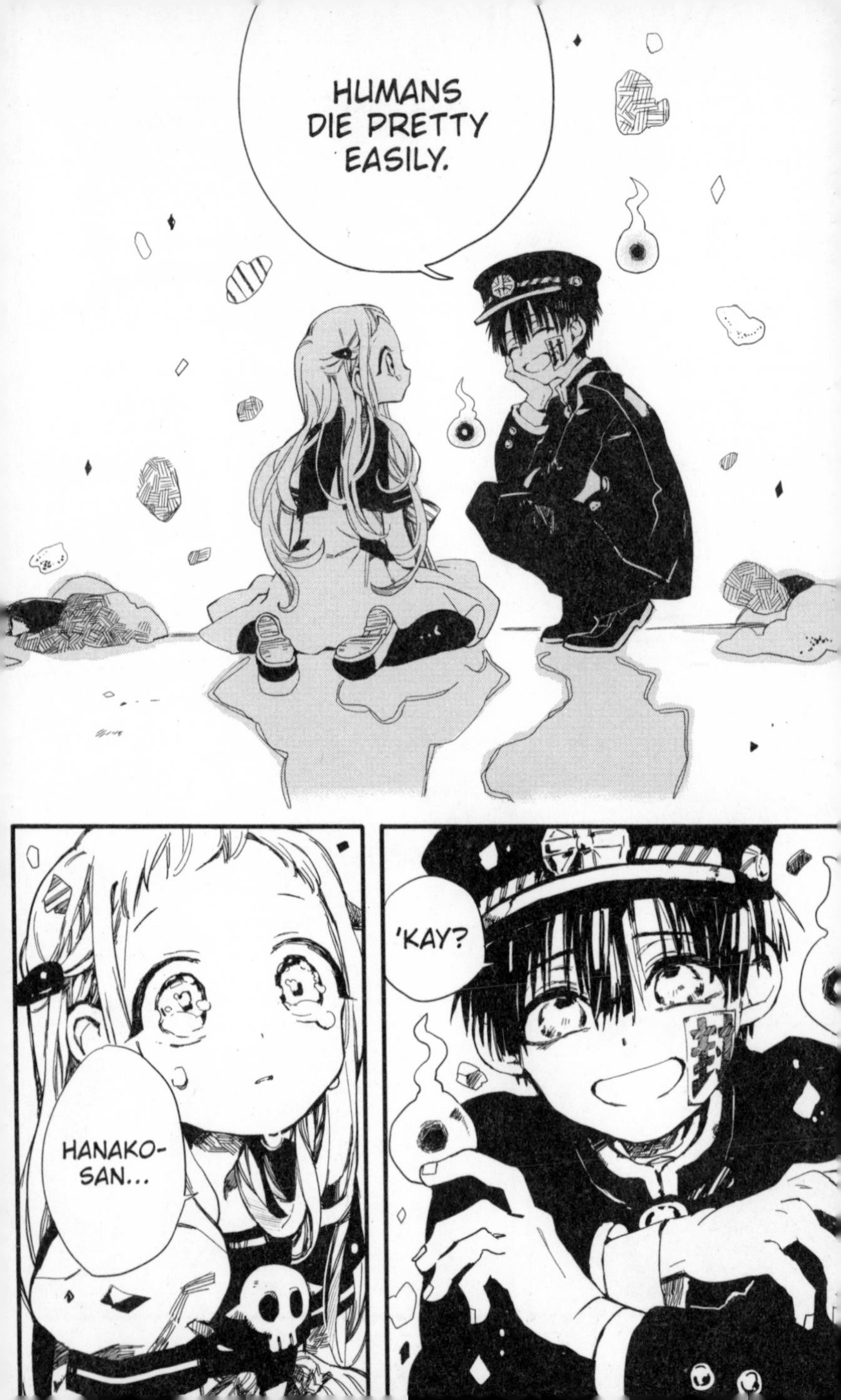
HUMANS DIE PRETTY EASILY.
'KAY?
HANAKO-SAN...

...HE DID IT AGAIN.

HE SAVED ME.

HM?

STARE

ボン

BOMP

OW!

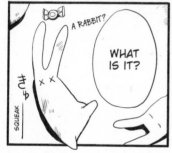

A RABBIT?

WHAT IS IT?

SQUEAK

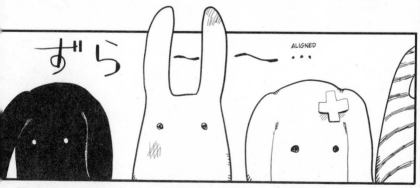

ずら

ALIGNED

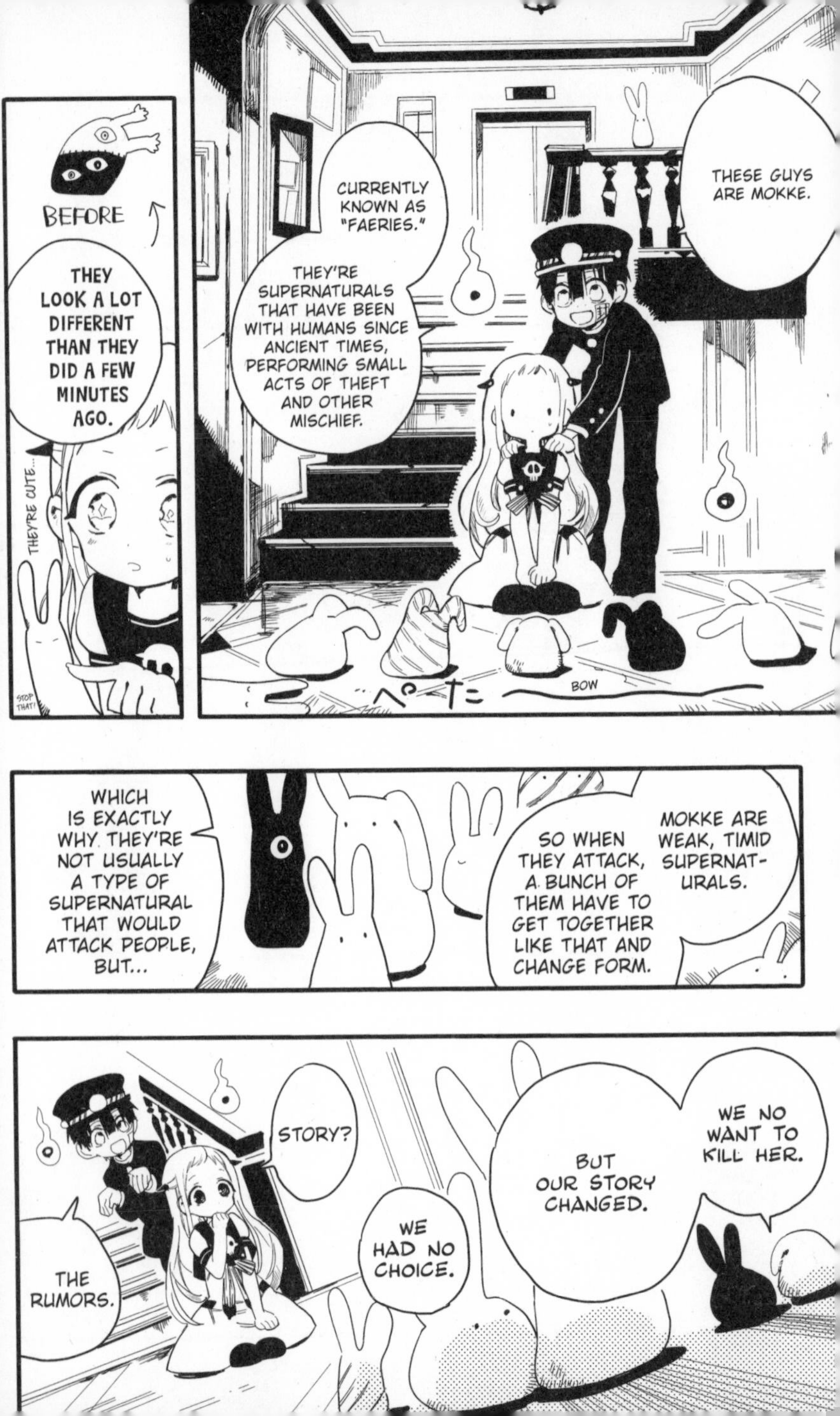

THESE GUYS ARE MOKKE.
CURRENTLY KNOWN AS "FAERIES."
THEY'RE SUPERNATURALS THAT HAVE BEEN WITH HUMANS SINCE ANCIENT TIMES, PERFORMING SMALL ACTS OF THEFT AND OTHER MISCHIEF.
BOW
BEFORE
THEY LOOK A LOT DIFFERENT THAN THEY DID A FEW MINUTES AGO.
THEY'RE CUTE...
STOP THAT!
MOKKE ARE WEAK, TIMID SUPERNATURALS.
SO WHEN THEY ATTACK, A BUNCH OF THEM HAVE TO GET TOGETHER LIKE THAT AND CHANGE FORM.
WHICH IS EXACTLY WHY THEY'RE NOT USUALLY A TYPE OF SUPERNATURAL THAT WOULD ATTACK PEOPLE, BUT...
WE NO WANT TO KILL HER.
BUT OUR STORY CHANGED.
WE HAD NO CHOICE.
STORY?
THE RUMORS.

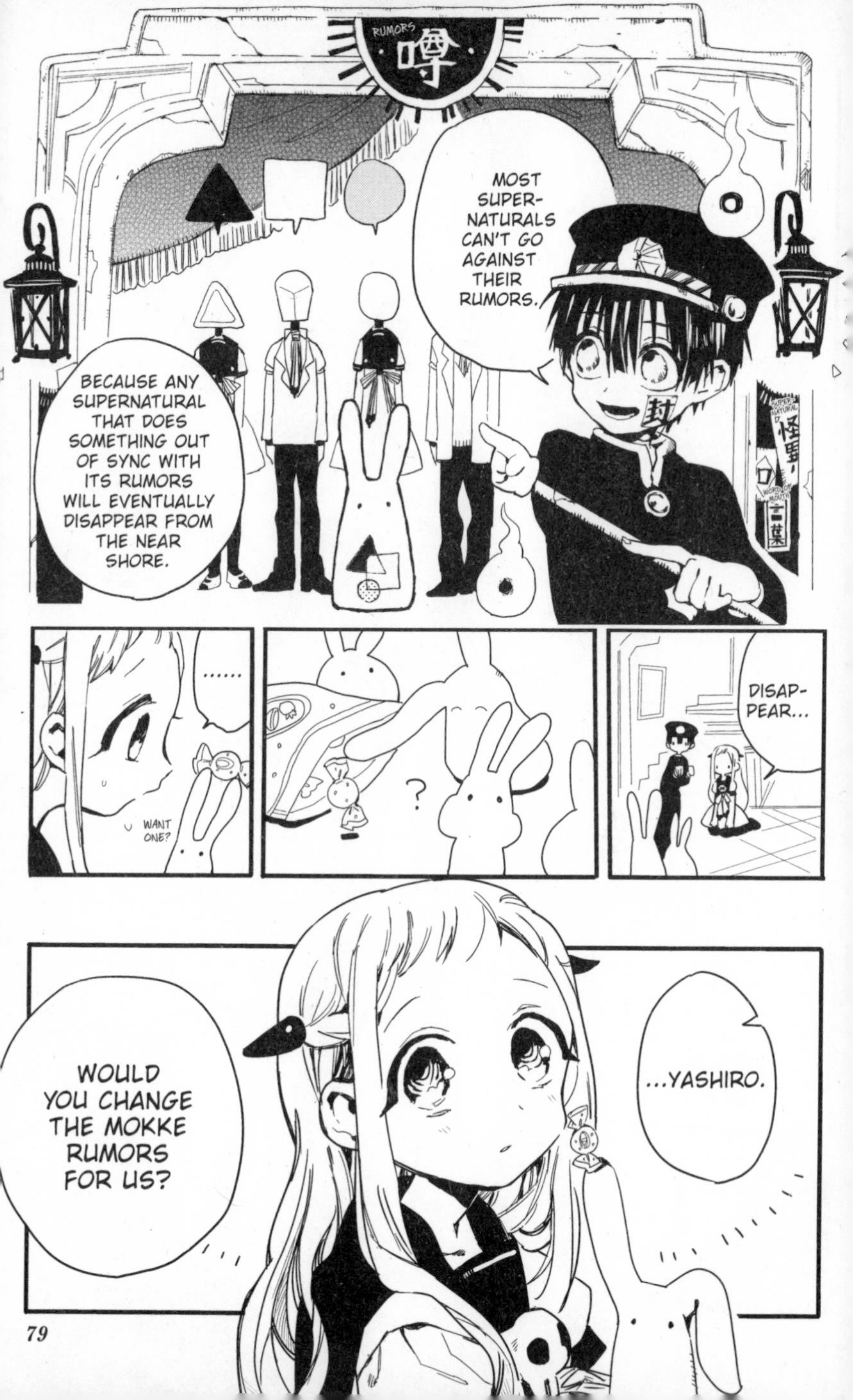
RUMORS
噂
MOST SUPER-NATURALS CAN'T GO AGAINST THEIR RUMORS.
SUPERNATURAL
怪異
WORD OF MOUTH
口
言葉
BECAUSE ANY SUPERNATURAL THAT DOES SOMETHING OUT OF SYNC WITH ITS RUMORS WILL EVENTUALLY DISAPPEAR FROM THE NEAR SHORE.
DISAP-PEAR...
?
......
WANT ONE?
...YASHIRO.
WOULD YOU CHANGE THE MOKKE RUMORS FOR US?

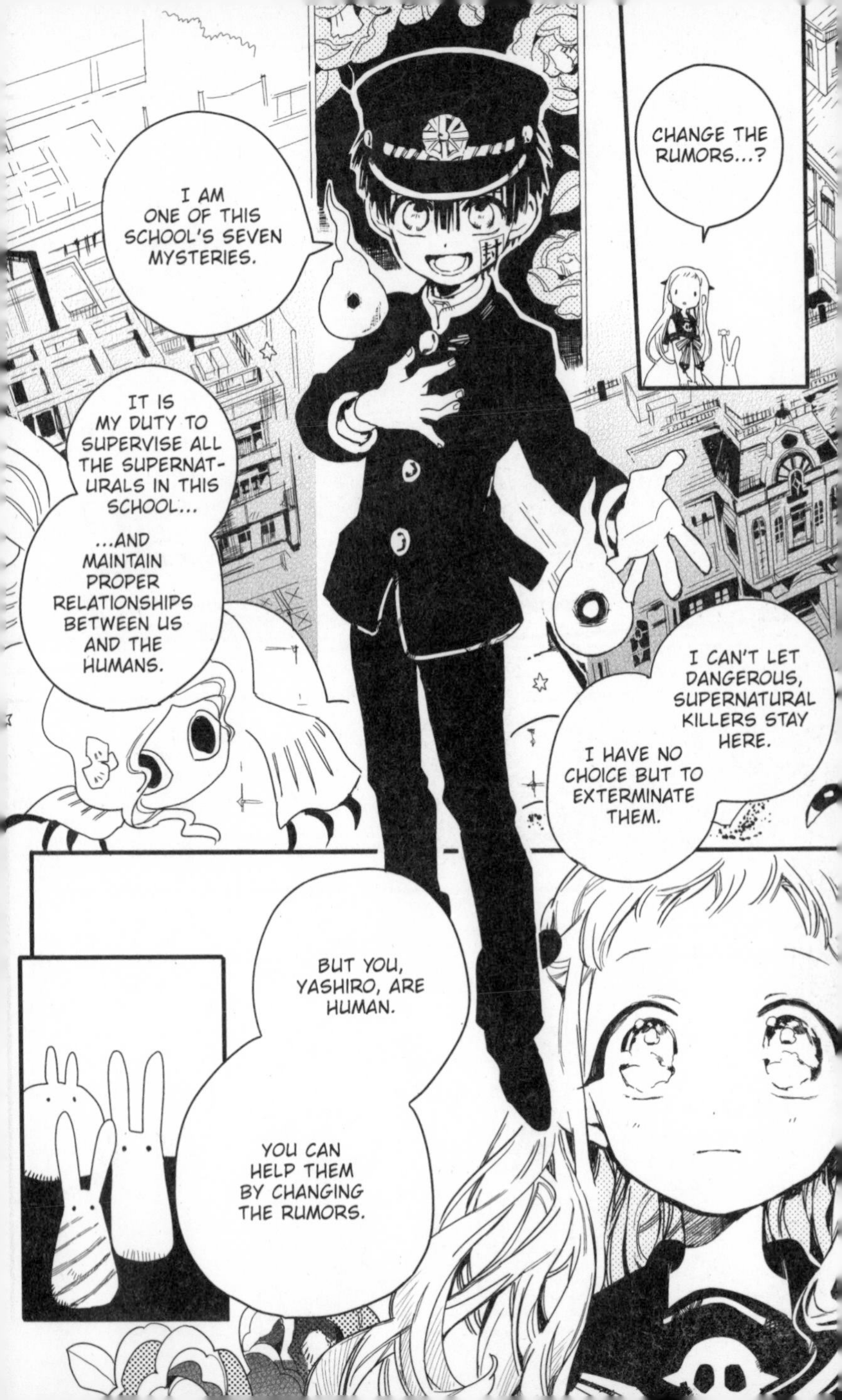
CHANGE THE RUMORS...?
I AM ONE OF THIS SCHOOL'S SEVEN MYSTERIES.
IT IS MY DUTY TO SUPERVISE ALL THE SUPERNAT-URALS IN THIS SCHOOL...
...AND MAINTAIN PROPER RELATIONSHIPS BETWEEN US AND THE HUMANS.
I CAN'T LET DANGEROUS, SUPERNATURAL KILLERS STAY HERE.
I HAVE NO CHOICE BUT TO EXTERMINATE THEM.
BUT YOU, YASHIRO, ARE HUMAN.
YOU CAN HELP THEM BY CHANGING THE RUMORS.

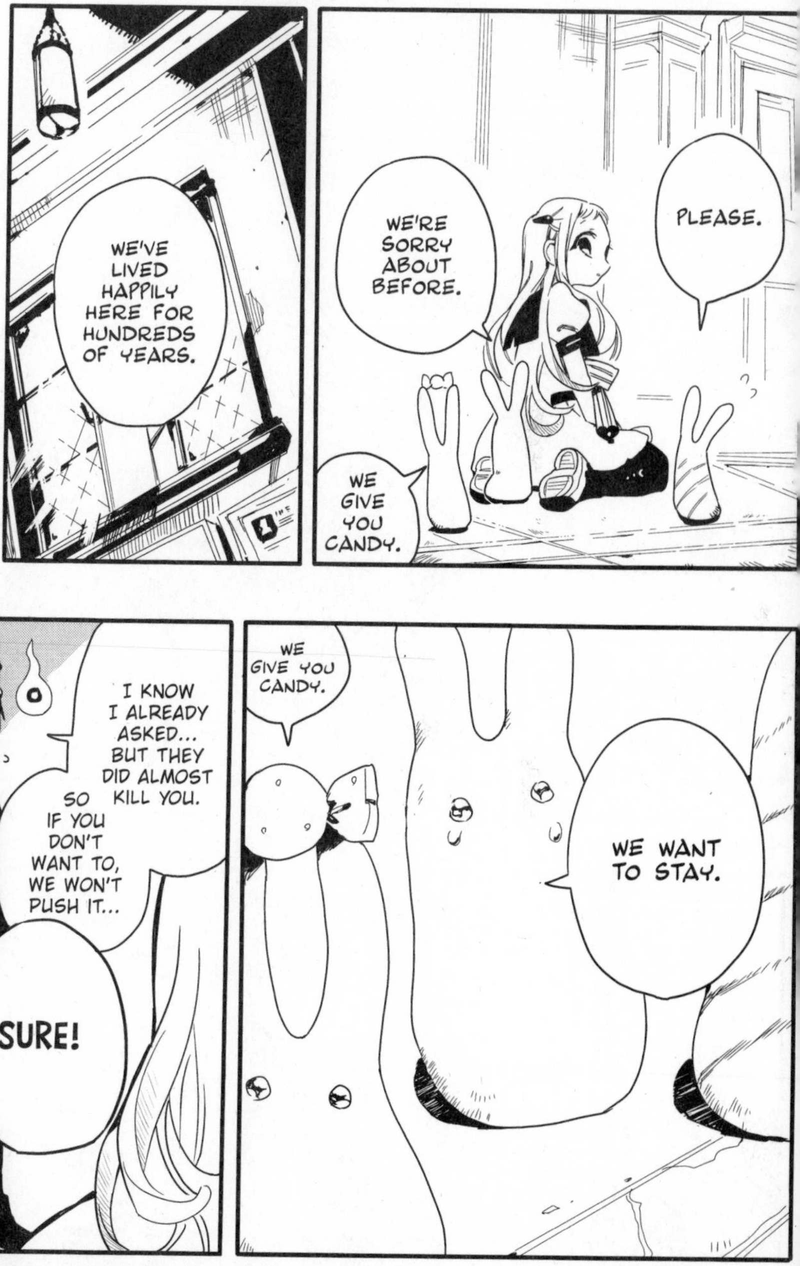
PLEASE.
WE'RE SORRY ABOUT BEFORE.
WE GIVE YOU CANDY.
WE'VE LIVED HAPPILY HERE FOR HUNDREDS OF YEARS.
WE WANT TO STAY.
WE GIVE YOU CANDY.
I KNOW I ALREADY ASKED... BUT THEY DID ALMOST KILL YOU.
SO IF YOU DON'T WANT TO, WE WON'T PUSH IT...
SURE!

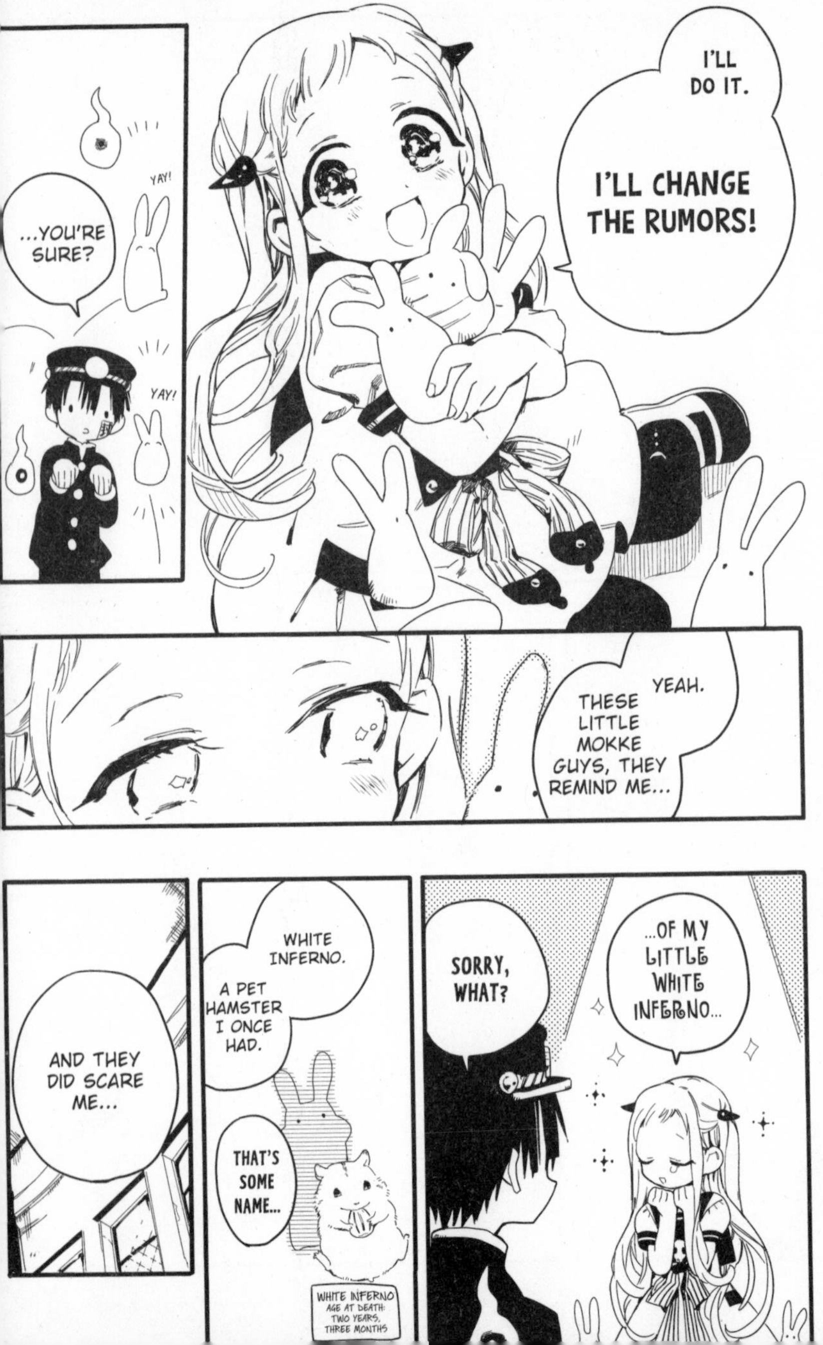
I'LL DO IT.
I'LL CHANGE THE RUMORS!
YAY!
...YOU'RE SURE?
YAY!
YEAH.
THESE LITTLE MOKKE GUYS, THEY REMIND ME...
...OF MY LITTLE WHITE INFERNO...
SORRY, WHAT?
WHITE INFERNO.
A PET HAMSTER I ONCE HAD.
THAT'S SOME NAME...
WHITE INFERNO AGE AT DEATH: TWO YEARS, THREE MONTHS
AND THEY DID SCARE ME...

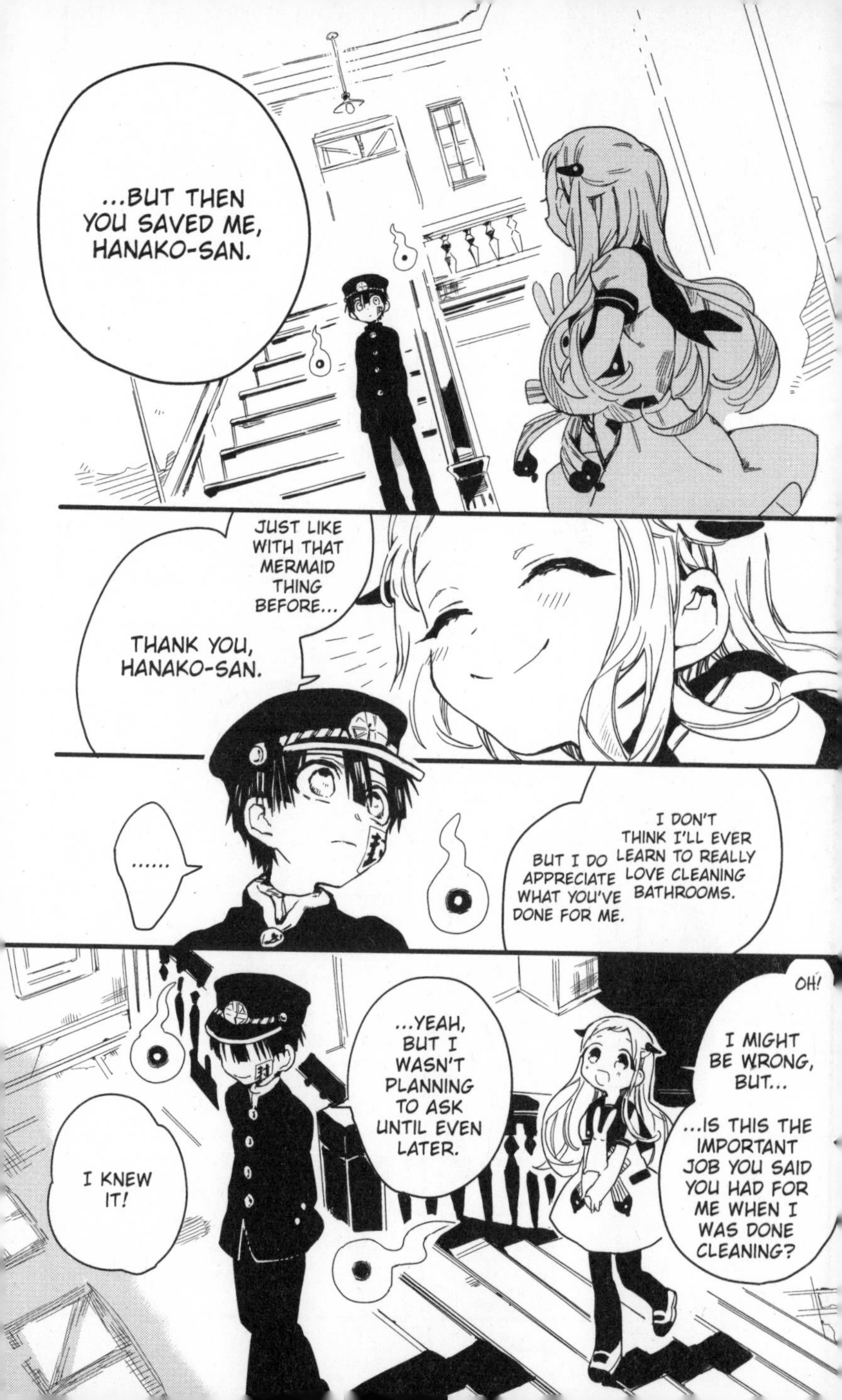
...BUT THEN YOU SAVED ME, HANAKO-SAN.
JUST LIKE WITH THAT MERMAID THING BEFORE...
THANK YOU, HANAKO-SAN.
I DON'T THINK I'LL EVER LEARN TO REALLY LOVE CLEANING BATHROOMS.
BUT I DO APPRECIATE WHAT YOU'VE DONE FOR ME.
......
OH!
I MIGHT BE WRONG, BUT...
...IS THIS THE IMPORTANT JOB YOU SAID YOU HAD FOR ME WHEN I WAS DONE CLEANING?
...YEAH, BUT I WASN'T PLANNING TO ASK UNTIL EVEN LATER.
I KNEW IT!

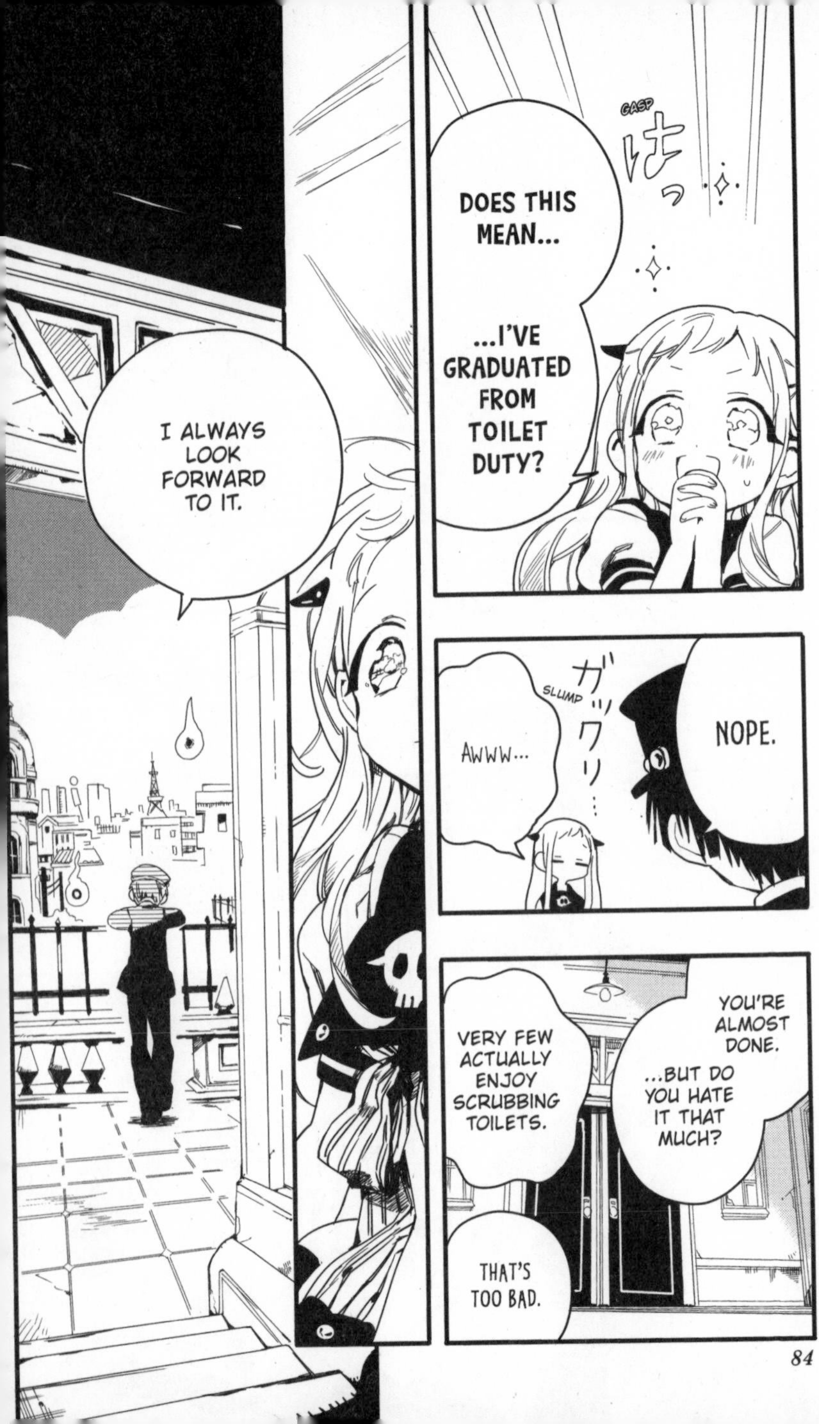
GASP
はっ
DOES THIS MEAN...
...I'VE GRADUATED FROM TOILET DUTY?
NOPE.
SLUMP
ガックリ...
AWWW...
YOU'RE ALMOST DONE.
...BUT DO YOU HATE IT THAT MUCH?
VERY FEW ACTUALLY ENJOY SCRUBBING TOILETS.
THAT'S TOO BAD.
I ALWAYS LOOK FORWARD TO IT.

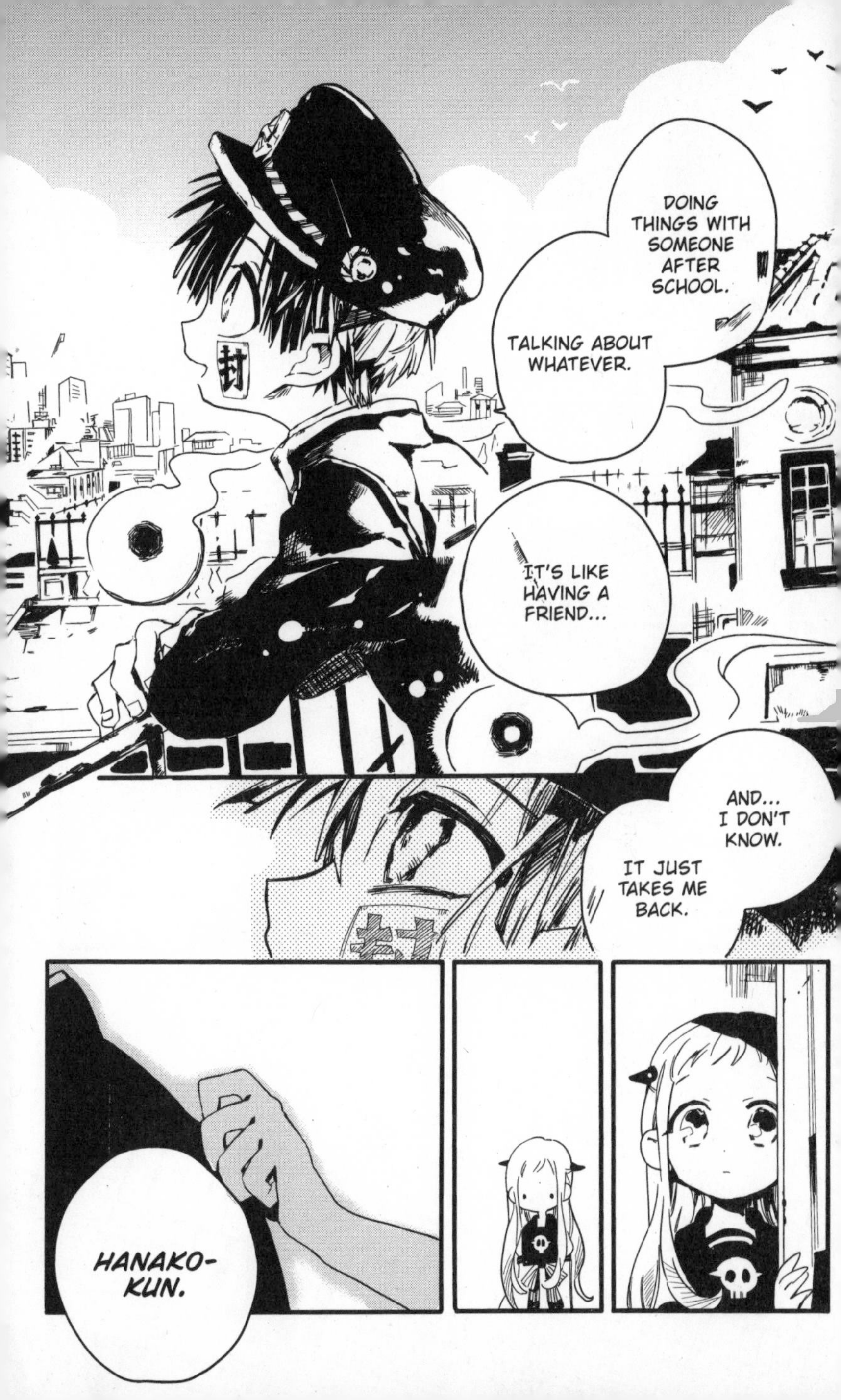
DOING THINGS WITH SOMEONE AFTER SCHOOL.
TALKING ABOUT WHATEVER.
IT'S LIKE HAVING A FRIEND...
AND... I DON'T KNOW.
IT JUST TAKES ME BACK.
HANAKO-KUN.

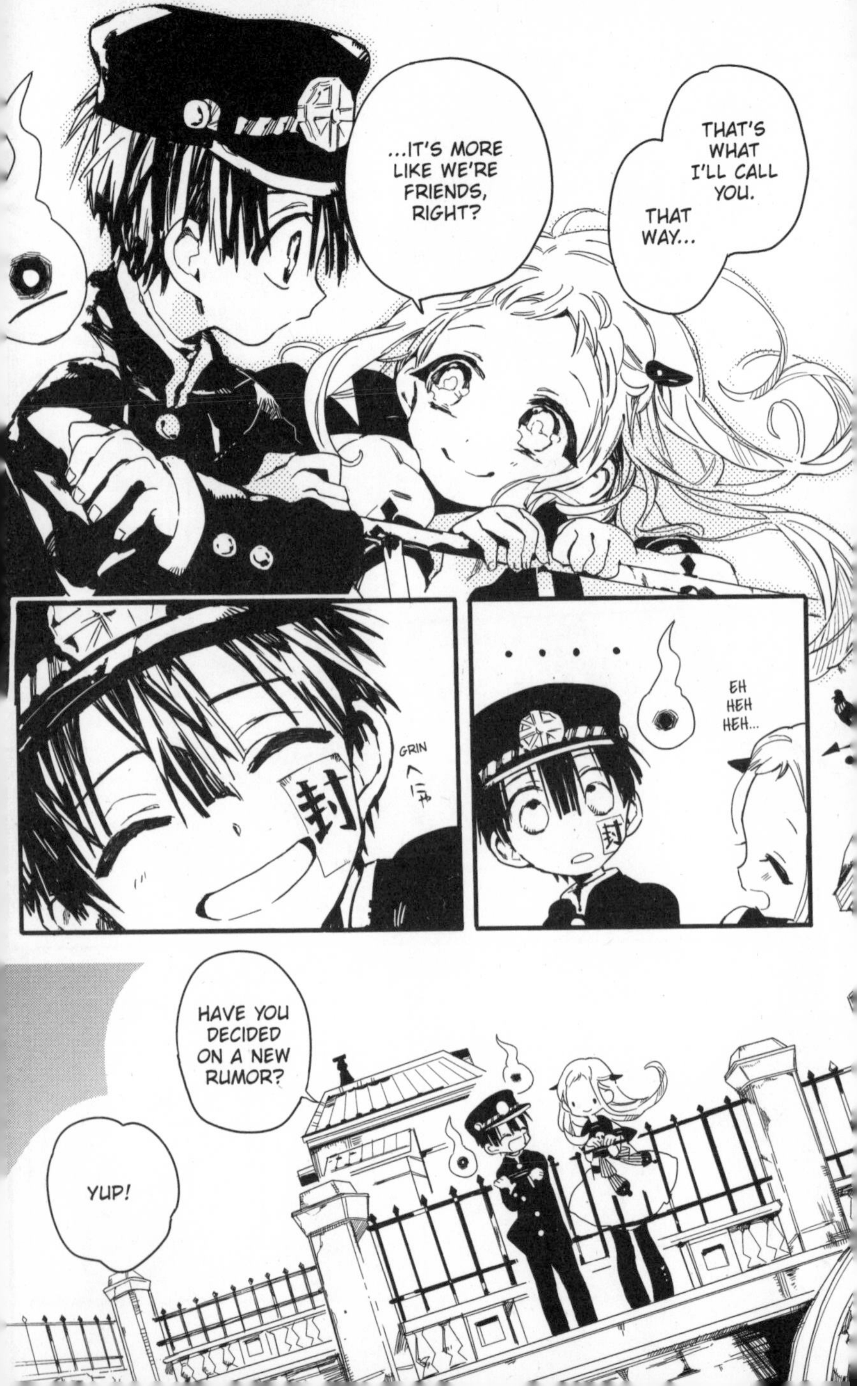
THAT'S WHAT I'LL CALL YOU.
THAT WAY...
...IT'S MORE LIKE WE'RE FRIENDS, RIGHT?
....
EH HEH HEH...
GRIN
HAVE YOU DECIDED ON A NEW RUMOR?
YUP!

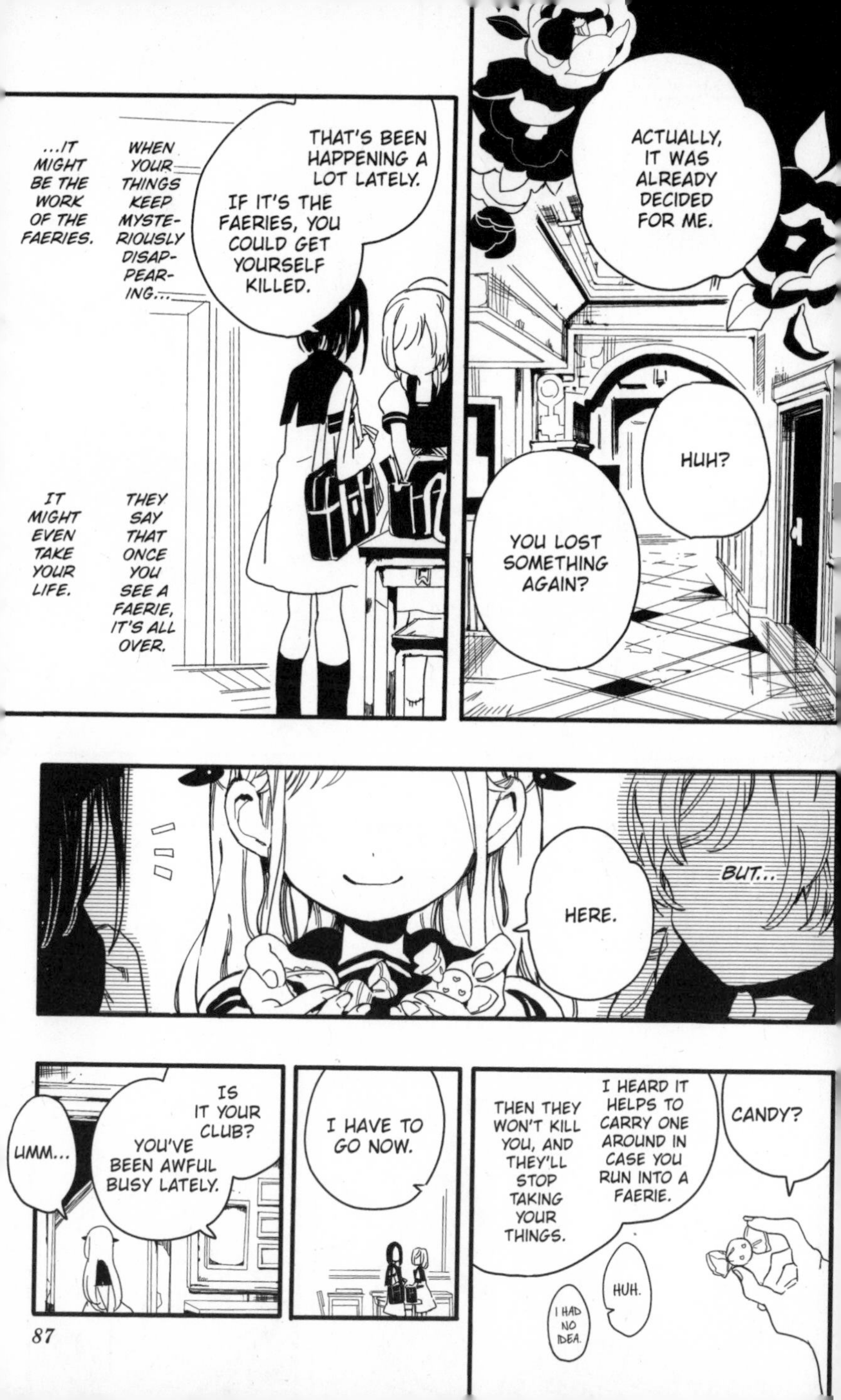
ACTUALLY, IT WAS ALREADY DECIDED FOR ME.
HUH?
YOU LOST SOMETHING AGAIN?
THAT'S BEEN HAPPENING A LOT LATELY.
IF IT'S THE FAERIES, YOU COULD GET YOURSELF KILLED.
WHEN YOUR THINGS KEEP MYSTE-RIOUSLY DISAP-PEAR-ING...
...IT MIGHT BE THE WORK OF THE FAERIES.
THEY SAY THAT ONCE YOU SEE A FAERIE, IT'S ALL OVER.
IT MIGHT EVEN TAKE YOUR LIFE.
BUT...
HERE.
CANDY?
I HEARD IT HELPS TO CARRY ONE AROUND IN CASE YOU RUN INTO A FAERIE.
THEN THEY WON'T KILL YOU, AND THEY'LL STOP TAKING YOUR THINGS.
HUH.
I HAD NO IDEA.
I HAVE TO GO NOW.
IS IT YOUR CLUB?
YOU'VE BEEN AWFUL BUSY LATELY.
UMM...

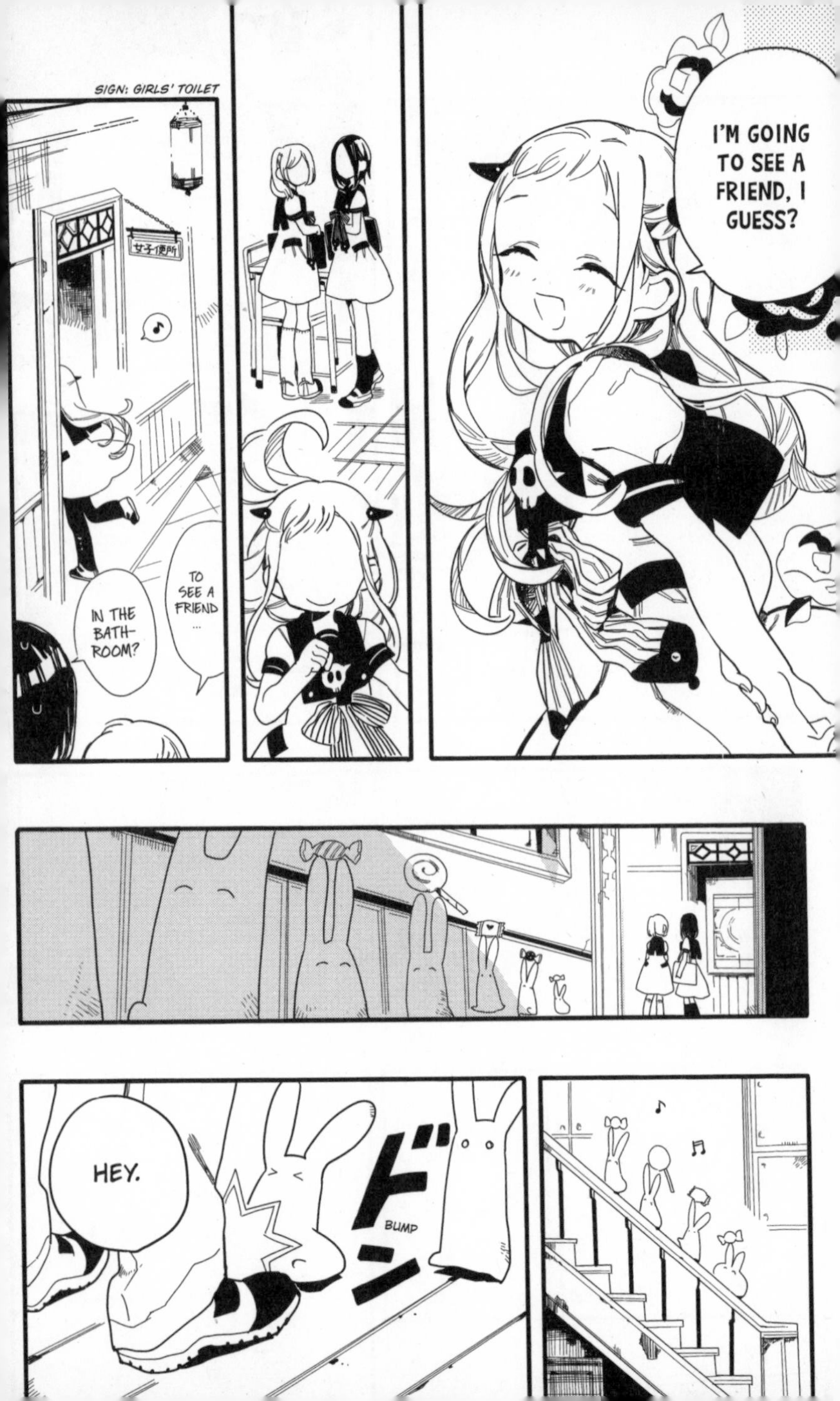
I'M GOING TO SEE A FRIEND, I GUESS?
TO SEE A FRIEND...
SIGN: GIRLS' TOILET
女子便所
IN THE BATH-ROOM?
HEY.
BUMP

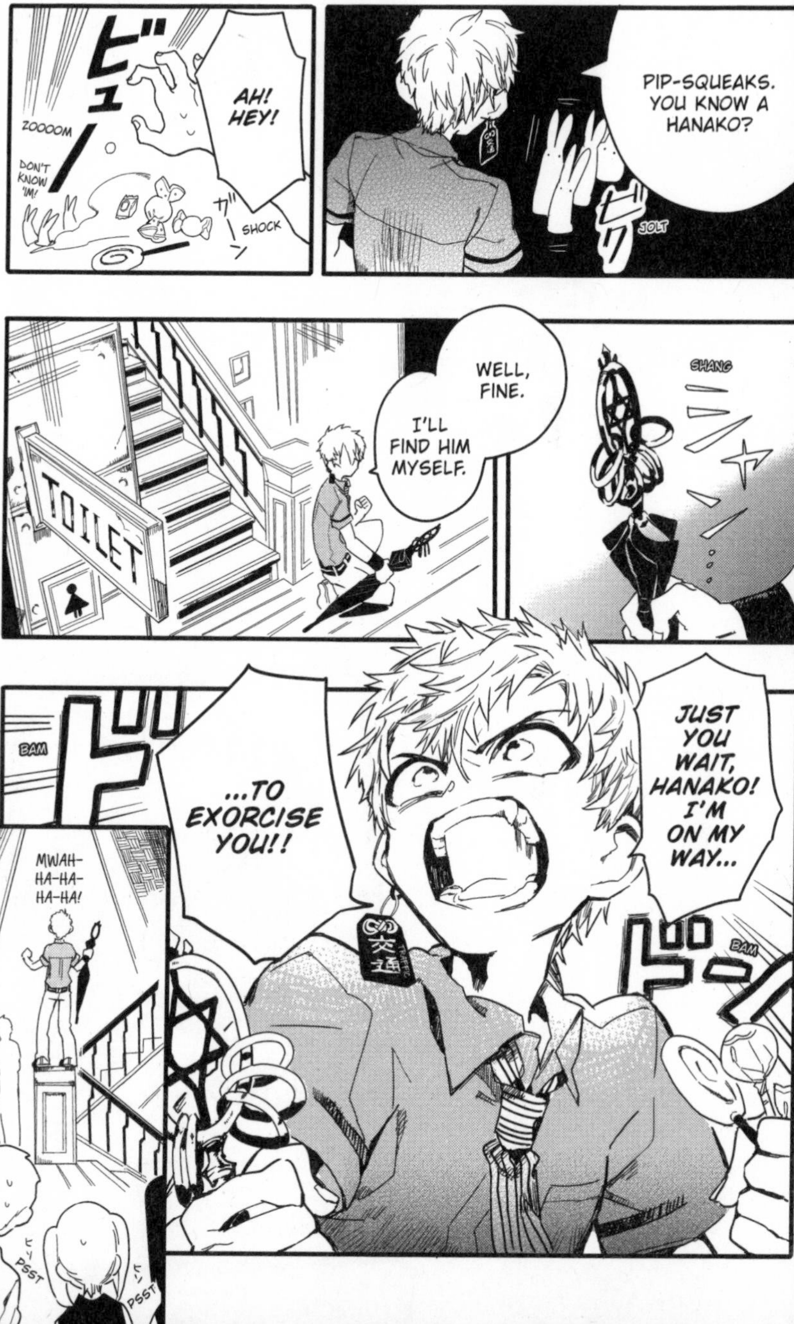

PIP-SQUEAKS. YOU KNOW A HANAKO?
JOLT
AH! HEY!
ZOOOOM
DON'T KNOW 'IM!
SHOCK
SHANG
WELL, FINE.
I'LL FIND HIM MYSELF.
TOILET
BAM
JUST YOU WAIT, HANAKO! I'M ON MY WAY...
...TO EXORCISE YOU!!
BAM
MWAH-HA-HA-HA-HA!
PSST
PSST

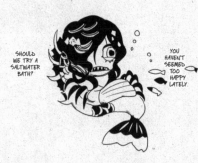

HER FISH ARE HELPFUL AND CARING.
YOU HAVEN'T SEEMED TOO HAPPY LATELY.
SHOULD WE TRY A SALTWATER BATH?

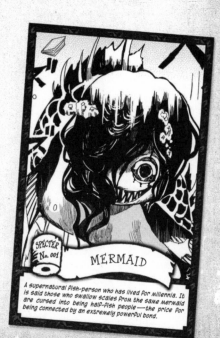

SPECTER No. 001
MERMAID
A supernatural fish-person who has lived for millennia. It is said those who swallow scales from the same mermaid are cursed into being half-fish people—the price for being connected by an extremely powerful bond.

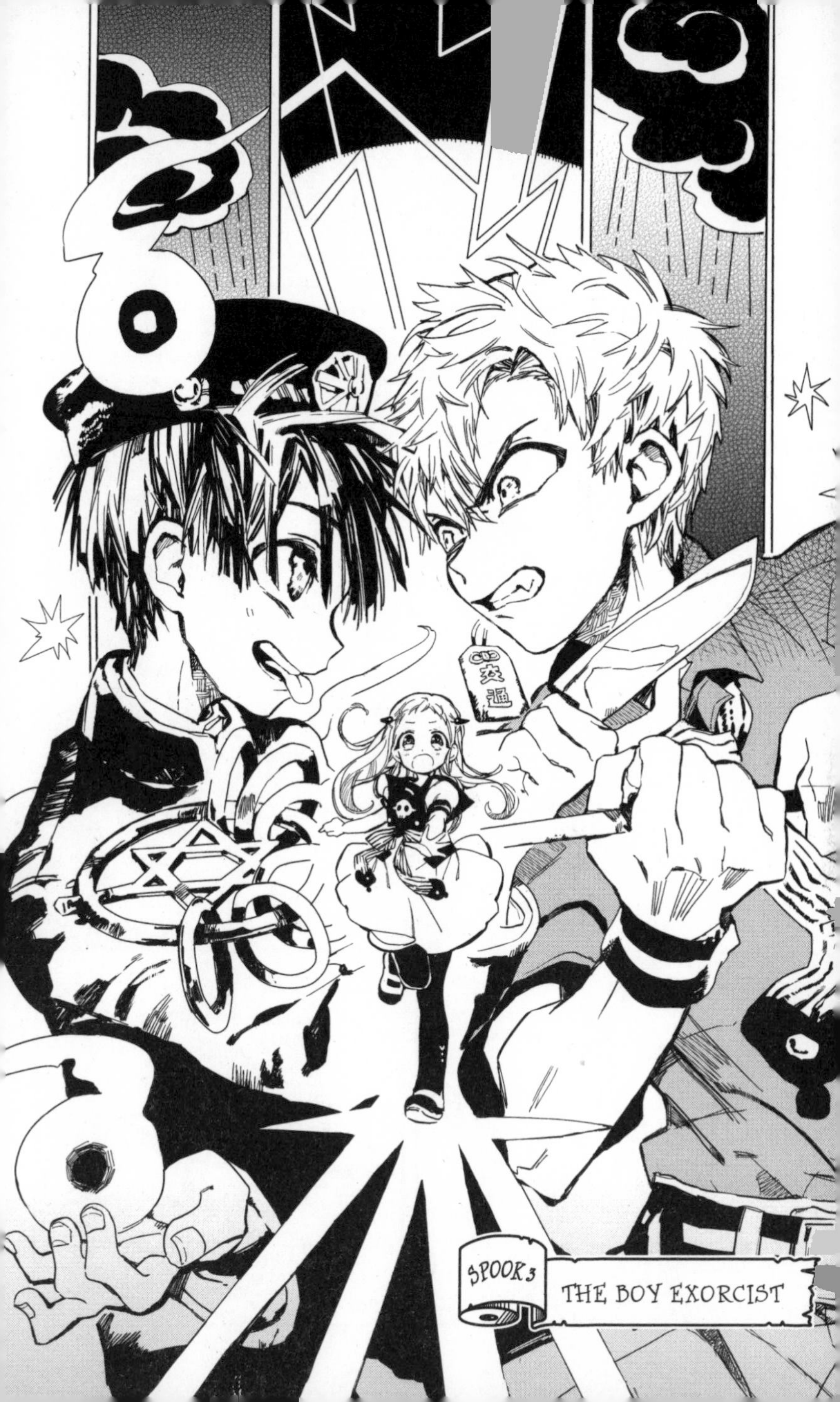
交通
SPOOK 3
THE BOY EXORCIST

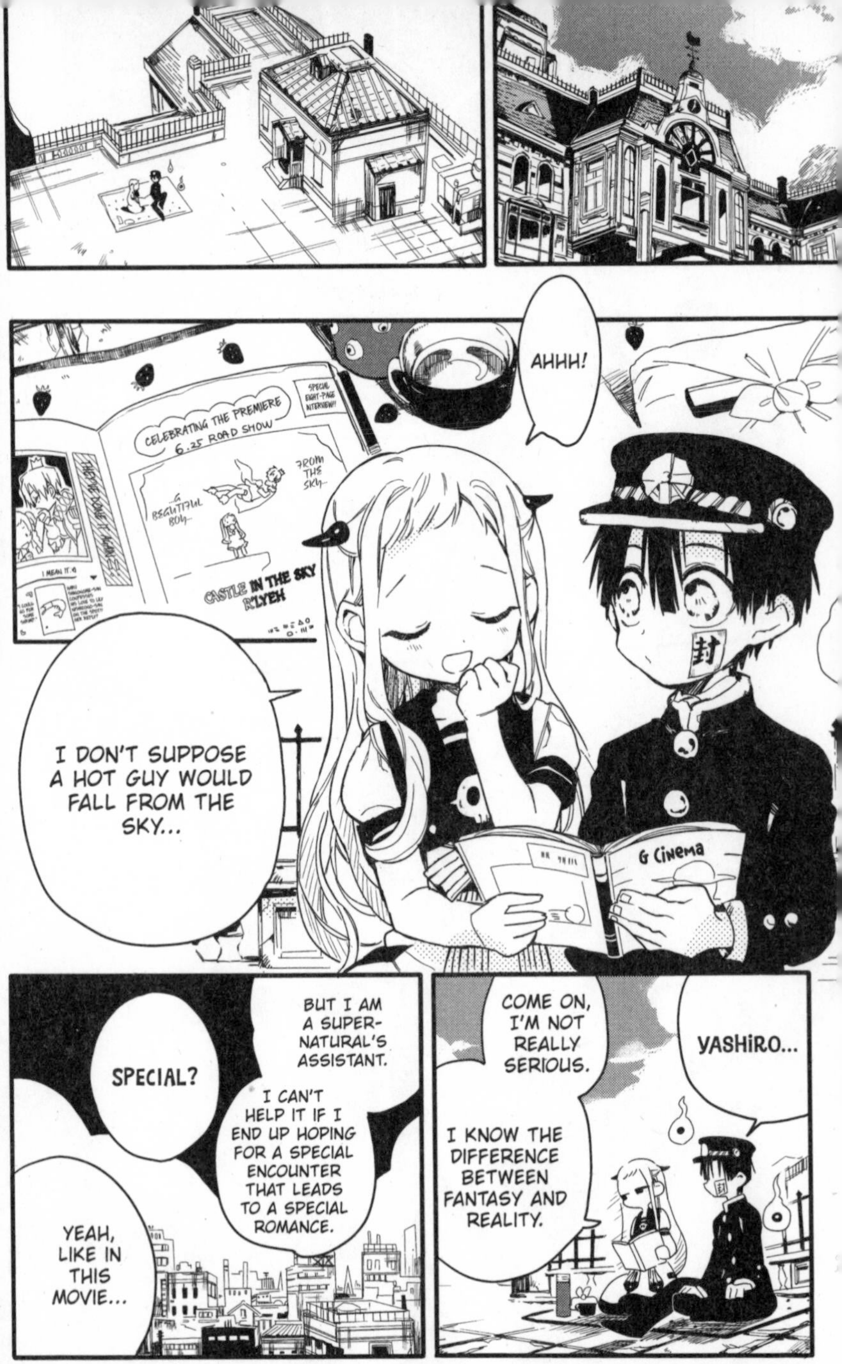
AHHH!
CELEBRATING THE PREMIERE
6.25 ROAD SHOW
SPECIAL EIGHT-PAGE INTERVIEW!!
FROM THE SKY...
CASTLE IN THE SKY R'LYEH
G Cinema
I DON'T SUPPOSE A HOT GUY WOULD FALL FROM THE SKY...
YASHIRO...
COME ON, I'M NOT REALLY SERIOUS.
I KNOW THE DIFFERENCE BETWEEN FANTASY AND REALITY.
BUT I AM A SUPER-NATURAL'S ASSISTANT.
I CAN'T HELP IT IF I END UP HOPING FOR A SPECIAL ENCOUNTER THAT LEADS TO A SPECIAL ROMANCE.
SPECIAL?
YEAH, LIKE IN THIS MOVIE...

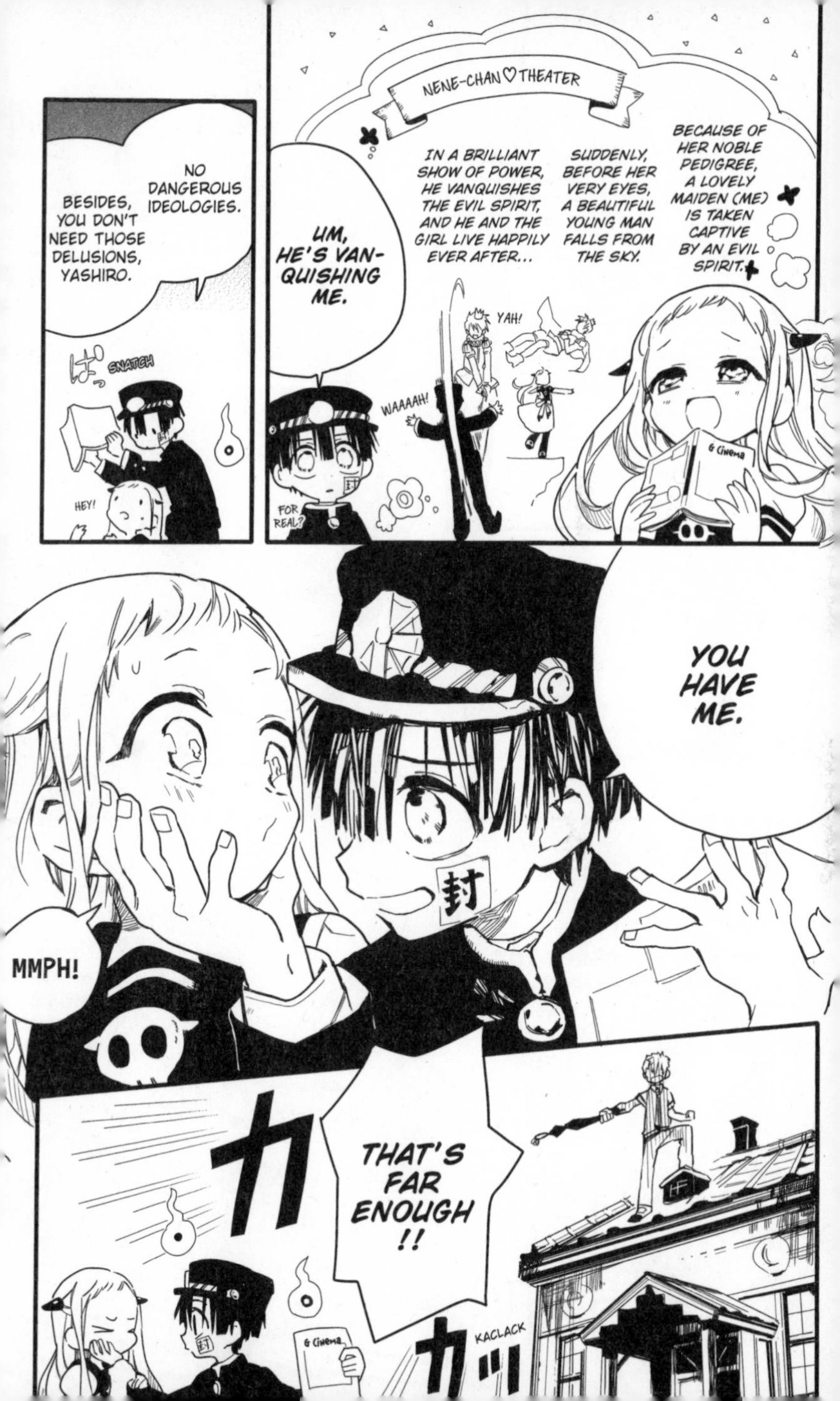
NENE-CHAN♡THEATER
BECAUSE OF HER NOBLE PEDIGREE, A LOVELY MAIDEN (ME) IS TAKEN CAPTIVE BY AN EVIL SPIRIT.
SUDDENLY, BEFORE HER VERY EYES, A BEAUTIFUL YOUNG MAN FALLS FROM THE SKY.
IN A BRILLIANT SHOW OF POWER, HE VANQUISHES THE EVIL SPIRIT, AND HE AND THE GIRL LIVE HAPPILY EVER AFTER...
YAH!
G Cinema
WAAAAH!
UM, HE'S VANQUISHING ME.
FOR REAL?
NO DANGEROUS IDEOLOGIES.
BESIDES, YOU DON'T NEED THOSE DELUSIONS, YASHIRO.
ぱっ SNATCH
HEY!
YOU HAVE ME.
MMPH!
THAT'S FAR ENOUGH!!
カッ KACLACK
カ
G Cinema

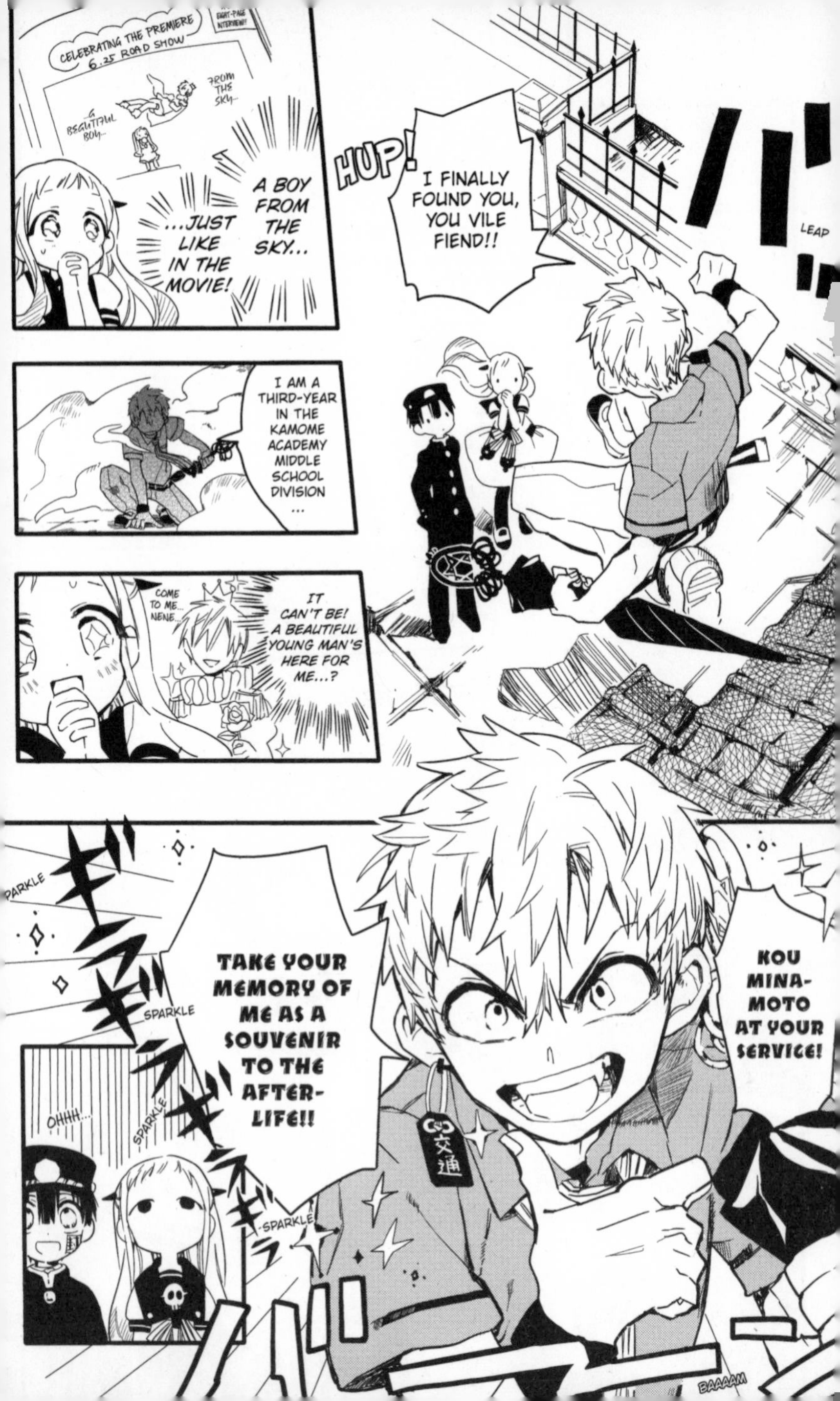
HUP!
I FINALLY FOUND YOU, YOU VILE FIEND!!
LEAP
EIGHT-PAGE INTERVIEW!!
CELEBRATING THE PREMIERE
6.25 ROAD SHOW
FROM THE SKY
...A BEAUTIFUL BOY...
A BOY FROM THE SKY...
...JUST LIKE IN THE MOVIE!
I AM A THIRD-YEAR IN THE KAMOME ACADEMY MIDDLE SCHOOL DIVISION ...
IT CAN'T BE! A BEAUTIFUL YOUNG MAN'S HERE FOR ME...?
COME TO ME... NENE...
KOU MINAMOTO AT YOUR SERVICE!
TAKE YOUR MEMORY OF ME AS A SOUVENIR TO THE AFTERLIFE!!
PARKLE
SPARKLE
SPARKLE
SPARKLE
BAAAAM
OHHH...

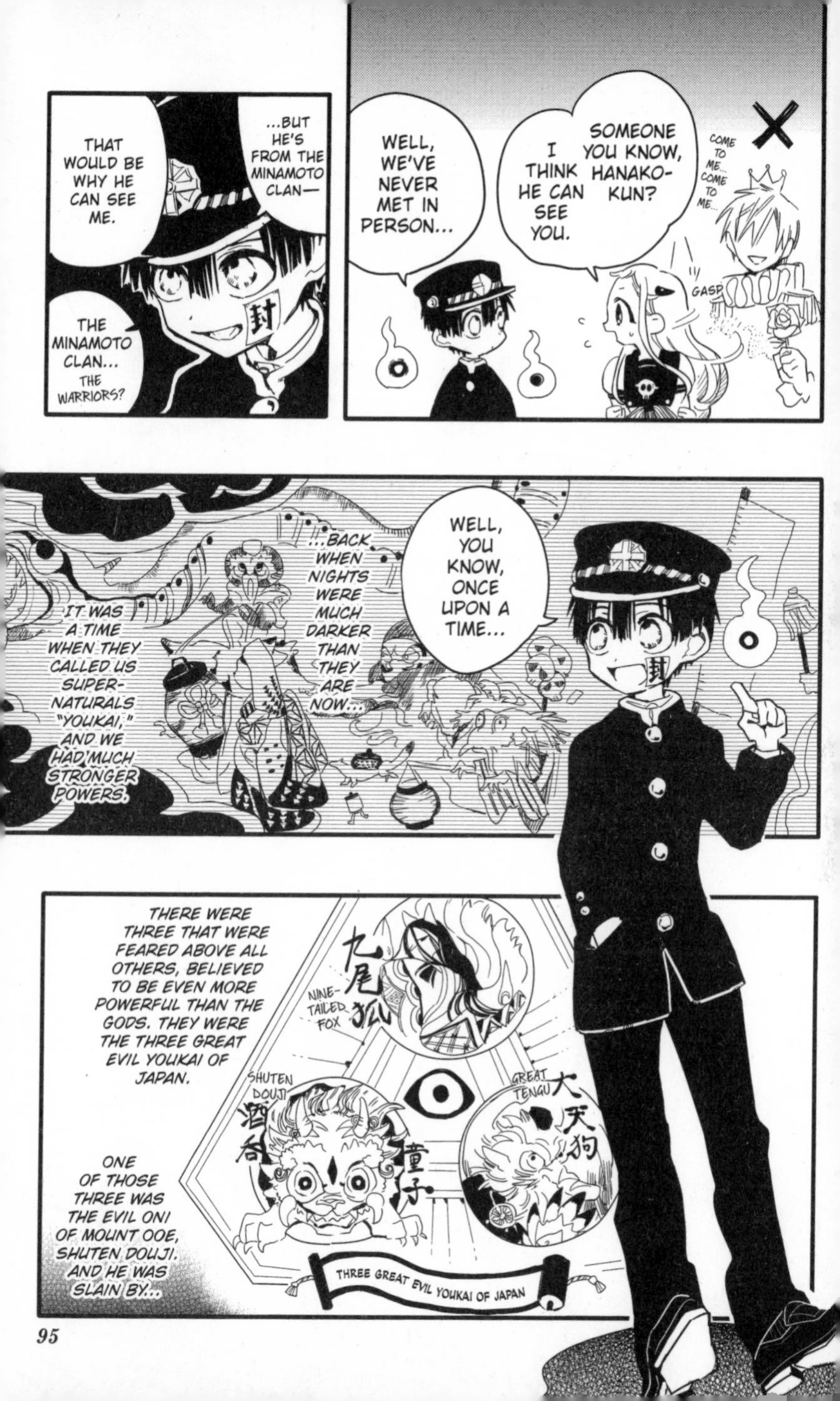
COME TO ME... COME TO ME...
GASP
SOMEONE YOU KNOW, HANAKO-KUN?
I THINK HE CAN SEE YOU.
WELL, WE'VE NEVER MET IN PERSON...
...BUT HE'S FROM THE MINAMOTO CLAN—
THAT WOULD BE WHY HE CAN SEE ME.
THE MINAMOTO CLAN... THE WARRIORS?
WELL, YOU KNOW, ONCE UPON A TIME...
...BACK WHEN NIGHTS WERE MUCH DARKER THAN THEY ARE NOW...
IT WAS A TIME WHEN THEY CALLED US SUPER-NATURALS "YOUKAI," AND WE HAD MUCH STRONGER POWERS.
THERE WERE THREE THAT WERE FEARED ABOVE ALL OTHERS, BELIEVED TO BE EVEN MORE POWERFUL THAN THE GODS. THEY WERE THE THREE GREAT EVIL YOUKAI OF JAPAN.
九尾狐
NINE-TAILED FOX
大天狗
GREAT TENGU
酒呑童子
SHUTEN DOUJI
THREE GREAT EVIL YOUKAI OF JAPAN
ONE OF THOSE THREE WAS THE EVIL ONI OF MOUNT OOE, SHUTEN DOUJI. AND HE WAS SLAIN BY...

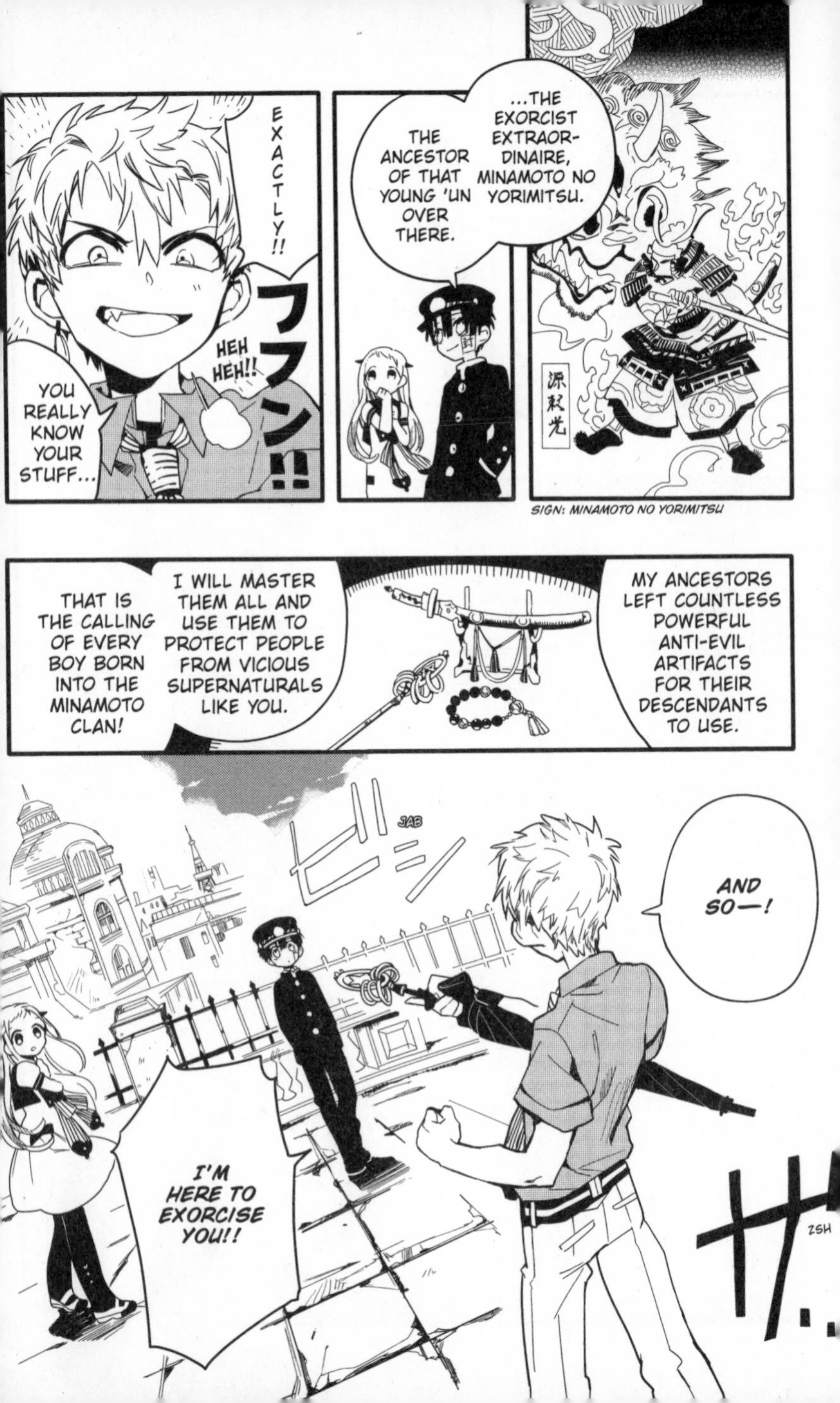
源頼光
SIGN: MINAMOTO NO YORIMITSU
...THE EXORCIST EXTRAOR-DINAIRE, MINAMOTO NO YORIMITSU.
THE ANCESTOR OF THAT YOUNG 'UN OVER THERE.
EXACTLY!!
フフン!!
HEH HEH!!
YOU REALLY KNOW YOUR STUFF...
MY ANCESTORS LEFT COUNTLESS POWERFUL ANTI-EVIL ARTIFACTS FOR THEIR DESCENDANTS TO USE.
I WILL MASTER THEM ALL AND USE THEM TO PROTECT PEOPLE FROM VICIOUS SUPERNATURALS LIKE YOU.
THAT IS THE CALLING OF EVERY BOY BORN INTO THE MINAMOTO CLAN!
AND SO—!
ビシッ
JAB
I'M HERE TO EXORCISE YOU!!
ザッ..
ZSH

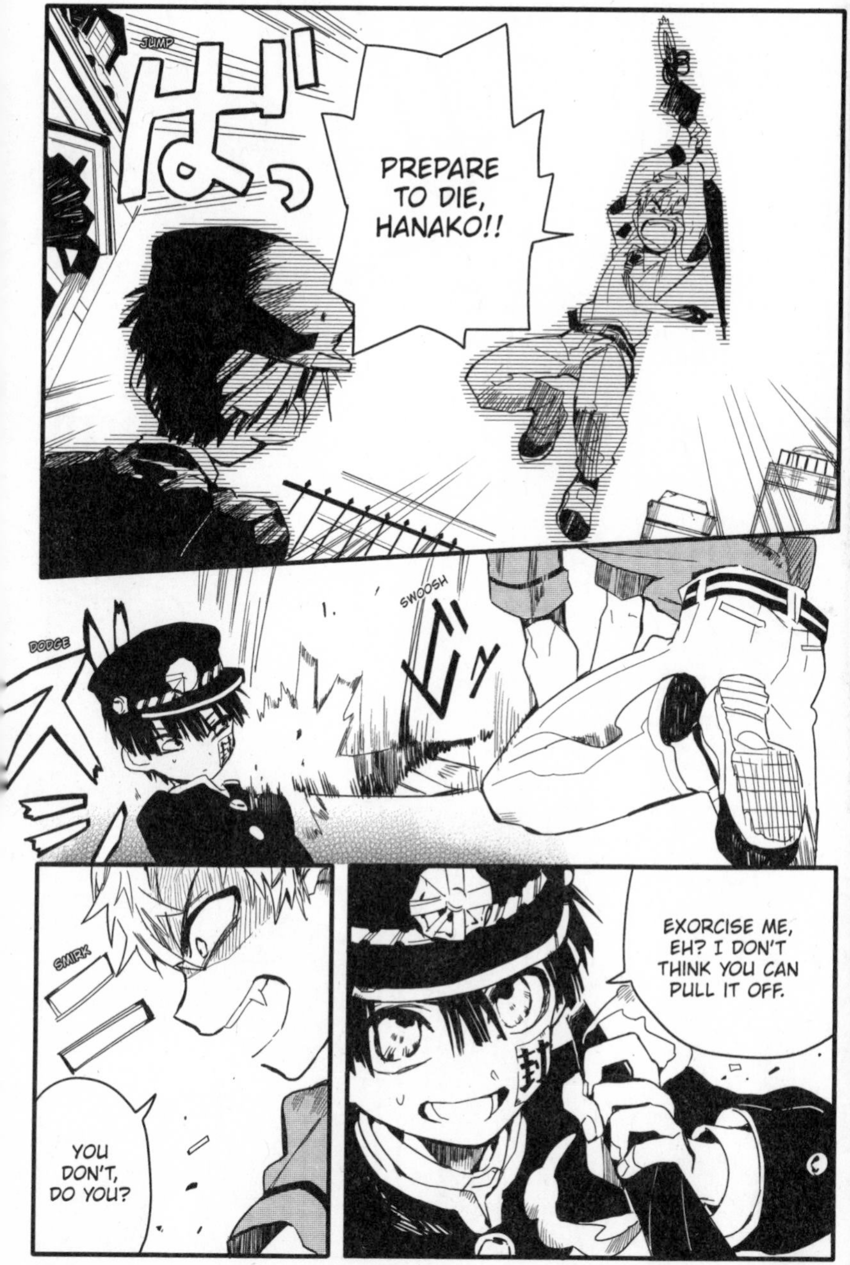
JUMP
ばっ
PREPARE TO DIE, HANAKO!!
SWOOSH
DODGE
EXORCISE ME, EH? I DON'T THINK YOU CAN PULL IT OFF.
SMIRK
YOU DON'T, DO YOU?

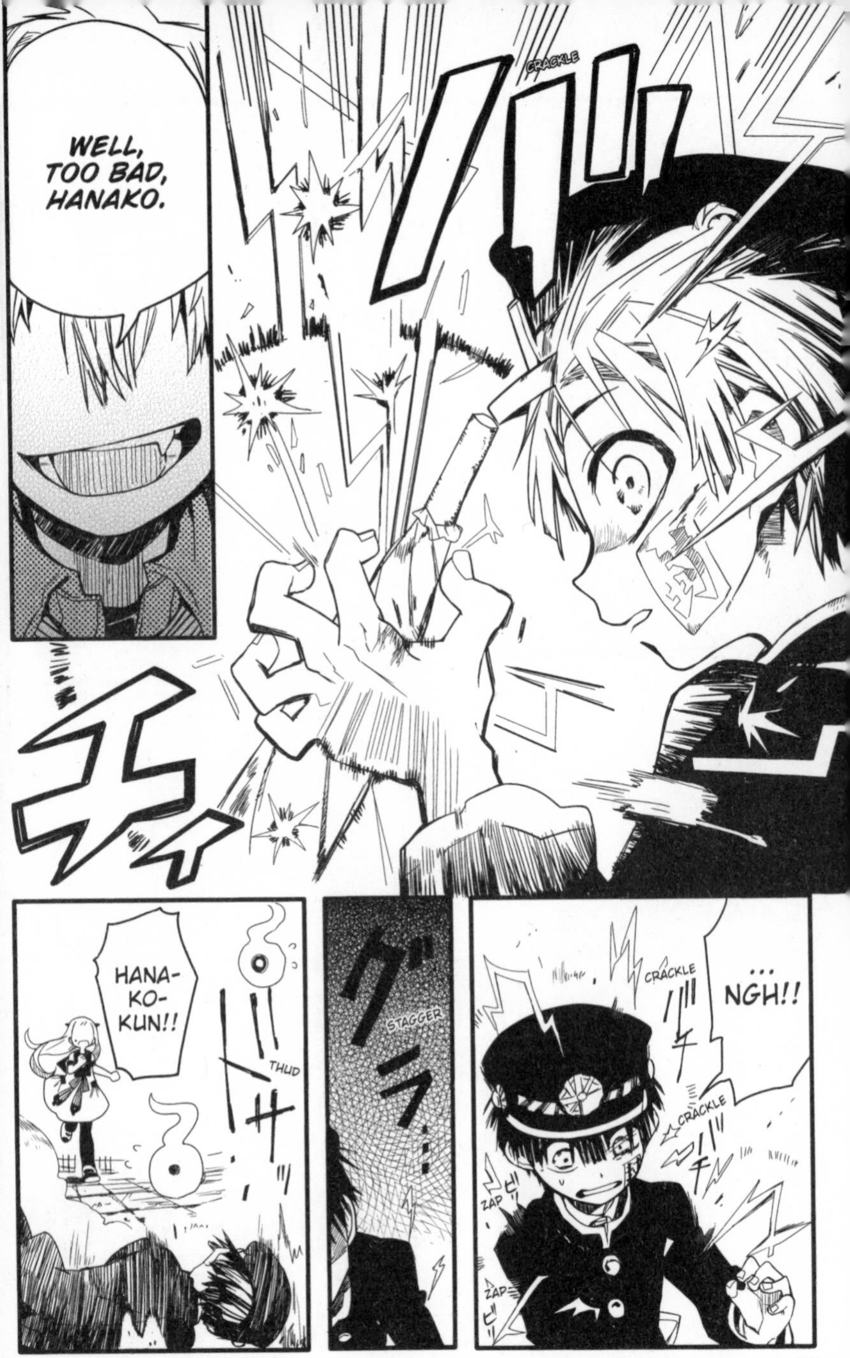
CRACKLE
WELL, TOO BAD, HANAKO.
CRACKLE
...NGH!!
CRACKLE
ZAP
ZAP
STAGGER
HANAKO-KUN!!
THUD

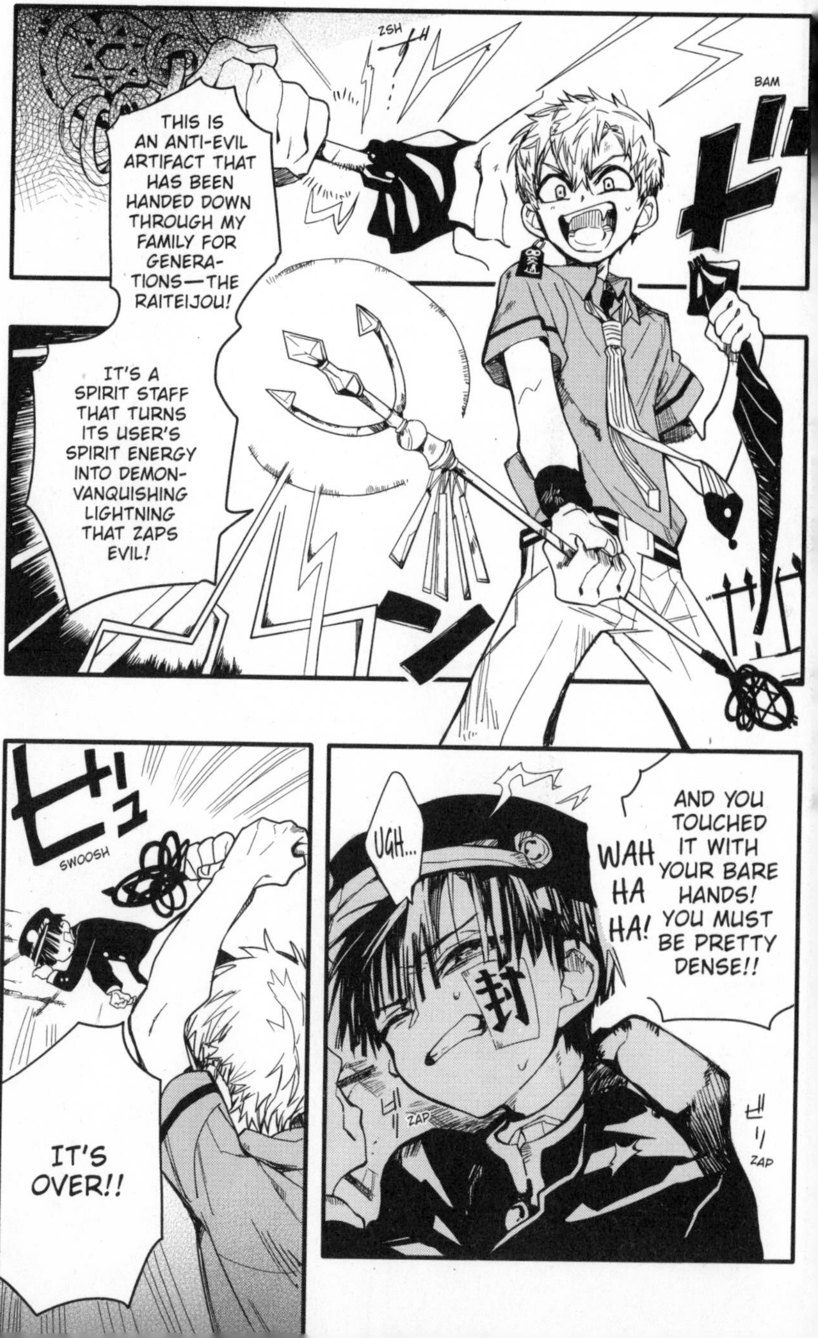
BAM
ZSH
THIS IS AN ANTI-EVIL ARTIFACT THAT HAS BEEN HANDED DOWN THROUGH MY FAMILY FOR GENERA-TIONS—THE RAITEIJOU!
IT'S A SPIRIT STAFF THAT TURNS ITS USER'S SPIRIT ENERGY INTO DEMON-VANQUISHING LIGHTNING THAT ZAPS EVIL!
AND YOU TOUCHED IT WITH YOUR BARE HANDS! YOU MUST BE PRETTY DENSE!!
WAH HA HA!
UGH...
ZAP
ZAP
SWOOSH
IT'S OVER!!

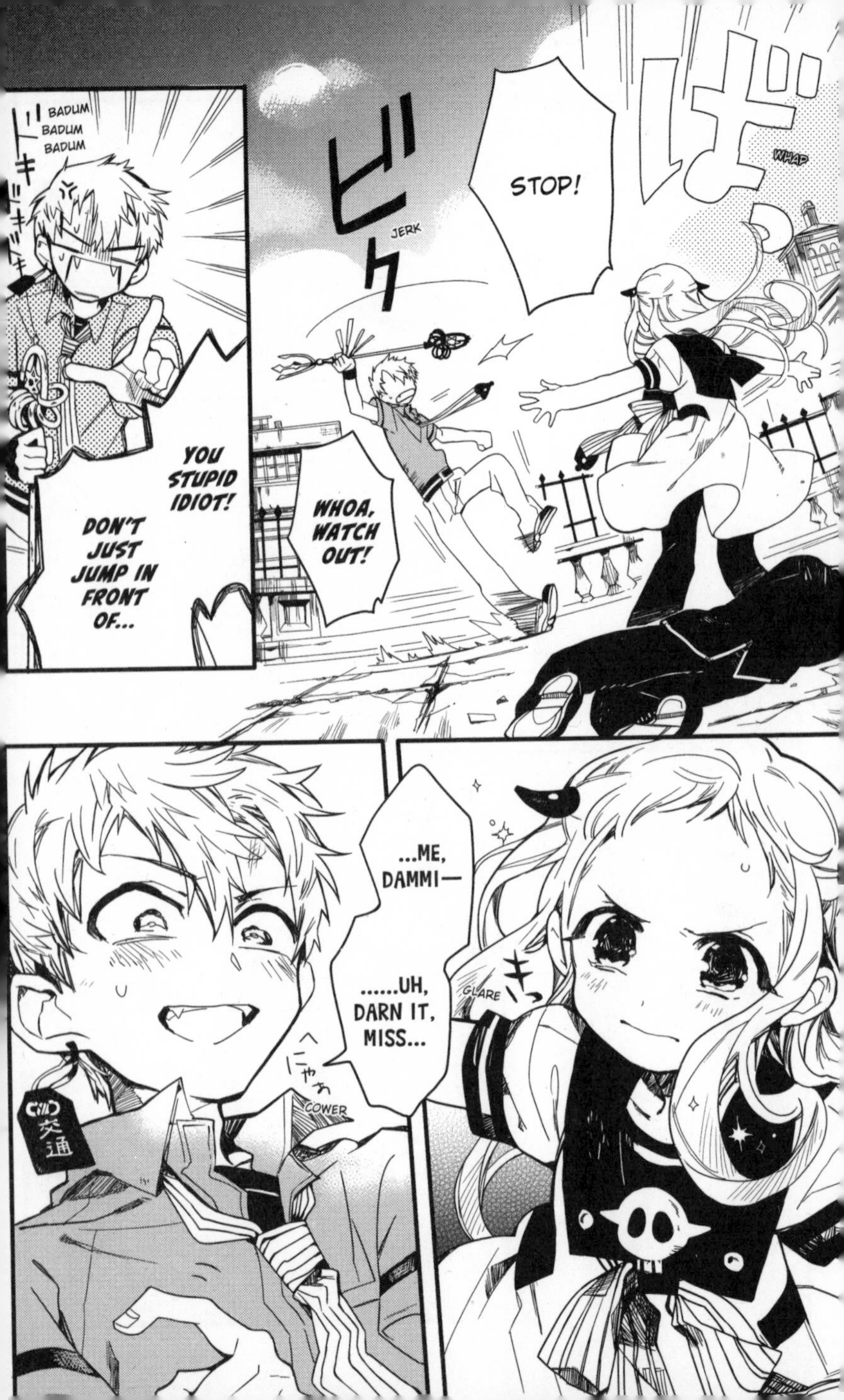
WHAP
STOP!
JERK
WHOA, WATCH OUT!
BADUM
BADUM
BADUM
YOU STUPID IDIOT!
DON'T JUST JUMP IN FRONT OF...
GLARE
...ME, DAMMI—
......UH, DARN IT, MISS...
COWER

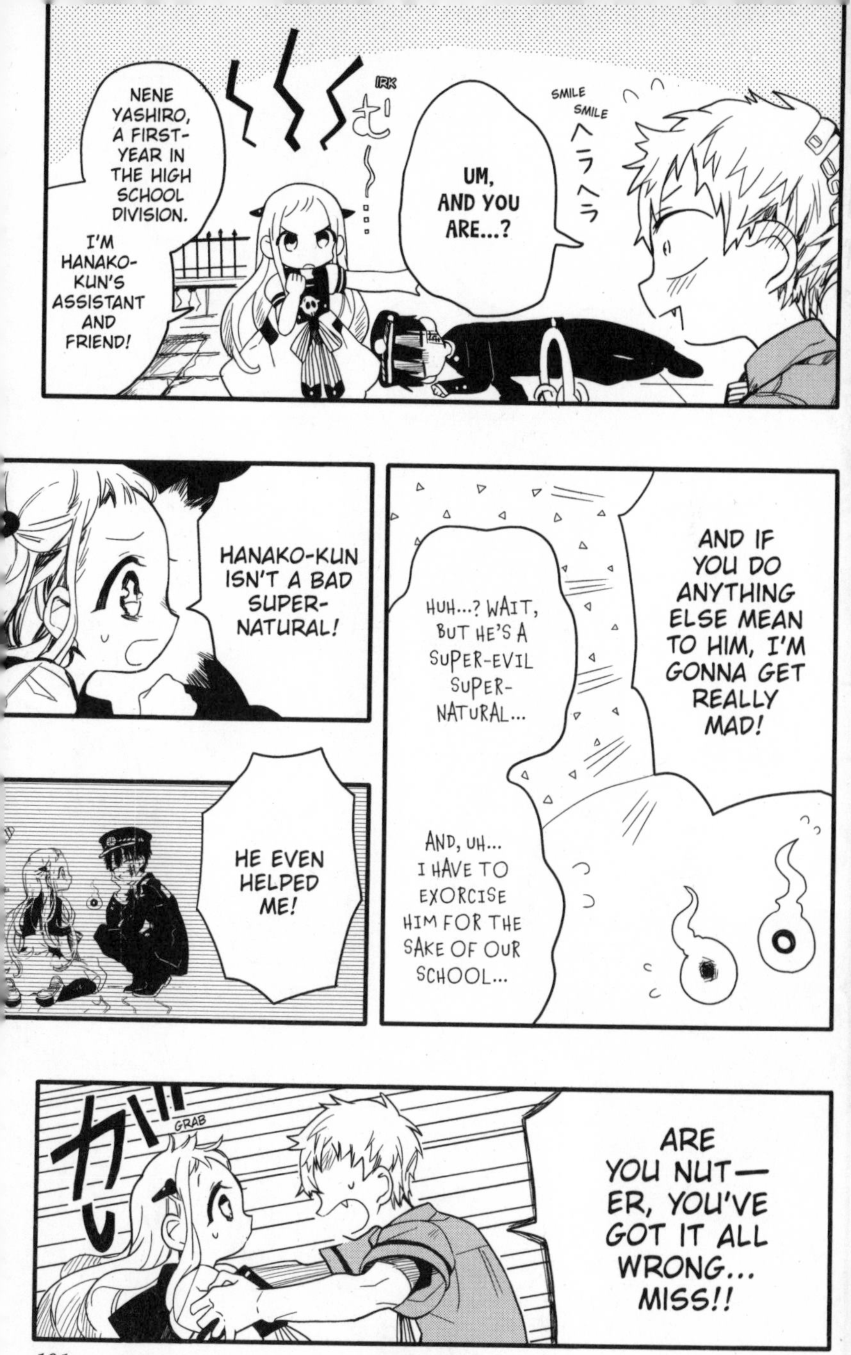
SMILE SMILE
UM, AND YOU ARE...?
IRK
NENE YASHIRO, A FIRST-YEAR IN THE HIGH SCHOOL DIVISION.
I'M HANAKO-KUN'S ASSISTANT AND FRIEND!
AND IF YOU DO ANYTHING ELSE MEAN TO HIM, I'M GONNA GET REALLY MAD!
HUH...? WAIT, BUT HE'S A SUPER-EVIL SUPER-NATURAL...
AND, UH... I HAVE TO EXORCISE HIM FOR THE SAKE OF OUR SCHOOL...
HANAKO-KUN ISN'T A BAD SUPER-NATURAL!
HE EVEN HELPED ME!
ARE YOU NUT— ER, YOU'VE GOT IT ALL WRONG... MISS!!
GRAB

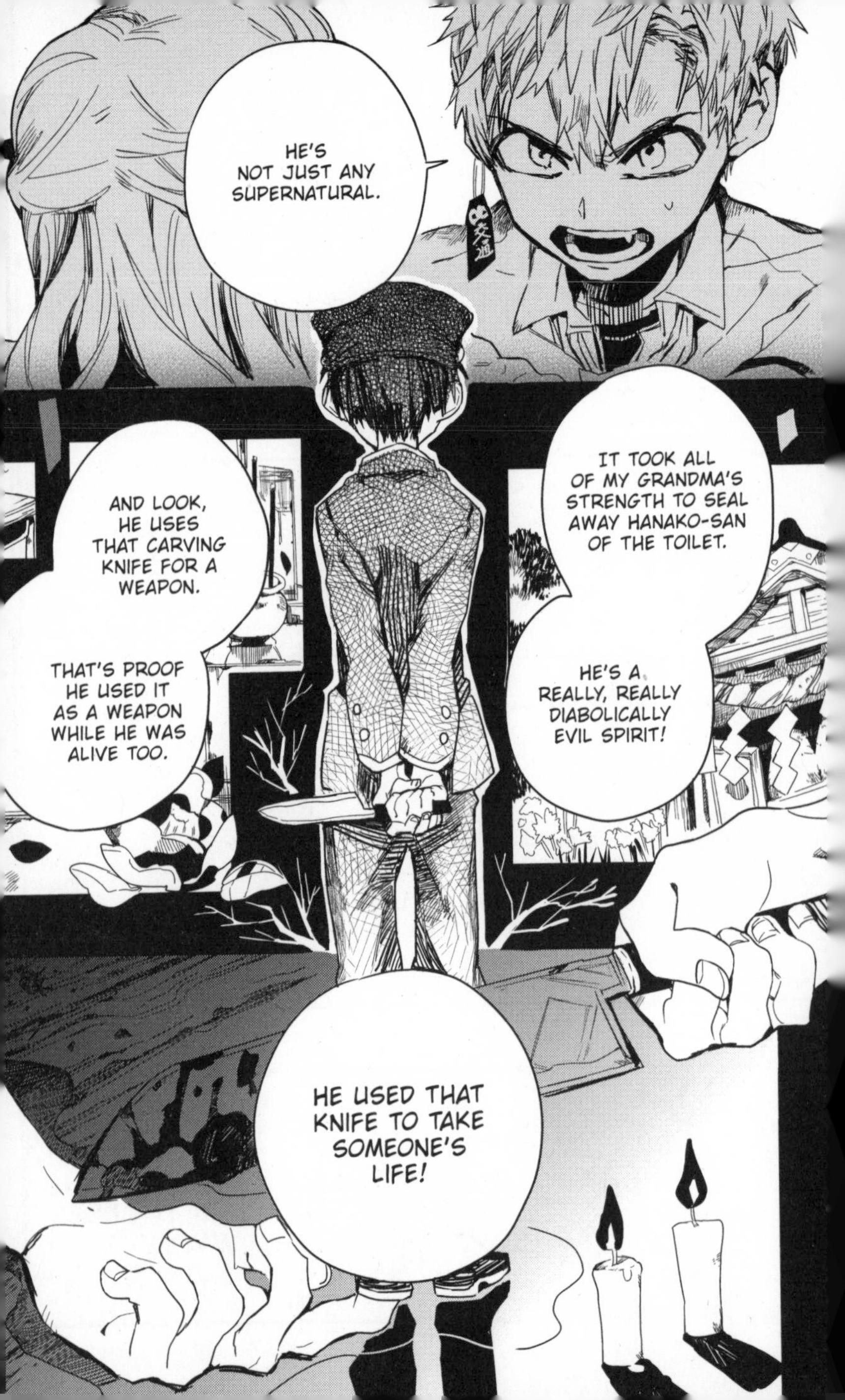
HE'S NOT JUST ANY SUPERNATURAL.
IT TOOK ALL OF MY GRANDMA'S STRENGTH TO SEAL AWAY HANAKO-SAN OF THE TOILET.
HE'S A REALLY, REALLY DIABOLICALLY EVIL SPIRIT!
AND LOOK, HE USES THAT CARVING KNIFE FOR A WEAPON.
THAT'S PROOF HE USED IT AS A WEAPON WHILE HE WAS ALIVE TOO.
HE USED THAT KNIFE TO TAKE SOMEONE'S LIFE!

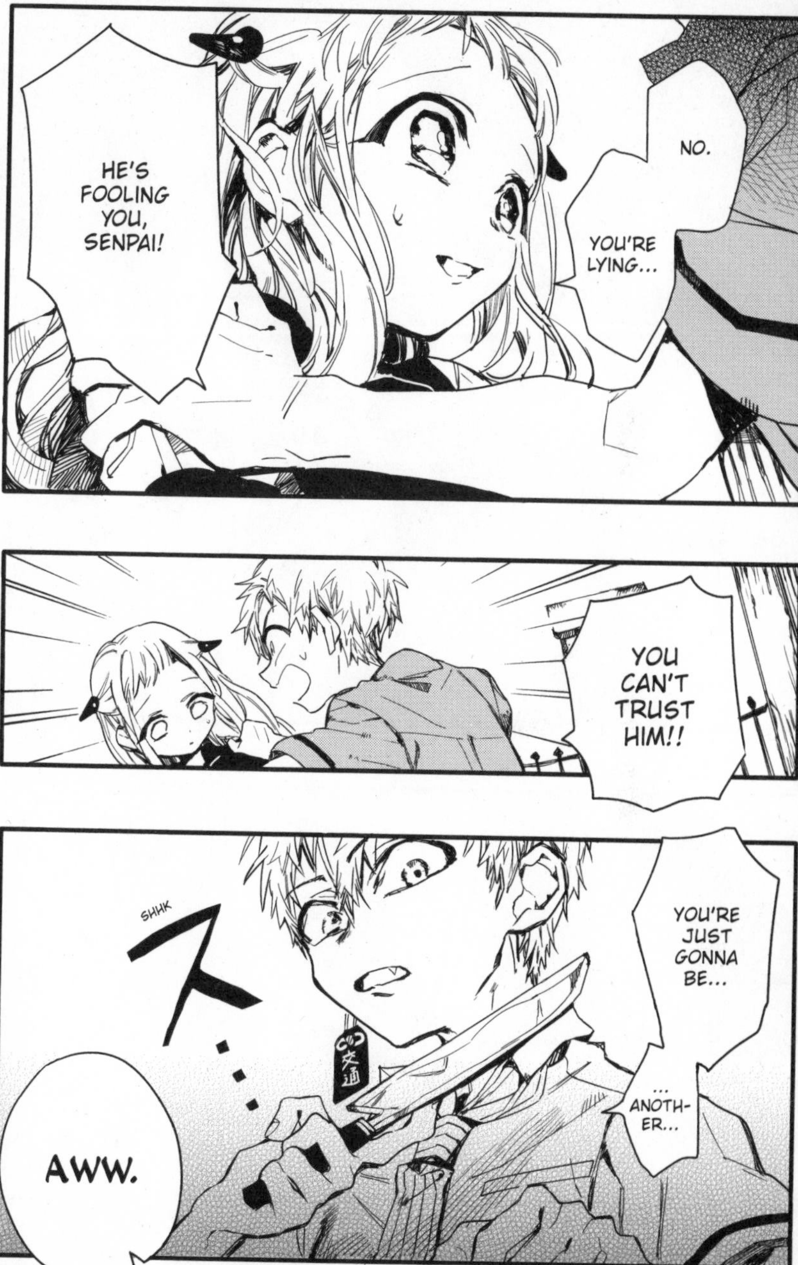
NO.
YOU'RE LYING...
HE'S FOOLING YOU, SENPAI!
YOU CAN'T TRUST HIM!!
YOU'RE JUST GONNA BE...
...ANOTH-ER...
SHHK
AWW.

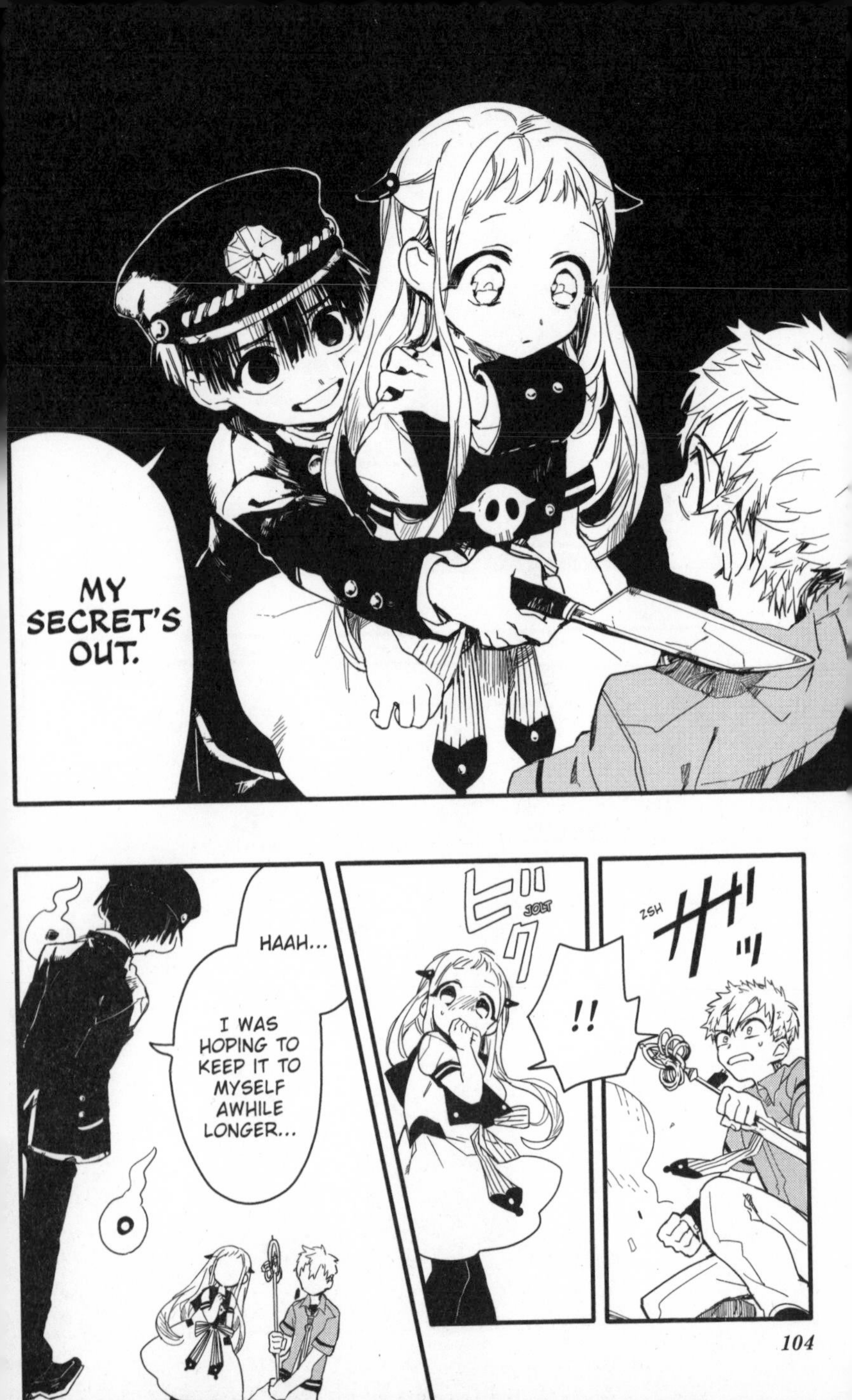
MY SECRET'S OUT.
ZSH
ザッ
JOLT
ビク
!!
HAAH...
I WAS HOPING TO KEEP IT TO MYSELF AWHILE LONGER...

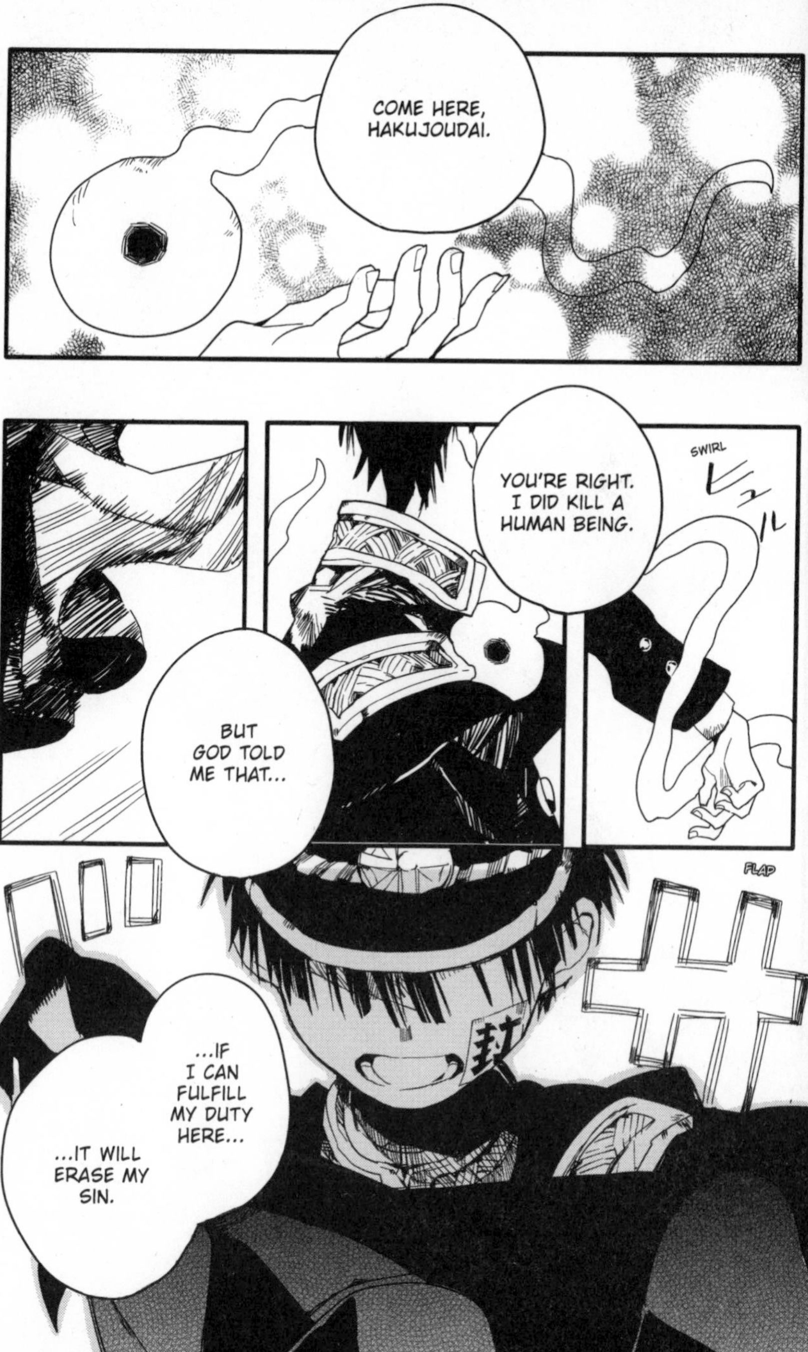

COME HERE, HAKUJOUDAI.
SWIRL
ヒュル
YOU'RE RIGHT. I DID KILL A HUMAN BEING.
BUT GOD TOLD ME THAT...
FLAP
...IF I CAN FULFILL MY DUTY HERE...
...IT WILL ERASE MY SIN.

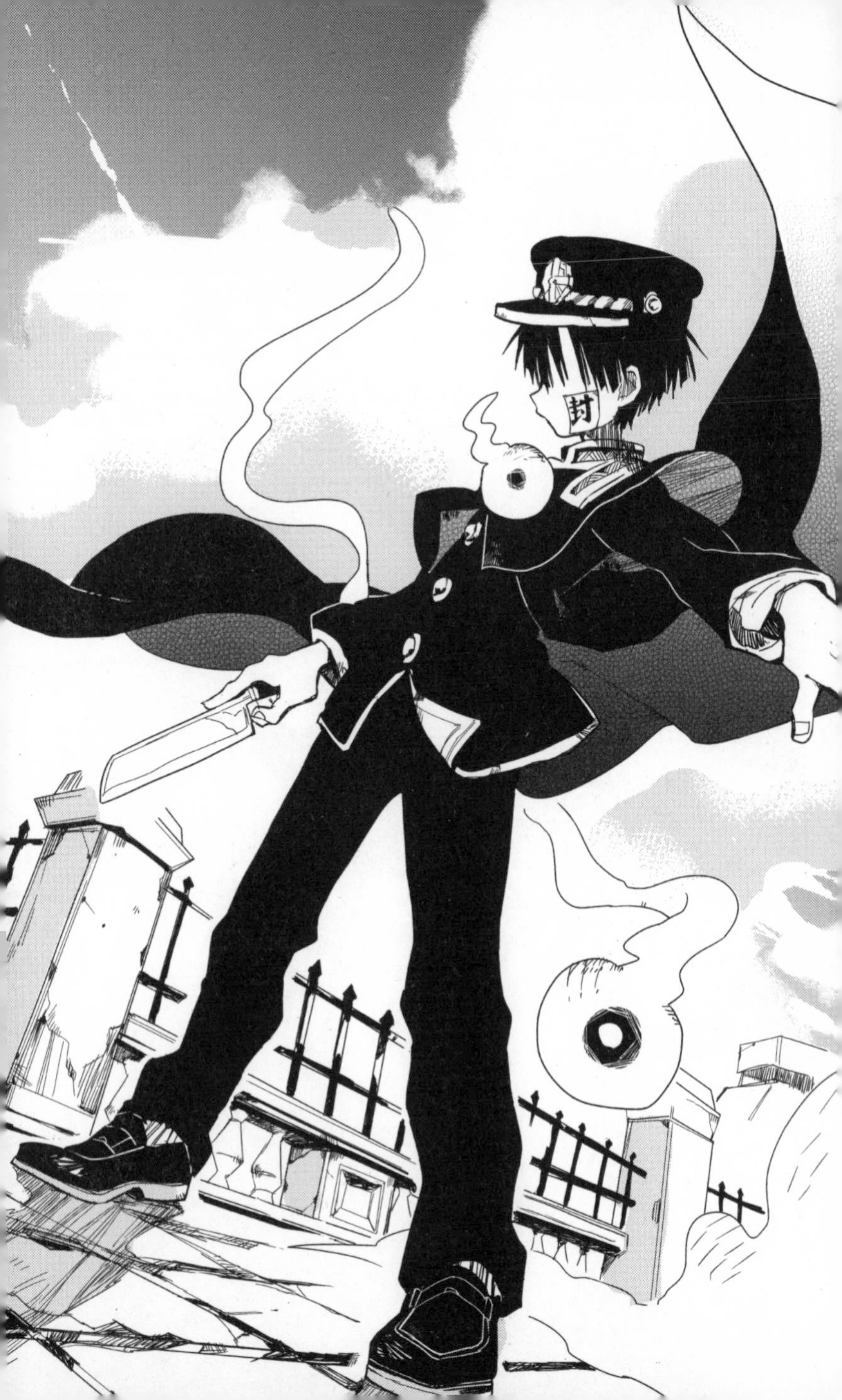
封

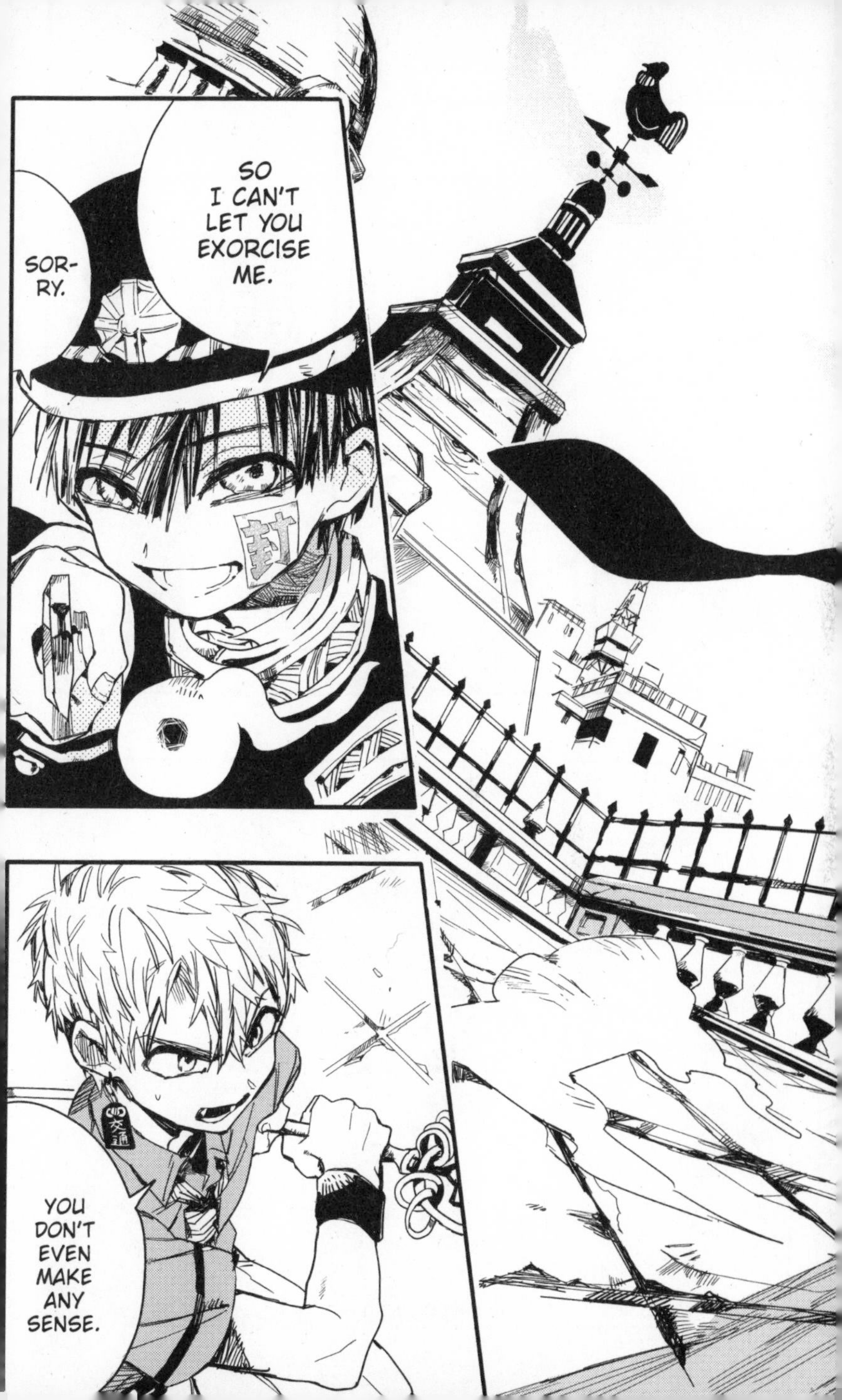
SO I CAN'T LET YOU EXORCISE ME.
SOR-RY.
YOU DON'T EVEN MAKE ANY SENSE.

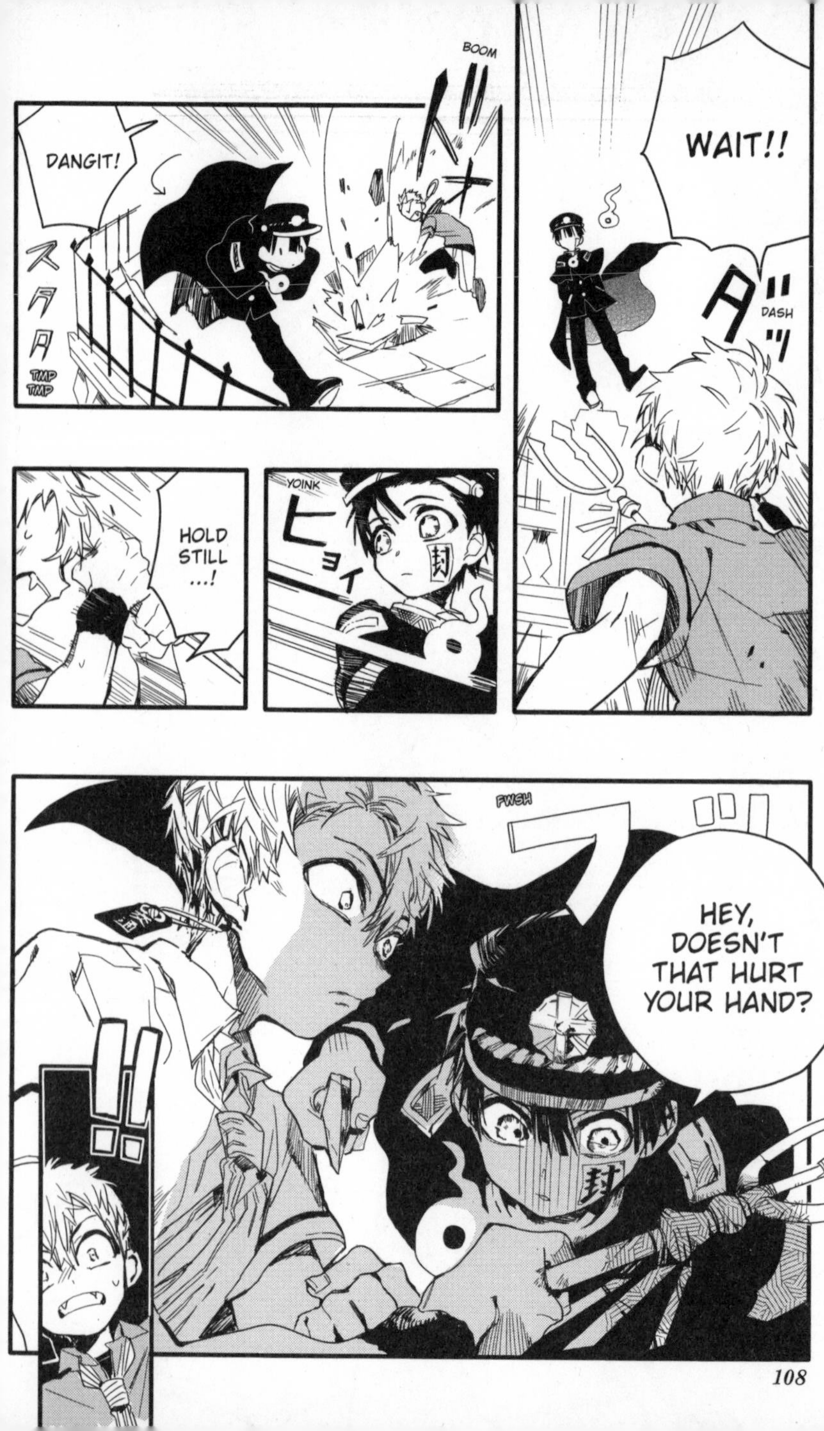
WAIT!!
DASH
BOOM
DANGIT!
TMP TMP
YOINK
HOLD STILL ...!
FWSH
HEY, DOESN'T THAT HURT YOUR HAND?

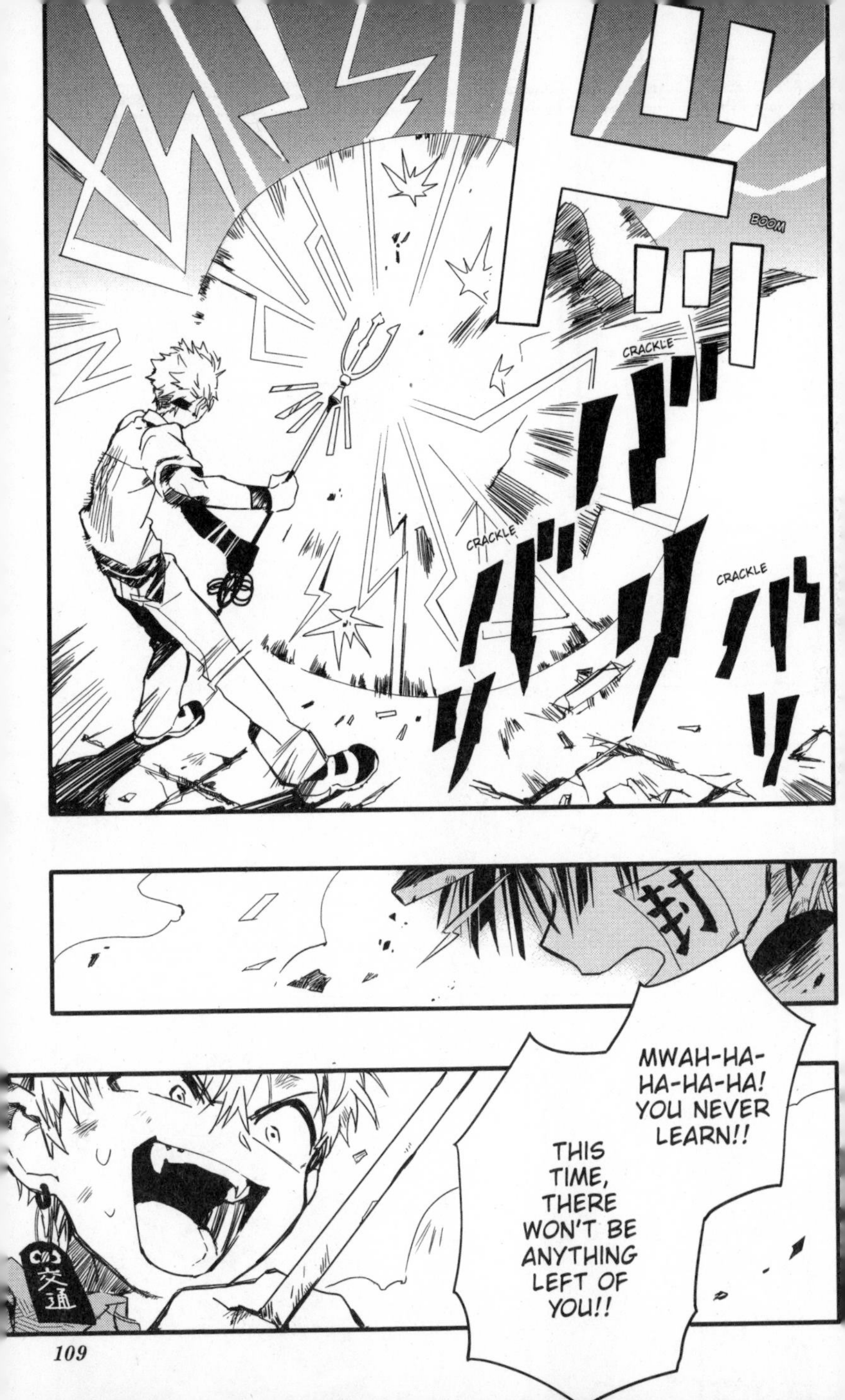
BOOM
CRACKLE
CRACKLE
CRACKLE
MWAH-HA-HA-HA-HA! YOU NEVER LEARN!!
THIS TIME, THERE WON'T BE ANYTHING LEFT OF YOU!!

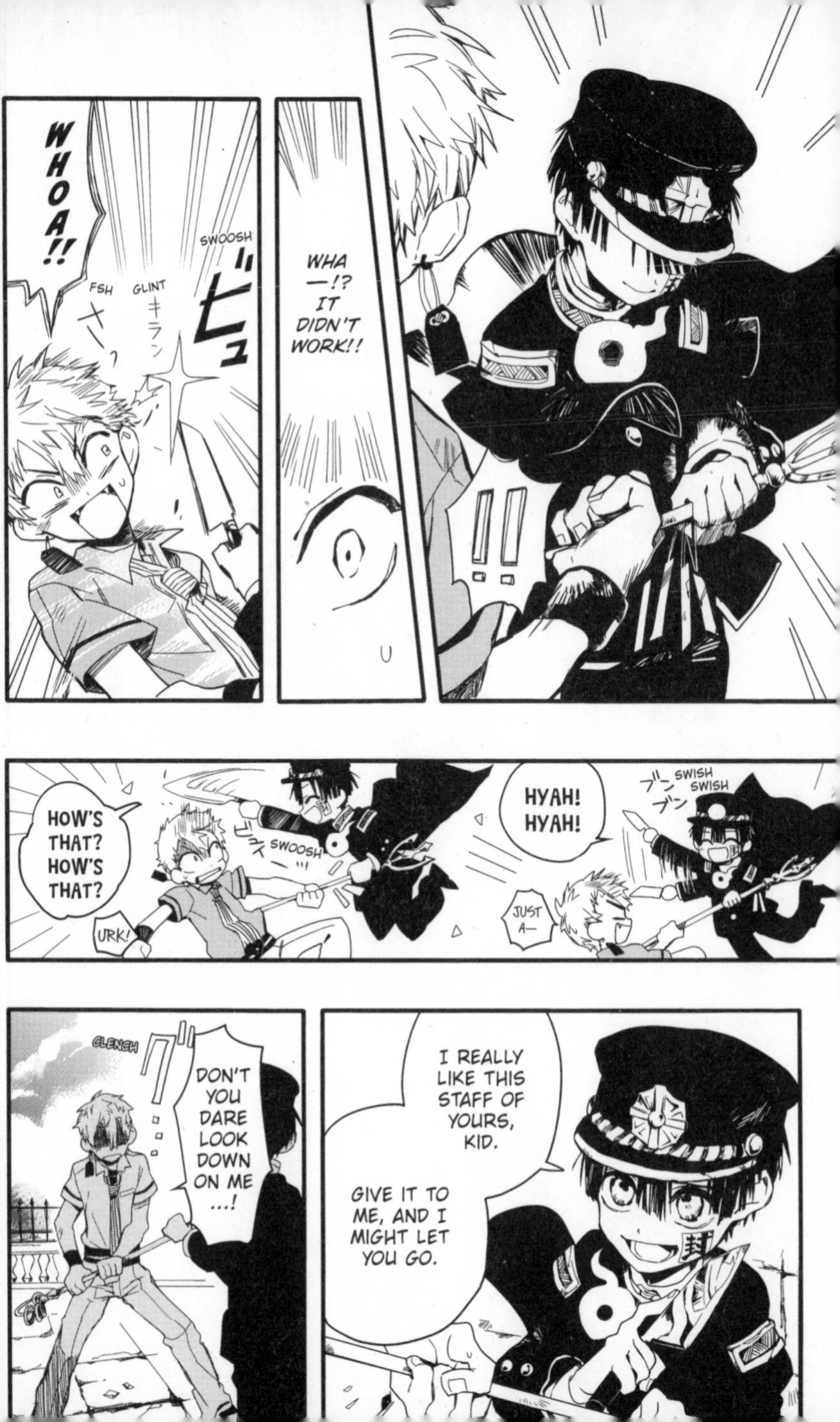
WHA—!? IT DIDN'T WORK!!
!!
WHOA!!
SWOOSH
ビュ
GLINT
キラン
FSH
さっ
SWISH SWISH
ブン ブン
HYAH! HYAH!
JUST A—
HOW'S THAT? HOW'S THAT?
SWOOSH
URK!
I REALLY LIKE THIS STAFF OF YOURS, KID.
GIVE IT TO ME, AND I MIGHT LET YOU GO.
CLENCH
DON'T YOU DARE LOOK DOWN ON ME ...!

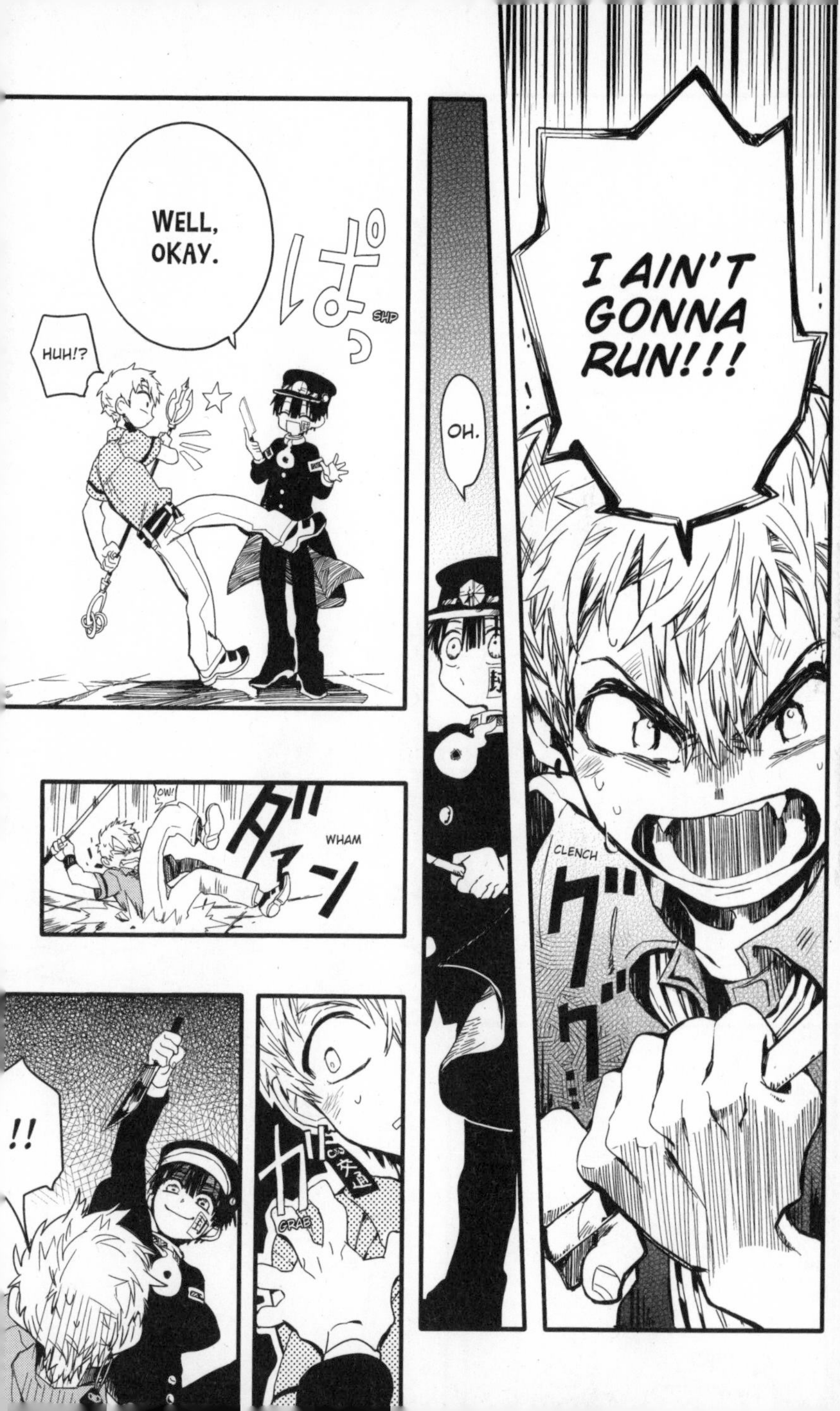

I AIN'T GONNA RUN!!!
CLENCH
OH.
WELL, OKAY.
SHP
HUH!?
OW!
WHAM
GRAB
!!

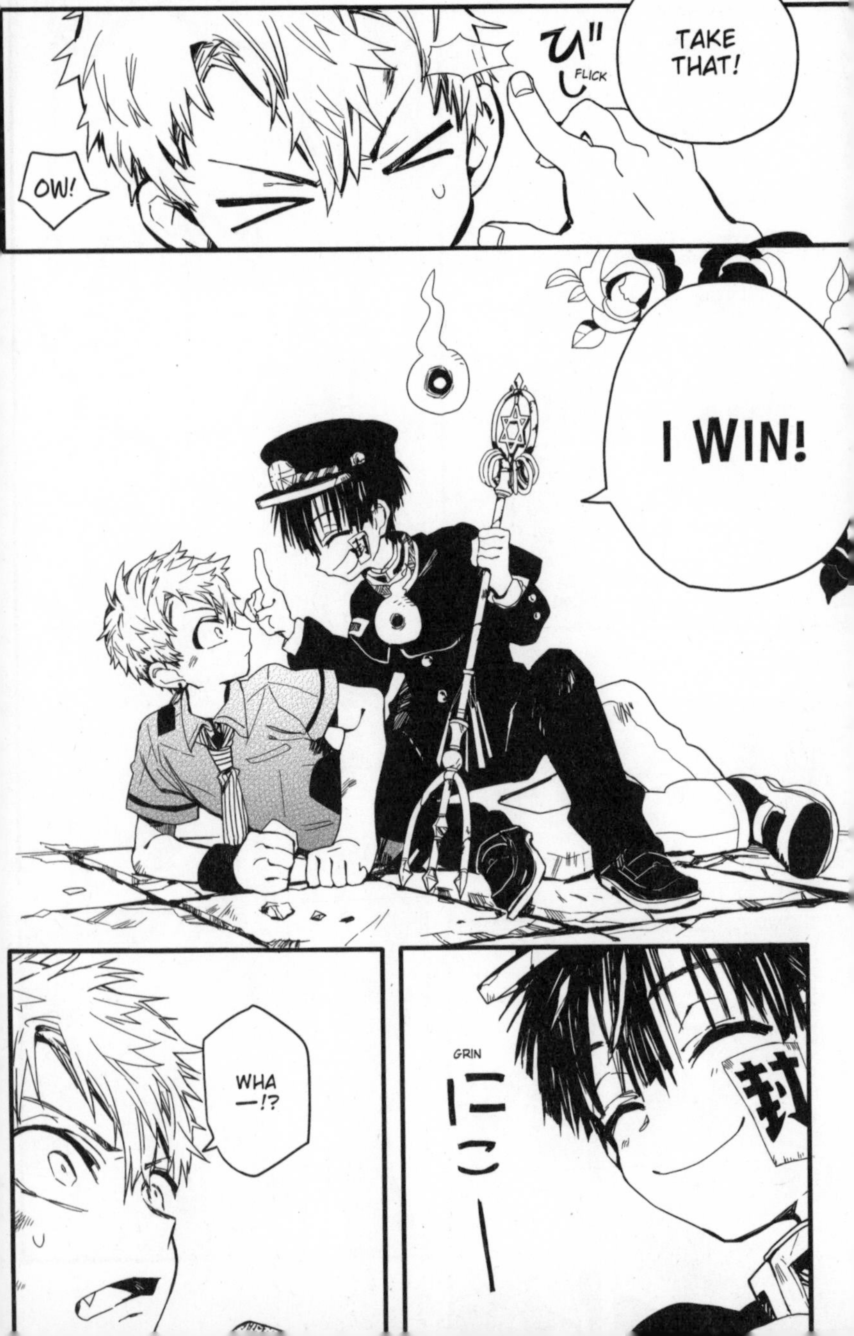
TAKE THAT!
ひ" FLICK
OW!
I WIN!
GRIN
にこー
WHA—!?

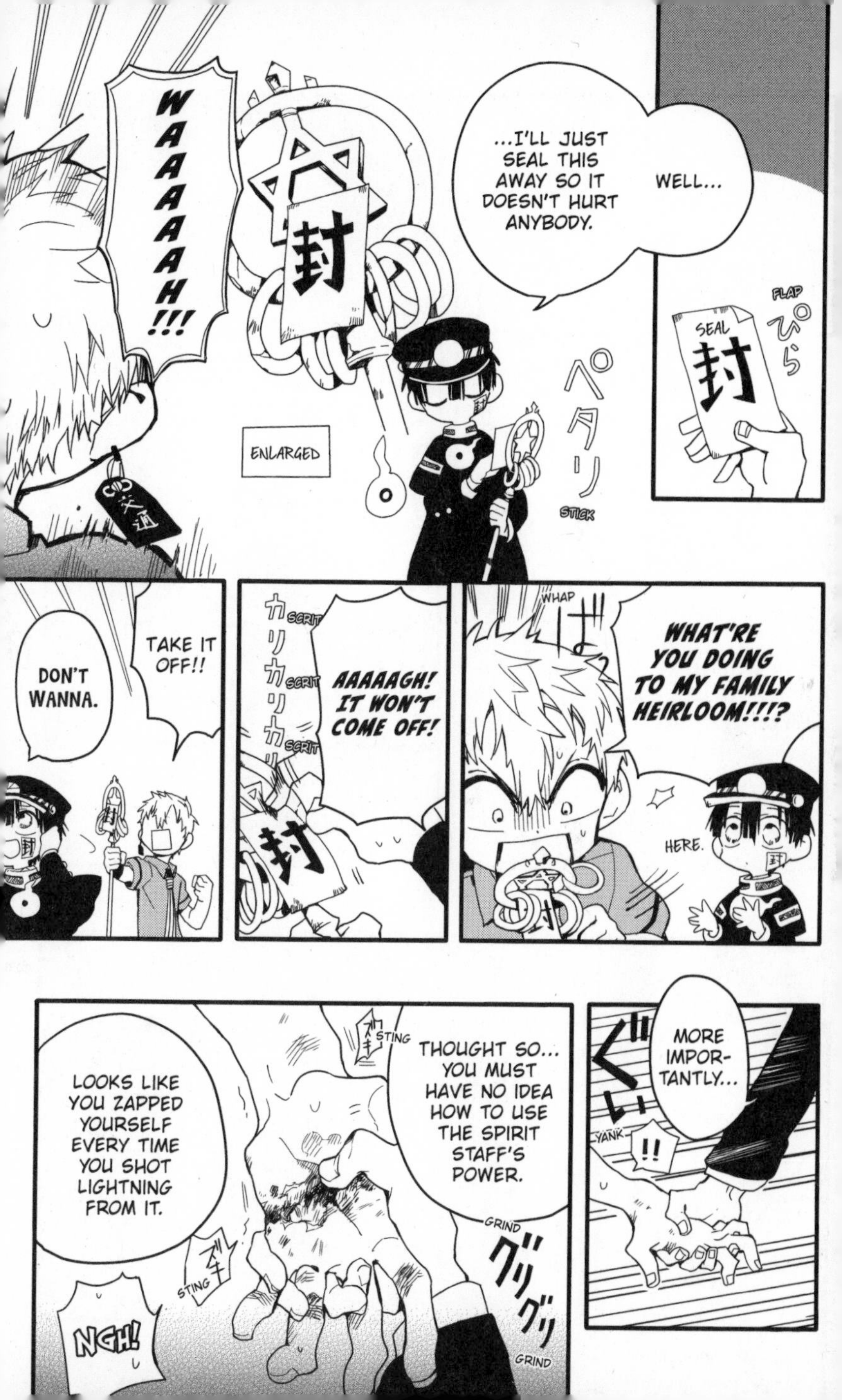
WELL...
FLAP
SEAL
...I'LL JUST SEAL THIS AWAY SO IT DOESN'T HURT ANYBODY.
STICK
WAAAAAAAH!!!
ENLARGED
WHAP
WHAT'RE YOU DOING TO MY FAMILY HEIRLOOM!!!?
HERE.
SCRIT
SCRIT
SCRIT
AAAAAGH! IT WON'T COME OFF!
TAKE IT OFF!!
DON'T WANNA.
MORE IMPORTANTLY...
YANK
!!
STING
THOUGHT SO... YOU MUST HAVE NO IDEA HOW TO USE THE SPIRIT STAFF'S POWER.
LOOKS LIKE YOU ZAPPED YOURSELF EVERY TIME YOU SHOT LIGHTNING FROM IT.
GRIND
GRIND
STING
NGH!

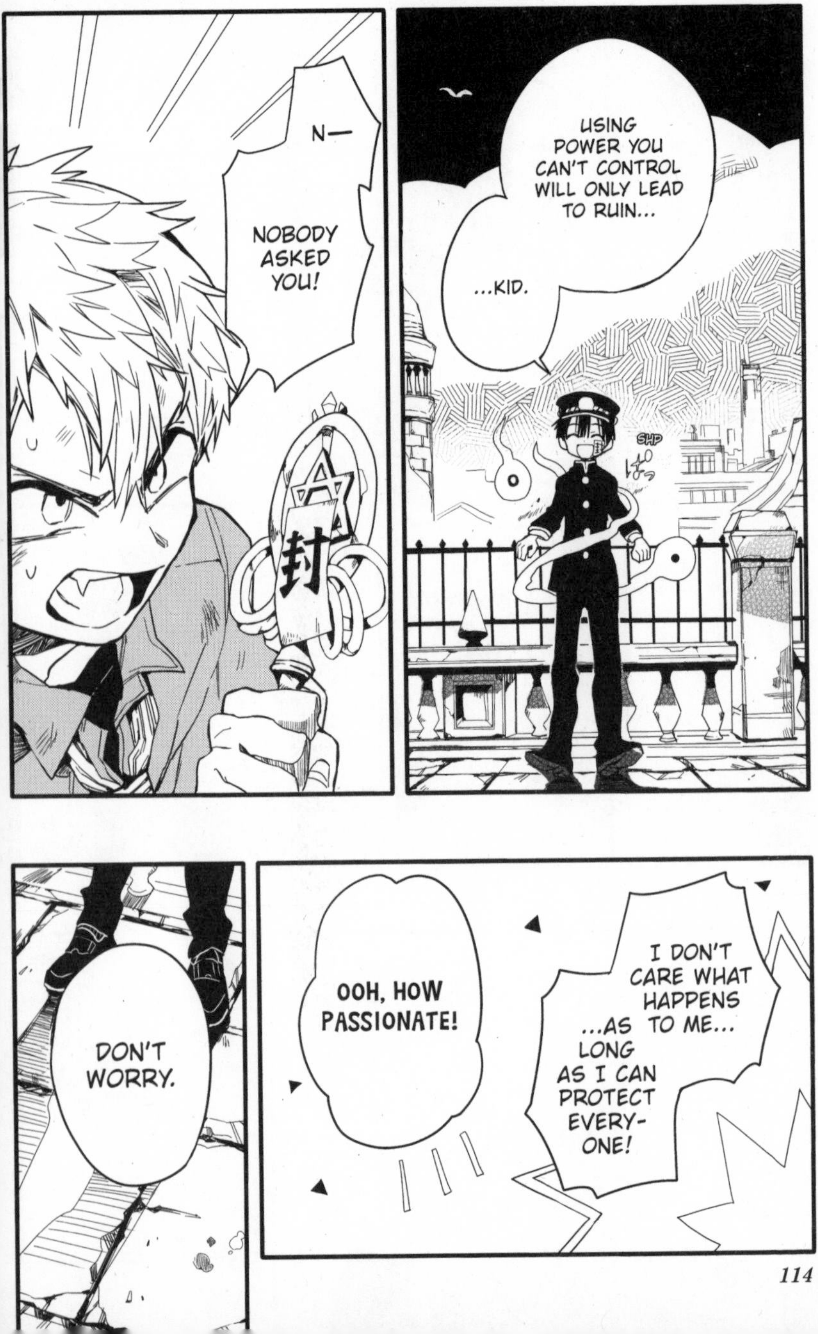
USING POWER YOU CAN'T CONTROL WILL ONLY LEAD TO RUIN...
...KID.
SHP
N—
NOBODY ASKED YOU!
I DON'T CARE WHAT HAPPENS TO ME...
...AS LONG AS I CAN PROTECT EVERY-ONE!
OOH, HOW PASSIONATE!
DON'T WORRY.

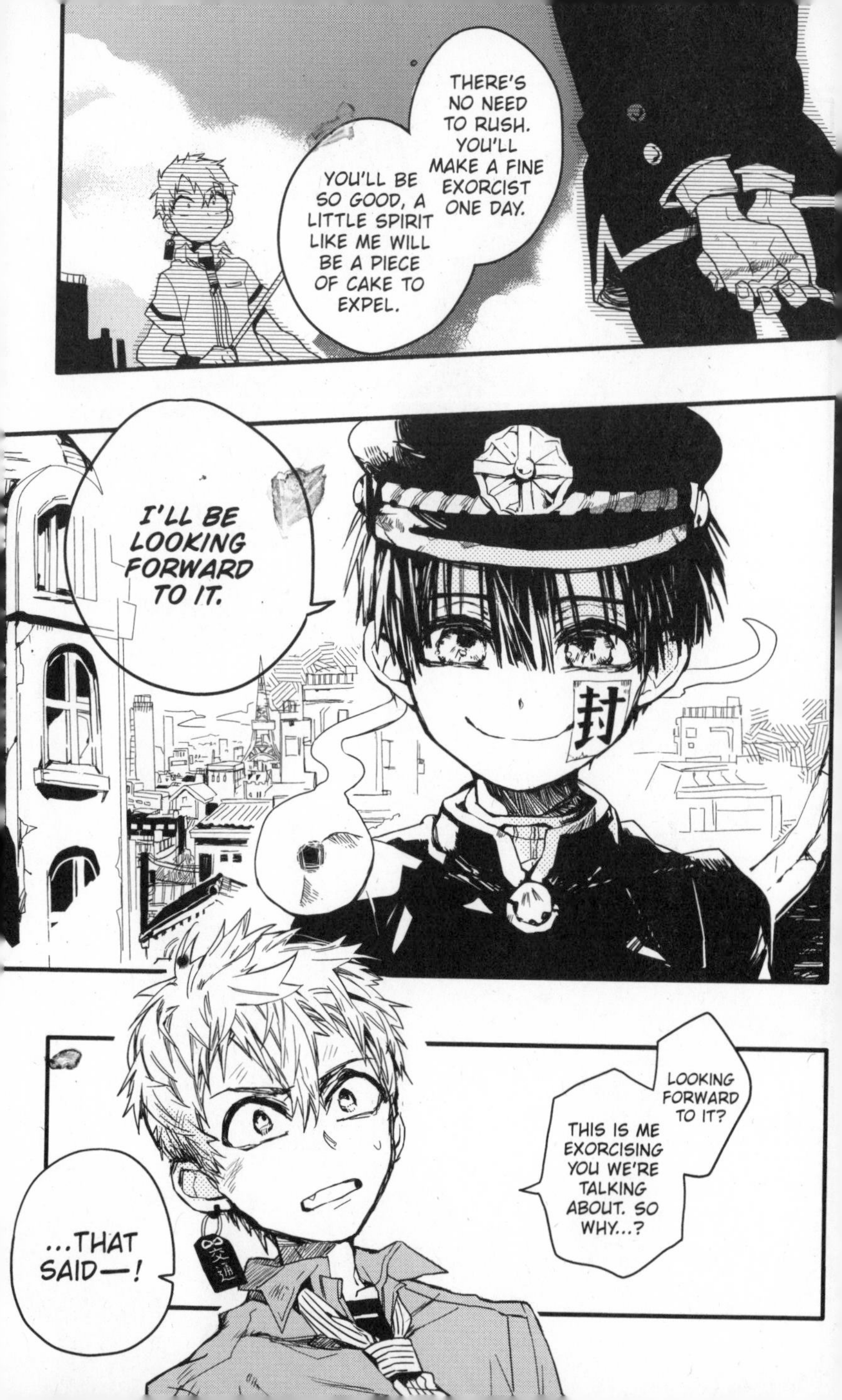
THERE'S NO NEED TO RUSH. YOU'LL MAKE A FINE EXORCIST ONE DAY.
YOU'LL BE SO GOOD, A LITTLE SPIRIT LIKE ME WILL BE A PIECE OF CAKE TO EXPEL.
I'LL BE LOOKING FORWARD TO IT.
LOOKING FORWARD TO IT?
THIS IS ME EXORCISING YOU WE'RE TALKING ABOUT. SO WHY...?
...THAT SAID—!

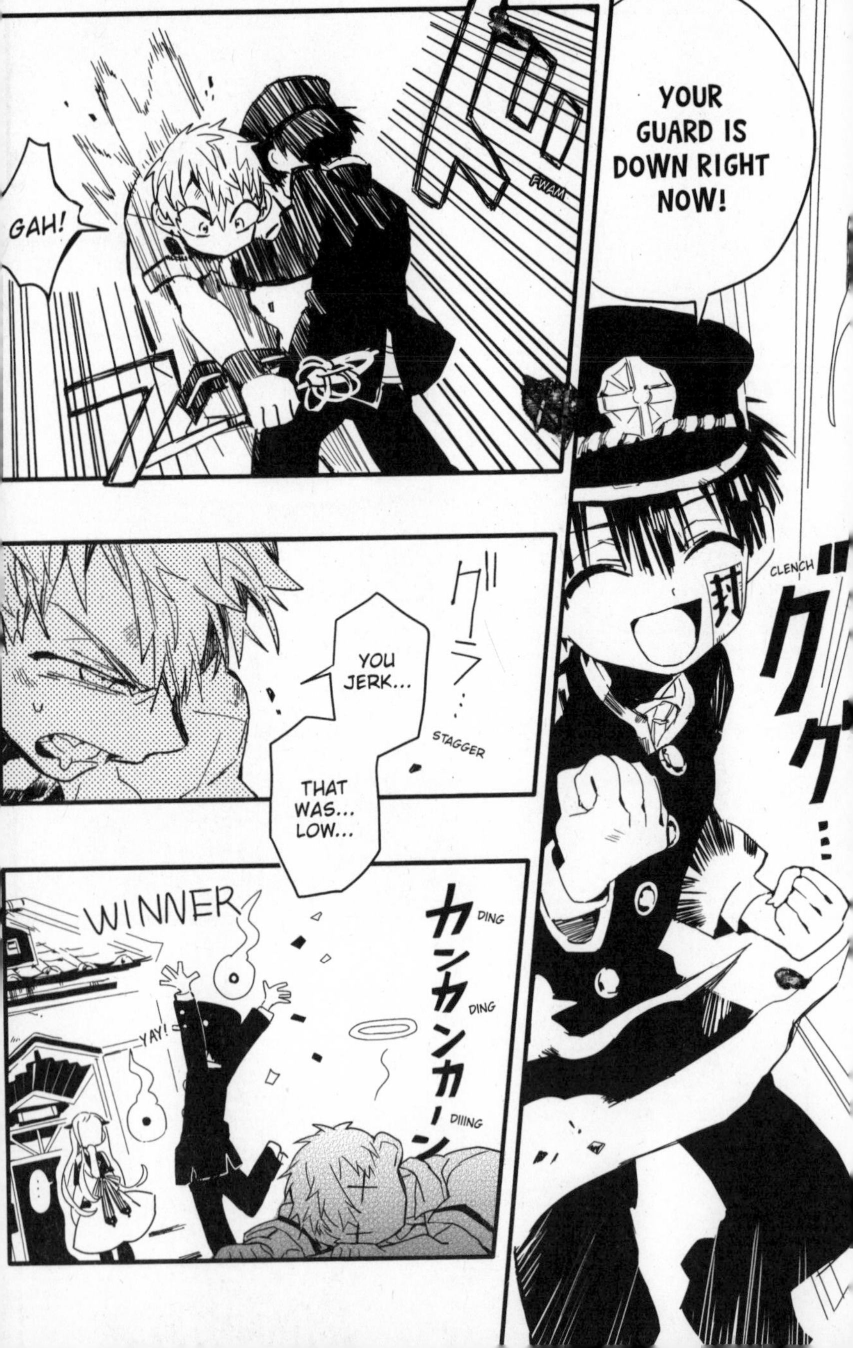
YOUR GUARD IS DOWN RIGHT NOW!
CLENCH
FWAM
GAH!
グラ
STAGGER
YOU JERK...
THAT WAS... LOW...
カンカンカーン
DING
DING
DIIING
WINNER
YAY!
...

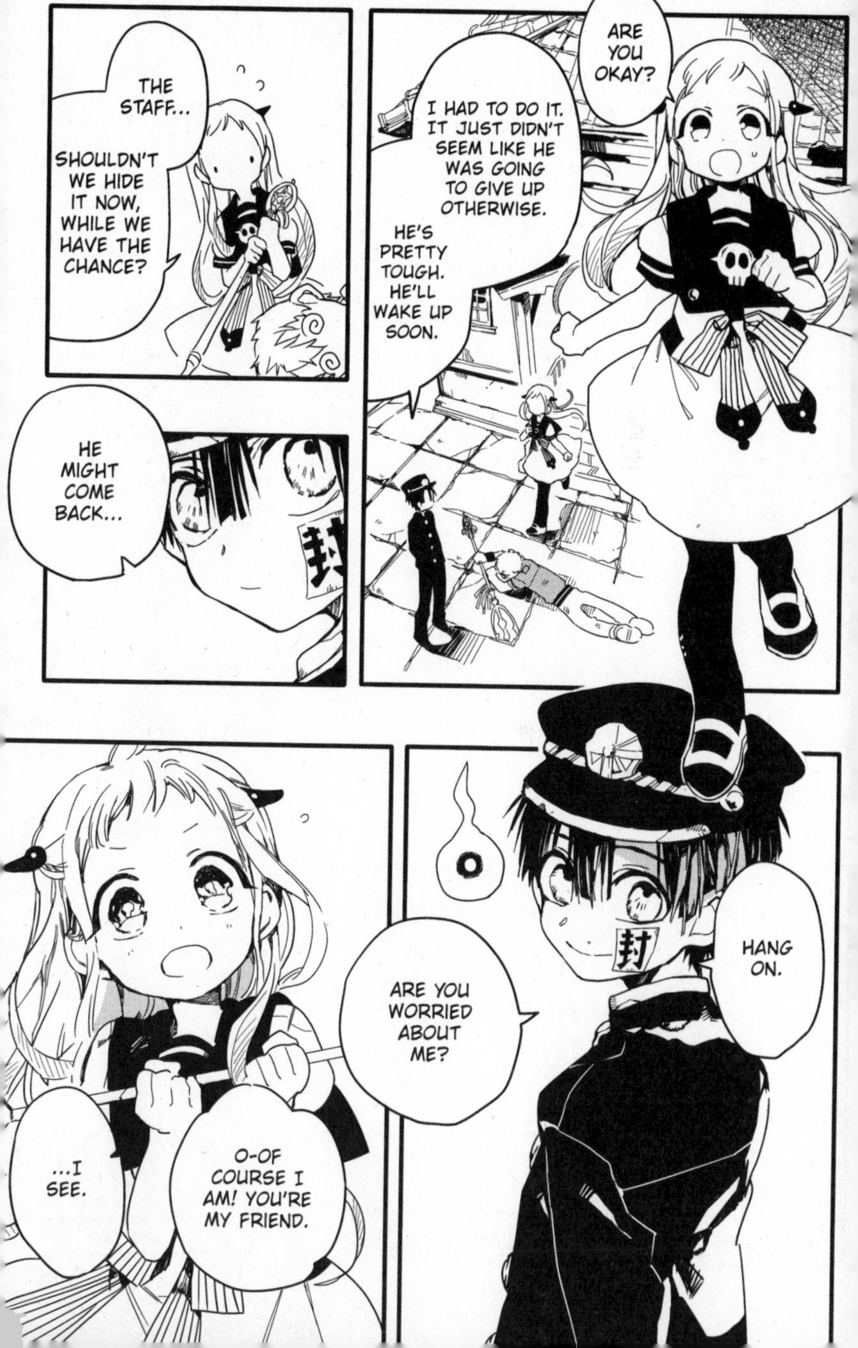
ARE YOU OKAY?
I HAD TO DO IT. IT JUST DIDN'T SEEM LIKE HE WAS GOING TO GIVE UP OTHERWISE.
HE'S PRETTY TOUGH. HE'LL WAKE UP SOON.
THE STAFF...
SHOULDN'T WE HIDE IT NOW, WHILE WE HAVE THE CHANCE?
HE MIGHT COME BACK...
HANG ON.
ARE YOU WORRIED ABOUT ME?
O-OF COURSE I AM! YOU'RE MY FRIEND.
...I SEE.

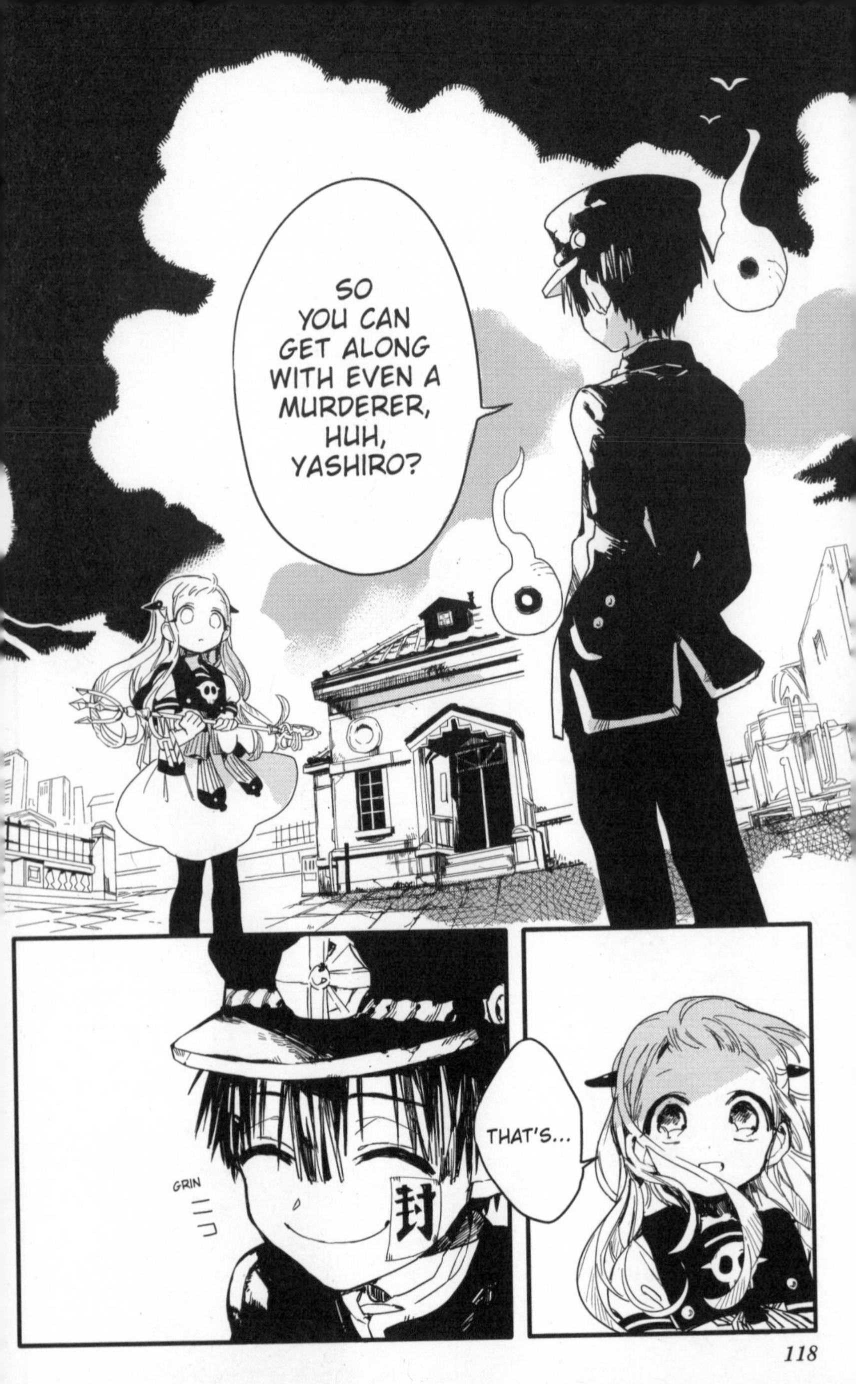
SO YOU CAN GET ALONG WITH EVEN A MURDERER, HUH, YASHIRO?
THAT'S...
封
GRIN
ニコ

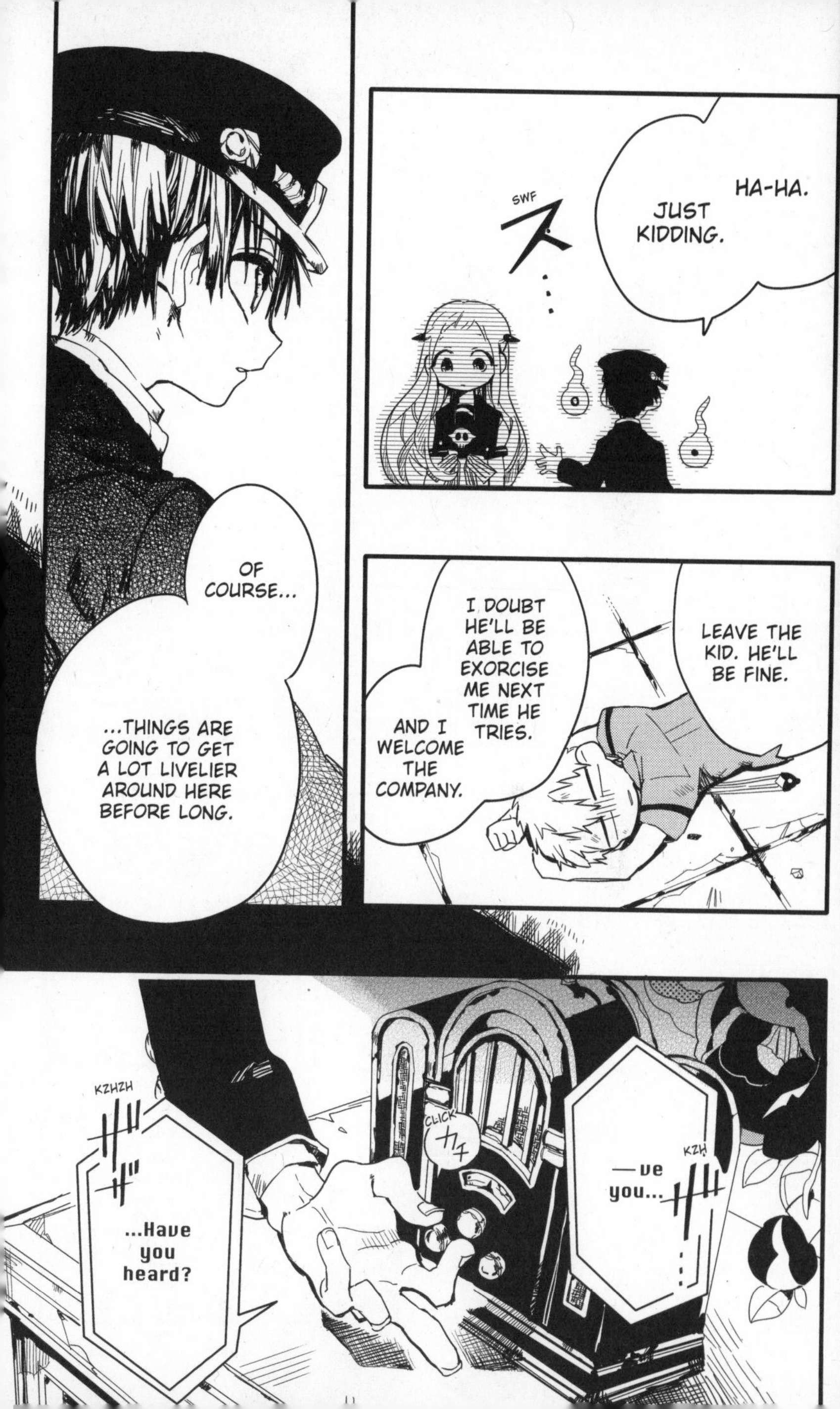
HA-HA.
JUST KIDDING.
SWF
...
LEAVE THE KID. HE'LL BE FINE.
I DOUBT HE'LL BE ABLE TO EXORCISE ME NEXT TIME HE TRIES.
AND I WELCOME THE COMPANY.
OF COURSE...
...THINGS ARE GOING TO GET A LOT LIVELIER AROUND HERE BEFORE LONG.
KZH
—ve you...
...
CLICK
KZHZH
...Have you heard?

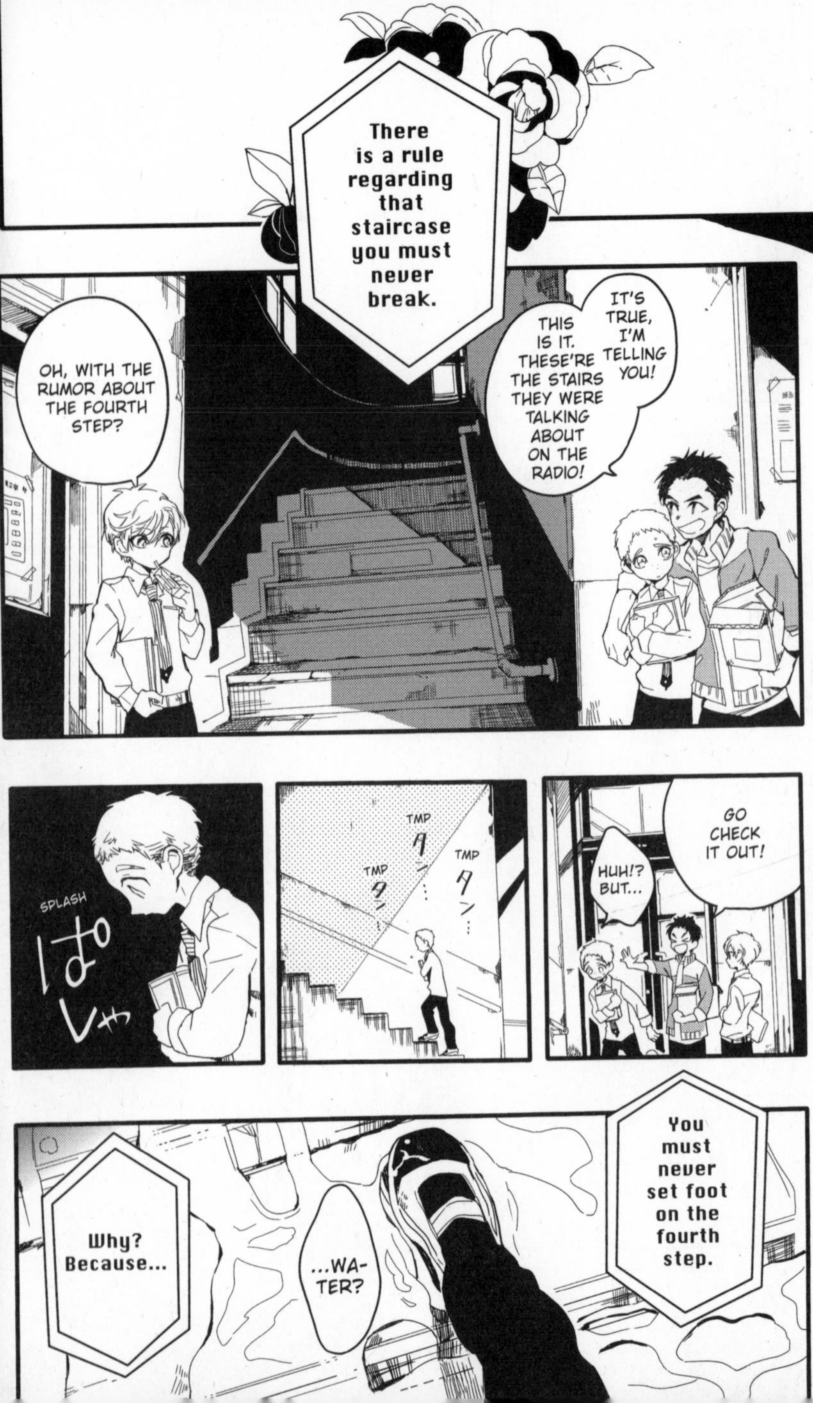
There is a rule regarding that staircase you must never break.
IT'S TRUE, I'M TELLING YOU!
THIS IS IT. THESE'RE THE STAIRS THEY WERE TALKING ABOUT ON THE RADIO!
OH, WITH THE RUMOR ABOUT THE FOURTH STEP?
GO CHECK IT OUT!
HUH!? BUT...
TMP タン…
TMP タン…
TMP タン
SPLASH ぱしゃ
You must never set foot on the fourth step.
...WA-TER?
Why? Because...

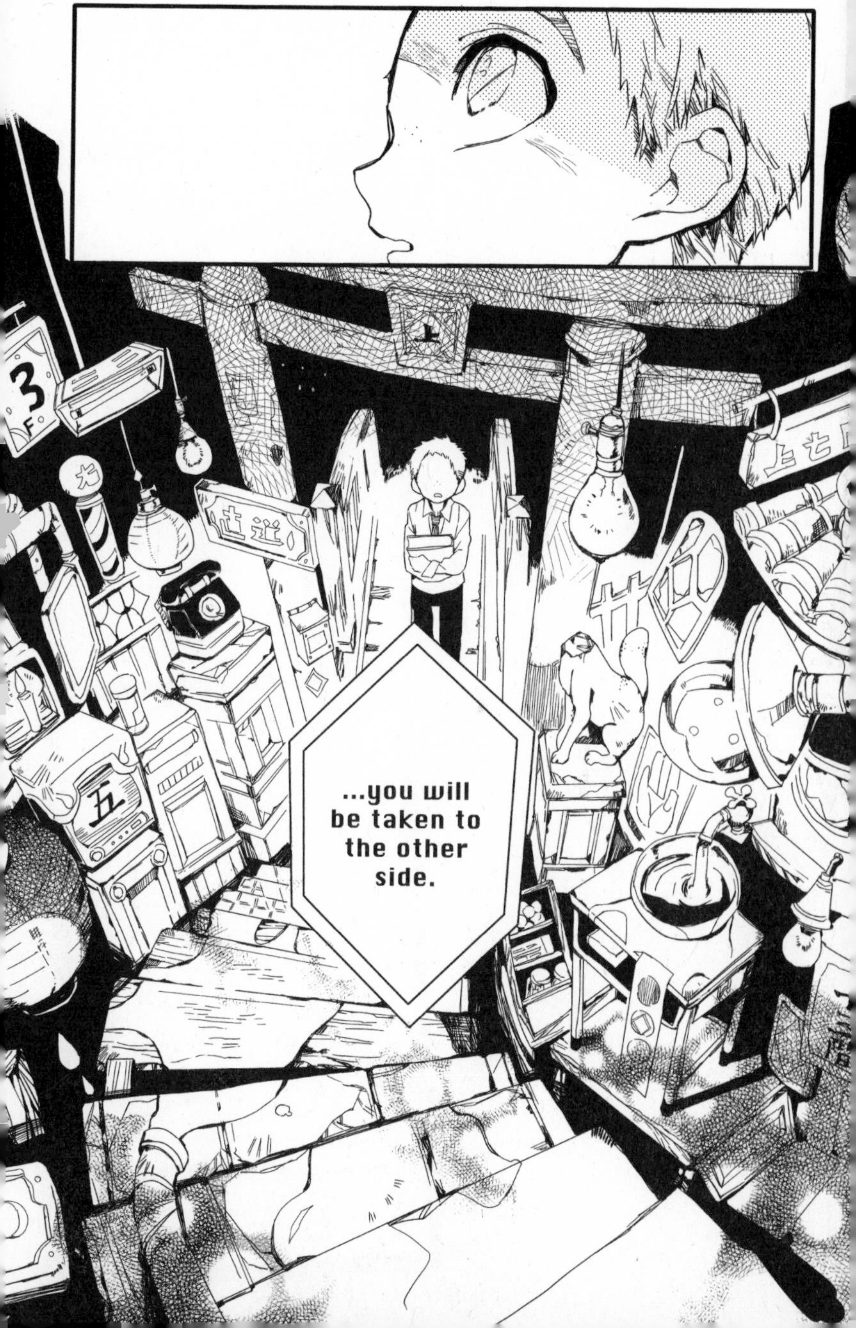
...you will be taken to the other side.

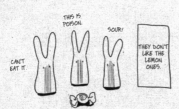

THEY DON'T LIKE THE LEMON ONES.
SOUR!
THIS IS POISON.
CAN'T EAT IT.

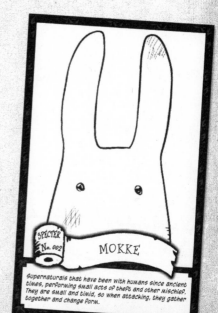

SPECTER No. 002
MOKKE
Supernaturals that have been with humans since ancient times, performing small acts of theft and other mischief. They are small and timid, so when attacking, they gather together and change form.

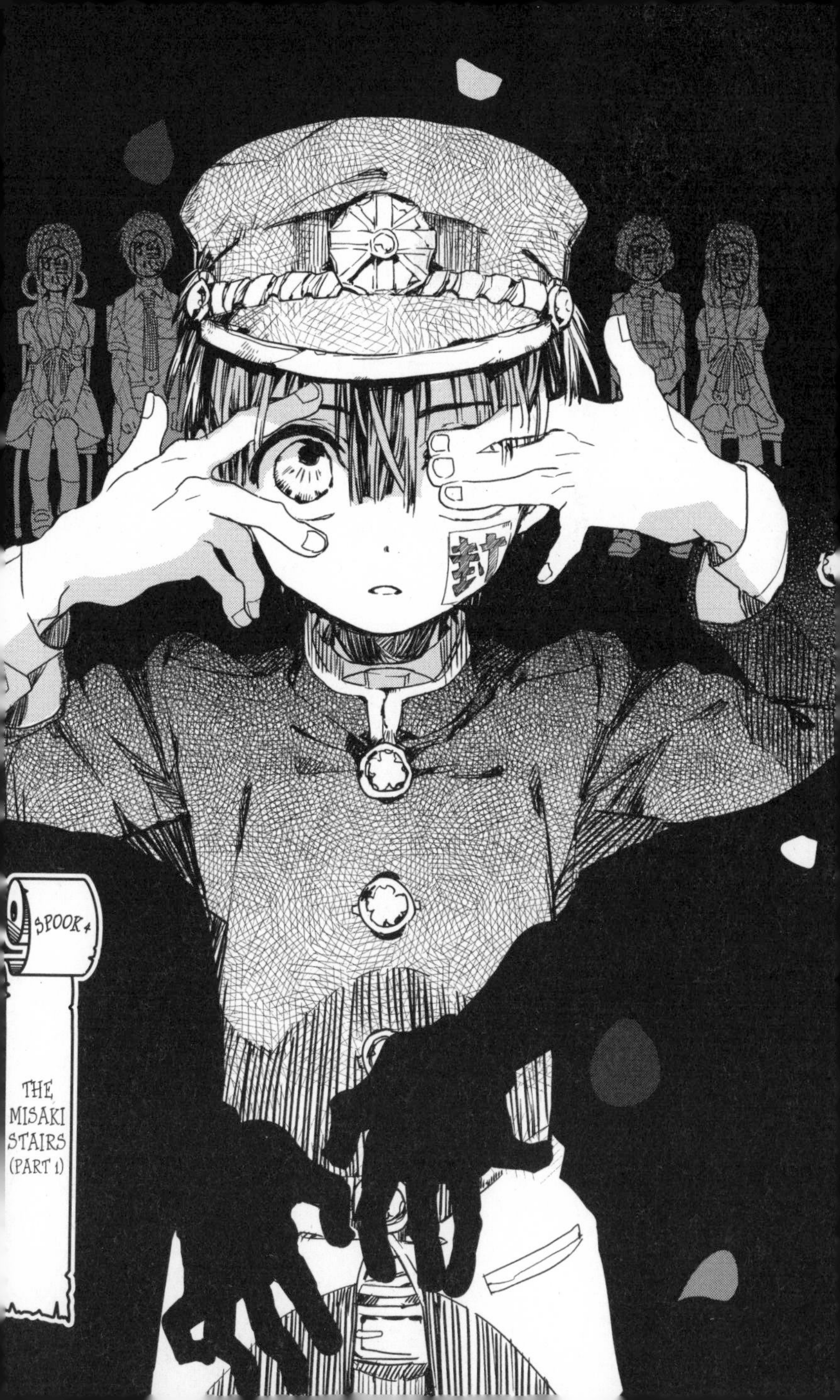
SPOOK 4
THE MISAKI STAIRS (PART 1)

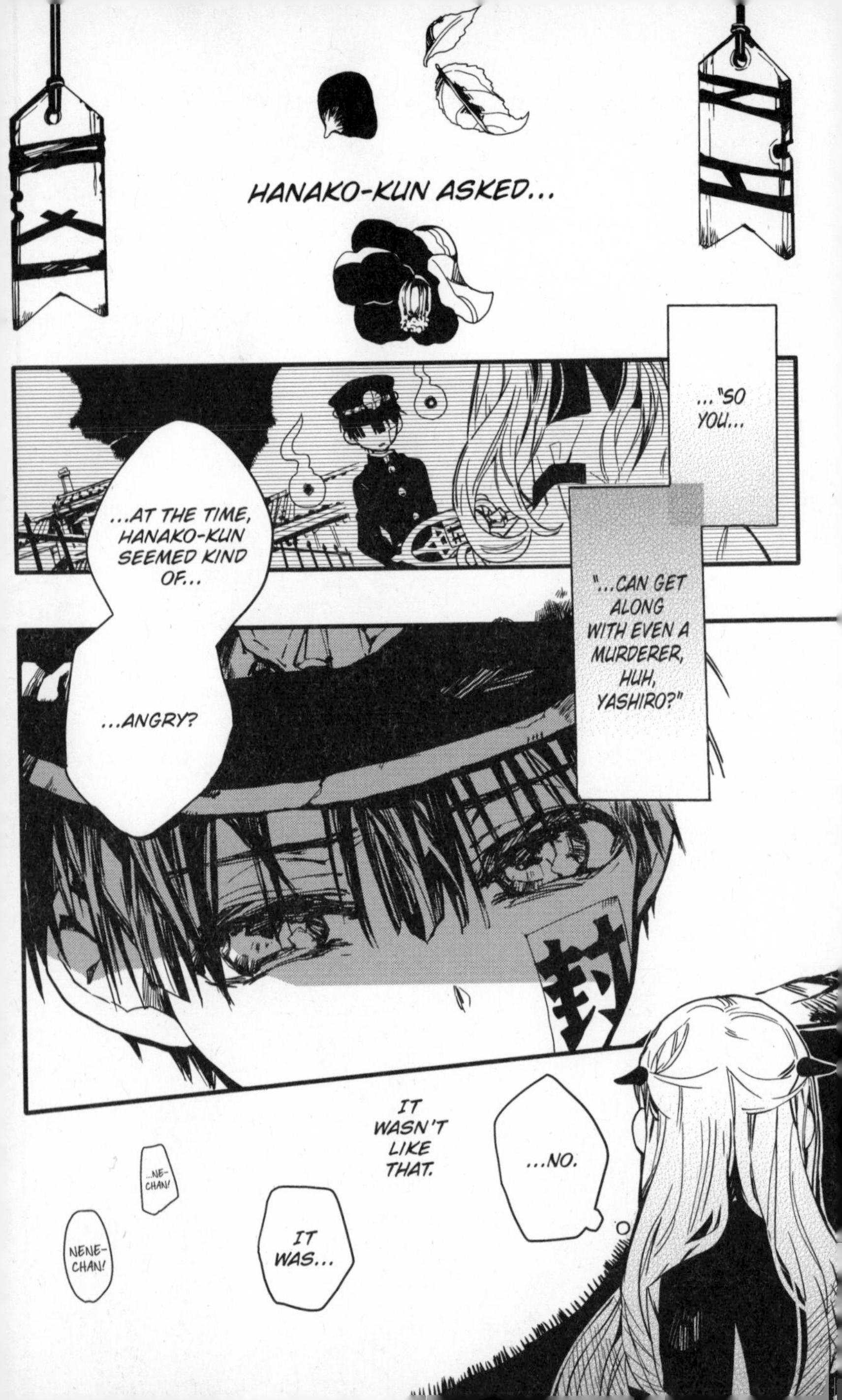
HANAKO-KUN ASKED...
..."SO YOU...
"...CAN GET ALONG WITH EVEN A MURDERER, HUH, YASHIRO?"
...AT THE TIME, HANAKO-KUN SEEMED KIND OF...
...ANGRY?
...NO.
IT WASN'T LIKE THAT.
IT WAS...
...NE-CHAN!
NENE-CHAN!

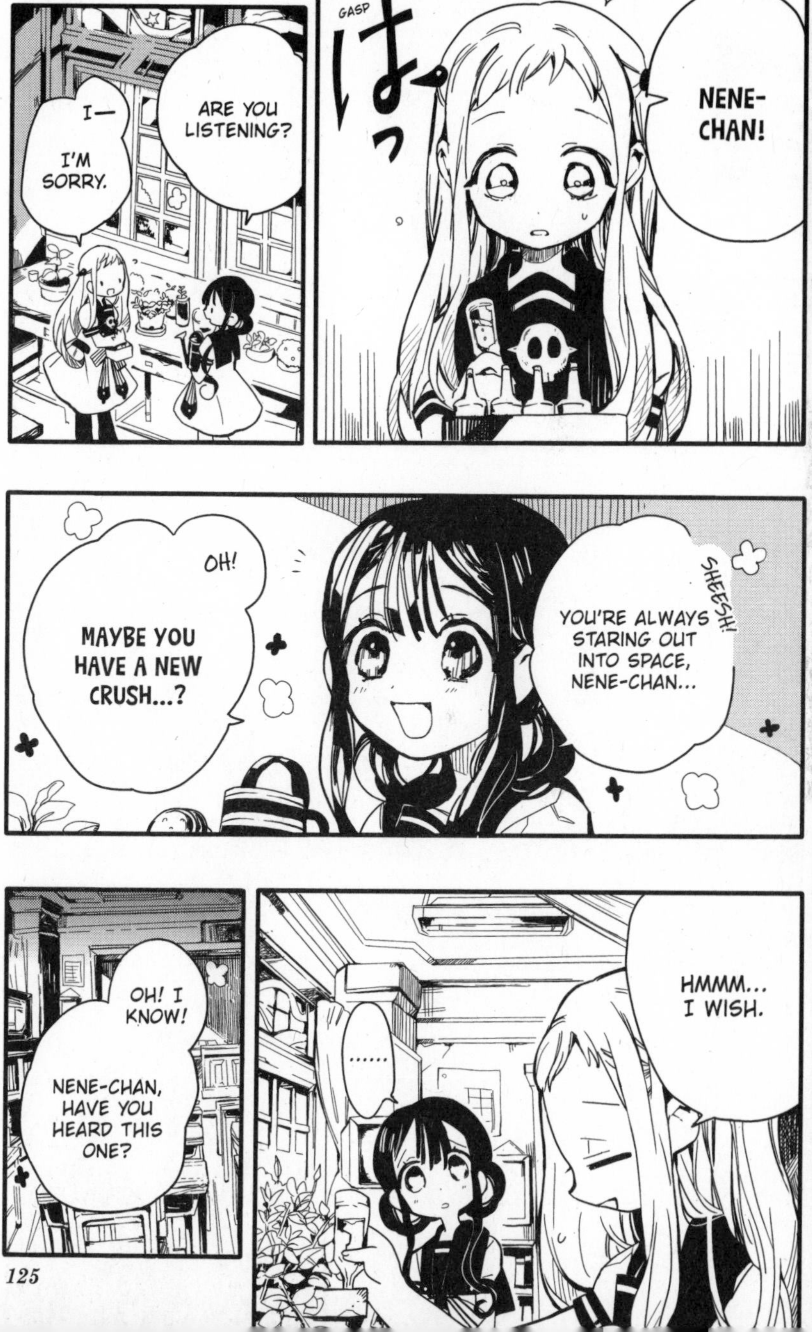

NENE-CHAN!
GASP
はっ
ARE YOU LISTENING?
I—
I'M SORRY.
SHEESH!
YOU'RE ALWAYS STARING OUT INTO SPACE, NENE-CHAN...
OH!
MAYBE YOU HAVE A NEW CRUSH...?
HMMM... I WISH.
......
OH! I KNOW!
NENE-CHAN, HAVE YOU HEARD THIS ONE?

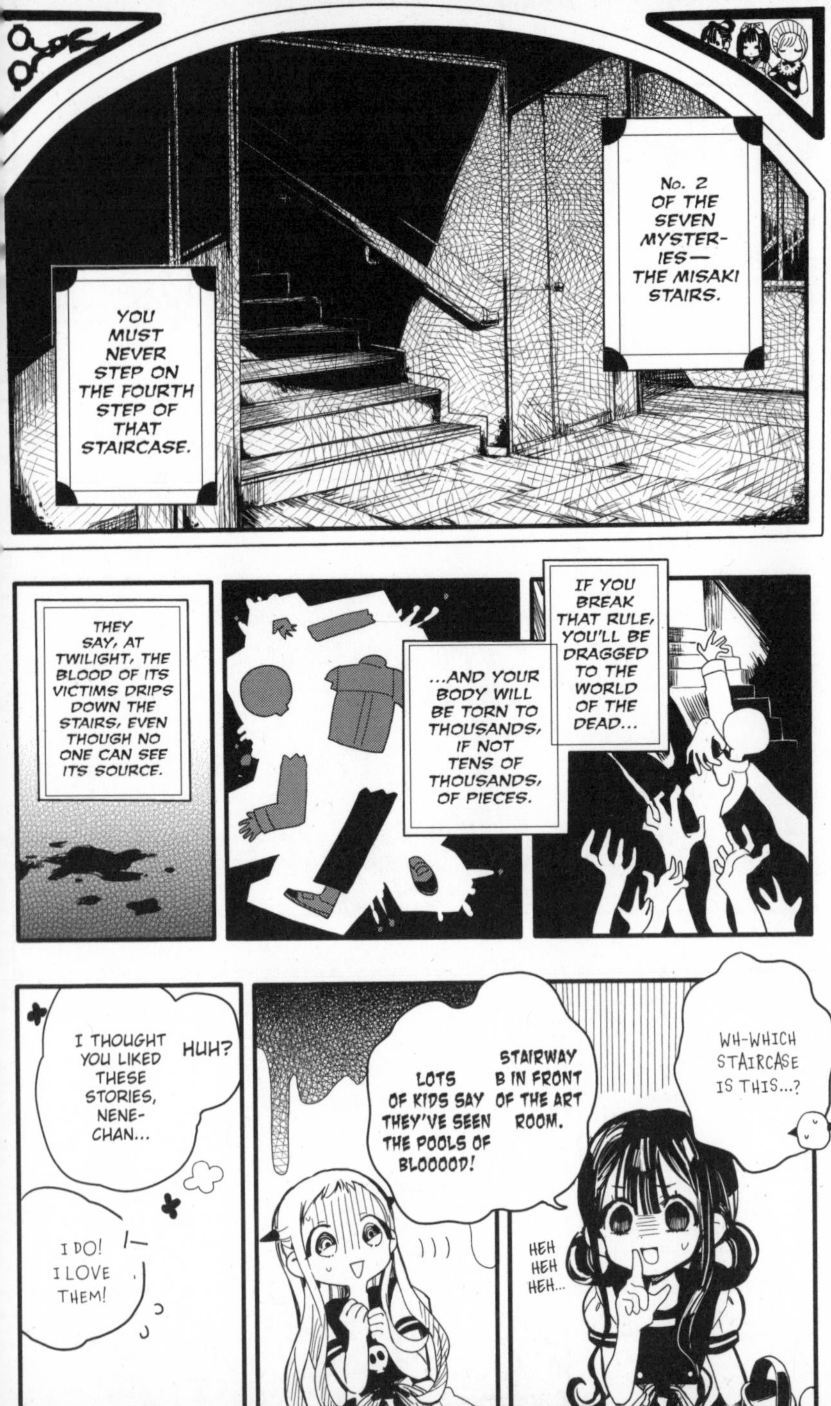

No. 2 OF THE SEVEN MYSTERIES—THE MISAKI STAIRS.
YOU MUST NEVER STEP ON THE FOURTH STEP OF THAT STAIRCASE.
IF YOU BREAK THAT RULE, YOU'LL BE DRAGGED TO THE WORLD OF THE DEAD...
...AND YOUR BODY WILL BE TORN TO THOUSANDS, IF NOT TENS OF THOUSANDS, OF PIECES.
THEY SAY, AT TWILIGHT, THE BLOOD OF ITS VICTIMS DRIPS DOWN THE STAIRS, EVEN THOUGH NO ONE CAN SEE ITS SOURCE.
WH-WHICH STAIRCASE IS THIS...?
HEH HEH HEH...
STAIRWAY B IN FRONT OF THE ART ROOM.
LOTS OF KIDS SAY THEY'VE SEEN THE POOLS OF BLOOOOD!
HUH?
I THOUGHT YOU LIKED THESE STORIES, NENE-CHAN...
I—
I DO! I LOVE THEM!

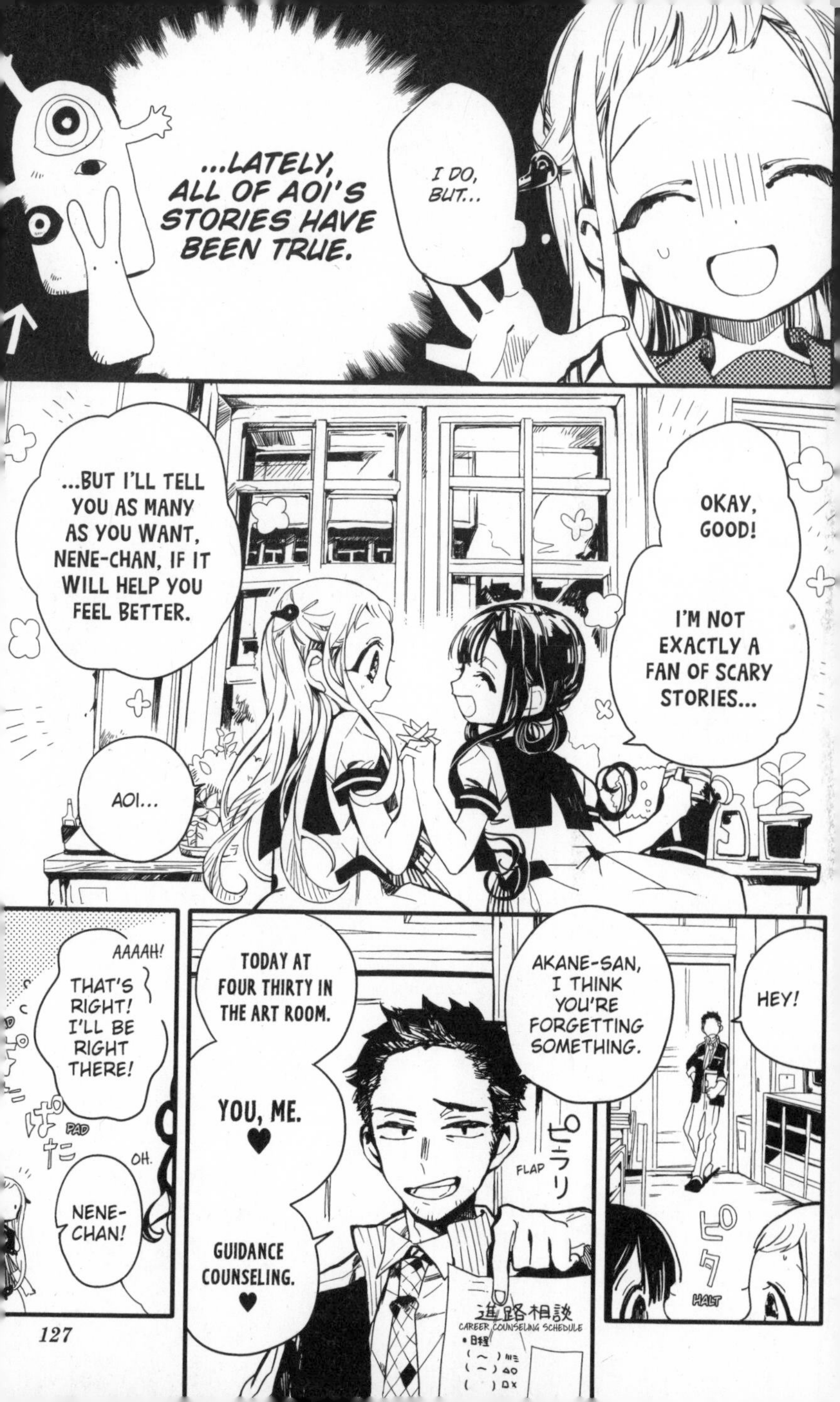
I DO, BUT...
...LATELY, ALL OF AOI'S STORIES HAVE BEEN TRUE.
OKAY, GOOD!
I'M NOT EXACTLY A FAN OF SCARY STORIES...
...BUT I'LL TELL YOU AS MANY AS YOU WANT, NENE-CHAN, IF IT WILL HELP YOU FEEL BETTER.
AOI...
HEY!
ピタ
HALT
AKANE-SAN, I THINK YOU'RE FORGETTING SOMETHING.
ピラリ
FLAP
TODAY AT FOUR THIRTY IN THE ART ROOM.
YOU, ME. ♥
GUIDANCE COUNSELING. ♥
進路相談
CAREER COUNSELING SCHEDULE
AAAAH!
THAT'S RIGHT! I'LL BE RIGHT THERE!
PAD
OH.
NENE-CHAN!

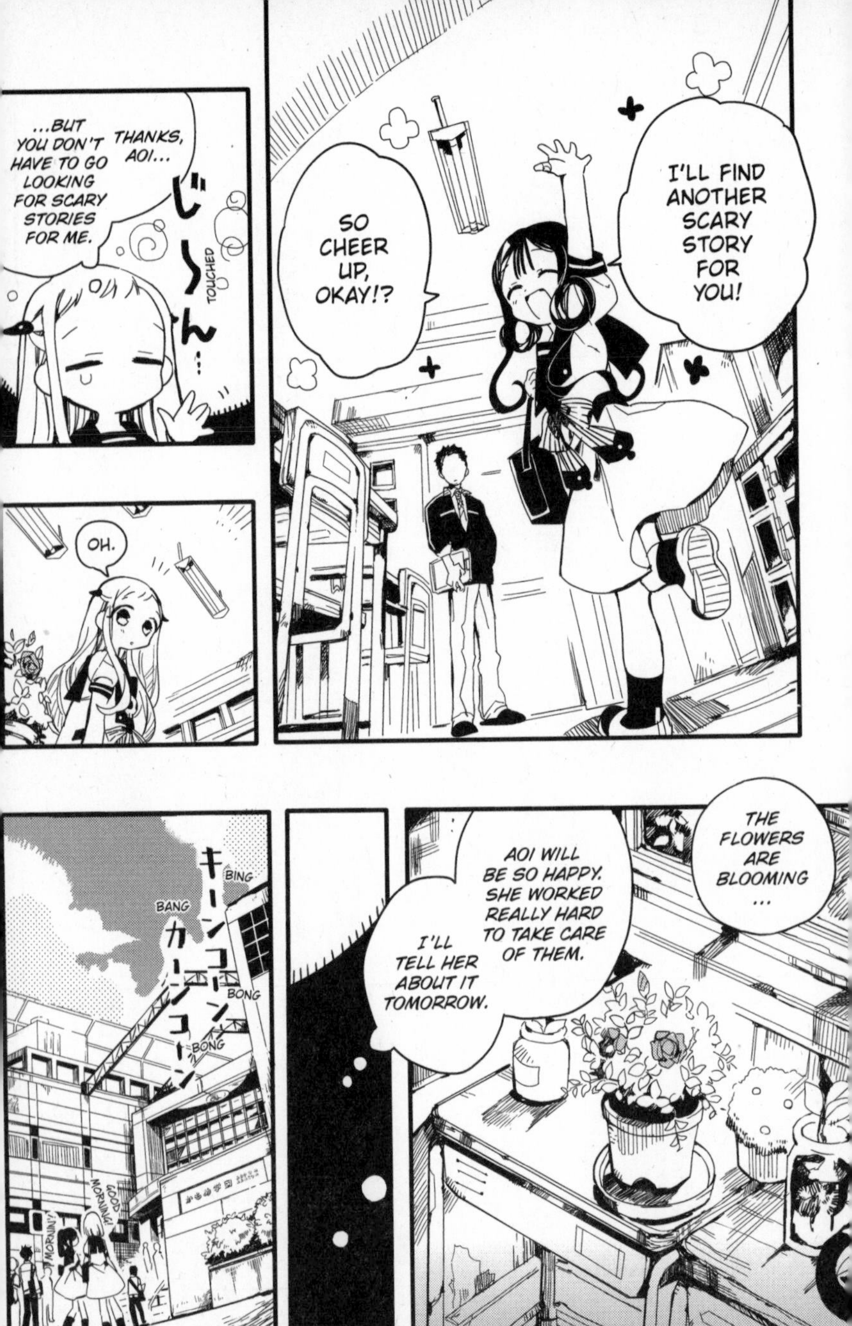
I'LL FIND ANOTHER SCARY STORY FOR YOU!
SO CHEER UP, OKAY!?
THANKS, AOI...
...BUT YOU DON'T HAVE TO GO LOOKING FOR SCARY STORIES FOR ME.
じ～ん…
TOUCHED
OH.
THE FLOWERS ARE BLOOMING...
AOI WILL BE SO HAPPY. SHE WORKED REALLY HARD TO TAKE CARE OF THEM.
I'LL TELL HER ABOUT IT TOMORROW.
キーンコーン
BING
BONG
カーンコーン
BANG
BONG
GOOD MORNING!
MORNIN'!
SIGN: KAMOME ACADEMY

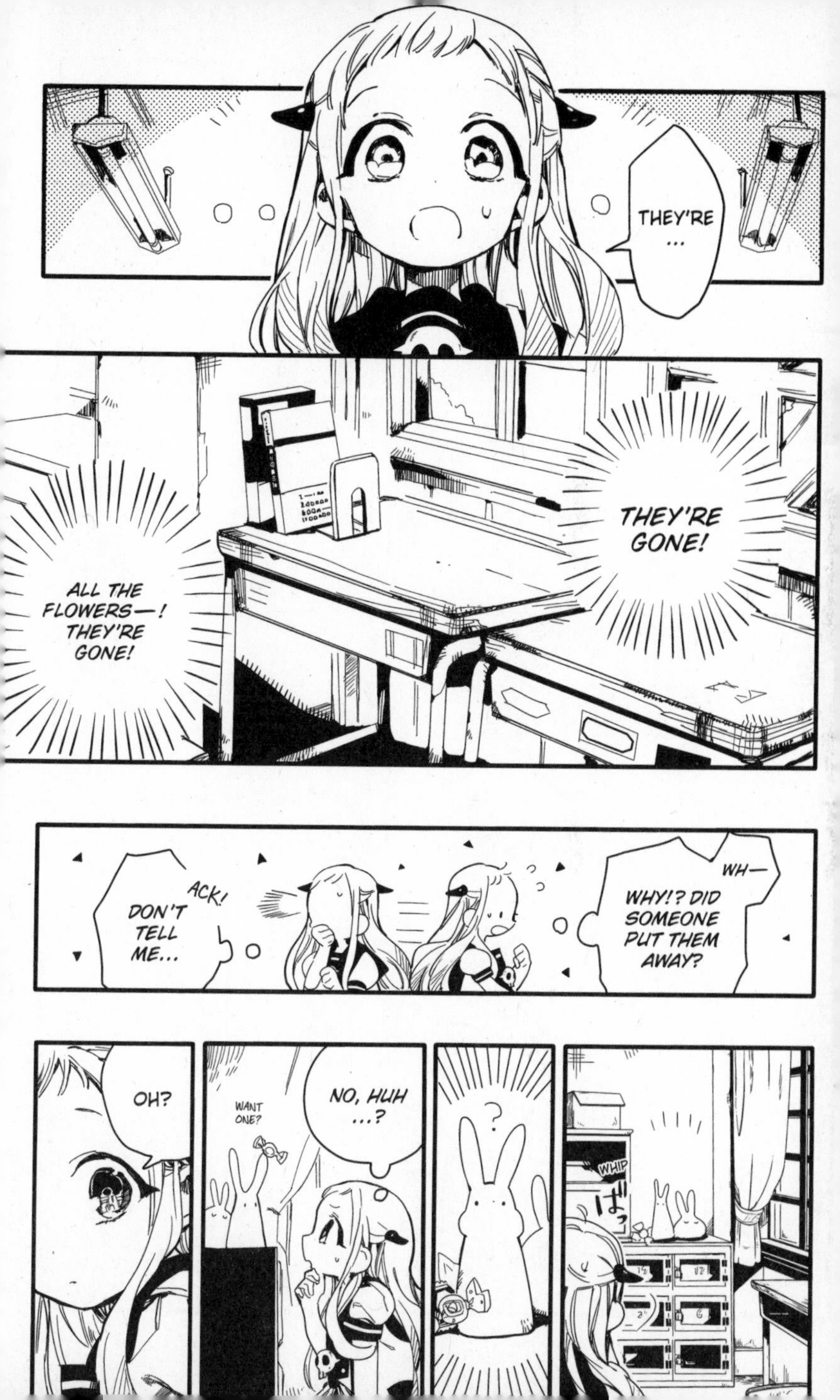
THEY'RE ...
THEY'RE GONE!
ALL THE FLOWERS—! THEY'RE GONE!
WH— WHY!? DID SOMEONE PUT THEM AWAY?
ACK! DON'T TELL ME...
WHIP
ばっ
?
NO, HUH ...?
WANT ONE?
OH?

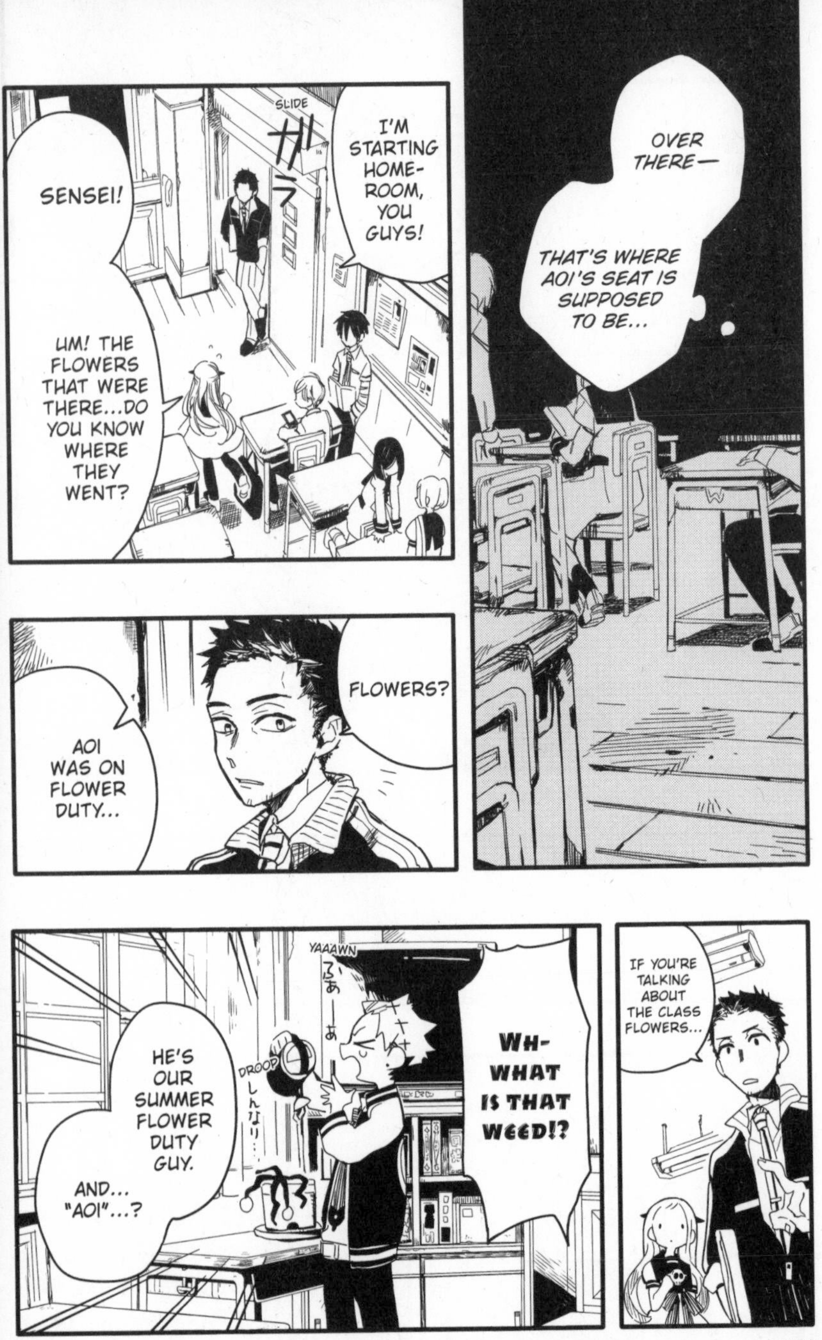
OVER THERE—
THAT'S WHERE AOI'S SEAT IS SUPPOSED TO BE...
SLIDE
ガラ
I'M STARTING HOME-ROOM, YOU GUYS!
SENSEI!
UM! THE FLOWERS THAT WERE THERE...DO YOU KNOW WHERE THEY WENT?
FLOWERS?
AOI WAS ON FLOWER DUTY...
IF YOU'RE TALKING ABOUT THE CLASS FLOWERS...
WH-WHAT IS THAT WEED!?
YAAAWN
ふあーあ
DROOP
しんなり…
HE'S OUR SUMMER FLOWER DUTY GUY.
AND... "AOI"...?

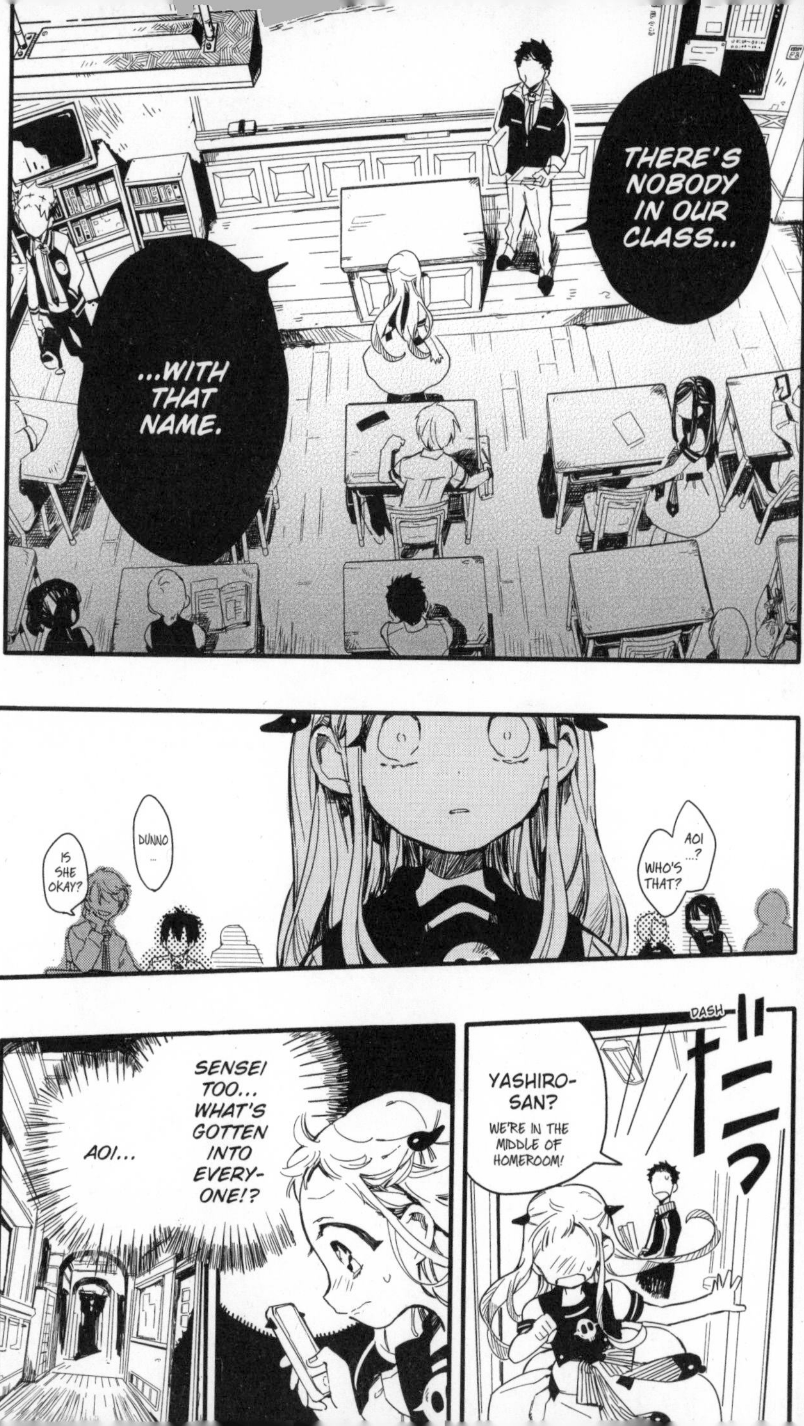
THERE'S NOBODY IN OUR CLASS...
...WITH THAT NAME.
AOI ...? WHO'S THAT?
DUNNO ...
IS SHE OKAY?
DASH
YASHIRO-SAN?
WE'RE IN THE MIDDLE OF HOMEROOM!
SENSEI TOO... WHAT'S GOTTEN INTO EVERY-ONE!?
AOI...

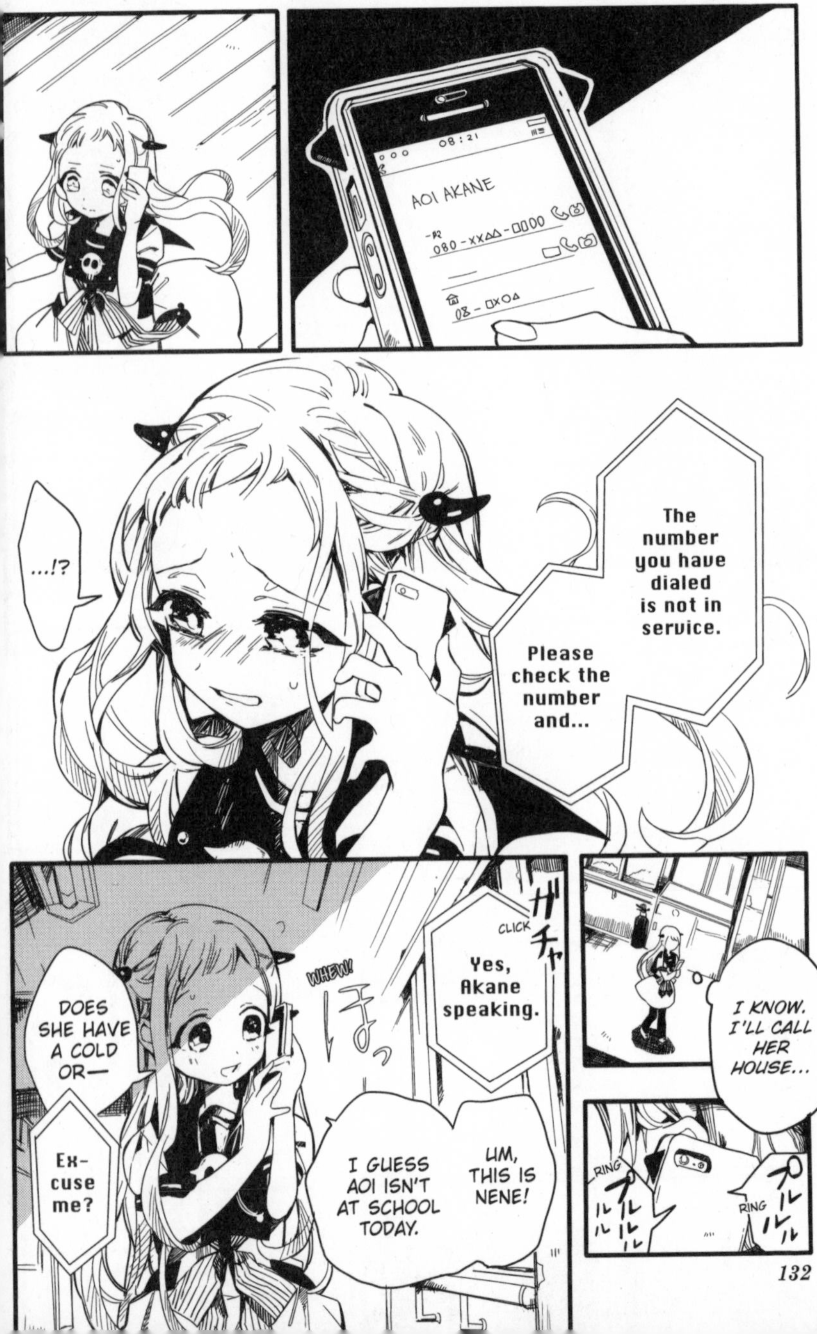

08:21
AOI AKANE
080-XX△△-□□00
08-□X○△
The number you have dialed is not in service.
Please check the number and...
...!?
I KNOW. I'LL CALL HER HOUSE...
RING
プルルル
RING
プルルル
CLICK
ガチャ
Yes, Akane speaking.
WHEW!
ほっ
UM, THIS IS NENE!
I GUESS AOI ISN'T AT SCHOOL TODAY.
DOES SHE HAVE A COLD OR—
Ex-cuse me?

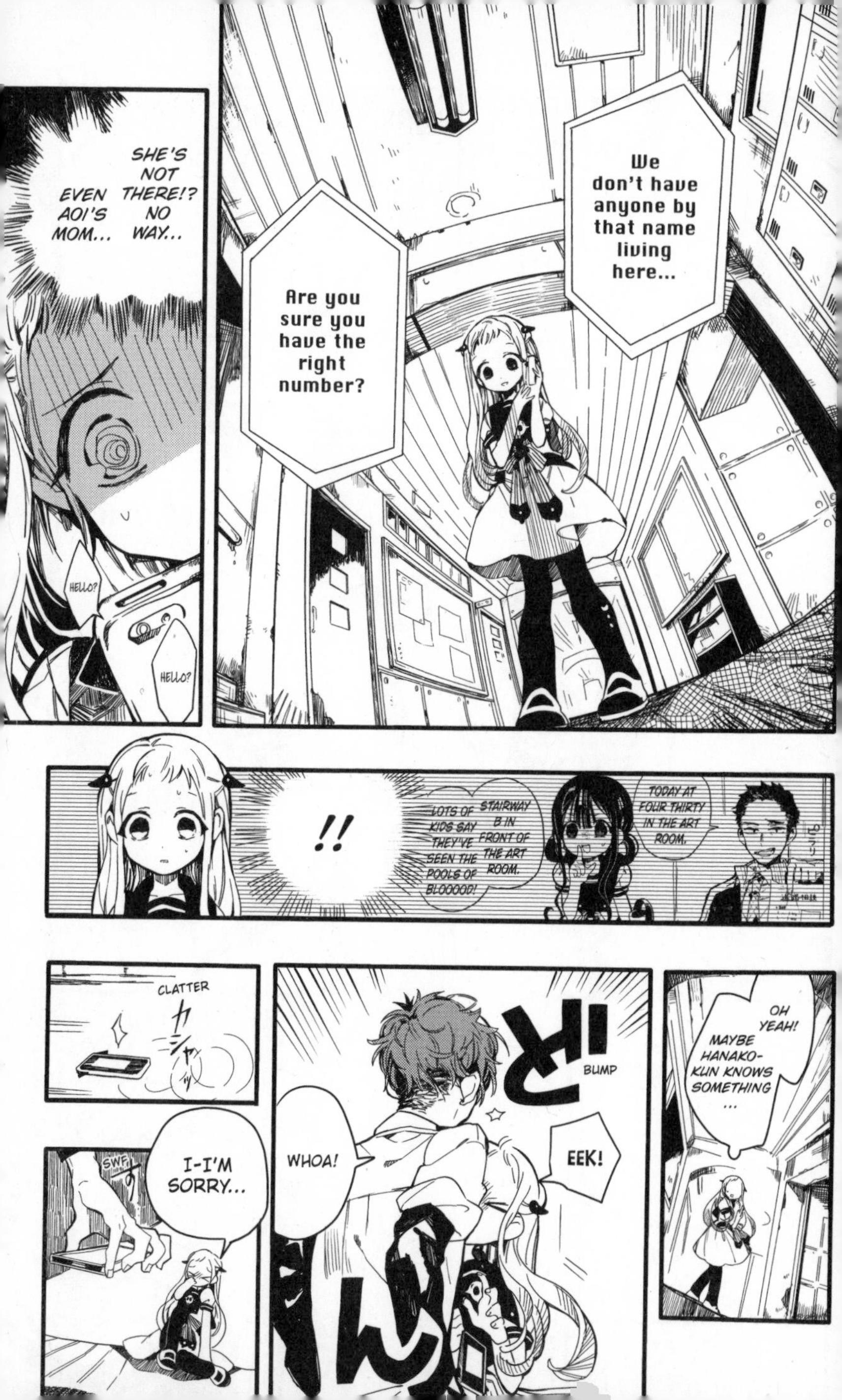
We don't have anyone by that name living here...
Are you sure you have the right number?
SHE'S NOT THERE!? NO WAY...
EVEN AOI'S MOM...
HELLO?
HELLO?
TODAY AT FOUR THIRTY IN THE ART ROOM.
STAIRWAY B IN FRONT OF THE ART ROOM.
LOTS OF KIDS SAY THEY'VE SEEN THE POOLS OF BLOOOOOD!
!!
OH YEAH! MAYBE HANAKO-KUN KNOWS SOMETHING...
BUMP
EEK!
WHOA!
CLATTER
SWF
I-I'M SORRY...

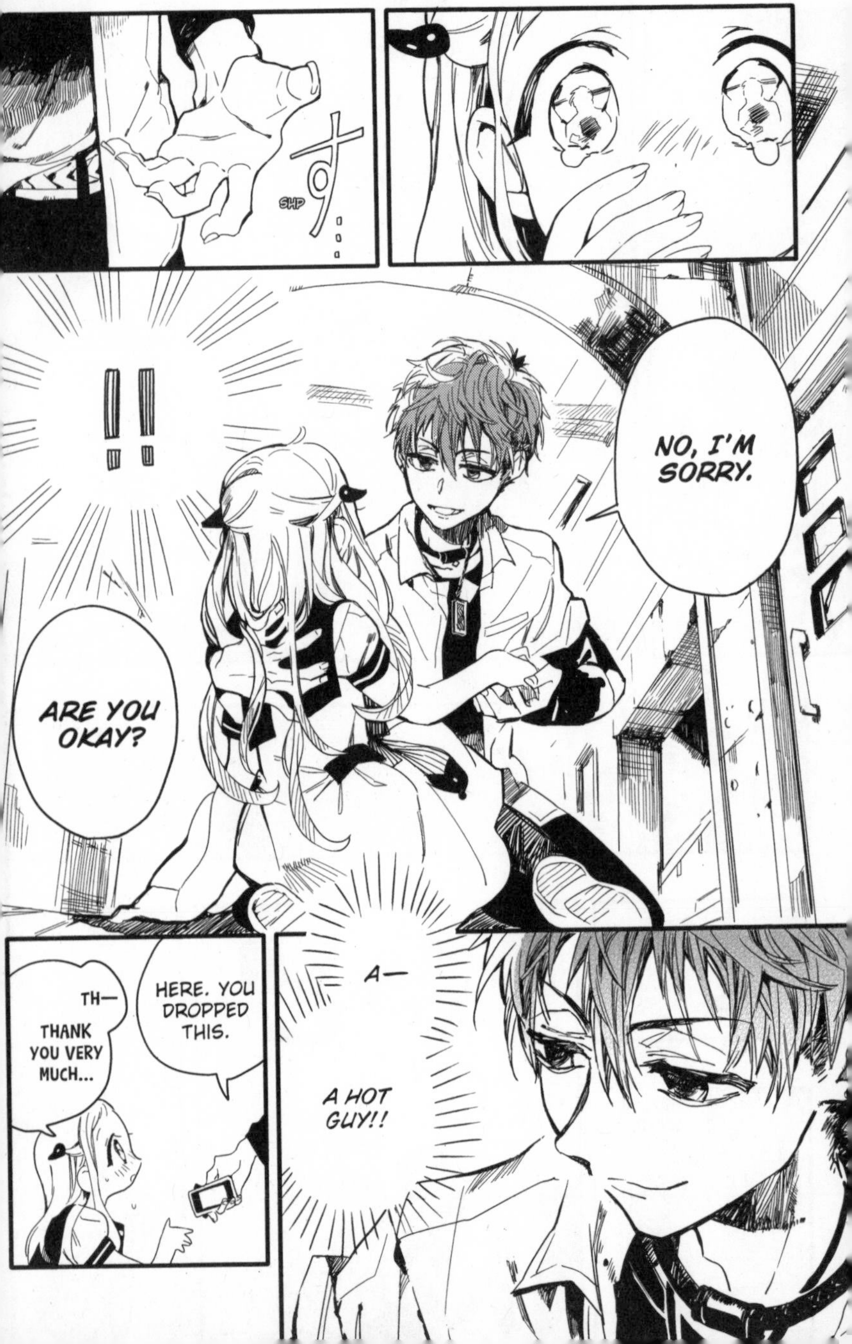
す
SHP
NO, I'M SORRY.
!!
ARE YOU OKAY?
A—
A HOT GUY!!
HERE. YOU DROPPED THIS.
TH—
THANK YOU VERY MUCH...

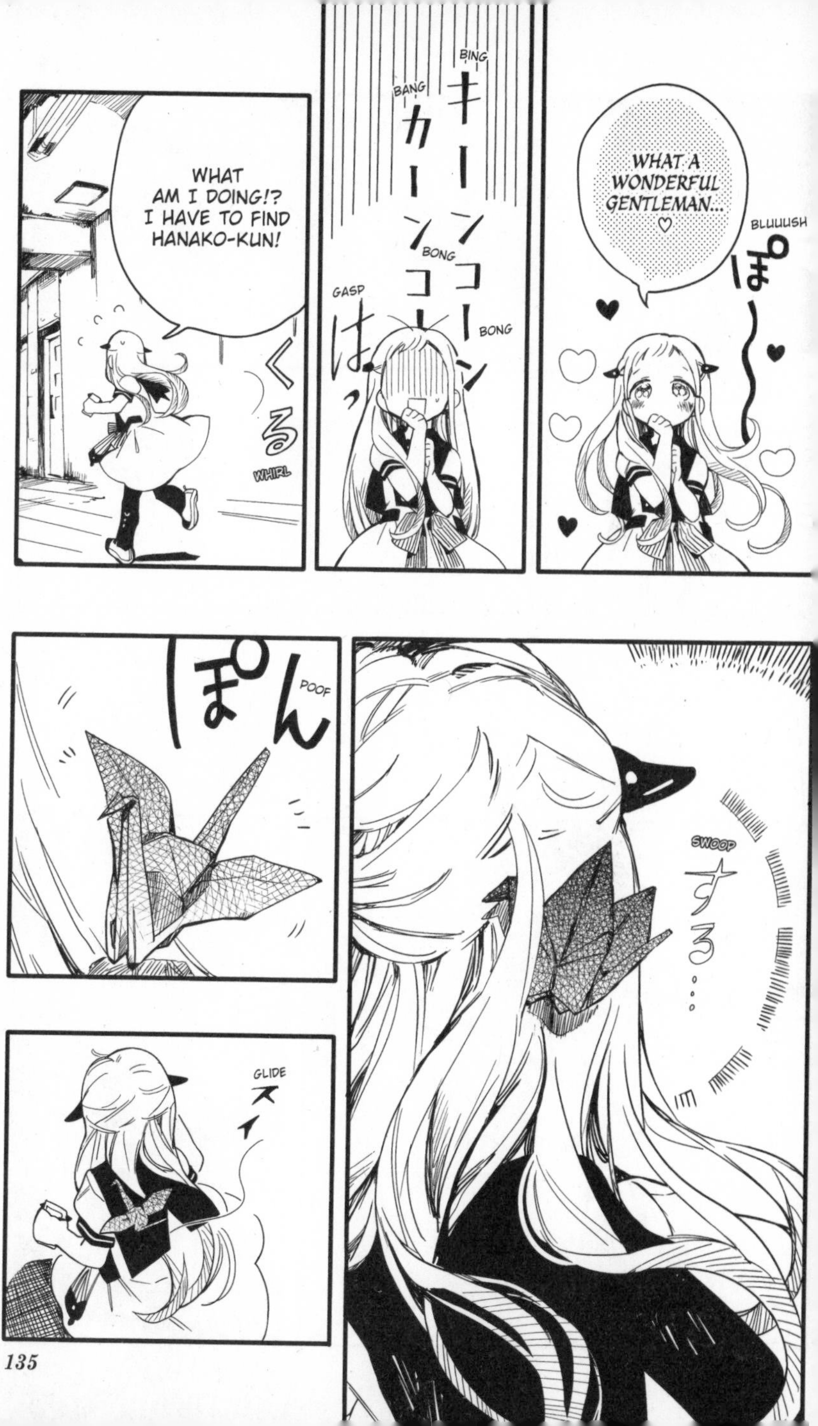

WHAT A WONDERFUL GENTLEMAN... ♡
BLUUUSH
ぽ〜
BING
BANG
キーンコーンカーンコーン
BONG
BONG
GASP
はっ
WHAT AM I DOING!? I HAVE TO FIND HANAKO-KUN!
くる
WHIRL
SWOOP
する…
ぽん
POOF
GLIDE
スイ

ス
SWF
カ
CAW
カ
CAW
SHE'S VANISHED?
GIRLS' TOILET
女子便所
清掃中

SIGN: CLEANING IN PROGRESS

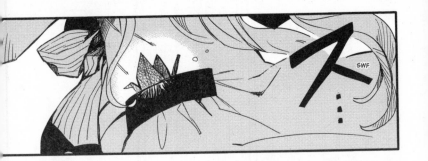

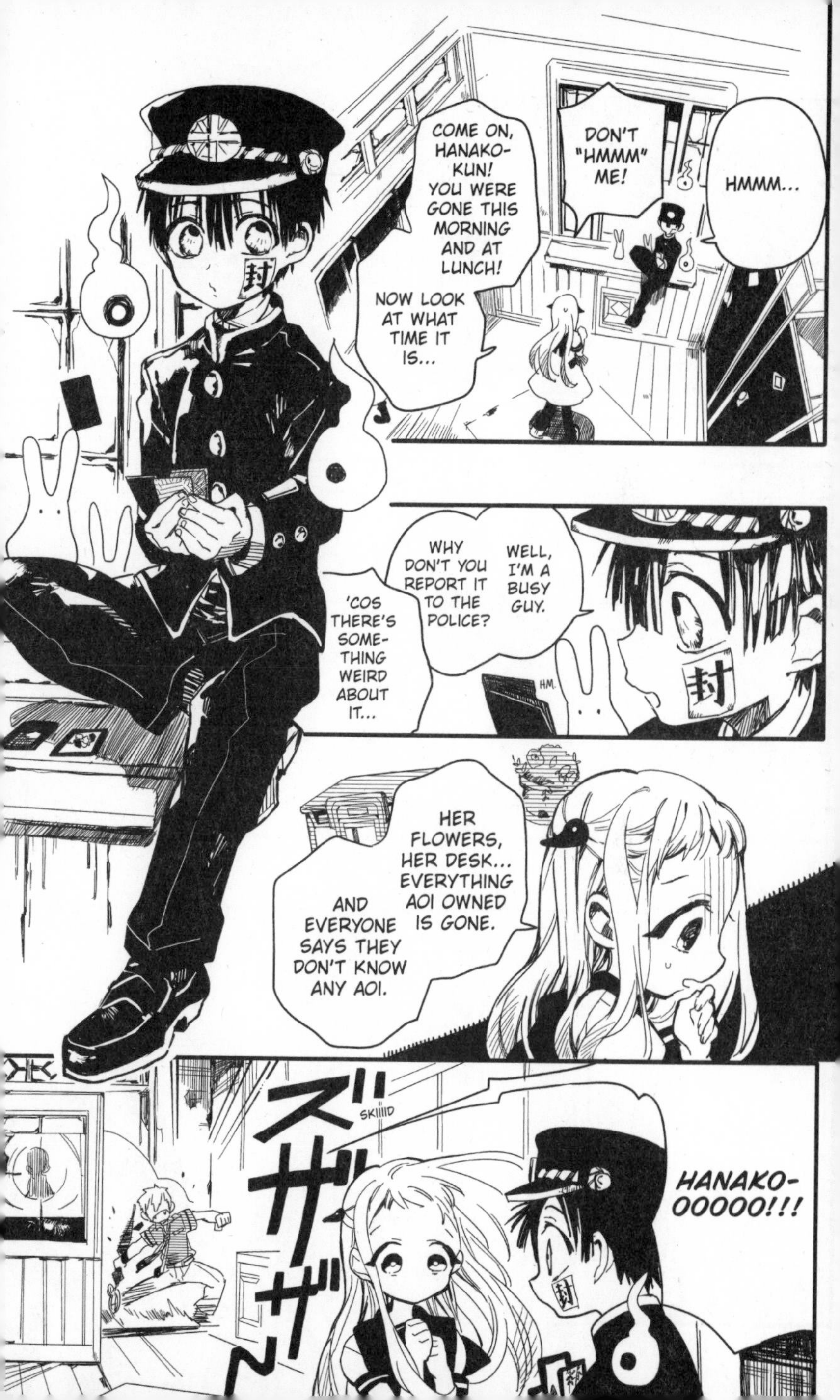
HMMM...
DON'T "HMMM" ME!
COME ON, HANAKO-KUN! YOU WERE GONE THIS MORNING AND AT LUNCH!
NOW LOOK AT WHAT TIME IT IS...
WELL, I'M A BUSY GUY.
HM.
WHY DON'T YOU REPORT IT TO THE POLICE?
'COS THERE'S SOME-THING WEIRD ABOUT IT...
HER FLOWERS, HER DESK... EVERYTHING AOI OWNED IS GONE.
AND EVERYONE SAYS THEY DON'T KNOW ANY AOI.
HANAKO-OOOOO!!!
ズザザ
SKIIIID

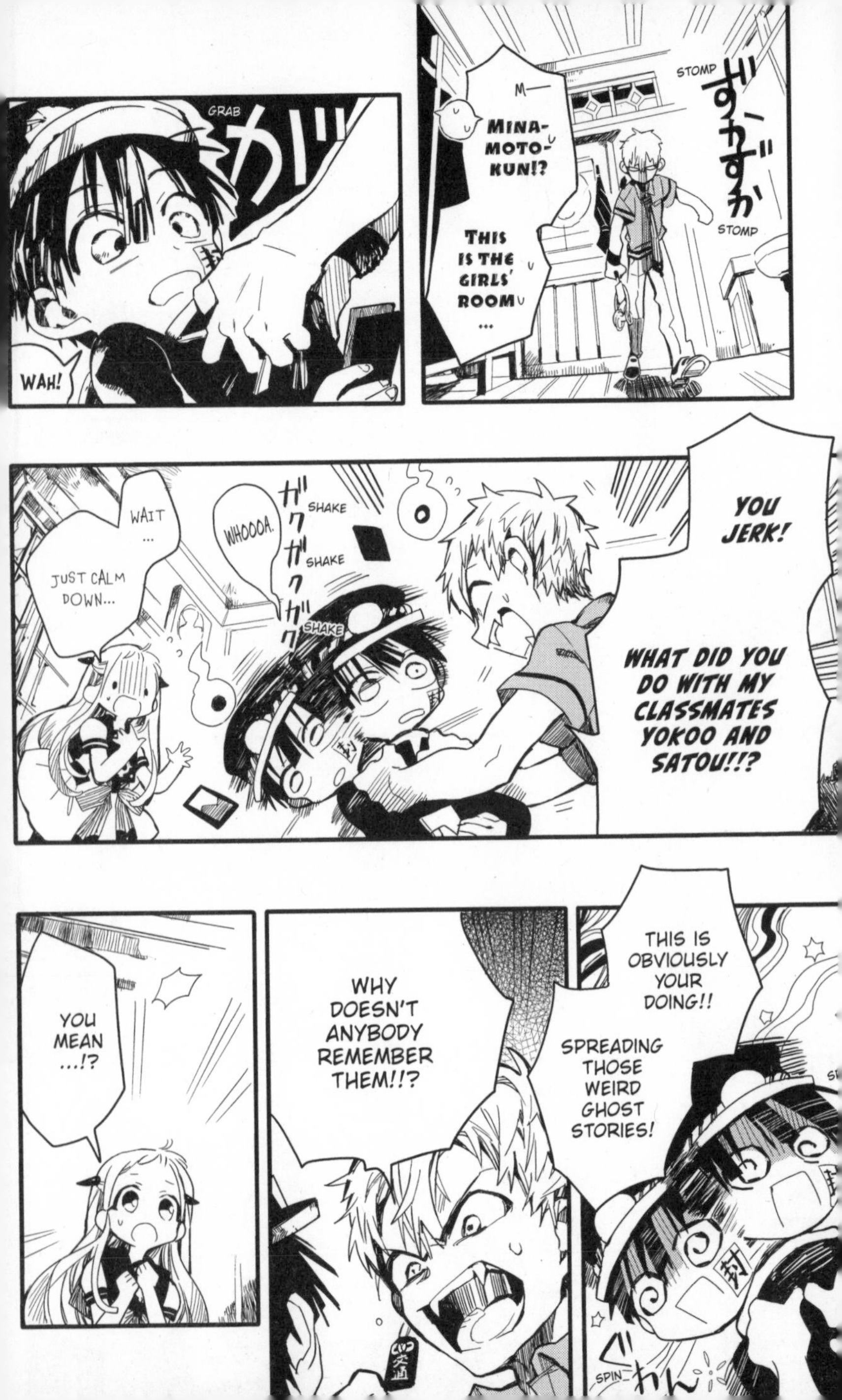
M—
MINA-MOTO-KUN!?
THIS IS THE GIRLS' ROOM ...
STOMP
ずかずか
STOMP
GRAB
ガッ
WAH!
YOU JERK!
WHAT DID YOU DO WITH MY CLASSMATES YOKOO AND SATOU!!?
ガクガクガク
SHAKE
SHAKE
SHAKE
WHOOOA.
WAIT ...
JUST CALM DOWN...
THIS IS OBVIOUSLY YOUR DOING!!
SPREADING THOSE WEIRD GHOST STORIES!
SPIN
ぐわん
WHY DOESN'T ANYBODY REMEMBER THEM!!?
YOU MEAN ...!?

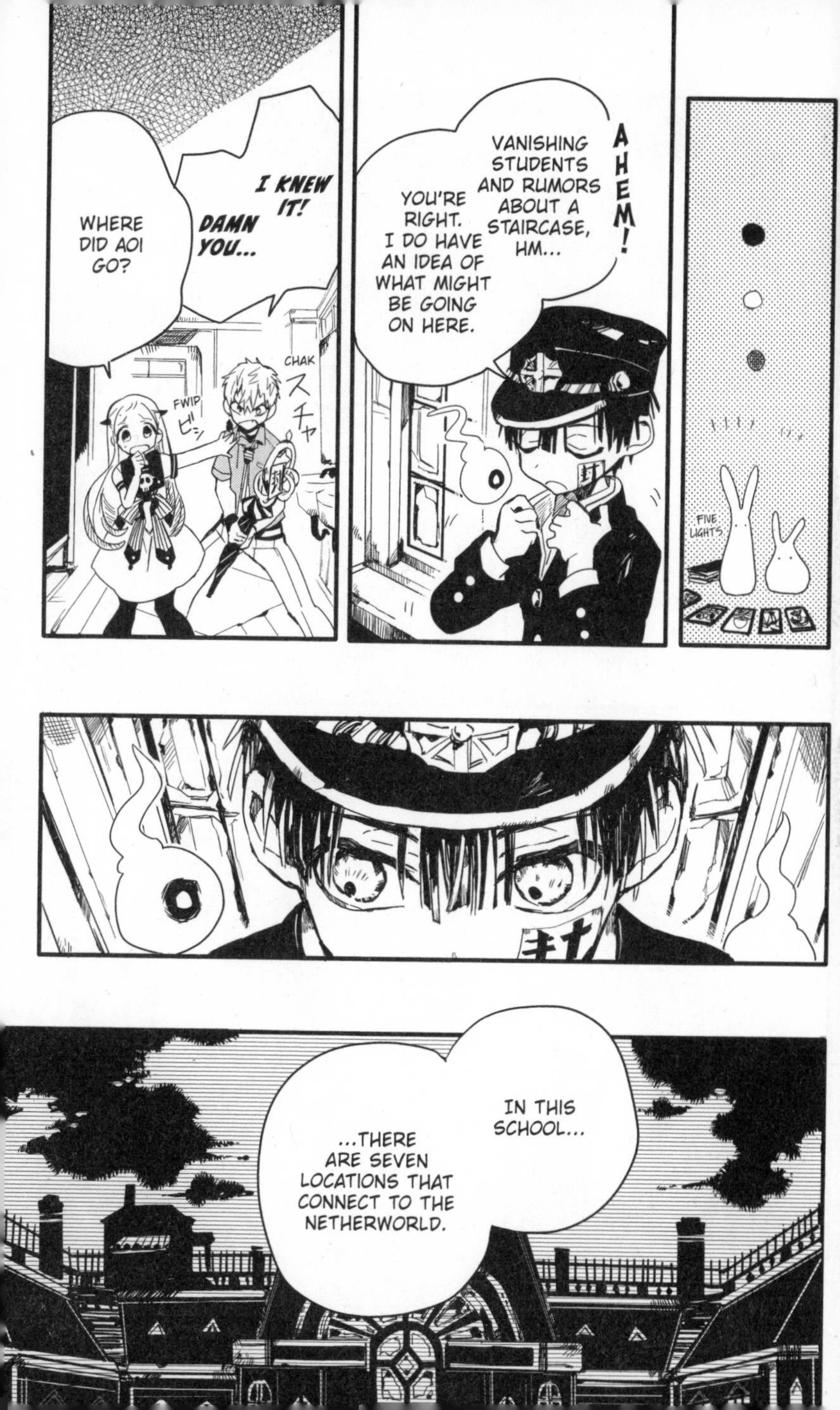
FIVE LIGHTS
AHEM!
VANISHING STUDENTS AND RUMORS ABOUT A STAIRCASE, HM...
YOU'RE RIGHT. I DO HAVE AN IDEA OF WHAT MIGHT BE GOING ON HERE.
DAMN YOU... I KNEW IT!
WHERE DID AOI GO?
CHAK
スチャ
FWIP
ビシッ
IN THIS SCHOOL...
...THERE ARE SEVEN LOCATIONS THAT CONNECT TO THE NETHERWORLD.

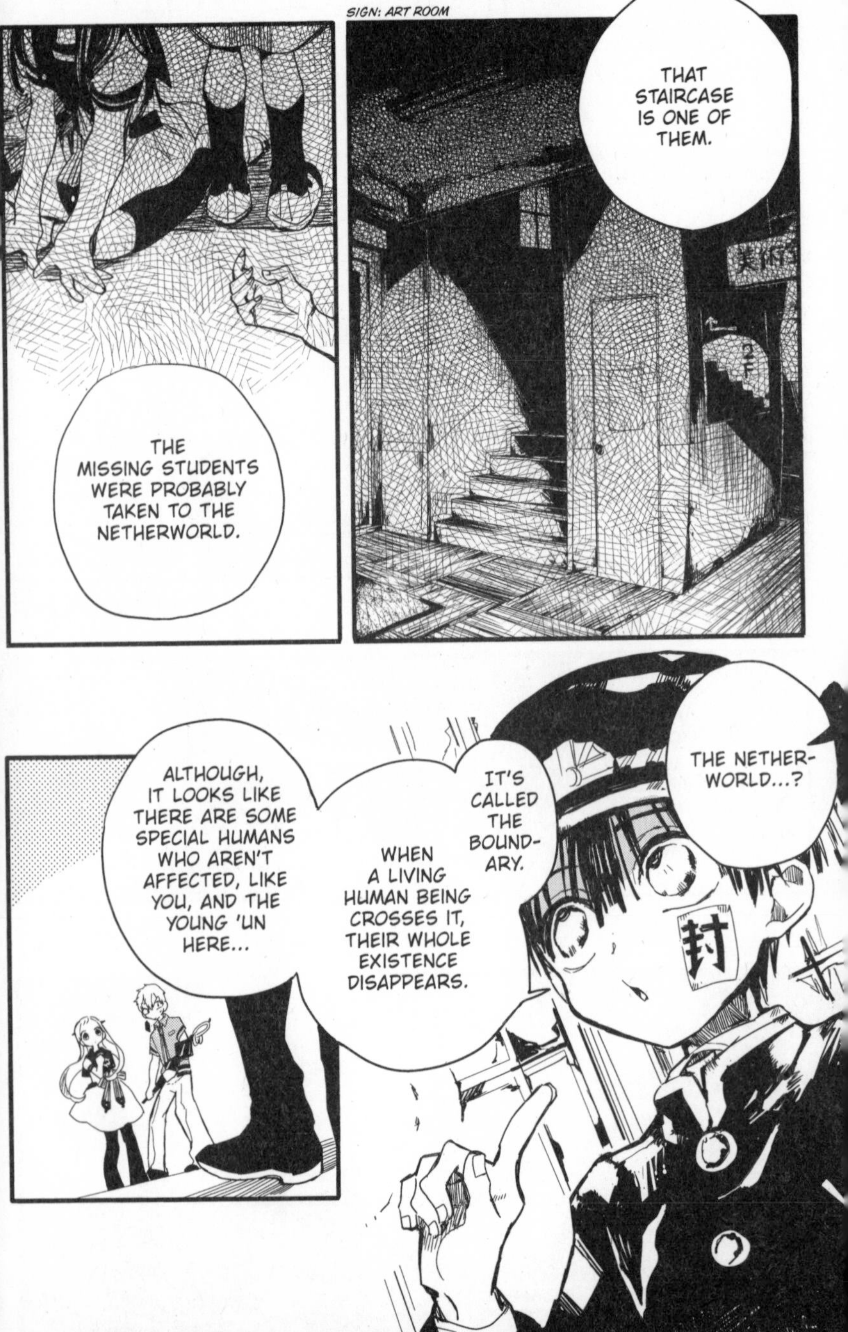
SIGN: ART ROOM
THAT STAIRCASE IS ONE OF THEM.
THE MISSING STUDENTS WERE PROBABLY TAKEN TO THE NETHERWORLD.
THE NETHER-WORLD...?
IT'S CALLED THE BOUND-ARY.
WHEN A LIVING HUMAN BEING CROSSES IT, THEIR WHOLE EXISTENCE DISAPPEARS.
ALTHOUGH, IT LOOKS LIKE THERE ARE SOME SPECIAL HUMANS WHO AREN'T AFFECTED, LIKE YOU, AND THE YOUNG 'UN HERE...

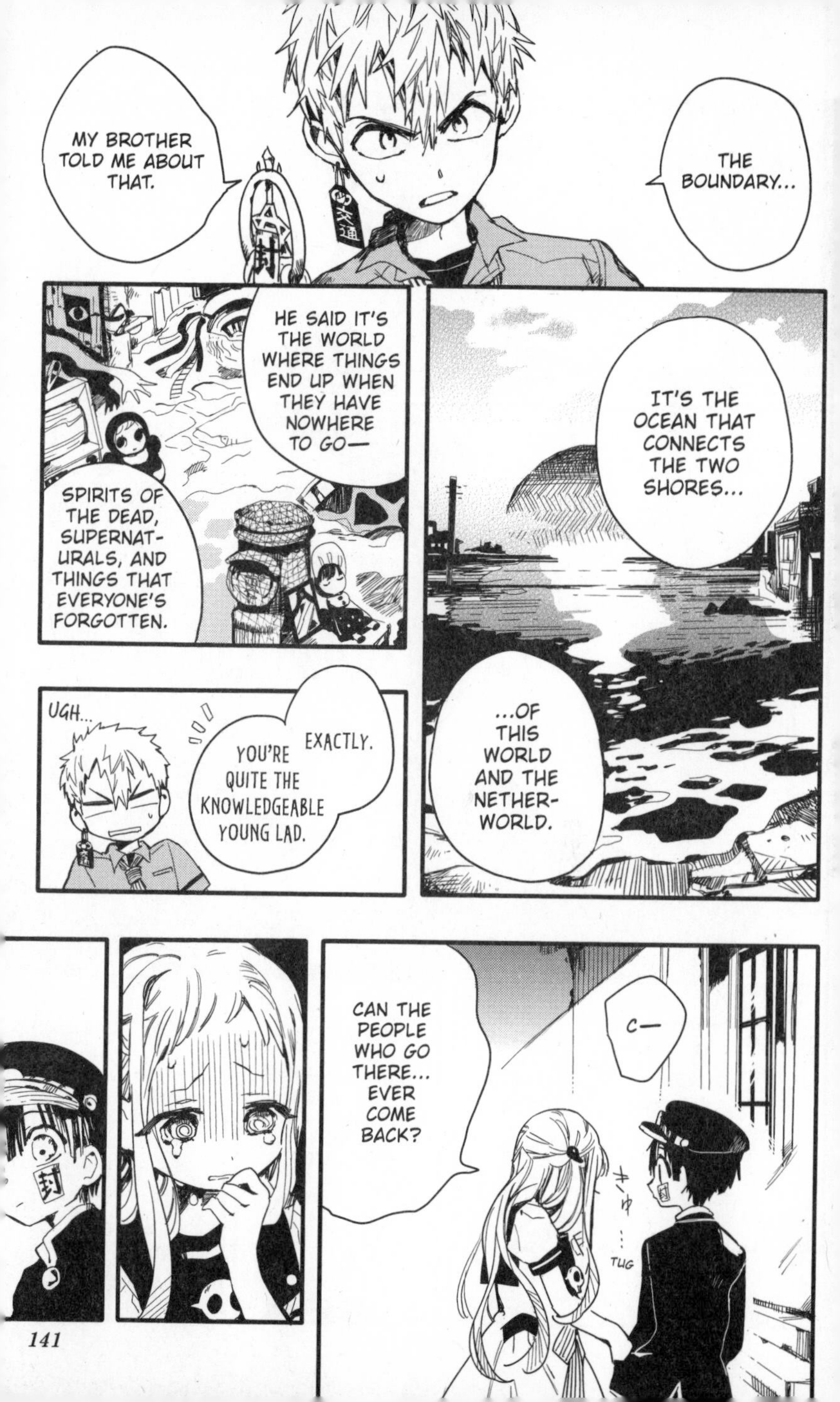

THE BOUNDARY...
MY BROTHER TOLD ME ABOUT THAT.
IT'S THE OCEAN THAT CONNECTS THE TWO SHORES...
...OF THIS WORLD AND THE NETHER-WORLD.
HE SAID IT'S THE WORLD WHERE THINGS END UP WHEN THEY HAVE NOWHERE TO GO—
SPIRITS OF THE DEAD, SUPERNAT-URALS, AND THINGS THAT EVERYONE'S FORGOTTEN.
EXACTLY.
YOU'RE QUITE THE KNOWLEDGEABLE YOUNG LAD.
UGH...
C—
CAN THE PEOPLE WHO GO THERE... EVER COME BACK?
キュ…
TUG

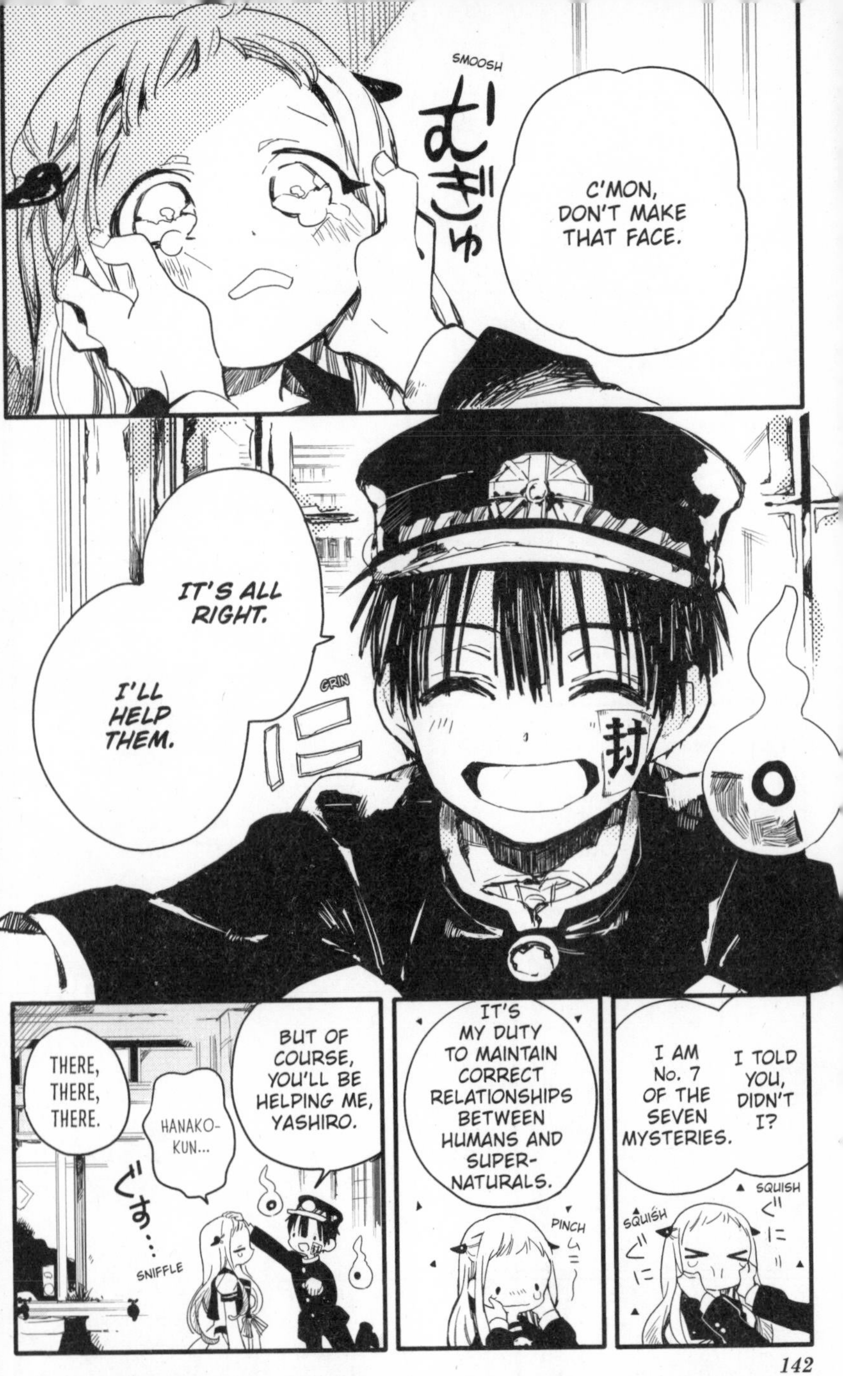

C'MON, DON'T MAKE THAT FACE.
SMOOSH
むぎゅ
IT'S ALL RIGHT.
I'LL HELP THEM.
GRIN
ニ
I TOLD YOU, DIDN'T I?
I AM No. 7 OF THE SEVEN MYSTERIES.
SQUISH
ぐに
SQUISH
ぐに
IT'S MY DUTY TO MAINTAIN CORRECT RELATIONSHIPS BETWEEN HUMANS AND SUPER-NATURALS.
PINCH
むに
BUT OF COURSE, YOU'LL BE HELPING ME, YASHIRO.
HANAKO-KUN...
THERE, THERE, THERE.
ぐす…
SNIFFLE

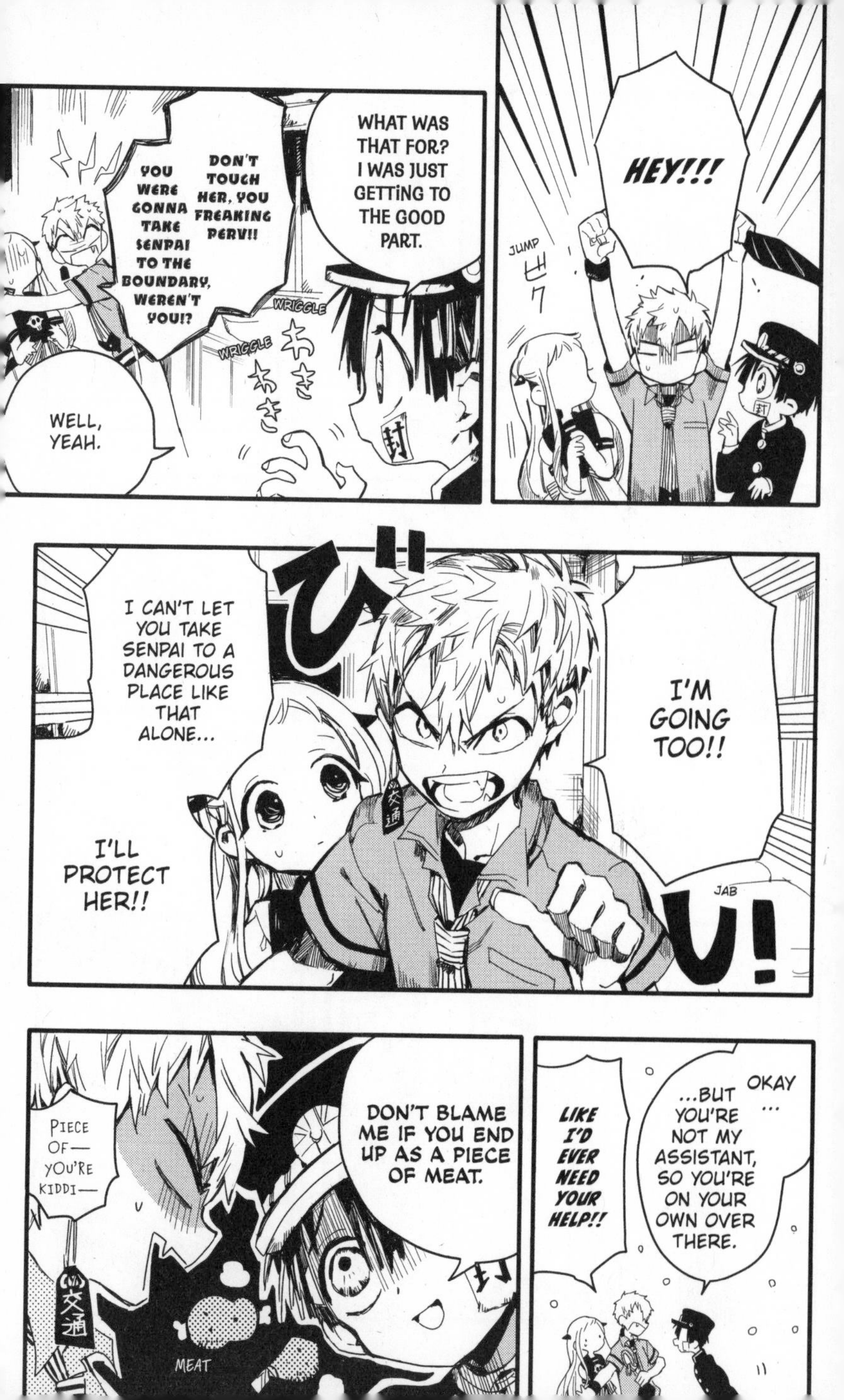
HEY!!!
JUMP
WHAT WAS THAT FOR? I WAS JUST GETTING TO THE GOOD PART.
DON'T TOUCH HER, YOU FREAKING PERV!!
YOU WERE GONNA TAKE SENPAI TO THE BOUNDARY, WEREN'T YOU!?
WRIGGLE
WRIGGLE
WELL, YEAH.
I'M GOING TOO!!
I CAN'T LET YOU TAKE SENPAI TO A DANGEROUS PLACE LIKE THAT ALONE...
I'LL PROTECT HER!!
JAB
OKAY...
...BUT YOU'RE NOT MY ASSISTANT, SO YOU'RE ON YOUR OWN OVER THERE.
LIKE I'D EVER NEED YOUR HELP!!
DON'T BLAME ME IF YOU END UP AS A PIECE OF MEAT.
PIECE OF— YOU'RE KIDDI—
MEAT

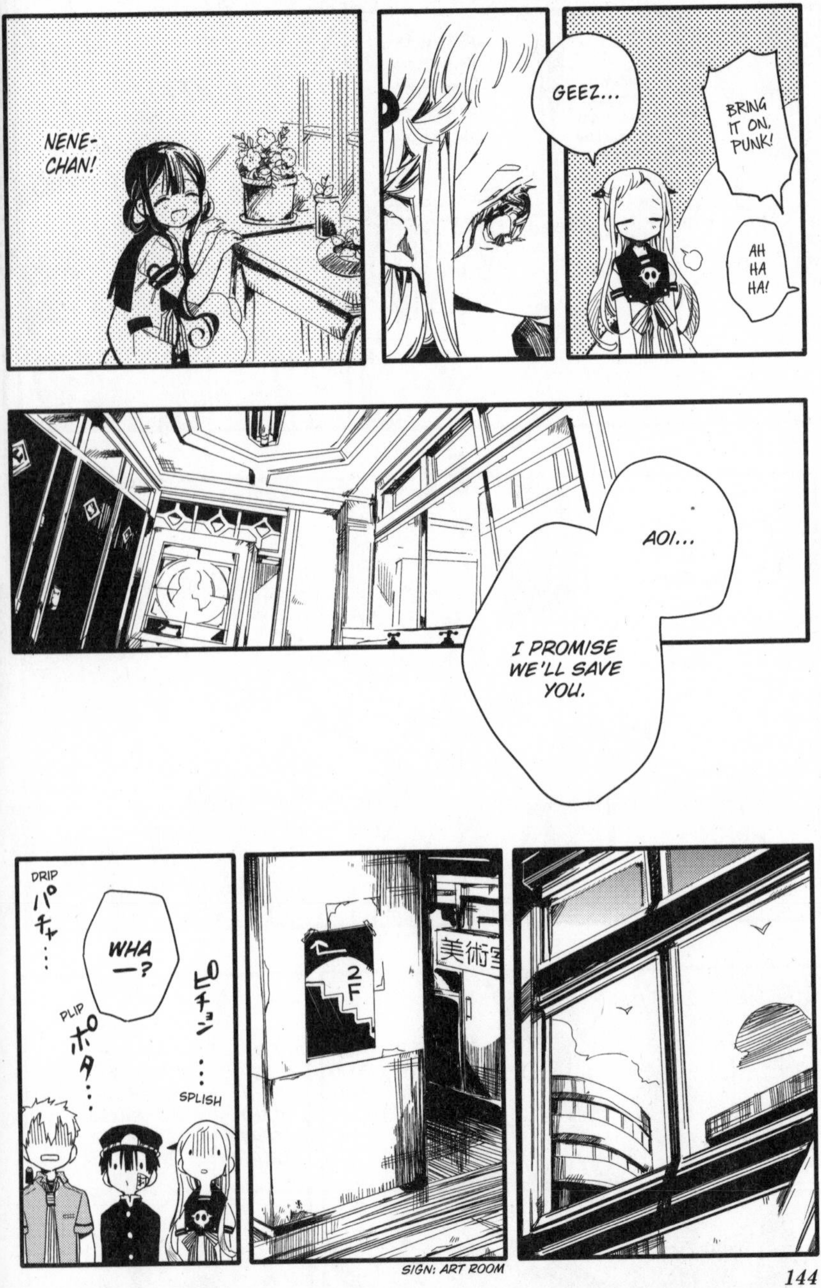
BRING IT ON, PUNK!
GEEZ...
AH HA HA!
NENE-CHAN!
AOI...
I PROMISE WE'LL SAVE YOU.
美術室
2F
ピチョン…
SPLISH
WHA—?
ポタ…
PLIP
パチャ…
DRIP
SIGN: ART ROOM

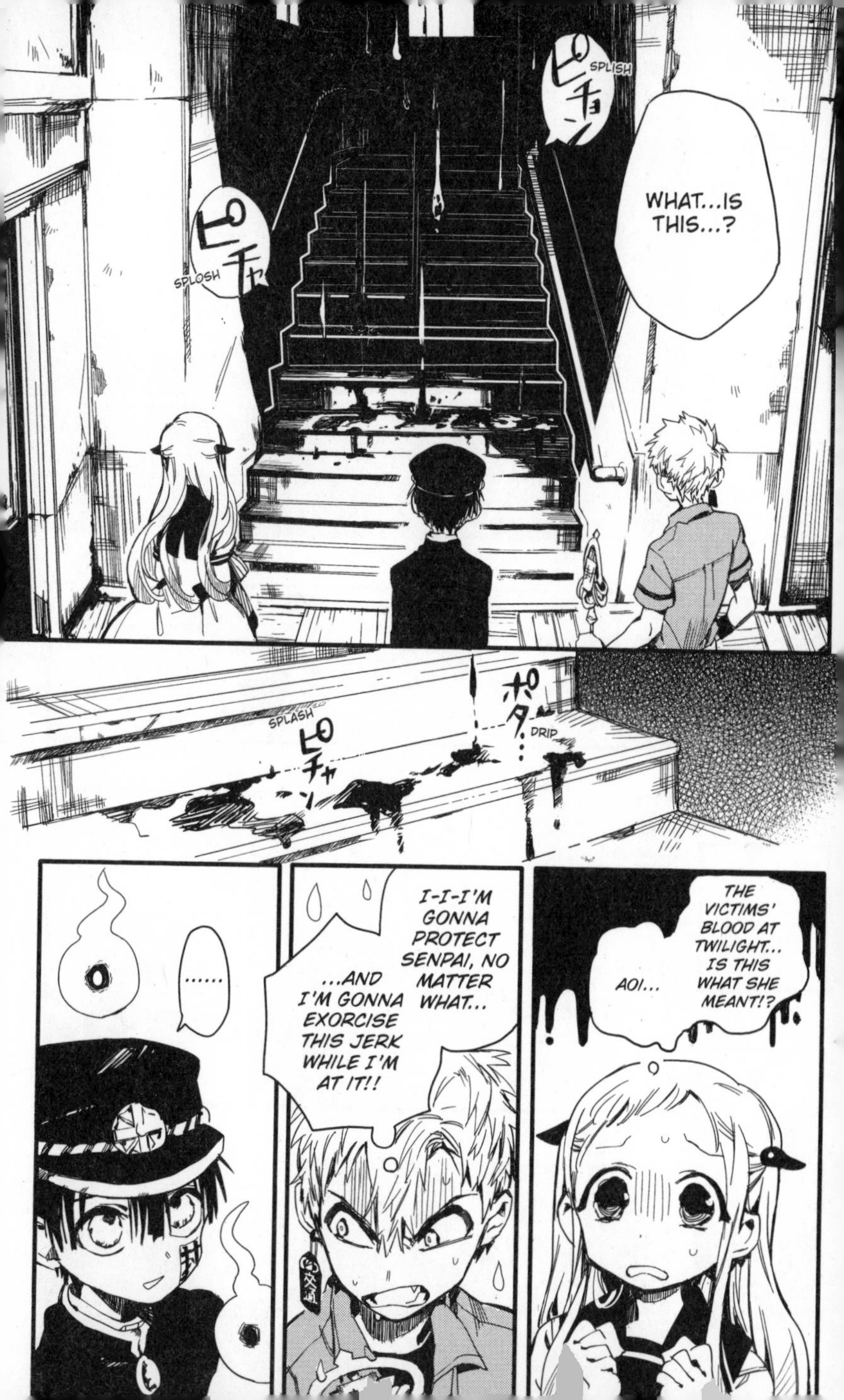

ピチョン
SPLISH
WHAT...IS THIS...?
ピチャ
SPLOSH
ポタ…
DRIP
ピチャン
SPLASH
THE VICTIMS' BLOOD AT TWILIGHT... IS THIS WHAT SHE MEANT!?
AOI...
I-I-I'M GONNA PROTECT SENPAI, NO MATTER WHAT...
...AND I'M GONNA EXORCISE THIS JERK WHILE I'M AT IT!!
......

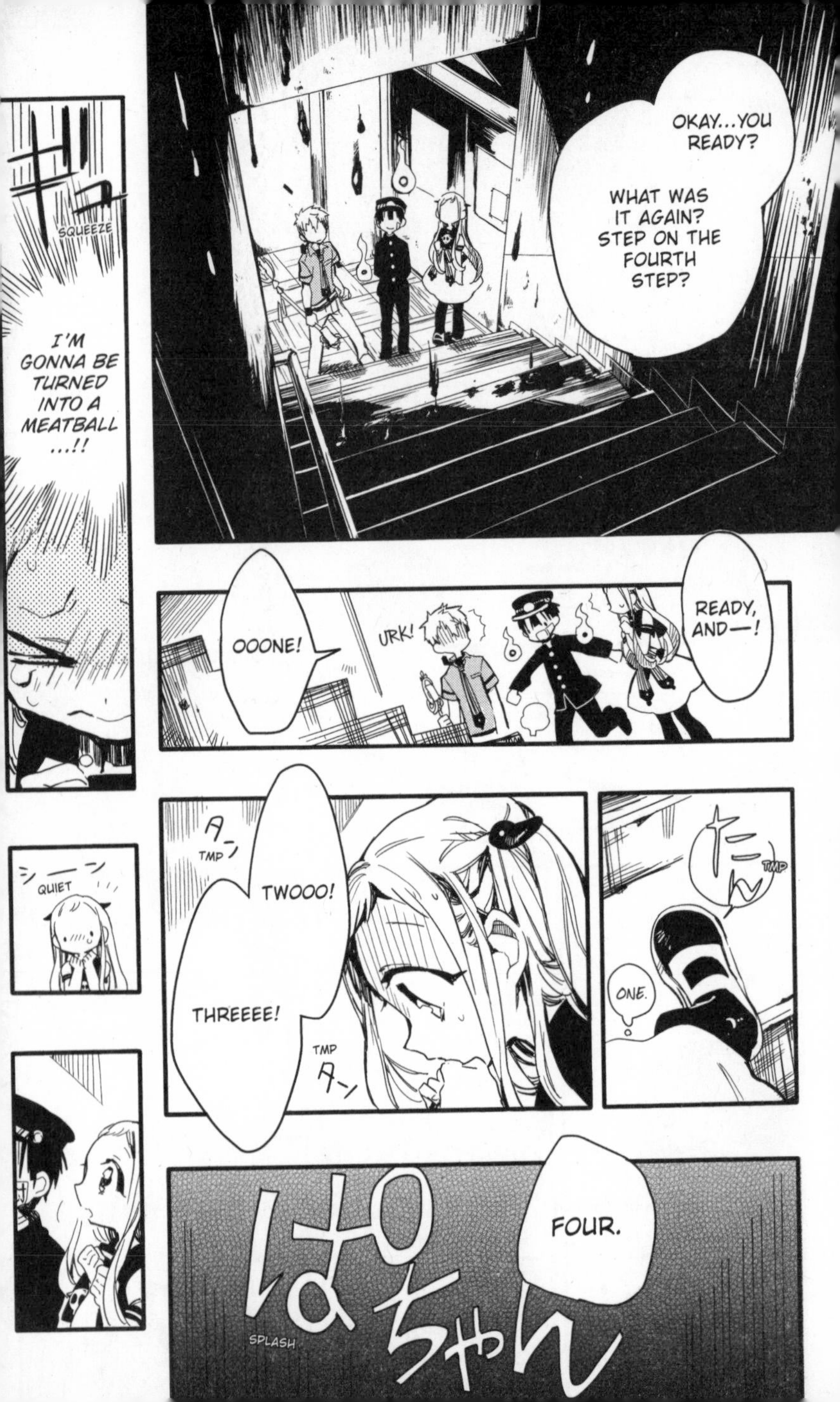
OKAY...YOU READY?
WHAT WAS IT AGAIN? STEP ON THE FOURTH STEP?
SQUEEZE
I'M GONNA BE TURNED INTO A MEATBALL ...!!
READY, AND—!
URK!
OOONE!
たーん
TMP
ONE.
タン
TMP
TWOOO!
THREEEE!
TMP
タン
シーーン
QUIET
FOUR.
ぱちゃん
SPLASH

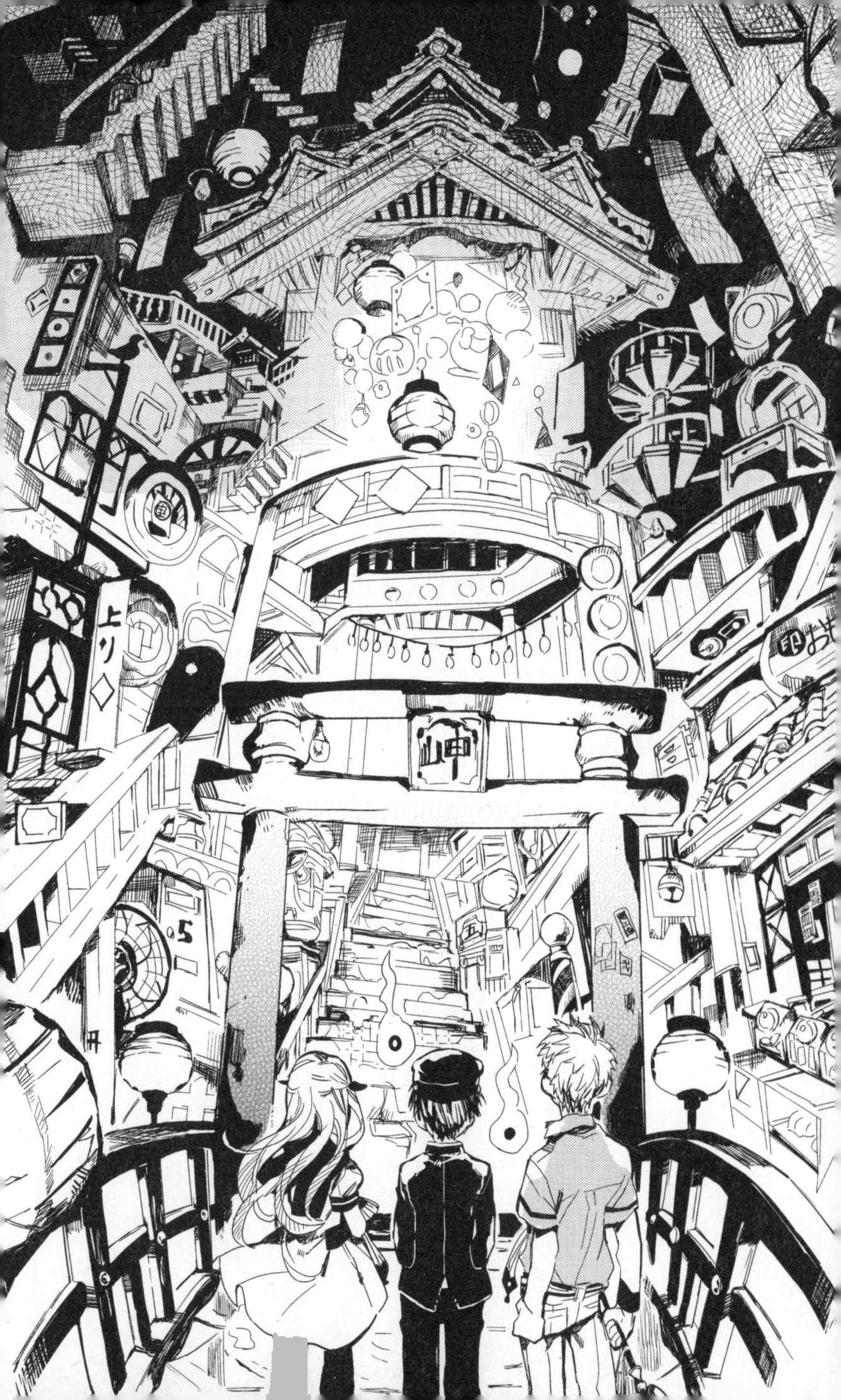

上り

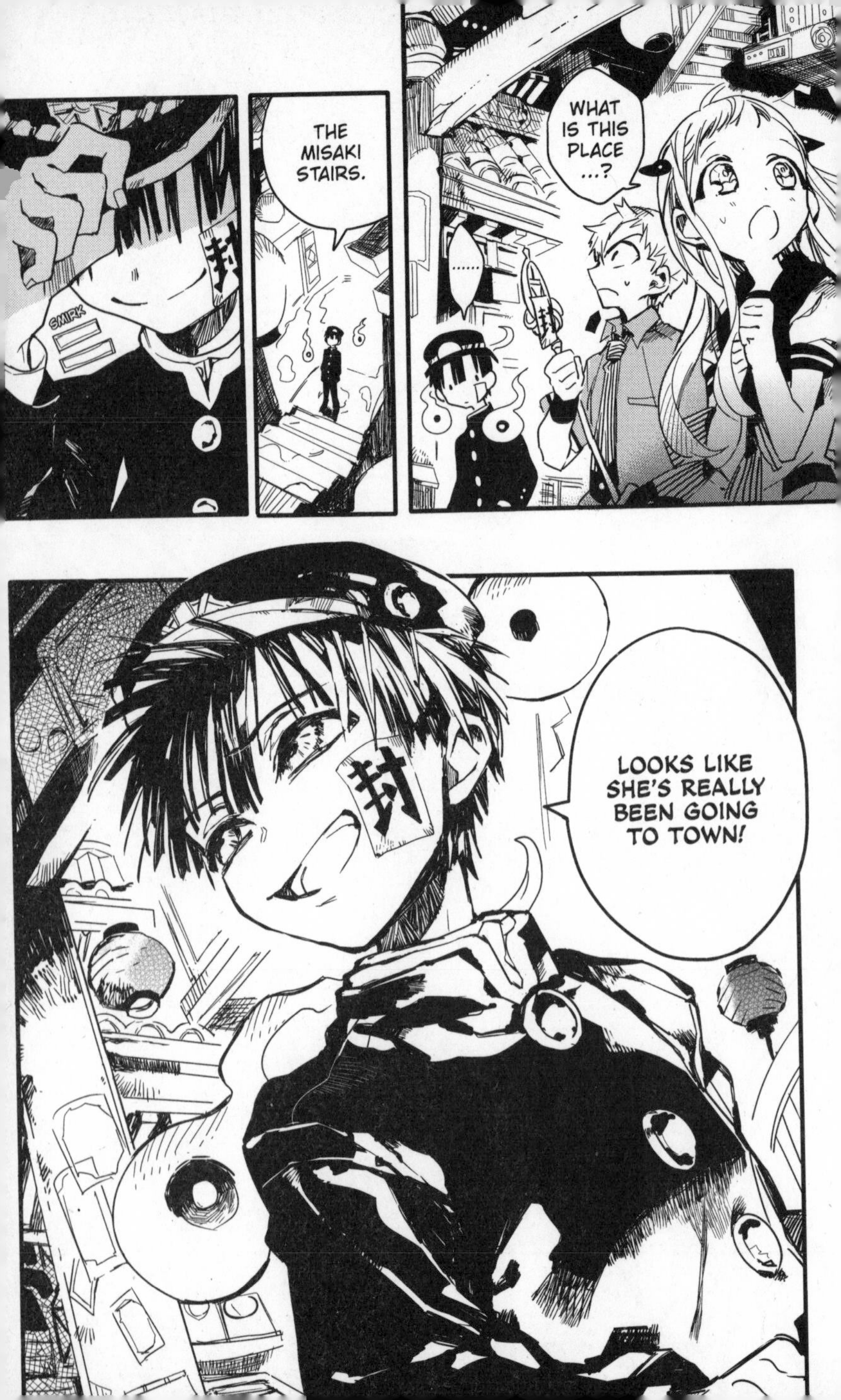
WHAT IS THIS PLACE ...?
......
THE MISAKI STAIRS.
SMIRK
LOOKS LIKE SHE'S REALLY BEEN GOING TO TOWN!

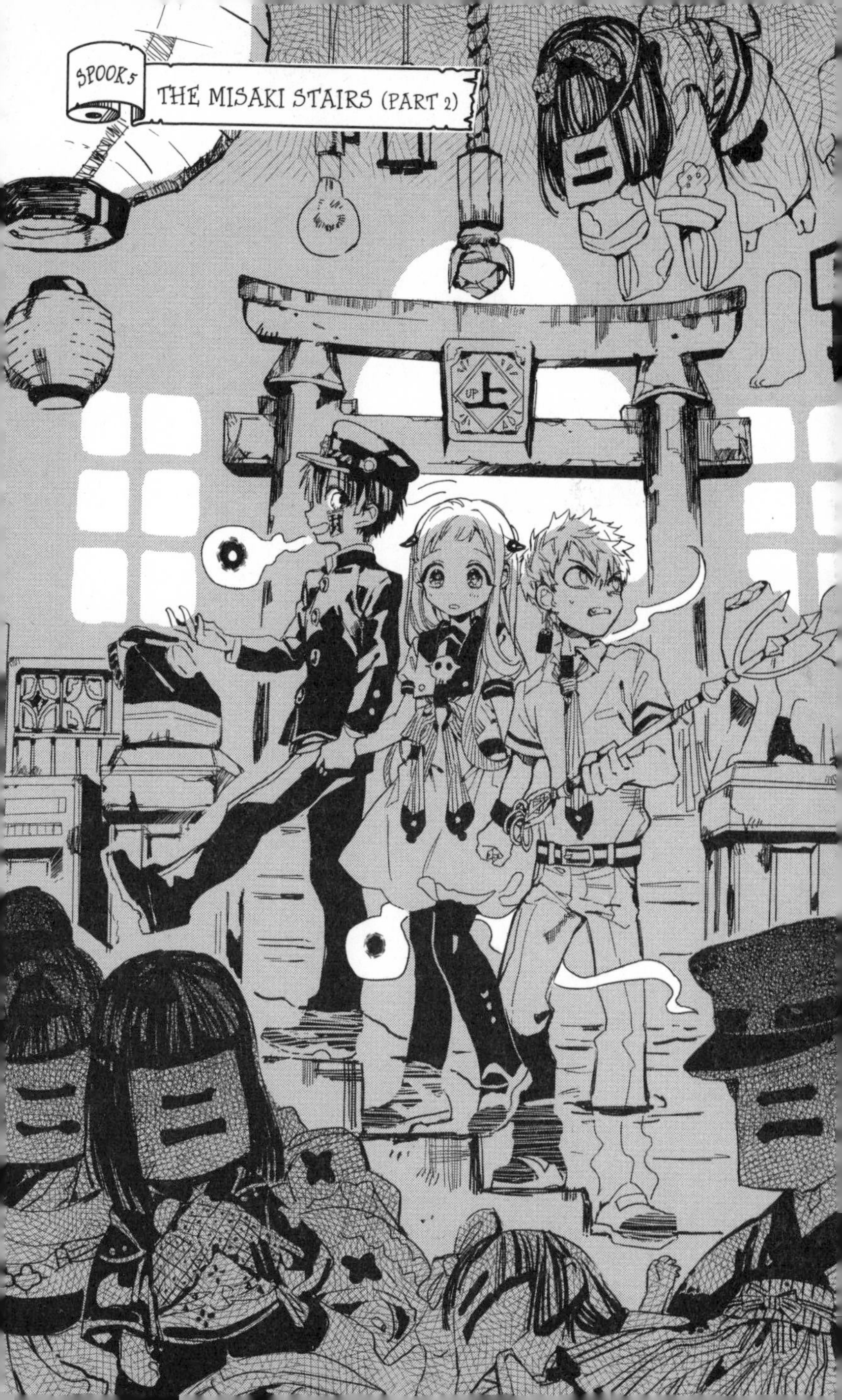
SPOOK 5
THE MISAKI STAIRS (PART 2)
UP 上

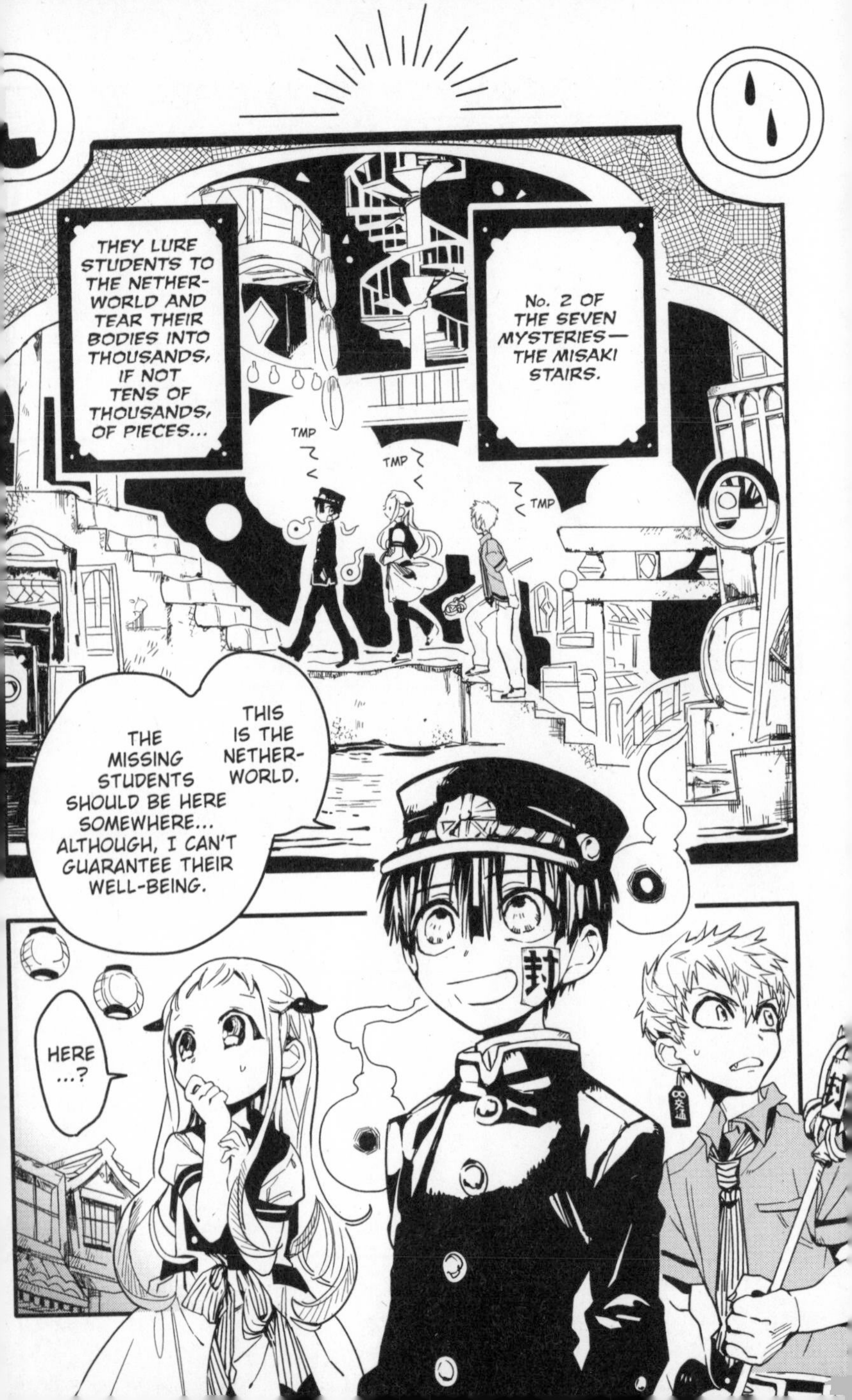
No. 2 OF THE SEVEN MYSTERIES— THE MISAKI STAIRS.
THEY LURE STUDENTS TO THE NETHER-WORLD AND TEAR THEIR BODIES INTO THOUSANDS, IF NOT TENS OF THOUSANDS, OF PIECES...
TMP
TMP
TMP
THIS IS THE NETHER-WORLD.
THE MISSING STUDENTS SHOULD BE HERE SOMEWHERE... ALTHOUGH, I CAN'T GUARANTEE THEIR WELL-BEING.
HERE ...?

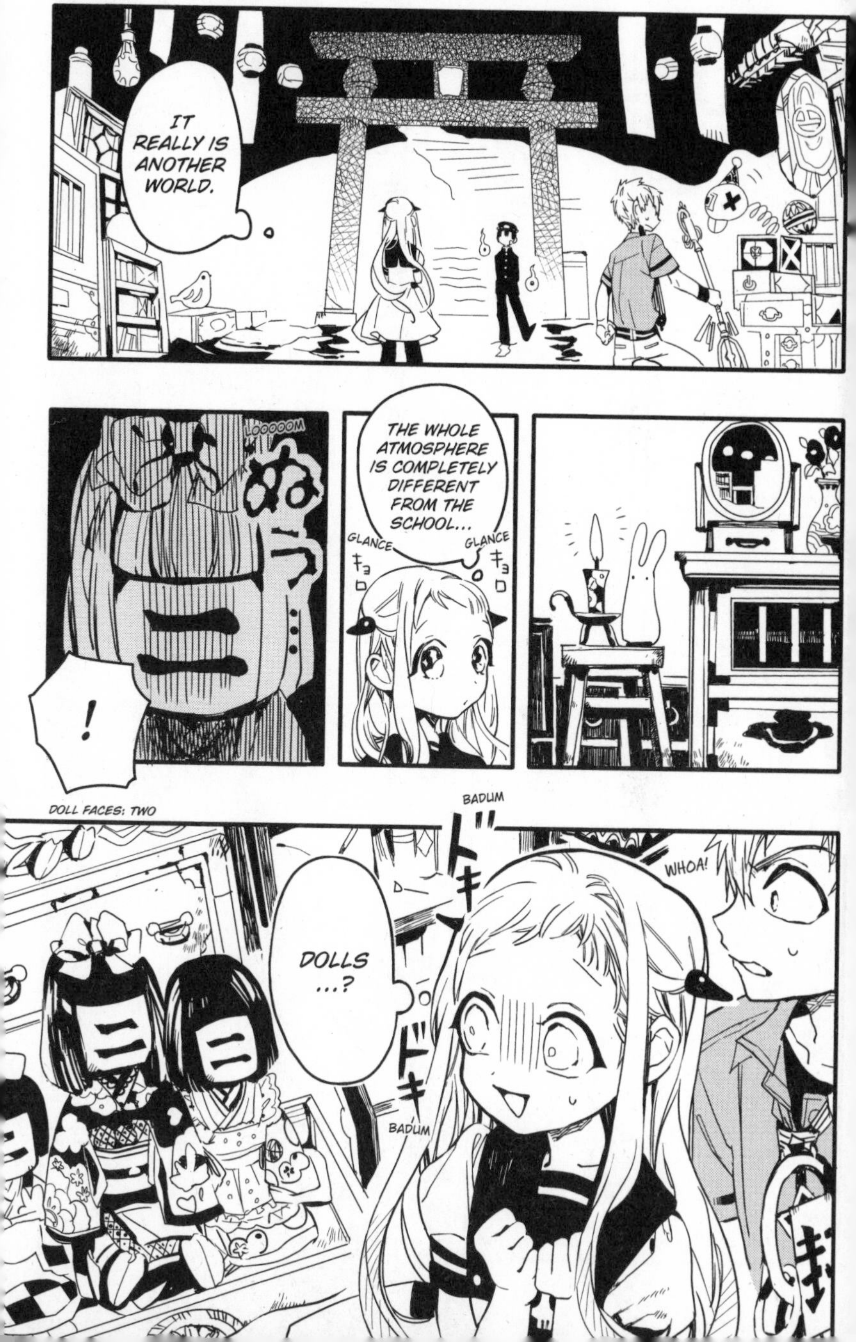
IT REALLY IS ANOTHER WORLD.
GLANCE
キョロ
THE WHOLE ATMOSPHERE IS COMPLETELY DIFFERENT FROM THE SCHOOL...
GLANCE
キョロ
LOOOOOM
ぬう
!
DOLL FACES: TWO
WHOA!
BADUM
ドキ
DOLLS ...?
ドキ
BADUM

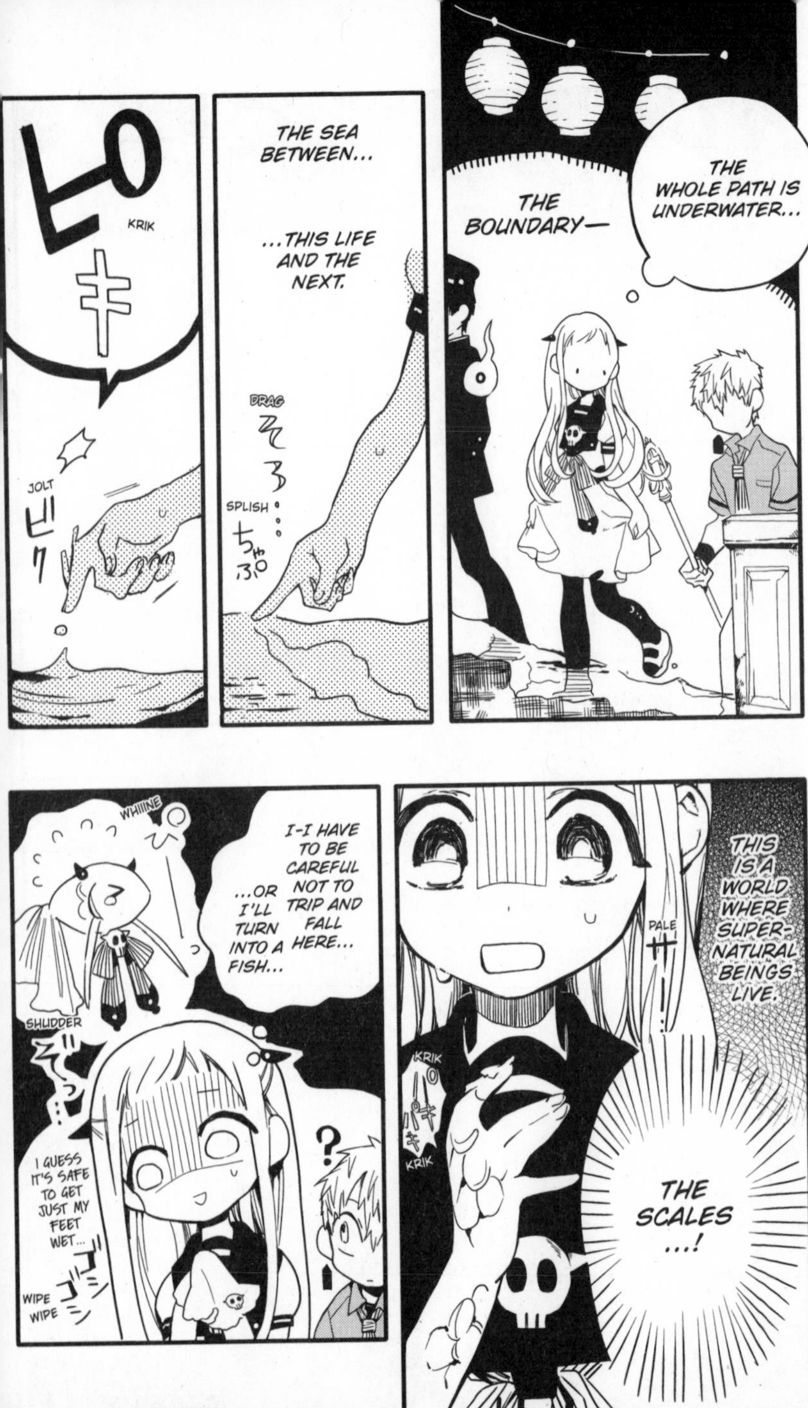
THE WHOLE PATH IS UNDERWATER...
THE BOUNDARY—
THE SEA BETWEEN...
...THIS LIFE AND THE NEXT.
DRAG
SPLISH
KRIK
JOLT
THIS IS A WORLD WHERE SUPER-NATURAL BEINGS LIVE.
PALE
THE SCALES...!
KRIK
KRIK
I-I HAVE TO BE CAREFUL NOT TO TRIP AND FALL HERE...
...OR I'LL TURN INTO A FISH...
WHIIINE
SHUDDER
?
I GUESS IT'S SAFE TO GET JUST MY FEET WET...
WIPE WIPE

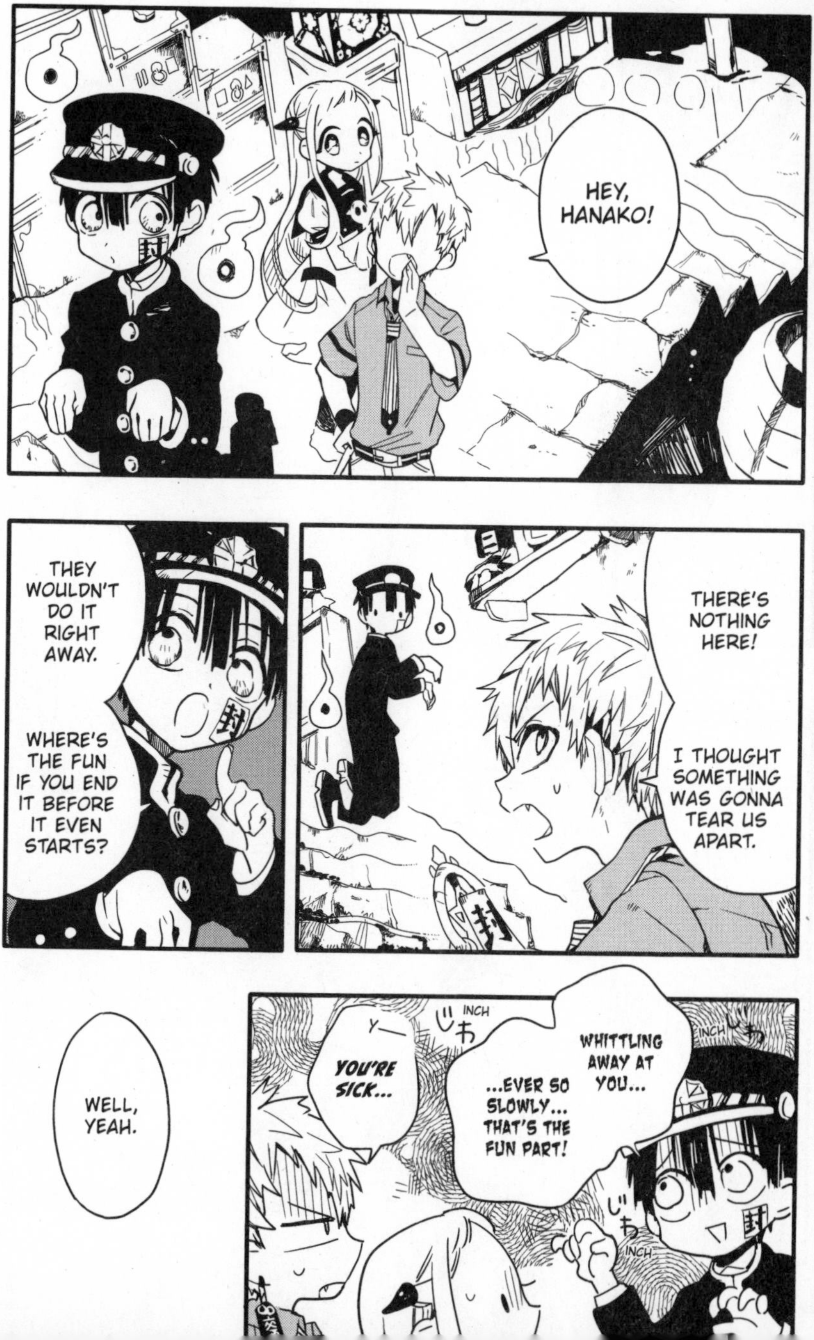
HEY, HANAKO!
THERE'S NOTHING HERE!
I THOUGHT SOMETHING WAS GONNA TEAR US APART.
THEY WOULDN'T DO IT RIGHT AWAY.
WHERE'S THE FUN IF YOU END IT BEFORE IT EVEN STARTS?
INCH
WHITTLING AWAY AT YOU...
INCH
...EVER SO SLOWLY... THAT'S THE FUN PART!
YOU'RE SICK...
INCH
WELL, YEAH.

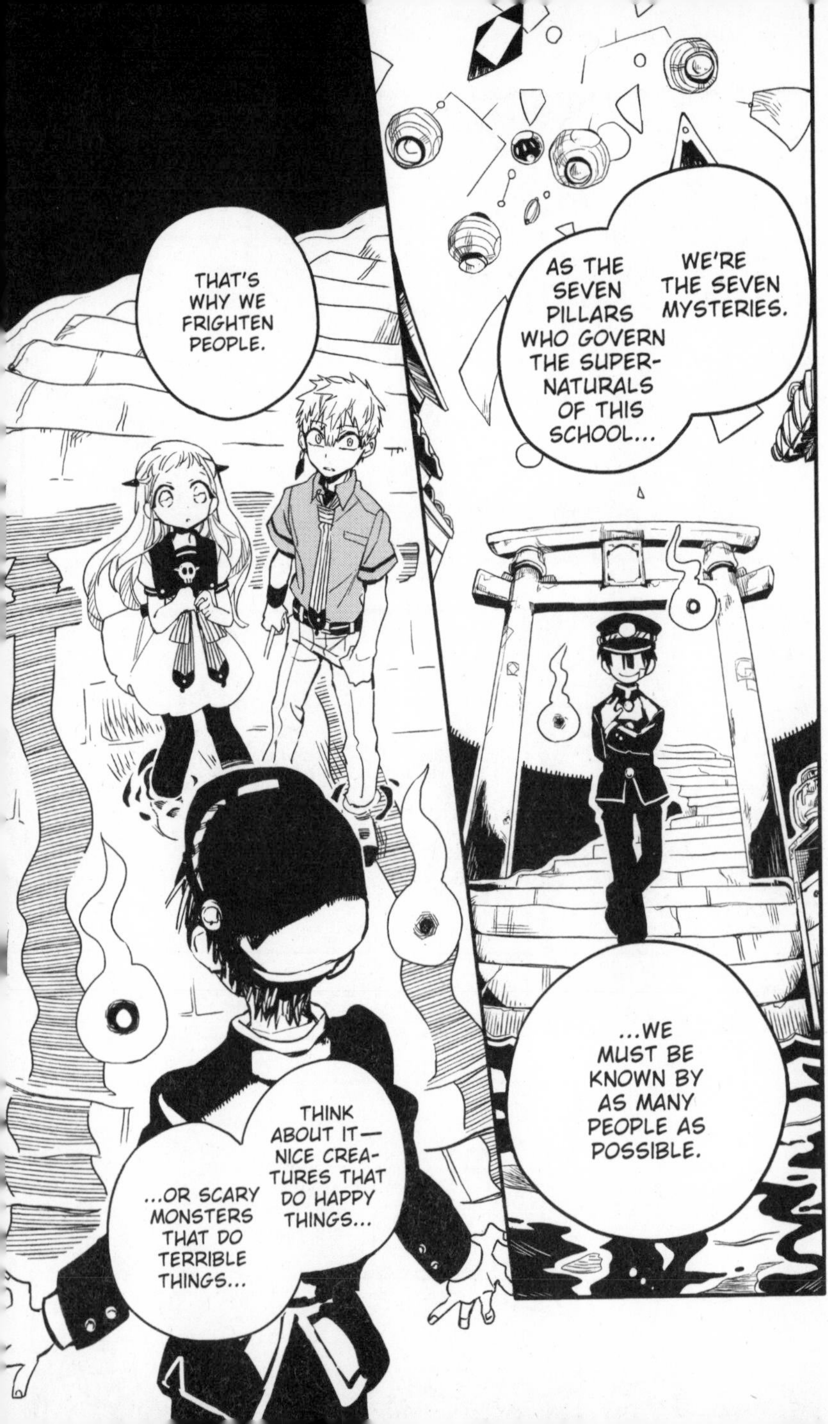
WE'RE THE SEVEN MYSTERIES.
AS THE SEVEN PILLARS WHO GOVERN THE SUPER-NATURALS OF THIS SCHOOL...
...WE MUST BE KNOWN BY AS MANY PEOPLE AS POSSIBLE.
THAT'S WHY WE FRIGHTEN PEOPLE.
THINK ABOUT IT—NICE CREA-TURES THAT DO HAPPY THINGS...
...OR SCARY MONSTERS THAT DO TERRIBLE THINGS...

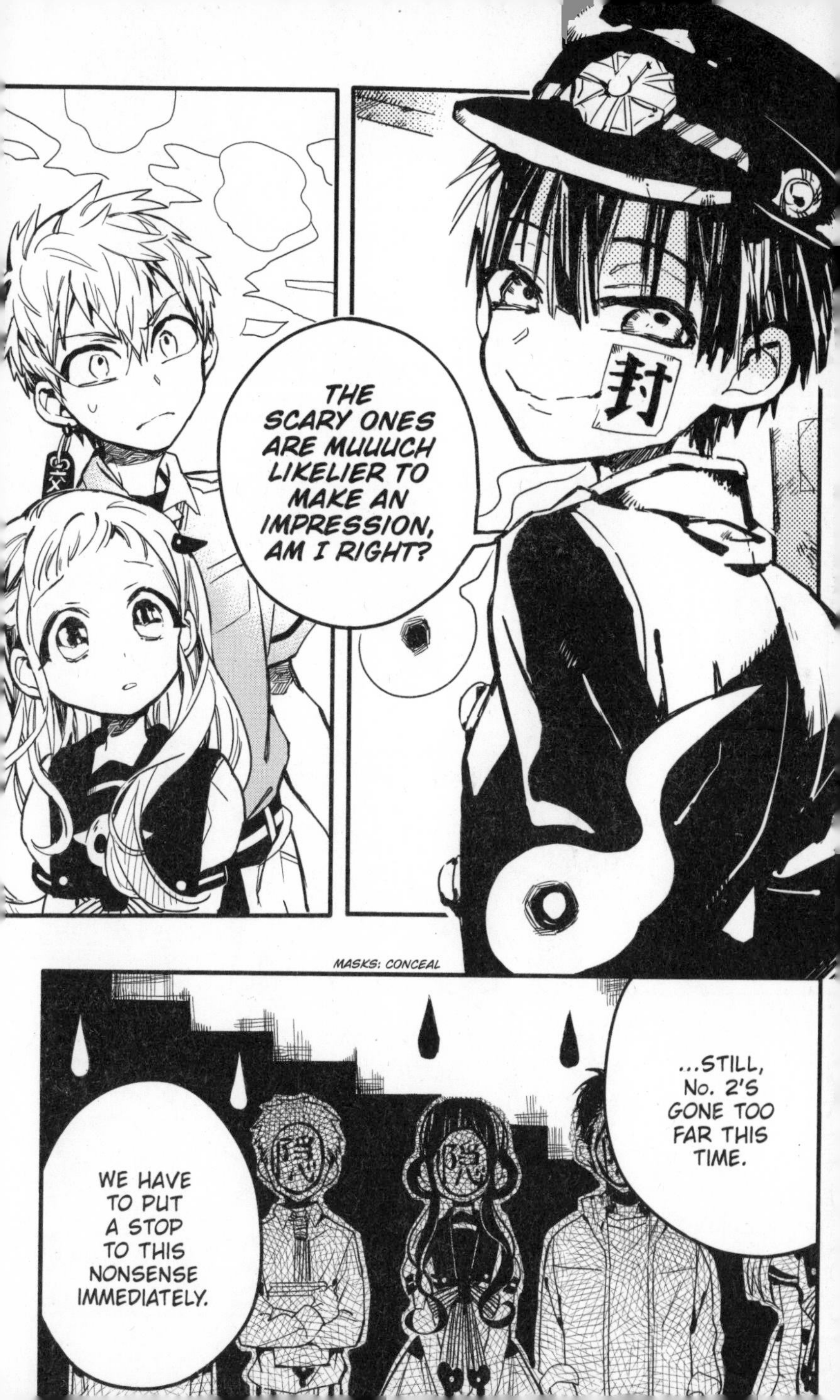
THE SCARY ONES ARE MUUUCH LIKELIER TO MAKE AN IMPRESSION, AM I RIGHT?
MASKS: CONCEAL
...STILL, No. 2'S GONE TOO FAR THIS TIME.
WE HAVE TO PUT A STOP TO THIS NONSENSE IMMEDIATELY.

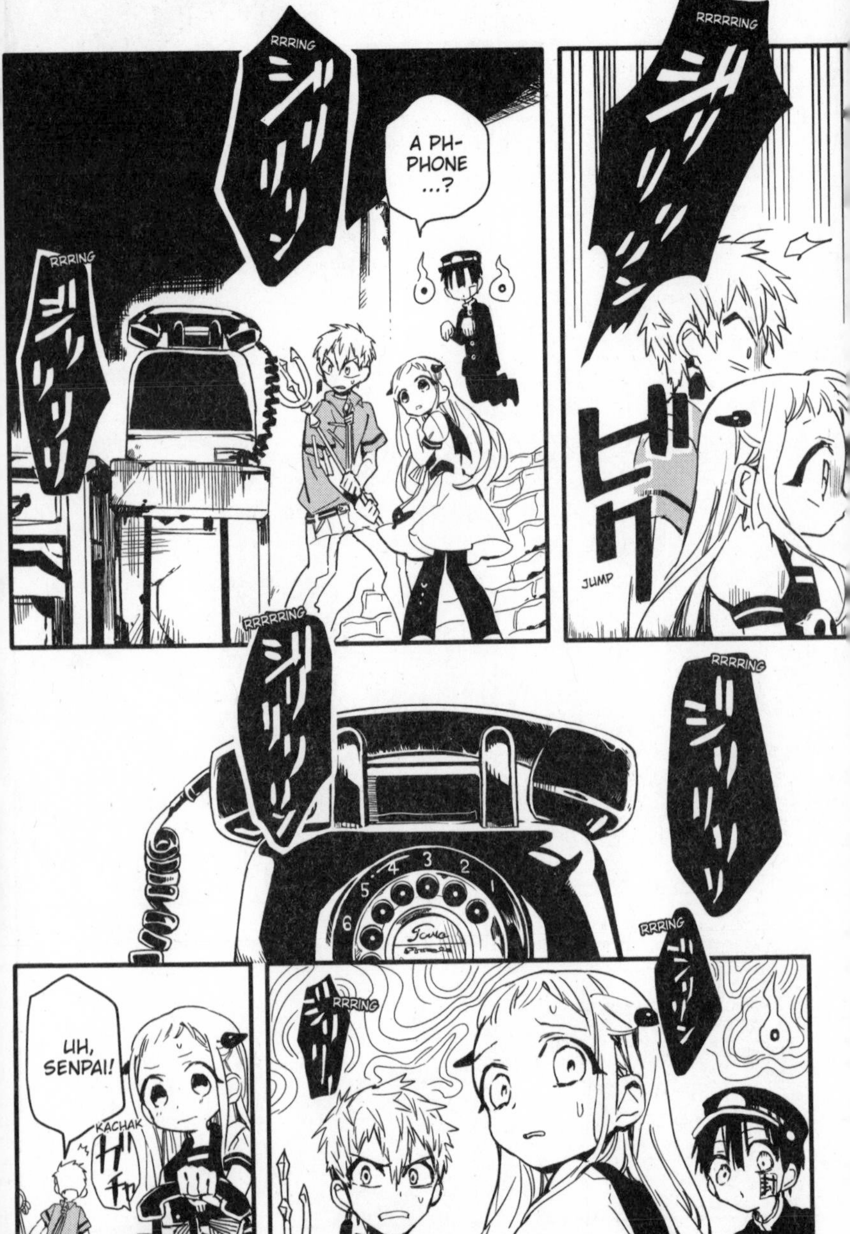
RRRRRING
JUMP
RRRING
A PH-
PHONE
...?
RRRING
RRRRING
RRRRRING
RRRING
RRRING
UH,
SENPAI!
KACHAK

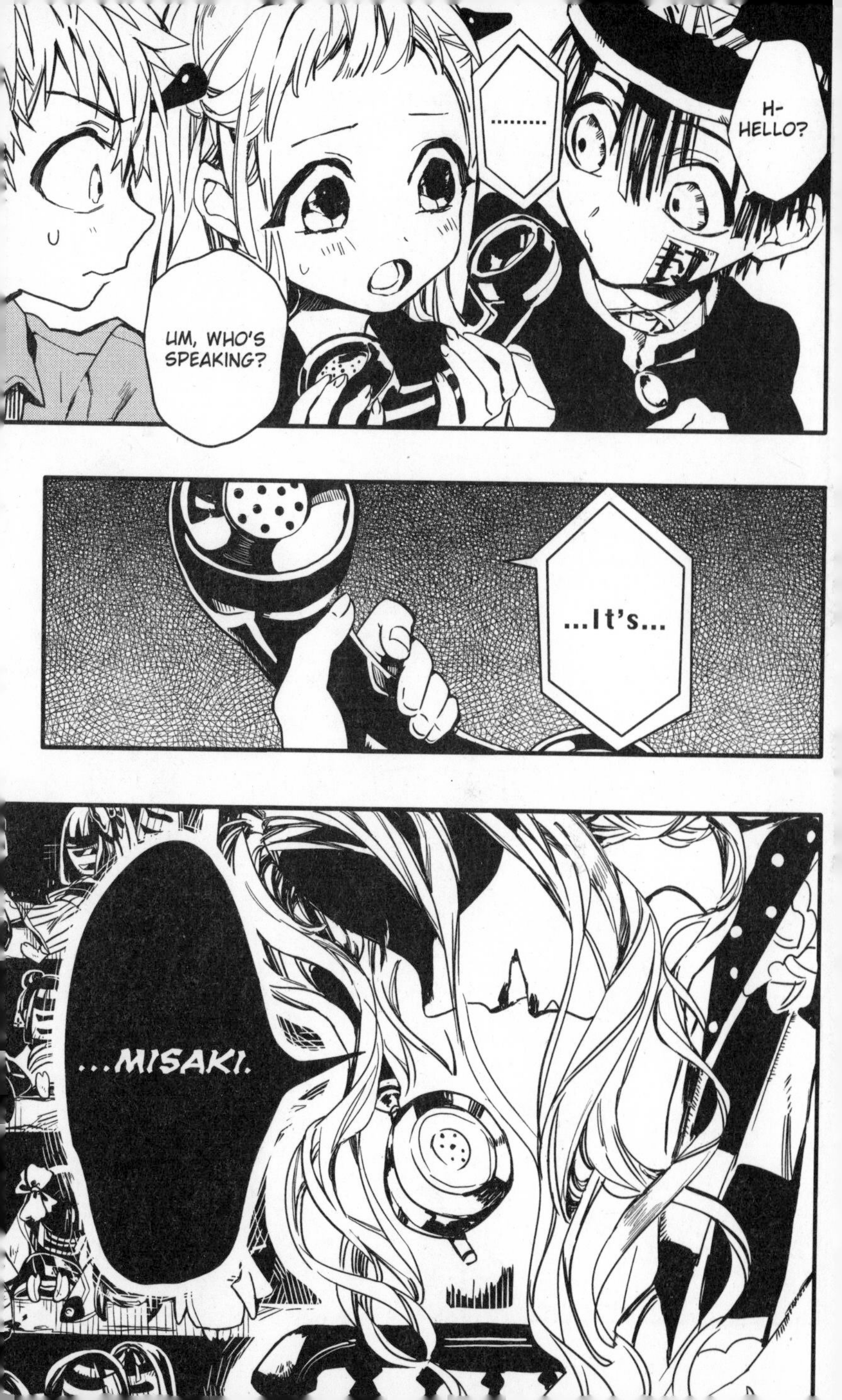
H- HELLO?
....
UM, WHO'S SPEAKING?
...It's...
...MISAKI.

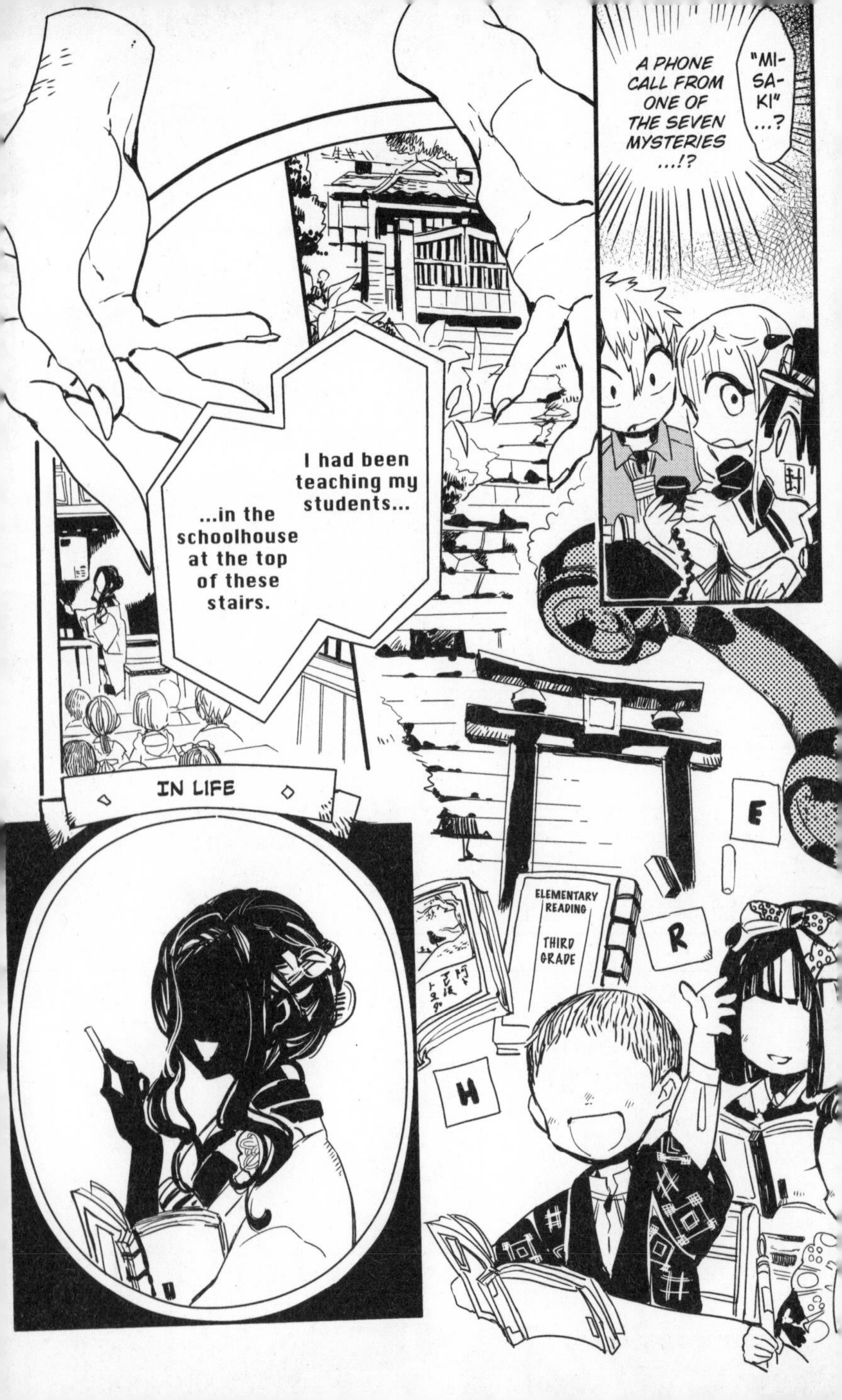

"MI-SA-KI"...?
A PHONE CALL FROM ONE OF THE SEVEN MYSTERIES ...!?
I had been teaching my students...
...in the schoolhouse at the top of these stairs.
IN LIFE
E
ELEMENTARY READING
THIRD GRADE
R
H

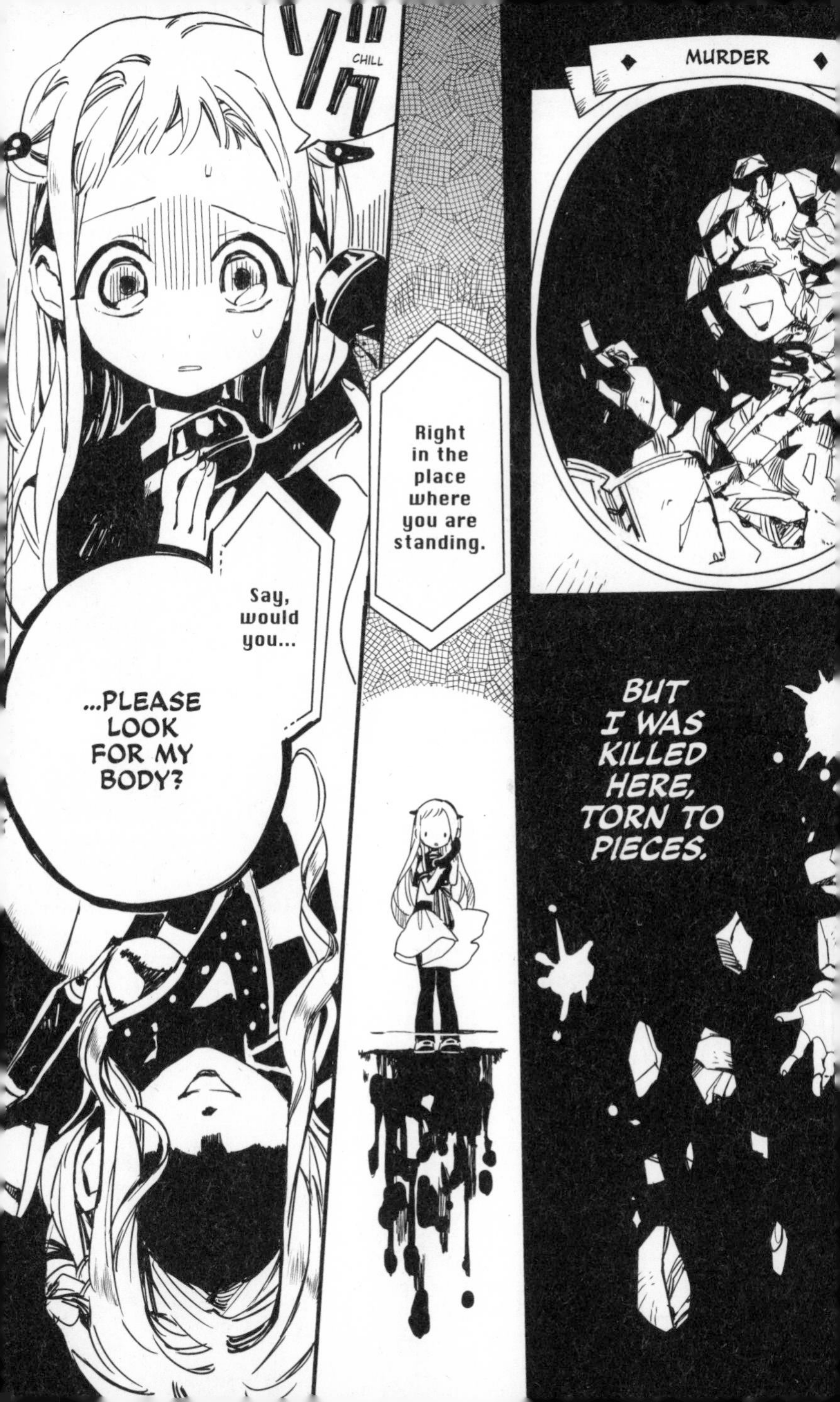
MURDER
BUT I WAS KILLED HERE, TORN TO PIECES.
Right in the place where you are standing.
CHILL
Say, would you...
...PLEASE LOOK FOR MY BODY?

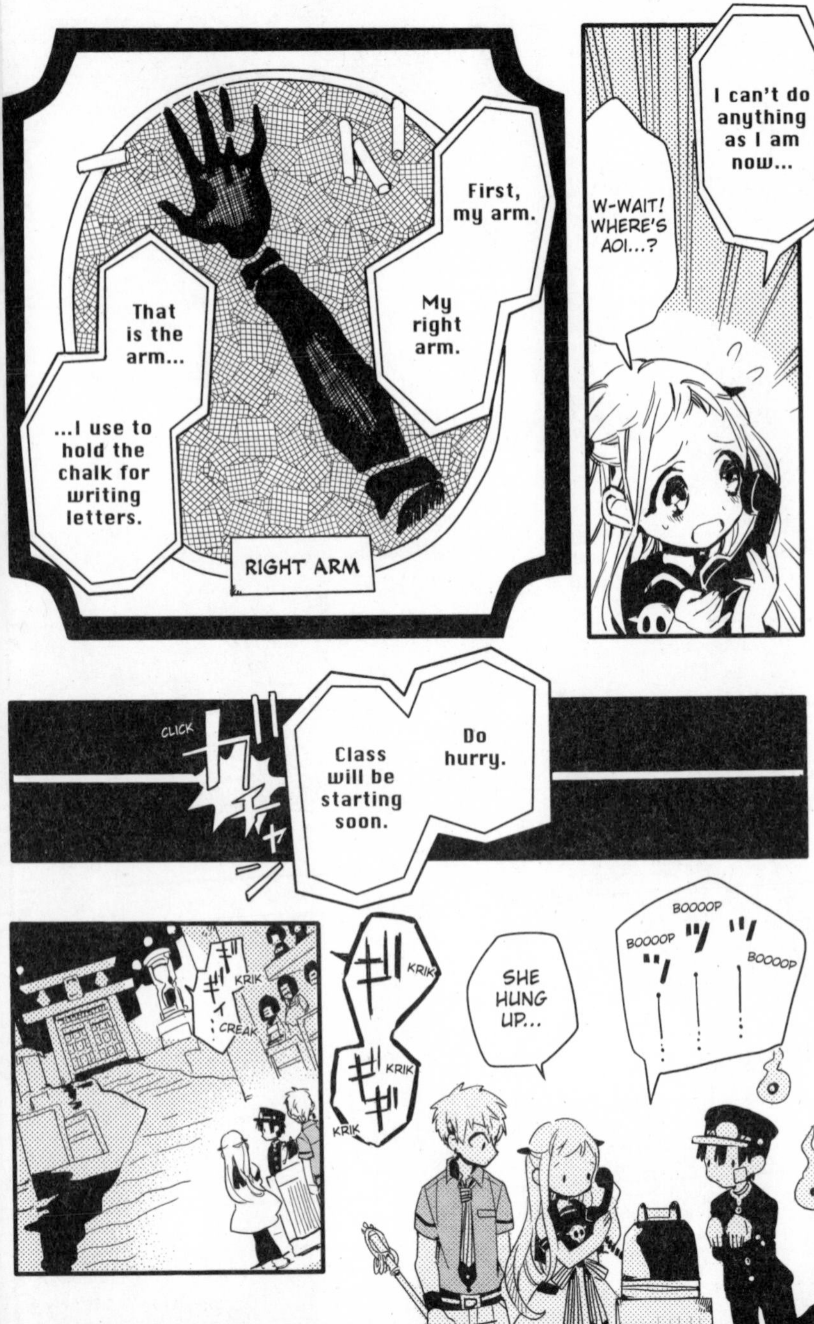

I can't do anything as I am now...
W-WAIT! WHERE'S AOI...?
First, my arm.
My right arm.
That is the arm...
...I use to hold the chalk for writing letters.
RIGHT ARM
Do hurry.
Class will be starting soon.
CLICK
BOOOOP
BOOOOP
BOOOOP
SHE HUNG UP...
KRIK
KRIK
KRIK
KRIK
CREAK

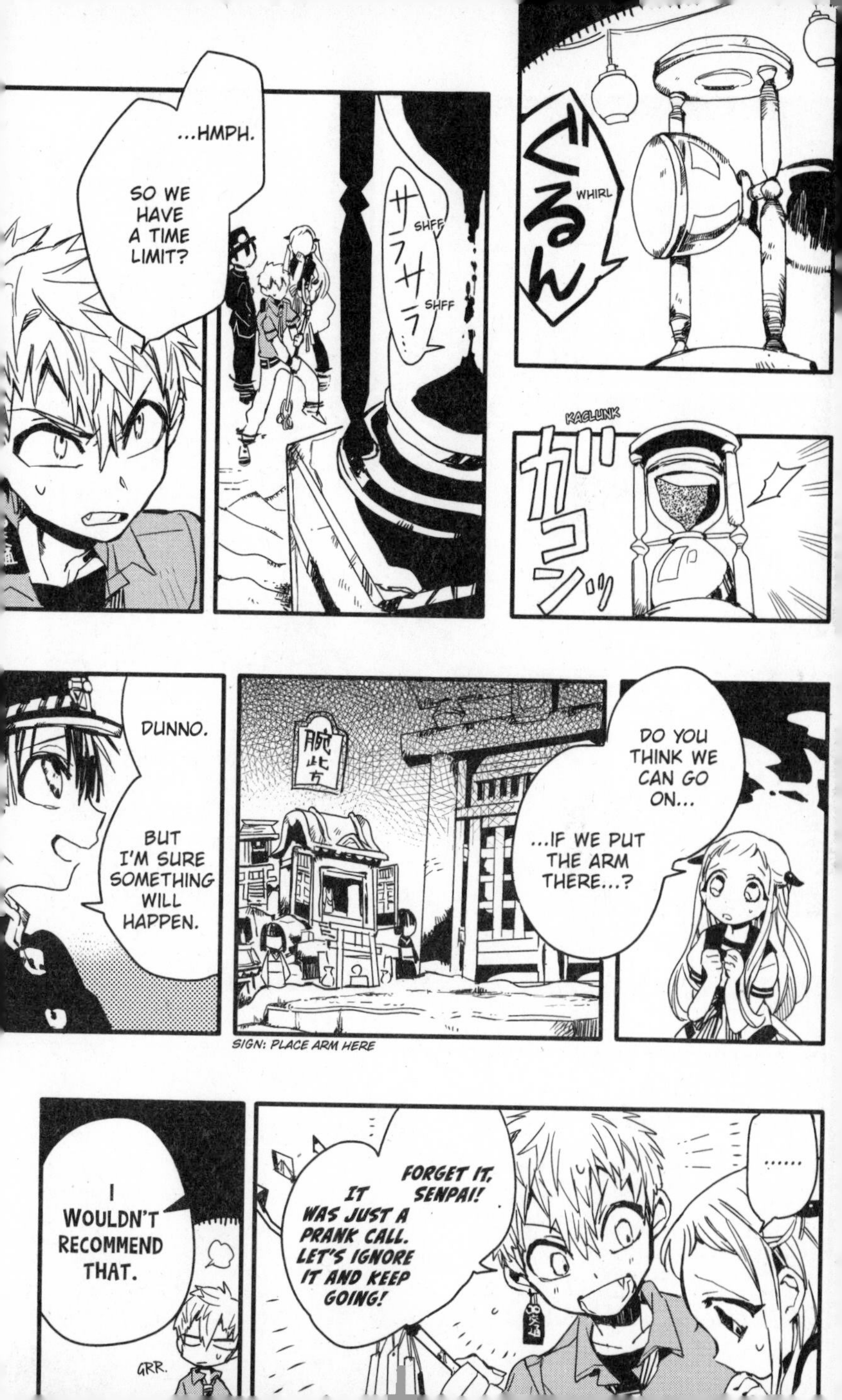

ぐるん
WHIRL
KAGLUNK
ガコンッ
サラサラ
SHFF
SHFF
...HMPH.
SO WE HAVE A TIME LIMIT?
DO YOU THINK WE CAN GO ON...
...IF WE PUT THE ARM THERE...?
腕此方
SIGN: PLACE ARM HERE
DUNNO.
BUT I'M SURE SOMETHING WILL HAPPEN.
......
FORGET IT, SENPAI!
IT WAS JUST A PRANK CALL. LET'S IGNORE IT AND KEEP GOING!
I WOULDN'T RECOMMEND THAT.
GRR.

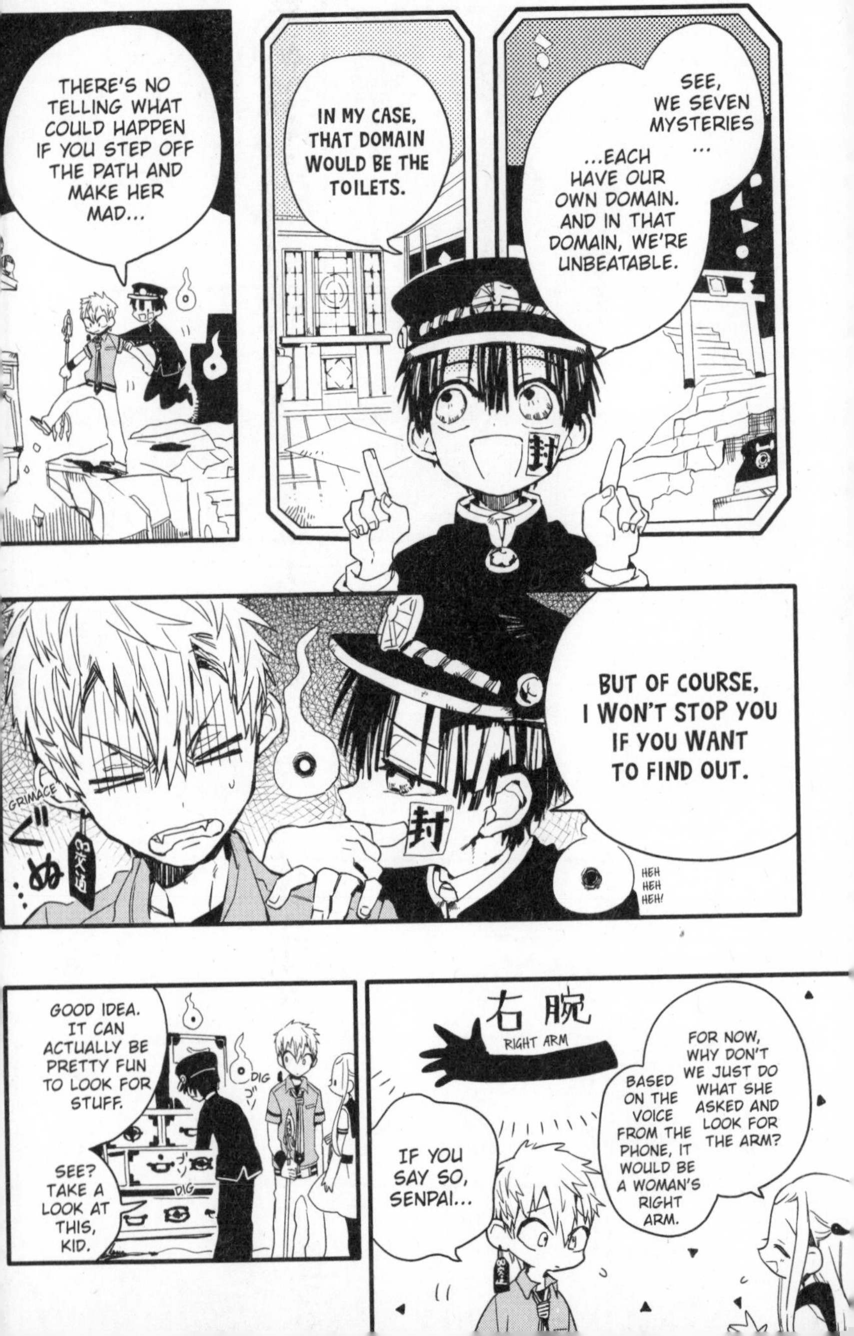
SEE, WE SEVEN MYSTERIES ...
...EACH HAVE OUR OWN DOMAIN. AND IN THAT DOMAIN, WE'RE UNBEATABLE.
IN MY CASE, THAT DOMAIN WOULD BE THE TOILETS.
THERE'S NO TELLING WHAT COULD HAPPEN IF YOU STEP OFF THE PATH AND MAKE HER MAD...
BUT OF COURSE, I WON'T STOP YOU IF YOU WANT TO FIND OUT.
HEH HEH HEH!
GRIMACE
ぐぬ
右腕
RIGHT ARM
FOR NOW, WHY DON'T WE JUST DO WHAT SHE ASKED AND LOOK FOR THE ARM?
BASED ON THE VOICE FROM THE PHONE, IT WOULD BE A WOMAN'S RIGHT ARM.
IF YOU SAY SO, SENPAI...
GOOD IDEA. IT CAN ACTUALLY BE PRETTY FUN TO LOOK FOR STUFF.
DIG
DIG
SEE? TAKE A LOOK AT THIS, KID.

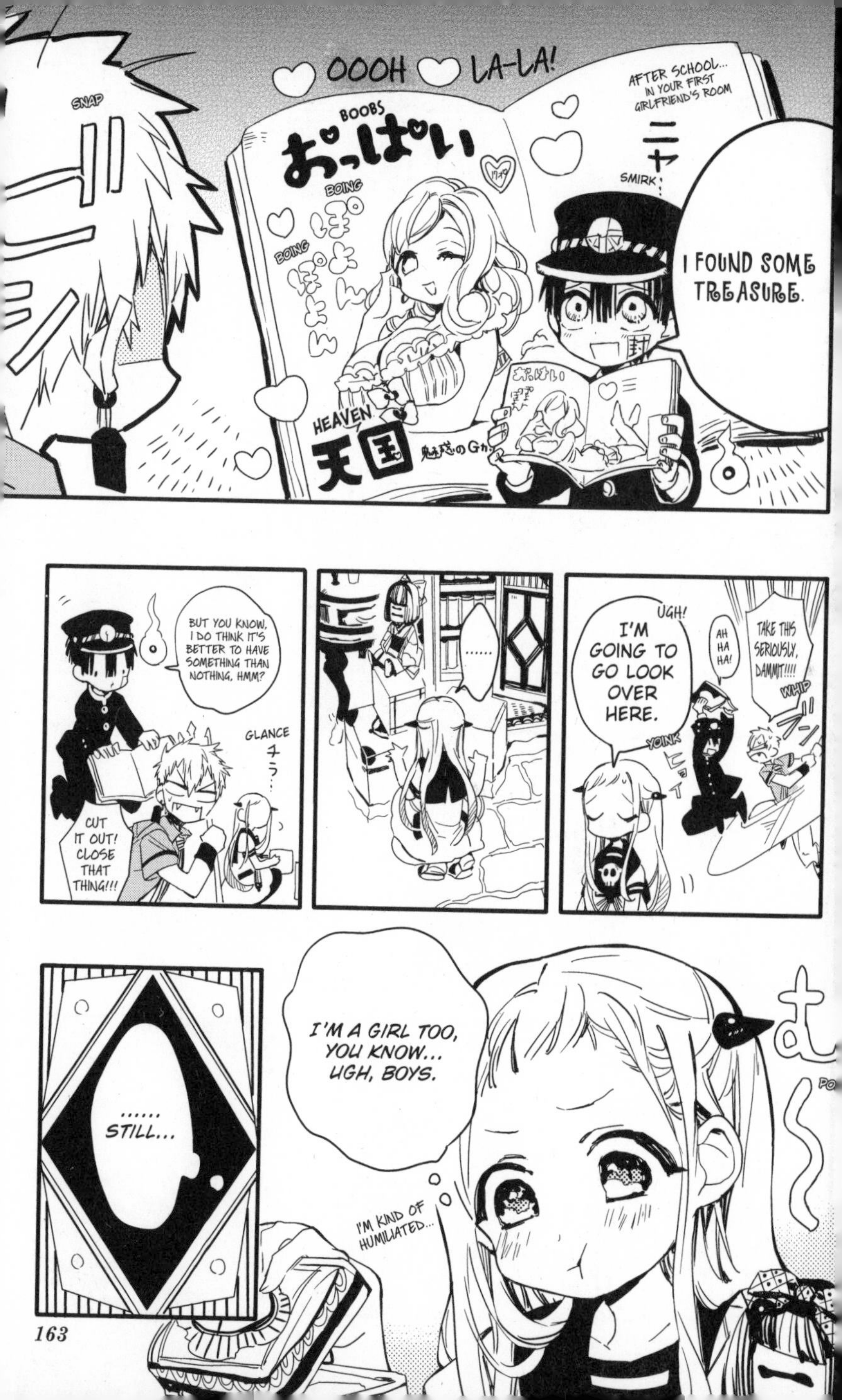
I FOUND SOME TREASURE.
AFTER SCHOOL... IN YOUR FIRST GIRLFRIEND'S ROOM
ニヤ
SMIRK
OOOH LA-LA!
BOOBS
おっぱい
BOING
BOING
ぽよんぽよん
HEAVEN
天国
SNAP
UGH!
TAKE THIS SERIOUSLY, DAMMIT!!!!
AH HA HA!
I'M GOING TO GO LOOK OVER HERE.
WHIP
YOINK
......
BUT YOU KNOW, I DO THINK IT'S BETTER TO HAVE SOMETHING THAN NOTHING, HMM?
GLANCE
チラ...
CUT IT OUT! CLOSE THAT THING!!!
I'M A GIRL TOO, YOU KNOW... UGH, BOYS.
I'M KIND OF HUMILIATED...
...... STILL...

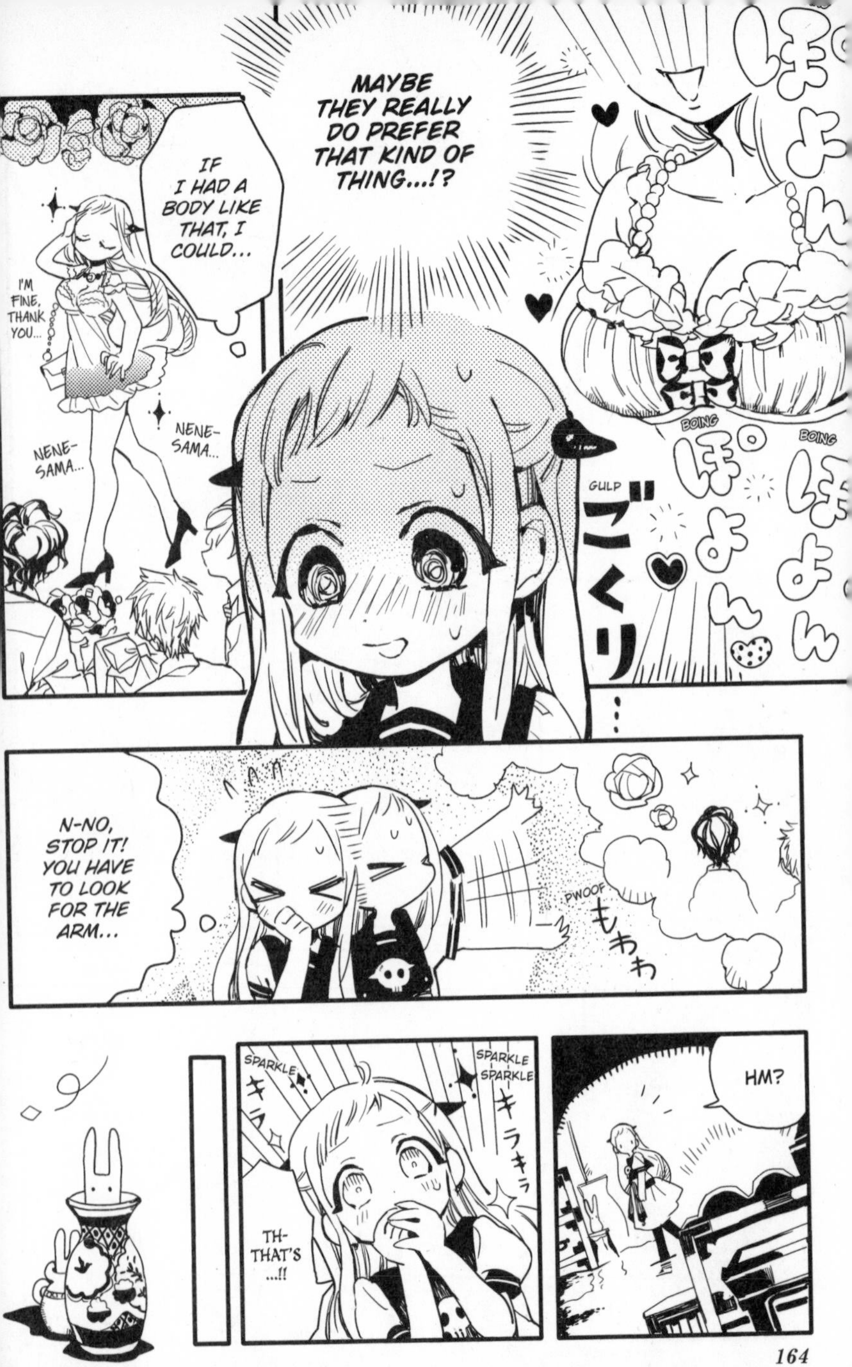
ぽよん
BOING
ぽよん
BOING
ぽよん
MAYBE THEY REALLY DO PREFER THAT KIND OF THING...!?
GULP
ごくり
IF I HAD A BODY LIKE THAT, I COULD...
NENE-SAMA...
I'M FINE, THANK YOU...
NENE-SAMA...
PWOOF
もわわ
N-NO, STOP IT! YOU HAVE TO LOOK FOR THE ARM...
HM?
SPARKLE SPARKLE
キラキラ
SPARKLE
キラ
TH-THAT'S ...!!

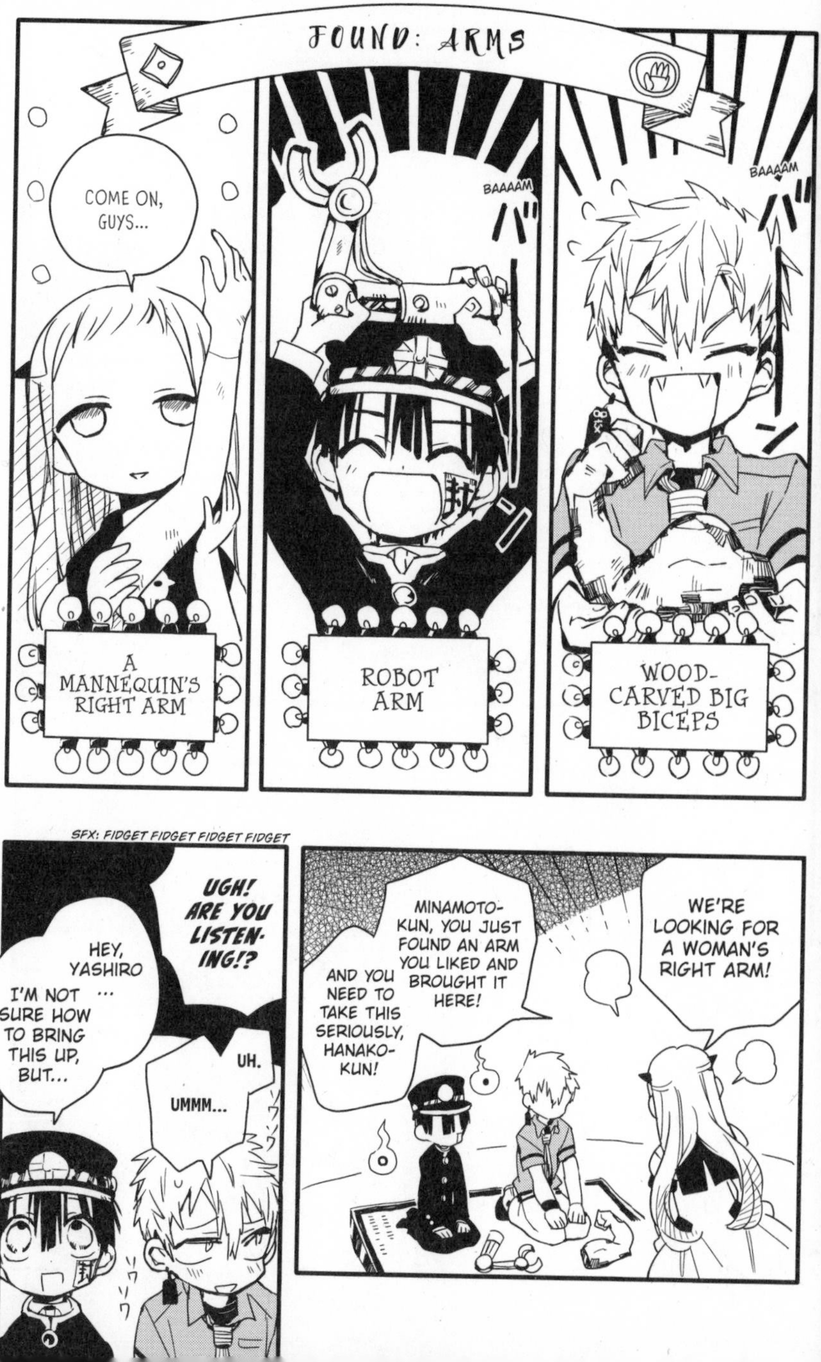
FOUND: ARMS
BAAAAM
WOOD-CARVED BIG BICEPS
BAAAAM
ROBOT ARM
COME ON, GUYS...
A MANNEQUIN'S RIGHT ARM
WE'RE LOOKING FOR A WOMAN'S RIGHT ARM!
MINAMOTO-KUN, YOU JUST FOUND AN ARM YOU LIKED AND BROUGHT IT HERE!
AND YOU NEED TO TAKE THIS SERIOUSLY, HANAKO-KUN!
SFX: FIDGET FIDGET FIDGET FIDGET
UGH! ARE YOU LISTENING!?
HEY, YASHIRO ... I'M NOT SURE HOW TO BRING THIS UP, BUT...
UH.
UMMM...

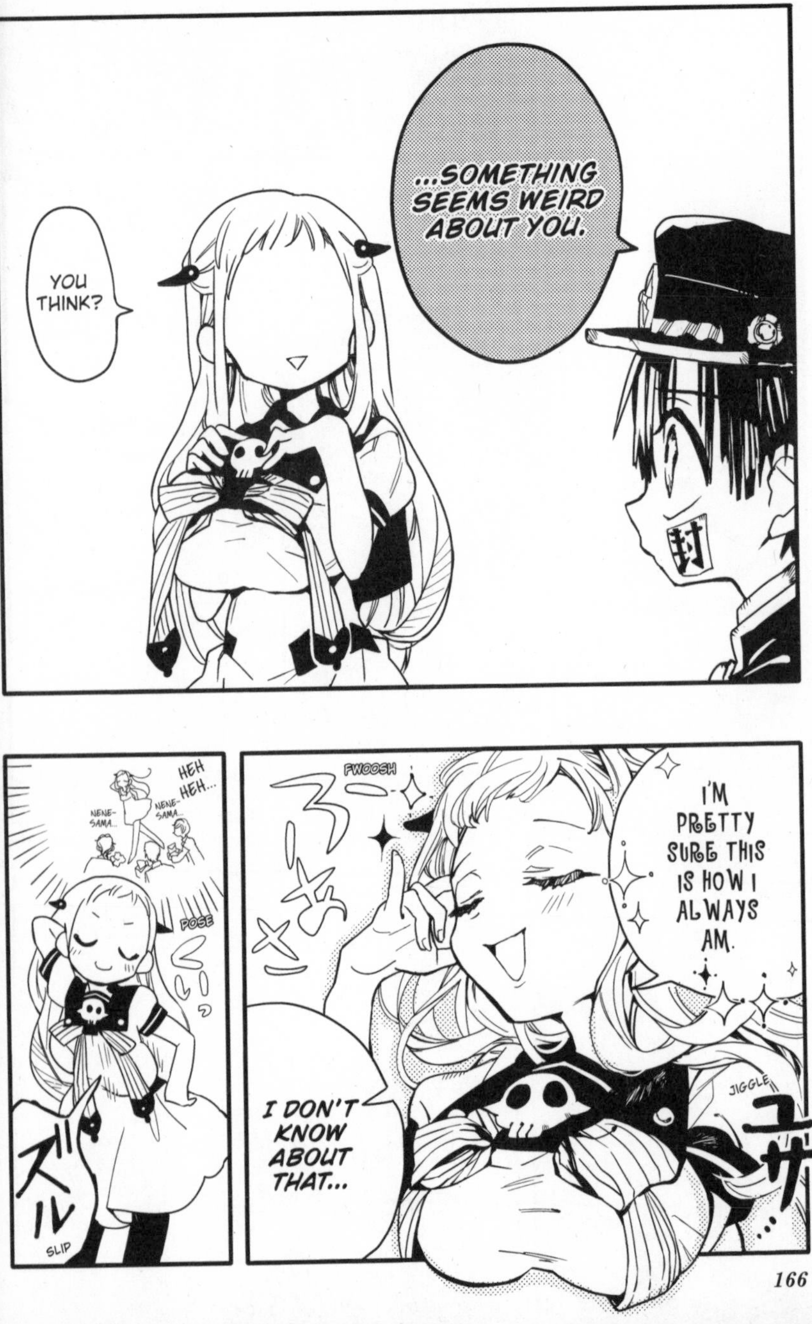
...SOMETHING SEEMS WEIRD ABOUT YOU.
YOU THINK?
I'M PRETTY SURE THIS IS HOW I ALWAYS AM.
FWOOSH
JIGGLE
I DON'T KNOW ABOUT THAT...
HEH HEH...
NENE-SAMA...
NENE-SAMA...
POSE
SLIP

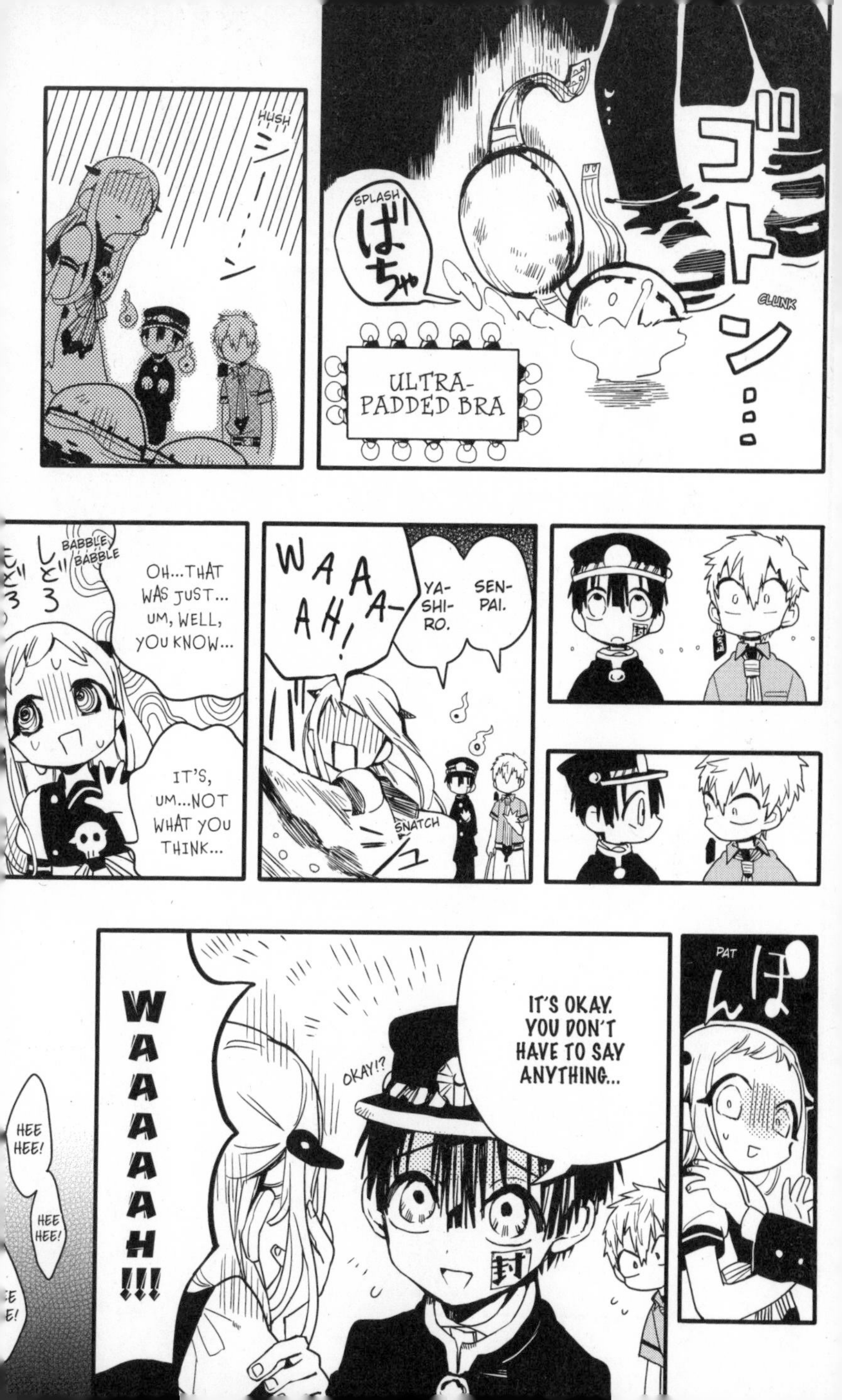
SPLASH
ULTRA-PADDED BRA
CLUNK
HUSH
WAAAA-AH!
YASHIRO-SENPAI.
SNATCH
BABBLE BABBLE
OH...THAT WAS JUST... UM, WELL, YOU KNOW...
IT'S, UM...NOT WHAT YOU THINK...
PAT
IT'S OKAY. YOU DON'T HAVE TO SAY ANYTHING...
OKAY!?
WAAAAAAAH!!!
HEE HEE!
HEE HEE!

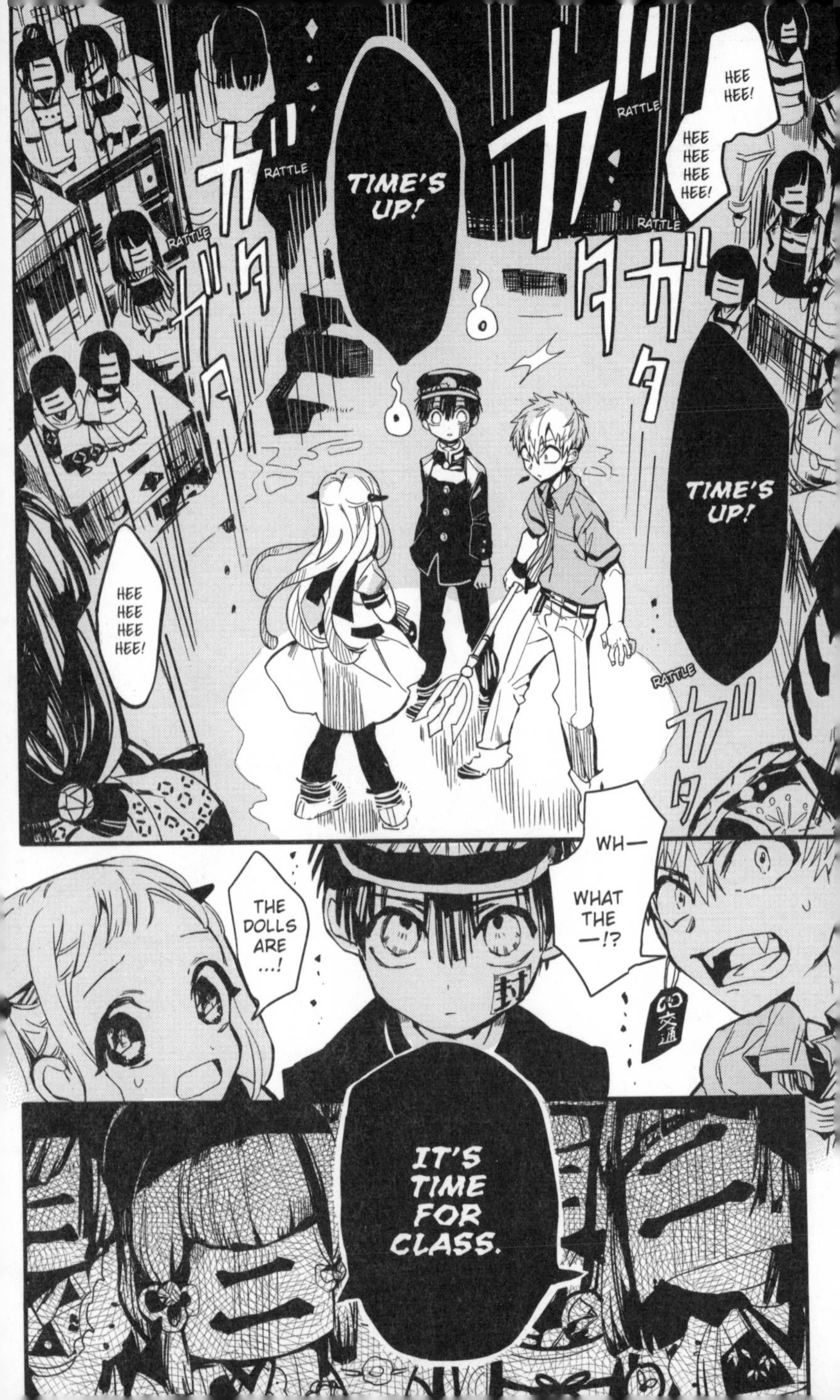
HEE HEE!
RATTLE
HEE HEE HEE HEE!
RATTLE
TIME'S UP!
RATTLE
RATTLE
TIME'S UP!
RATTLE
HEE HEE HEE HEE!
WH— WHAT THE—!?
THE DOLLS ARE ...!
IT'S TIME FOR CLASS.

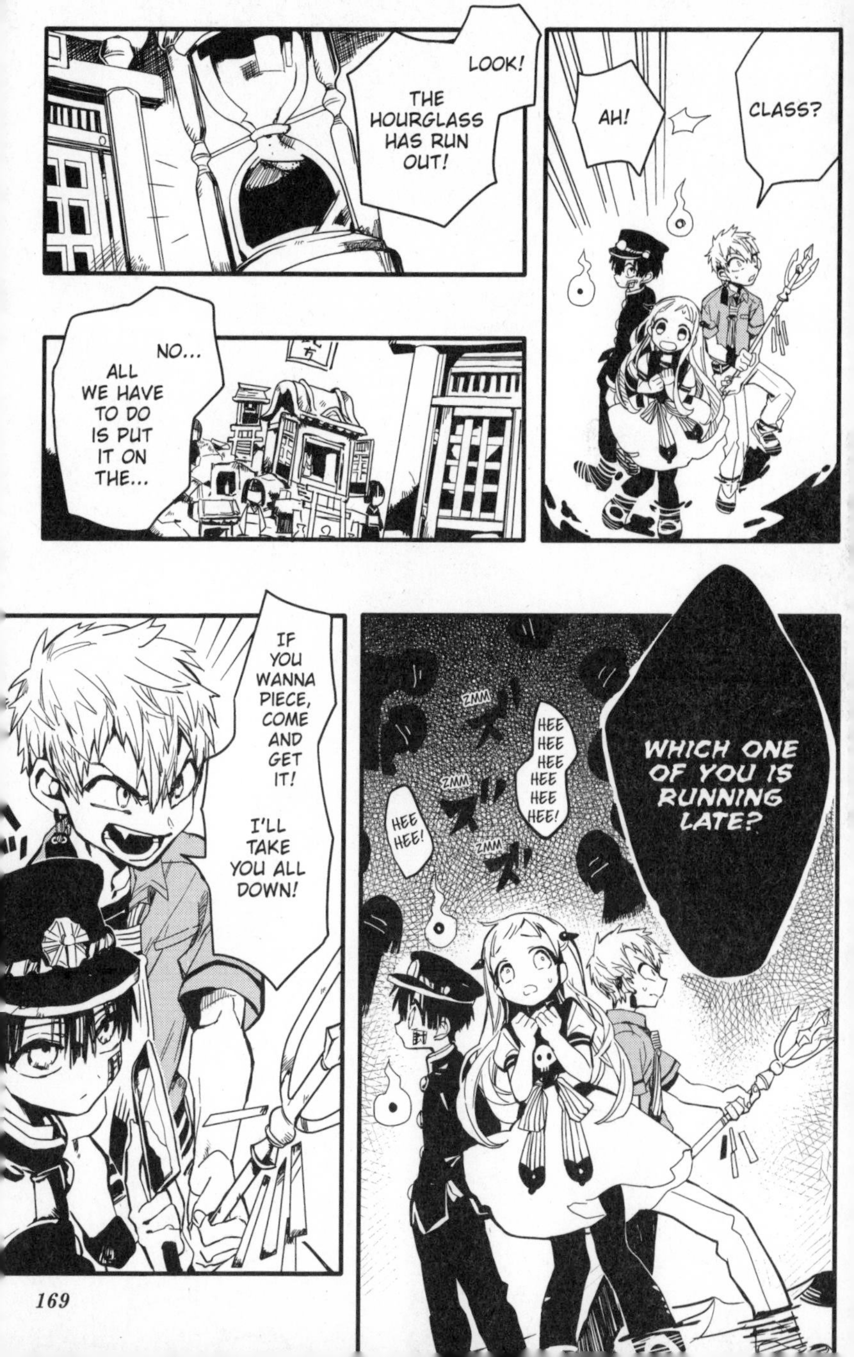
CLASS?
AH!
LOOK!
THE HOURGLASS HAS RUN OUT!
NO...
ALL WE HAVE TO DO IS PUT IT ON THE...
WHICH ONE OF YOU IS RUNNING LATE?
HEE HEE HEE HEE HEE HEE!
ZMM
ZMM
HEE HEE!
ZMM
IF YOU WANNA PIECE, COME AND GET IT!
I'LL TAKE YOU ALL DOWN!

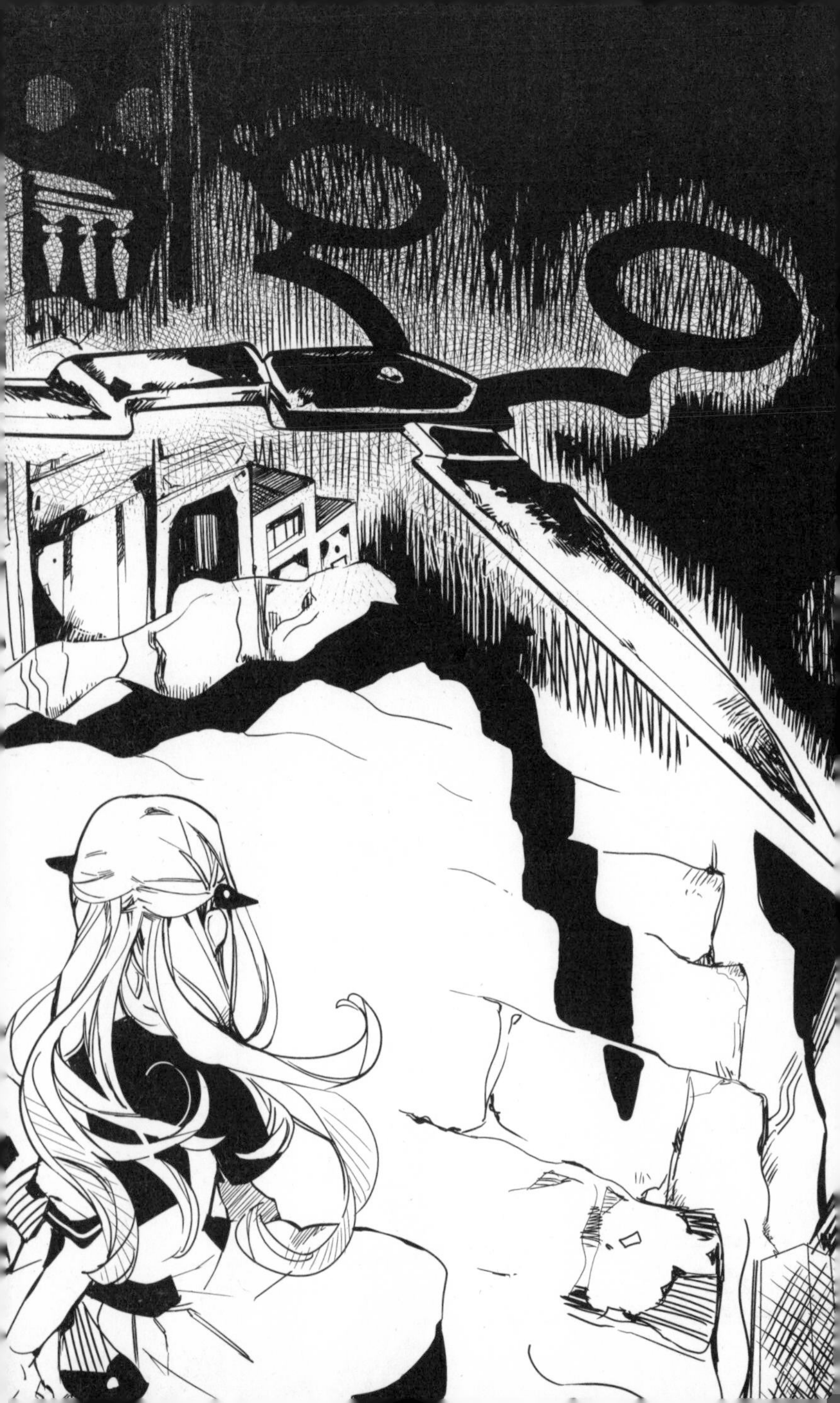

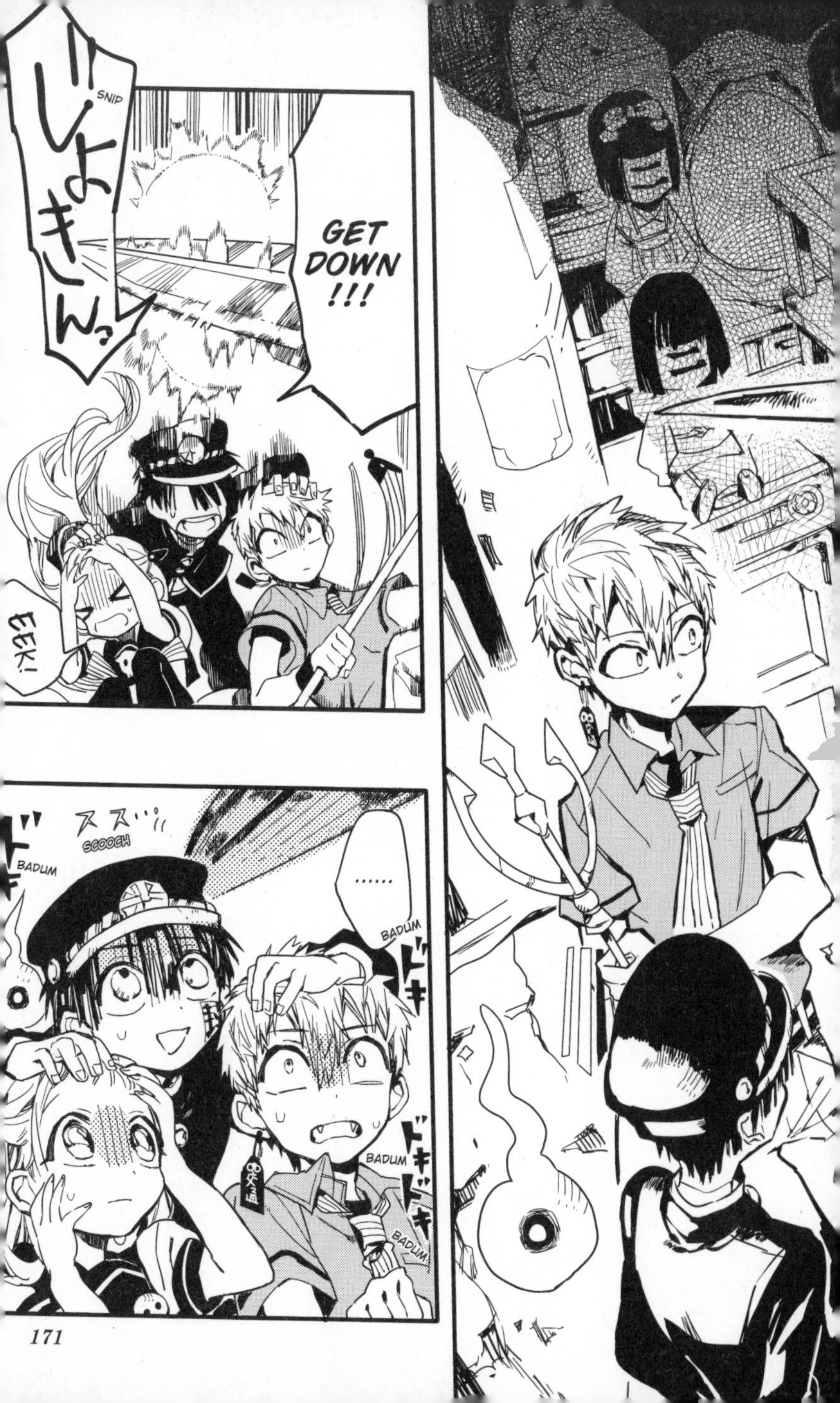
GET DOWN!!!
じょきんっ
SNIP
EEK!
……
ドキ
BADUM
ドキドキ
BADUM
BADUM
スス…
SCOOCH
ドキ
BADUM

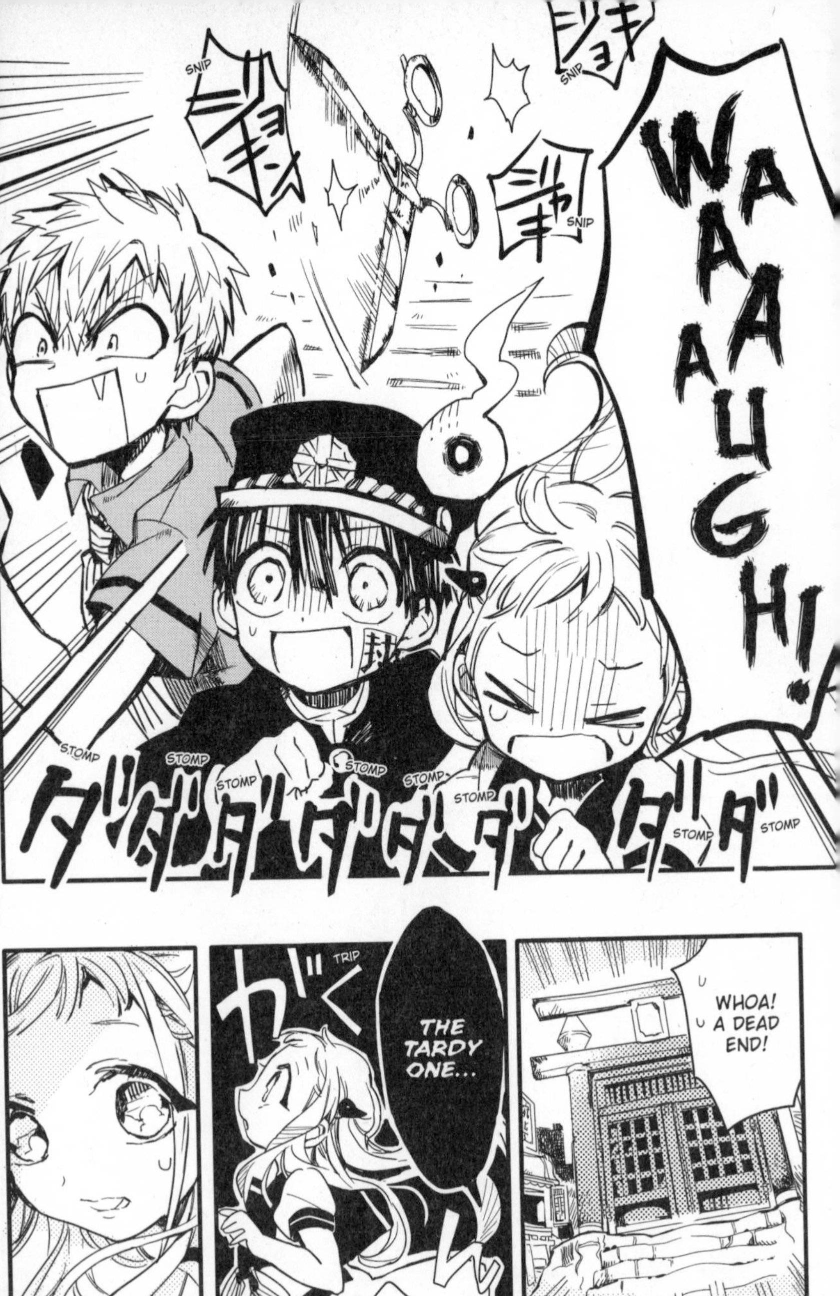
SNIP
WAAAAUGH!!
SNIP
SNIP
STOMP
STOMP
STOMP
STOMP
STOMP
STOMP
STOMP
STOMP
STOMP
WHOA! A DEAD END!
TRIP
THE TARDY ONE...
ACK!

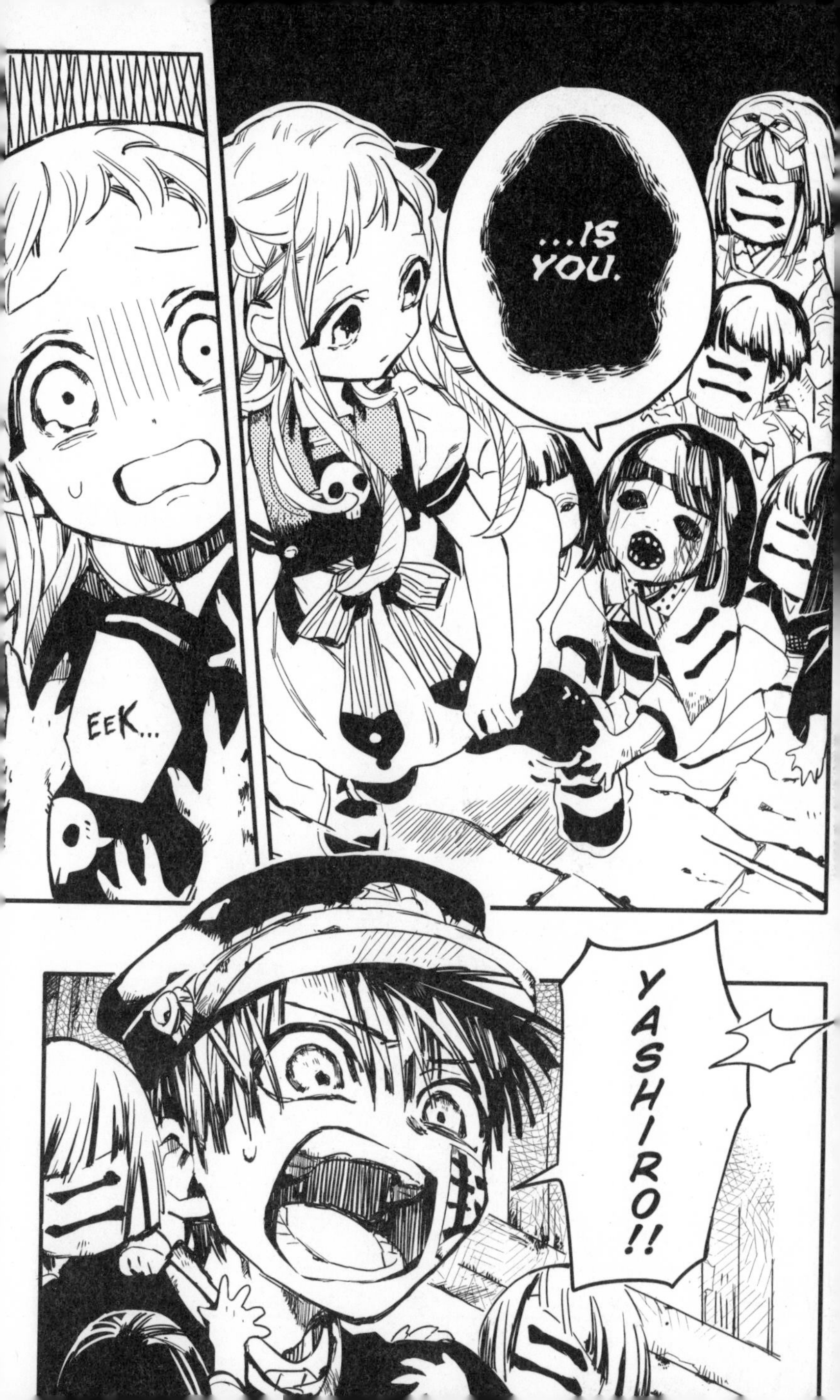
...IS YOU.
EEK...
YASHIRO!!

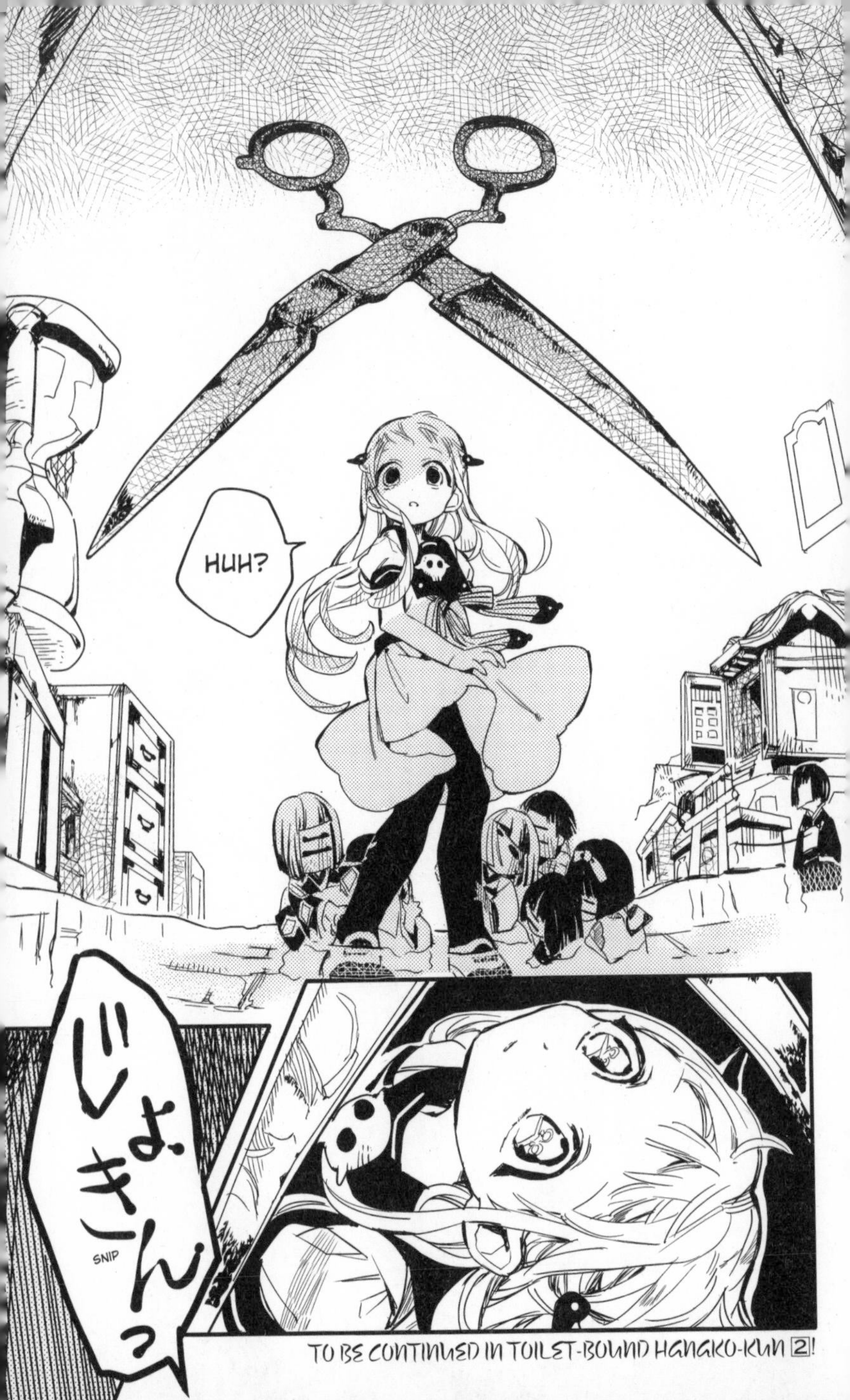
HUH?
じょきんっ
SNIP

TO BE CONTINUED IN TOILET-BOUND HANAKO-KUN 2!

BONUS MANGA

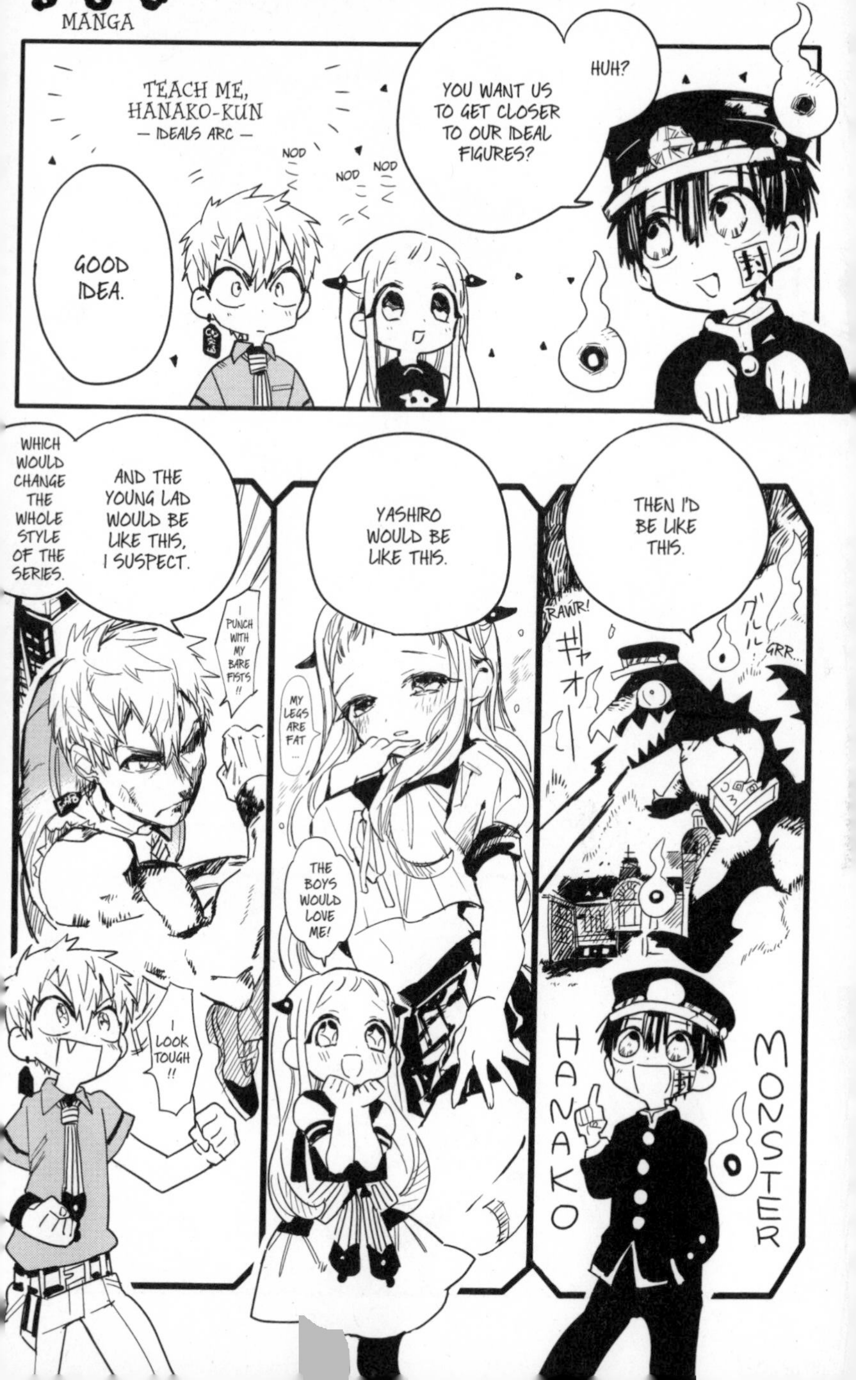
TEACH ME, HANAKO-KUN
— IDEALS ARC —
HUH?
YOU WANT US TO GET CLOSER TO OUR IDEAL FIGURES?
NOD
NOD
NOD
GOOD IDEA.
THEN I'D BE LIKE THIS.
RAWR!
GRR...
HANAKO MONSTER
YASHIRO WOULD BE LIKE THIS.
MY LEGS ARE FAT...
THE BOYS WOULD LOVE ME!
AND THE YOUNG LAD WOULD BE LIKE THIS, I SUSPECT.
WHICH WOULD CHANGE THE WHOLE STYLE OF THE SERIES.
I PUNCH WITH MY BARE FISTS!!
I LOOK TOUGH!!

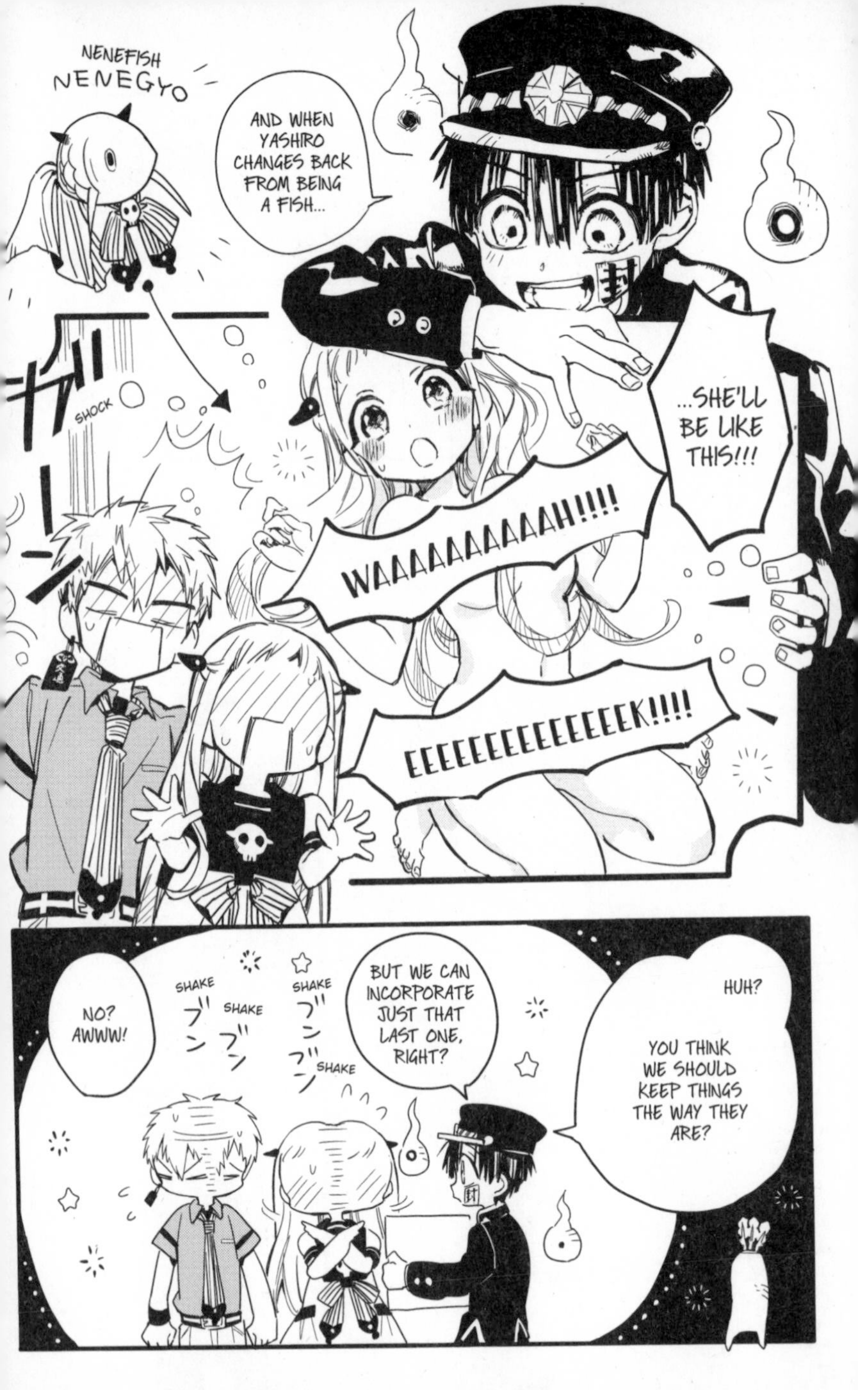
AND WHEN YASHIRO CHANGES BACK FROM BEING A FISH...
NENEFISH
NENEGYO
...SHE'LL BE LIKE THIS!!!
WAAAAAAAAAAH!!!!
EEEEEEEEEEEEEEK!!!!
SHOCK
HUH?
YOU THINK WE SHOULD KEEP THINGS THE WAY THEY ARE?
BUT WE CAN INCORPORATE JUST THAT LAST ONE, RIGHT?
SHAKE
SHAKE
SHAKE
SHAKE
NO? AWWW!

TRANSLATION NOTES

Common Honorifics

no honorific: Indicates familiarity or closeness; if used without permission or reason, addressing someone in this manner would constitute an insult.

-san: The Japanese equivalent of Mr./Mrs./Miss. If a situation calls for politeness, this is the fail-safe honorific.

-sama: Conveys great respect; may also indicate that the social status of the speaker is lower than that of the addressee.

-kun: Used most often when referring to boys, this indicates affection or familiarity. Occasionally used by older men among their peers, but it may also be used by anyone referring to a person of lower standing.

-chan: An affectionate honorific indicating famil-iarity used mostly in reference to girls; also used in reference to cute persons or animals of either gender.

-senpai: A suffix used to address upperclassmen or more experienced coworkers.

-sensei: A respectful term for teachers, artists, or high-level professionals.

Page 7

Hanako-san of the Toilet is a famous school ghost story all over Japan. According to legend, this ghost can be summoned by knocking on the door of her bathroom stall, just as Nene did. However, as the *-ko* ending to the name implies, the general stories of Hanako are about a little girl (which would also be why she is usually found in the girls' restroom). The famous image of Hanako wears a red skirt and has her hair cut in a bob. It may also be worth noting this Hanako has a sticker on his face with the kanji character for "seal," as in "to seal or lock away." Clearly, he hasn't been fully sealed away, or he wouldn't appear at all, so either the sealing attempt failed or some of his powers have been locked away.

Page 23

As the name suggests, a **character bento** is a lunch (*bento*) made to look like characters. They can be preexisting characters or original characters. Usually, these characters are cute and friendly, but of course, it all depends on the tastes of the cook.

Page 27

Kokeshi are simple wooden dolls characterized by their lack of arms and legs. The cylindrical torso is traditionally decorated with a floral pattern and the head with basic features.

Page 67

Haniwa clay figurines are made from terracotta clay and used for rituals and funerals between the third and sixth centuries in Japan. This boy seems to have named his "**Hanitaro**," where the ending *-taro* means "eldest son."

Page 95

Oni are demons from Japanese folklore similar to trolls, typically portrayed with horns growing from their heads, whereas *tengu* are another type of otherworldly creature, often with features that take after birds of prey.

Page 89

This young man is wearing a **protective charm** as an earring, of a type that can be purchased in shrines all over Japan. Shrines sell amulets for all kinds of things—to help a student do well on tests, to help a mother safely give birth to a new child, to help a single person find a significant other, etc. Based on the label, it would seem this particular amulet contains a prayer for safety in traffic. Perhaps this boy is concerned about getting safely from one place to another.

Page 99

Literally, **Raiteijou** means "thunder staff." It may be a reference to Vajra, a Sanskrit word meaning "diamond" or "thunderbolt," which is also a type of weapon.

Page 139

Apparently, Hanako is "busy" playing *hanafuda* with the mokke. **Hanafuda** is a Japanese card game where the objective is to accumulate points by collecting matching cards. **"Five lights"** means the player has collected five cards in the light suit.

Page 147

Misaki is Japanese for "promontory," as in a piece of land jutting out into the ocean. In this case, these stairs are jutting out into the ocean between this life and the next. The word *misaki* has other meanings as well: For example, it is a name for the servants, such as foxes or crows, that appear to herald the coming of a supernatural being such as a god. It can also refer to the spirit of someone who died an unnatural death, which may be why, when someone kills themself, it is sometimes said the *misaki* called to them.

Toilet-bound Hanako-Kun 1

AidaIro

Translation: Alethea Nibley and Athena Nibley
Lettering: Jesse Moriarty, Tania Biswas

JIBAKU SHONEN HANAKO-KUN Volume 1 ©2015 AidaIro / SQUARE ENIX CO., LTD.
First published in Japan in 2015 by SQUARE ENIX CO., LTD. English translation rights arranged with SQUARE ENIX CO., LTD. and Yen Press, LLC through Tuttle-Mori Agency, Inc.

English translation © 2017 by SQUARE ENIX CO., LTD.

Yen Press
150 West 30th Street, 19th Floor
New York, NY 10001

Visit us at yenpress.com • facebook.com/yenpress • twitter.com/yenpress • yenpress.tumblr.com • instagram.com/yenpress

First Yen Press Print Edition: January 2020
Originally published as an ebook in August 2017 by Yen Press.

Yen Press is an imprint of Yen Press, LLC.
The Yen Press name and logo are trademarks of Yen Press, LLC.

The publisher is not responsible for websites (or their content) that are not owned by the publisher.

Library of Congress Control Number: 2019953610

ISBN: 978-1-9753-3287-7 (paperback)

10

TPA

Printed in South Korea